The Archaeology of
Ancient Indian Cities

DILIP K. CHAKRABARTI

DELHI
OXFORD UNIVERSITY PRESS
CALCUTTA CHENNAI MUMBAI
1997

Oxford University Press, Great Clarendon Street, Oxford OX2 6DP

Oxford New York
Athens Auckland Bangkok Calcutta
Cape Town Chennai Dar es Salaam Delhi
Florence Hong Kong Istanbul Karachi
Kuala Lumpur Madrid Melbourne Mexico City
Mumbai Nairobi Paris Singapore
Taipei Tokyo Toronto
and associates in
Berlin Ibadan

ISBN 0 19 564174 4

Printed at Rajkamal Electric Press, Delhi 110033
and published by Manzar Khan, Oxford University Press
YMCA Library Building, Jai Singh Road, New Delhi 110001

To
the memory of
NIHARRANJAN RAY,
from a recalcitrant student

Contents

Preface   xiii

1. INTRODUCTION   1

2. BACKGROUND AND ORIGIN OF THE INDUS CIVILIZATION   11
   Background   11
   Origin   46

3. HARAPPAN SETTLEMENTS   53
   North Afghanistan and Baluchistan   53
   Sind   59
       Mohenjodaro   61
       Chanhudaro   76
       Ali Murad   77
       Kot Diji   77
       Ahladino   78
   Cholistan   78
   Western Panjab   82
       Harappa   82
   Rajasthan, Haryana, East Panjab and U.P.   86
       Kalibangan   89
       Banawali   92
   Kutch, Kathiawar and Mainland Gujarat   94
       Sindhi Harappan and Sorath Harappan?   95
       Lothal   97
       Rangpur, Surkotada and Dholavira   102
   Aspects of Harappan Urbanism   106
       Some Features of Distribution and Size   106
       Chronology   111
       Elements of Planning   115
       Social Framework   122

4. PRELUDE TO EARLY HISTORIC URBAN GROWTH   124
   Decline of the Harappan Civilization   124
       The Late Harappans   129

Hypothesis Regarding the End of Harappan Urbanism 138
The Neolithic-Chalcolithic Cultures outside the
Harappan Orbit 141
    Northwest Frontier and Kashmir 141
    Northeast Rajasthan 143
    Southeast Rajasthan 145
    Malwa 148
    Maharashtra 150
    Karnataka, Tamil Nadu and Andhra 154
    Eastern India 156
    Upper Gangetic Valley 160
    General Discussion 162
Hypothesis Regarding the Origin of the Neolithic-
Chalcolithic Cultures in Inner India 164
Towards Early History in the Gangetic Valley:
The Iron Age 167

5. EARLY HISTORICAL CITIES 170
Northwest 170
    Charsada 172
    Taxila 174
Kashmir 181
Panjab Plains 182
Sind 183
Indo-Gangetic Divide 184
    Rupar 185
    Sugh, Sunet, Agroha, Sanghol, Thaneshwar and
    Rangmahal 185
The U.P. Himalayan and Sub-Himalayan Belt 186
Upper Gangetic Valley 187
    Hastinapur 187
    Indraprastha 188
    Atranjikhera 188
    Mathura 189
    Kampil 191
    Sankisa 191
    Kanauj 191
    Chakranagar 192
    Ahichchhatra 192
    Saketa-Ayodhya 193

Hulaskhera   194
Kausambi   194
Bhita   198
Sringaverapura   199
Middle Gangetic Valley (Eastern U.P. and Bihar)   200
Rajghat   200
Khairadih   201
Narhan   202
Jhusi and Ghosi   202
Saheth-Maheth   202
Ganwaria   204
Tilaura Kot   205
Lauriya-Nandangarh   205
Balirajgarh   206
Katragarh   206
Basarh   206
Maner and Manjhi   209
Patna   209
Rajgir   212
Champa   215
Lower Gangetic Valley (West Bengal and Bangladesh)   216
Mahasthangarh   216
Bangarh   217
Wari-Bateshwar   217
Tamluk   218
Chandraketugarh   218
Mangalkot, Dihar and Pokharna   218
Brahmaputra Valley (Assam)   219
Rajasthan   219
Bairat   220
Rairh   220
Sambhar   221
Nagari   221
Madhya Pradesh   221
Besnagar   221
Pawaya   223
Ujjain   223
Malhar   225
Other Sites   225
Gujarat   226

Broach	226
Other Sites	227
Maharashtra	228
Karnataka	230
Kerala	231
Tamilnadu	232
Andhra	234
Nagarjunakonda	235
Satanikota	237
Vengi	238
Other Andhra Sites	238
Orissa	240
Jaugada	240
Sisupalgarh	240
Aspects of the Early Historic Urban Pattern	242
Pattern of Growth	242
Elements of Size and Planning	249
Literary Data on Town-Planning	255
Urban character	258
6. PROBLEMS AND PERSPECTIVES	263
References	279
Index	293

List of Maps

1.	General distribution of sites mentioned in Chapter 2	12
2a-b.	Site distribution area in Cholistan (after Mughal 1992)	18, 20
2c.	The suggested Indus-Hakra flows during the period of the Indus civilization (after Flam 1981)	25
3.	General distribution of sites mentioned in Chapter 3	54
4.	General distribution of sites mentioned in Chapter 4	125
5.	General distribution of sites mentioned in Chapter 5	171

List of Figures

(between pp. 146 and 147)

1. Site plans of Mohenjodaro and Harappa (after the Archaeological Survey of India—hereafter ASI)
2. The 'citadel' area of Mohenjodaro (after Wheeler 1953)
3. HR area, Mohenjodaro (after the ASI)
4. The 'citadel' area of Harappa (after the ASI)
5. The general site-plan of Harappa (after Kenoyer 1991)
6. Site plan of Kalibangan (after the ASI)
7. Site plan of Banawali (after the ASI)
8. Site plan of Lothal (after the ASI)
9. Site plan of Surkotada (after the ASI)
10. Site plan of Dholivara (after the ASI)
11. The general site plan of Taxila (after the ASI)
12. Site plan of Taxila, Sirkap (after the ASI)
13. Basic plan of Tulamba (after Alexander Cunningham)
14. Basic plan of Kanauj (after Alexander Cunningham)
15. Basic plan of Sankisa (after Alexander Cunningham)
16. Basic plan of Ahichchhatra (after Alexander Cunningham)
17. Basic plan of Masaon-dih (after Alexander Cunningham)
18. Basic plan of Khairadih (after Alexander Cunningham)
19. Basic plan of Sravasti (after the ASI)
20. Basic plan of Kausambi (after Alexander Cunningham)
21. Basic plan of Sarnath-Varanasi (after Alexander Cunnigham)
22. Basic plan of Mathura (after Piggott 1945)
23. Site plan of Mathura (after M.C.Joshi 1989)
24. Basic plan of Mahasthangarh (after Alexander Cunningham)
25. Site plan of Rajgir (after the ASI)
26. Site plan of Balirajgarh (after the ASI)
27. Site plan of Ujjayini (after the ASI)
28. Site plan of Nagarjunakonda (after the ASI)
29. Site plan of Satanikota (after the ASI)
30. Basic plan of Adam (after the ASI)
31. Basic plan of Sisupalgarh (after the ASI)
32. Site plan of Ayodhya (after Alexander Cunningham)

Preface

This book offers a systematic evaluation of archaeological data on the early urban history of India. It does so in terms of two major periods (protohistoric and early historic, coming down to about AD 300 and later) and all major areas of the subcontinent from where some data are available. In the process the book discusses some of the cardinal issues of South Asian archaeology—the problems of the origin and decline of the Indus civilization; the issue of its merger in the main flow of India's later cultural development; the archaeological basis of its long chronology; aspects of the Indus urbanism; the reason for the growth of neolithic-chalcolithic communities in all major agricultural regions of the subcontinent, especially inner India; the patterns and problems of urban growth in the early historic period on the subcontinental scale, etc. In each case the concern is with understanding the situation at the grassroots level within an essentially South Asian framework. In fact, this may be the first work which puts forward a cogent and well-argued case for a totally indigenous framework for the archaeological cultural development of the subcontinent from the period of the Indus civilization onwards. If this work leads, among other things, to detailed research on the settlement perspectives of different areas, I shall consider my work useful.

This work has its origin in my Ph.D. dissertation, 'Early Urban Centres in India, an Archaeological Perspective, *c.* 2500 BC–*c.* AD 300', submitted to the University of Calcutta in 1972 under the supervision of the late Professor Niharranjan Ray. The present work was written in 1992–93 and the fact that the task was not put off further was due to the insistence of Dr Nayanjot Lahiri, to whom I am extremely grateful.

In a work of this kind the list of references and illustrations is almost endless but I have tried to keep it to the minimum.

Chapter One

Introduction

The more purposeful academic attempts to understand ancient Indian cities like those of C.P.V. Ayyar (1915) and B.B. Dutt (1925) were based essentially either on the traditional Indian principles of the modes of urban layout as embodied in different *Vastusastra* texts (for a comprehensive analysis, see T. Bhattacharya, 1963) or on the old literature (the old Tamil literature in the case of Ayyar). Though not in the form of a monograph, A.K. Coomaraswamy (1930, 1931) attempted an analysis of the early historical cities of India and their associated architecture primarily on the basis of the *Jatakas* and other Buddhist texts and different representations of cities, palaces and houses in early Buddhist art. In later years the books by Stuart Piggott (1945), Amita Ray (1964), U.N. Roy (1965) and B.N. Puri (1966) contained much that was relevant to the theme.

The modern archaeological interest in the investigation of the phenomenon of early Indian cities dates from 1972–73 when, on the basis of my Ph.D. dissertation completed at Calcutta University in 1972, I published two articles, one trying to analyze the concept of urban revolution in the Indian context and the other trying to delineate the main political phases of India's early historic urban growth (Chakrabarti 1972–73, 1974). The first of these articles had also the privilege of being commented on by several leading Indian archaeologists including A. Ghosh who published soon afterwards a full-length study on this topic entitled *The City in Early Historic India* (A. Ghosh 1973). Although this volume by one of the most important archaeologists of post-Independence India contains a deep insight into various issues linked to the growth of early historic Indian cities, a detailed and region-by-region discussion of archaeological data was not within its scope, nor was it concerned in detail with the physical features of these cities. In 1981 V. Thakur (1981) published a book entitled *Urbanisation in Ancient India* where the focus was more general and literary than archaeological and specific. In 1984 Kameshwar Prasad (1984) published *Cities, Crafts and Commerce under the Kushans* which cited the archaeological data on cities of the early centuries AD. In 1986 M. Lal (1986) tried to examine the role of iron in the clearance of forests and the growth of cities in the Gangetic valley on the basis of his two earlier publications on the subject (M. Lal 1984a 1984b). In 1987 R.S. Sharma (1987) in his *Urban Decay in India (c. 300–c. 1000 AD)* tried to argue that the early historic cities of the country declined along with the decline of trade economy which reached its high water-mark during the Kushan period. In 1988 G. Erdosy (1988) assessed the problem of urbanization in early historic India against the background of his studies on the ancient settlement in the Allahabad–Kausambi region. In the same year I added some comments on 'the phenomenon of urbanization' in my book *Theoretical Issues in Indian Archaeology* (Chakrabarti 1988a) and on the rural-urban dichotomy in ancient India in a volume published by the Department of Ancient History and Archaeology of Allahabad University (Chakrabarti 1988b). In 1989 F.R. Allchin (1989) published an article entitled 'City and State Formation in Early Historic South Asia' which he followed up with an article published in 1990 entitled 'Patterns of City Formation in Early Historic South Asia' (Allchin 1990). In the field of ancient textual studies a significant contribution was made by K.T.S. Sarao (1989, 1990), especially in his *Urban Centres and Urbanisation as Reflected in the Pali Vinaya and Sutta Pitakas* (Sarao 1990).

This research survey may not be exhaustive but it serves the purpose of narrating the broad trend of urban studies in the context of ancient India.

Among modern sociologists K. Davies (1966) has asserted that 'the earliest urban centres are called "cities" mainly by the courtesy of the archaeologists' (Davies 1966: xi). In relation to their modern counterparts they were incomparably small, with a maximum of a few thousand inhabitants; they were what Davies (1966: xi) calls 'mere urban islands in a vast sea of rurality'. However the criteria of urbanism as a way of life proposed by L. Wirth (1938: 8), i.e. size, density and heterogeneity, hold true in both the ancient and modern contexts, and though affecting only a small part of the country's total population, these early cities, once they came into being, were repositories of what Robert Redfield (1963: 41–2) characterizes as the 'Great Tradition' of their respective civilizations. There is much truth in Oswald Spengler's remark, 'every spring time of a culture is *ipso facto* the spring time of a new city-type and civism' (Spengler 1954: 91), or that of Redfield, 'cities remain the symbols and carriers of civilization wherever they appear' (Redfield 1962: 327).

As early as in the beginning of this century, Emile Durkheim (1900, 1964 reprint: 361) suggested as one of the tasks of the sociologists to investigate 'what circumstances give birth to villages and then to cities, and from what the development of urban centres derives'. However, theoretical concern with the first urban growth in the history of the world was not clearly manifest in archaeological literature till V. Gordon Childe in his book *Man Makes Himself*, first published in 1936, coined the term 'Urban Revolution' to emphasize its importance and formulated a theoretical scheme to account for its occurrence (Childe 1941: chapter 7). In 1950 he delineated the basic features of the civilization accompanying the first urban growth on the basis of archaeological data. Thus, the study of urban growth in archaeological literature is initially linked to the writings of Childe.

His theoretical scheme to account for the first urban phenomena laid stress on technology as its prime force:

The thousand years or so immediately preceding 3000 BC were perhaps more fruitful in inventions and discoveries than any period of human history prior to the sixteenth century AD. Its achievements made possible that economic reorganization of society that I term the Urban Revolution (Childe 1952: 69).

Among these inventions the copper-bronze metallurgy, 'the first approximation to international science', as Childe calls it (1952: 78), was the most important. In addition, there was the invention of the wheel and wheeled transport, sailboats, ploughs, etc. The period was also characterized by an expanded foreign trade, a logical outcome of the development of metallurgy demanding diverse ores from diverse regions and the beginning of the exact sciences like astronomy which was obviously bound up with extensive plough agriculture calling for a knowledge of seasonal variations. The comparative self-sufficiency of the earlier peasant communities broke down and the way was paved for the development of a new settlement pattern and a new arrangement of society.

Childe (1950) further suggested ten traits of urban revolution: (1) a new magnitude of human settlement, (2) the central accumulation of capital through tribute and taxation, (3) monumental public works, (4) the art of writing, (5) the beginning of the exact and predictive sciences like arithmetic, geometry and astronomy, (6) a greatly expanded foreign trade implying the development of economic institutions, (7) the growth of full-time specialists in different crafts such as metal-working, (8) a privileged ruling class, (9) the birth of a state or organization of society on the basis of residence instead of or on top of the basis of kinship, and (10) the reappearance of naturalistic art.

An alternative approach to urban studies in archaeology soon became evident in the writings of the Chicago school of oriental archaeologists. In 1950 in his book *The Near East and the Foundations for Civilization* R.J. Braidwood (1950:41) characterized civilization in eight ways which did not differ significantly from the indices offered by Childe: (1) fully efficient food production, (2) cities, urbanization, (3) formal political state, (4) formal political laws—a new sense of moral order, (5) formal projects and works, (6) classes and hierarchies, (7) writing, and (8) monumentality in art. However, in the same publication, Braidwood (1950: 42) wrote the following:

We do not believe there was a second change in kind in the technologico-economic realm as civilization and the pre-civilizational phases of food-production were differences in degree. This emphasis on cultural growth and process as civilization appeared makes our interpretation different from that of Childe. . . . The great change between pre-civilization and civilized human life came in those realms of culture other than the technological and economic.

This set the tone of subsequent writings on the issue by archaeologists and other scholars throughout the fifties and sixties. Whether or not writing was an index of civilization and cities came to be hotly debated in the context of the 'pre-pottery A' stage of Jericho in the eighth millennium BC. Kathleen Kenyon (1956) and Mortimer Wheeler (1956) assigned an urban status to this level of the site on the basis of its monumental architecture which comprised a rock-cut ditch and a stone wall with round towers and inner stairways for manning the defences around the settlement. This was criticized by Braidwood (1957) and Childe (1957) but the same problem arose in the mid-sixties when James Mellart decided to describe the neolithic Catal Huyuk (*c*. 6500 BC) as the 'world's oldest city' (Mellart 1966, 1965).

Another issue which agitated scholars was the suitability of the term itself. They could not be sure if the change was as precipitous as Childe's use of the term 'revolution' would imply. Lewis Mumford in his *The City in History* (Mumford 1961: 51) points out that though

the term does justice to the active and critically important role of the city it does not accurately indicate the process, for a revolution implies turning things upside down, and a progressive movement away from outworn institutions that have been left behind. . . . The rise of the city, so far from wiping out earlier elements in the culture, actually brought them together and increased their efficiency and scope.

H. Frankfort (1951: 38, fn 3) objects to the word because he believes that by its use 'an impression of violent, and especially of purposeful change is made which the facts do not suggest'. R. Redfield (1962 ix) accepts the word 'revolution' but 'with hesitation' and prefers 'transformation' instead. Glyn Daniel (1968: 26) suggests the use of the word 'synoecism'. Childe (1958: 89) himself admits that 'the process is so finely divided in the successive building levels that it seems arbitrary to fix the exact critical point at which quantity passed over into quality, when the Revolution was accomplished'. While analysing the ancient Egyptian centres J. A. Wilson (1963: 34) has even gone to the extent of arguing that 'one may accept a truth in Childe's "Urban Revolution" provided that it is understood that it was not "urban" and was not a "revolution"'. However, as R.M. Adams (1965: 9) points out, the term has its advantages. 'Among its important advantages are that it places stress on the transformative character of the change, that it suggests at least relative rapidity, and that it specifies a restricted, urban locus within which the process was concentrated.'

The third issue was related to the enumeration of the ten traits associated with urban revolution by Childe. This enumeration, according to Adams (1965: 10), gave us a 'mixed bag of characteristics'. Among the features listed by Childe, monumental architecture could have existed— and, in fact, did exist—in non-civilized contexts. The trait like the beginning of the exact and predictive sciences may be 'largely matters of interpretation from evidence that is at least fragmentary and ambiguous' (Adams 1965: 11). Generally speaking, these indices were the results of a cumulative process where, apart from the distinctions in degree, the distinctions in kind are hard to arrive at. And not all of them seem to have been equally significant either. For instance, Redfield (1965: 24) is doubtful of the significance of the re-appearance of naturalistic art. So is Adams (1965: 11): 'its initial appearance, in so far as it deals with the human figure—for example, is at least not immediately apparent'. He goes on to write:

A more basic objection to any such listing is that its eclecticism embraces fundamental contradictions as to purpose. Childe echoes Morgan in seeking to identify the Urban Revolution by a series of traits whose vestiges the specialist can conveniently recognize. This was a reasonable procedure for Morgan's purpose, the initial delineation of a succession of stages, but with Childe, on the other hand, we enter an era in which emphasis shifted toward providing accounts with explanatory powers as well (Adams 1965: 11).

In brief, what Adams (1965: 11) seeks to emphasize is that the term Urban Revolution implies a focus on 'ordered systematic processes of change through time' and as such its identifying characteristics 'need to be more than loosely associated features'.

The final issue of controversy in this field in the mid-sixties and earlier, centred around the problem of the urban growth-process, and in this field too Adams was emphatic in his criticism of Childe's idea. Following Braidwood who disputed the assumption of the supremacy of the technological factor in the process of urban revolution, Adams (1960a: 153) characterized urban revolution as 'pre-eminently a social process'. Agricultural surplus was necessary but 'its essential element was a whole series of new institutions and the vastly greater size and complexity of the social unit, rather than basic innovations in subsistence' (Adams 1960a: 154). To prove his point Adams (1960b: 31–2) further argued that metallurgy came to be fully developed in Early Dynastic Mesopotamia only when cities were already a normal feature of Mesopotamian social life. He also posed the problem of Egypt where the decisive stage of early Pharaonic power was accompanied by 'little more in the way of technological superiority, in other words, may have had little to do with the processes which brought the city into being'. In a similar vein Mumford gave precedence to social-institutional changes and argued that it was the institution of kingship which was the most important single factor in the establishment of cities. In his concluding address at a symposium on urbanization and cultural development in the ancient Near East held at the Oriental Institute of Chicago University in 1958 he argued: 'I suggest that the key-agent in the foundation of the early city is the king and that one of the attributes of Ptah, that he founded cities, is in fact an all but universal attribute of kings' (Mumford 1960: 233).

Although T. Jacobsen (1960: 243) commented that the king as a city-builder appeared later in Egyptian literary records, a general association between the foundation of cities and the state-power is widely accepted. For instance, in the context of south Turkmenia, V.M. Masson (1968) felt that it was preferable to give priority 'not so much to a process of urbanization but to the emergence of a stratified society as an essential element in the process of social change in prehistory'. It may also be added here that the notion of technology-induced surplus leading by itself, outside any social-institutional framework, to social change was questioned quite early by H.W. Pearson (1957).

Since the early seventies two trends have increasingly become signi–
ficant in this field of archeological study. The first one is rooted in
attempts to study early urban centres in their settlement perspectives
whereas the second one has tried to understand the early urban growth
process through the application of a systems theory. A major milestone
in the history of the settlement approach is the publication of *Man,
Settlement and Urbanism* (Ucko, Tringham and Dimbleby 1972), the
result of a London seminar on settlements and urbanization in 1970. In
the context of ancient Mesopotamia the more modern studies from this
point of view include R.M. Adams' *Heartland of Cities, Surveys of
Ancient Settlement and Land Use on the Central Floodplain of the Euphrates* (Adams 1981) and H.J. Nissen's *The Early History of the Ancient
Near East, 9000–2000* BC (Nissen 1988). Nissen draws attention to the
concept of the *centre* and *surroundings* and explains the reasons why
(Nissen 1988: 10):

The terms *village, city,* and *state,* which are normally used in the archaeological
literature, are so changeable that one would really prefer to do without them.
Their definition becomes easier if we follow the example of settlement research-
ers, who assess the importance of a settlement by its relationship to its (settled)
surroundings. The main terms that must then be used are *centre* and *surroundings,* which together form a compact system, insofar as both parts of a settlement
system are permanently dependent on each other.

A concise discussion on the significance of the systems theory in this
context is offered by Colin Renfrew in *Approaches to Social Archaeology*
(Renfrew 1984: especially 248 ff) and Renfrew and Paul Bahn in
Archaeology, Theories, Methods and Practice (Renfrew and Bahn 1991:
421 ff). In the chapter on 'culture systems and the multiplier effect' in
Approaches to Social Archaeology one of the citations Renfrew gives as
an introduction to the theme of the chapter is from Kent Flannery:

It is vain to hope for the discovery of the first domestic corn cob, the first pottery
vessel, the first hieroglyphic, or the first site where some other major break-
through occurred. Such deviations from the pre-existing pattern almost certainly
took place in such a minor accidental way that these traces are not recoverable.
More worthwhile would be an investigation of the mutual casual processes that
amplify these tiny deviations into major changes in prehistoric culture (cited in
Renfrew 1984: 258).

The basic advantage of this systems approach or thinking may also be
best expressed in Flannery's words:

For one thing it does not attribute cultural evolution to 'discrepancies', 'inventions', 'expressions' or 'genius', but instead enables us to treat prehistoric

cultures as systems. It stimulates enquiry into the mechanisms that counteract change to amplify it, which ultimately tells us something about the nature of adaptation. Most importantly, it allows us to view change not as something arising *de novo*, but in terms of quite minor deviations in one overall part of a previously existing system, that once set in motion can expand greatly because of positive feedback (cited in Renfrew 1984: 267).

Renfrew's own case-study is in the context of the third millennium BC. Aegean where he broke the components of the six subsystems (subsistence, technological, social, cognitive/projective, external exchange, population) of culture into many detailed and specific formulations which he described as 'factors and interactions in the third millennium Aegean'. Change towards the origin of the state and civilization came as a result of the 'multiplier effect' where two subsystems entered 'into a mutual deviation-amplifying relationship' overcoming 'the innate conservative homeostasis of culture' and eventually leading to a morphogenesis or the emergence of totally new forms.

This certainly is a major analytical method which makes possible the appreciation of cultural change within the internal framework of that culture itself without taking recourse to such plainly crude assumptions as ethnicity, diffusion, etc., which has often been the case in the Indian context.

... the approach does offer a practical framework for the analysis of the articulation of the various components of the society. And it does lend itself very readily to computer modelling and simulation (Renfrew and Bahn 1991: 422).

As far as the earlier controversy between Childe and the Chicago school regarding the primacy or otherwise of technological factors is concerned, Renfrew could offer pertinent comments from the point of view of the 'systems thinking':

Since civilization, with its artificial environment, does imply some specialization, every civilization must have an economy which has progressed in some sense *beyond a subsistence economy*. But this does not mean that the growth of civilization was 'caused' by improved food production techniques, which may indeed in some cases have long been available. In many cases, I suggest, it did in fact come about through innovations in such techniques *coupled with* social and other developments which at the same time made these subsistence improvements both possible and desirable (Renfrew 1984: 277).

From this point of view he finds Adams' primary emphasis on transformation in the realm of social organization as a point of view tending towards the other extreme, as opposed to the primacy of the technological factor.

... we shall not expect the archeological record for the early development of a civilization to show greatly improved production techniques (e.g. irrigation) and 'surplus' storage facilities arising prior to, or without evidence of social stratification (e.g. palaces) or religious specialization (e.g. temples). Nor shall we, in the cases where the successful transition to civilization was later accomplished, expect these social and religious advantages to have developed markedly without developments also in food production. On the contrary, the two were linked by the multiplier effect, and it was their coupled expansion which led to rapid changes in the culture in general (Renfrew 1984: 278).

As a methodological proposition 'systems thinking' is certainly attractive because this in a sense takes our attention away from the invocation of sundry external causes. A culture becomes something to be understood in terms of the culture itself. Renfrew, for instance, tries to account for the birth of the Early Bronze Age Cycladic civilization by underlining the possible multiplier effect caused by vine cultivation which was linked to the manufacture of drinking vessels and, at a remove, religion; or by the production of, and trade in, daggers which was related to the development of better boats, the longships. But perhaps what is more significant in such contexts is not the solution of the initial problem itself but the building up, bit by bit, of what is called the 'system trajectory' covering the six subsystems. Depending on the quality and quantity of the data available this can be a valuable exercise in the explanation of any cultural change in the past. In the context of prehistoric Baluchistan, Jim Shaffer (1978) attempted this, and although this did not lead to any particularly path-breaking conclusions, it made possible the appreciation of the prehistoric Baluchi situation within the framework of Baluchistan itself. More recently, Erdosy (1988: 87 ff), in his discussion on 'the emergence of civilization' in the Gangetic valley, apparently accepts the logic of systematic thinking, but as far as I can understand it, he does not attempt at any point to build up or outline the 'system trajectory' in the context of the Gangetic valley. On the contrary, he refers to such issues as internal or external stresses, 'late Vedic society in archaeology', 'the Indo-Aryan contribution', etc.—in fact, the kind of issues which, one would have thought, formed no part of 'systematic thinking'. This is a good example of what Paul Courbin (1988: 35) expressed by writing, 'practice contrasts with the theory that has been repeated a thousand times', and has regrettably added nothing to his otherwise laudable settlement survey of the Allahabad district.

My aim in the present work is to undertake a study of the cities of tne Indus civilization and the subsequent early historic phase in different parts of India through an analysis of their background, physical features and historical contexts. Some theoretical ideas regarding early urban growth have been incorporated in this chapter as a general methodological backdrop to the Indian situation. The various debates specific to the Indian situation will be taken up in their appropriate contexts, and if any theoretical preferences are expressed here, it is due to the belief that the appearance of writing in the historical and archaeological records is a crucial dividing line between the pre-urban and urban situations in a given cultural context. I am aware that the appearance of writing was not a sudden or arbitrary event (Schmandt-Besserat 1992) but that does not make the appearance of literati as a class less significant. Secondly, I do not propose to offer any specific definition of a 'city', although the criteria of size, density, the presence of literati, various crafts specializations, etc. will be borne in mind when surveying the mass of Indian archaeological data in different regions. I have tried to take into consideration the settlement distributions of various periods and areas and to relate the 'cities' to these distributions. Despite the lack of definite knowledge, discussions along this line would, if nothing else, serve to pinpoint the lacunae in our understanding of the subject.

Chapter Two

Background and Origin of the Indus Civilization

BACKGROUND

The circumstances of the discovery and the first announcement of the Indus civilization (Chakrabarti 1988) do not concern us here. What does concern us here, especially to appreciate how the study of the background of this civilization has proceeded since then, is what John Marshall, the man who organized the first systematic phase of excavations at the Harappan sites, wrote while editing the first major report on that work *Mohenjodaro and the Indus Civilization*. In his introduction to this three volume report he wrote extensively on the distinct and unique character of the civilization, taking care to point out how it corresponded in its general features with the 'Chalcolithic cultures of Western Asia and Egypt'.

In other respects, however, it was peculiar to Sind and Panjab and as distinctive of those regions as the Sumerian culture was of Mesopotamia or the Egyptian of the Valley of the Nile. Thus, to mention only a few salient points, the use of cotton for textiles was exclusively restricted at this period to India and was not extended to the Western world until two or three thousand years later. Again there is nothing that we know of in prehistoric Egypt or Mesopotamia or anywhere else in Western Asia to compare with the well-built baths and commodious houses of the citizens of Mohenjodaro. In those countries, much money and thought were lavished on the building of magnificent temples for the gods and on the palaces and tombs of kings, but the rest of the people seemingly had to content themselves with insignificant dwellings of mud. In the Indus valley, the picture is reversed and the finest structures are those erected for the convenience of the citizens. Temples, palaces, and tombs there may of course have been, but if so, they are still undiscovered or so like other edifices are not to be readily distinguishable from them. At Ur, it is true, Mr Woolley has unearthed a group of moderate-sized houses of burnt brick which constitutes a notable exception to the general rule; but these disclose such a striking similarity to the small and rather loosely built structures of the latest levels at Mohenjodaro, that there can be little doubt as to the influence under which they were erected. Be this,

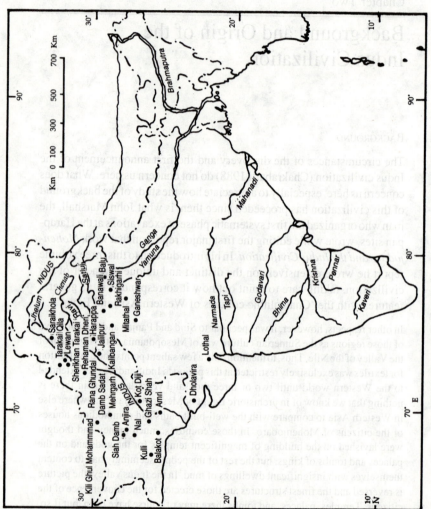

Map 1: General distribution of sites mentioned in Chapter 2

however, as it may, we are justified in seeing in the Great Bath of Mohenjodaro and in its roomy and serviceable houses, with their ubiquitous wells and bathrooms and elaborate systems of drainage, evidence that the ordinary towns people enjoyed here a degree of comfort and luxury unexampled in other parts of the then civilized world.

Equally peculiar to the Indus Valley and stamped with an individual character of their own are its art and religion. Nothing that we know of in other countries at this period bears any resemblance, in point of style, to the miniature faience models of rams, dogs and other animals or to the intaglio engravings on the seals, the best of which—notably the humped and short-horned bulls—are distinguished by a breadth of treatment and a feeling for line and plastic form that has rarely been surpassed in glyptic art; nor would it be possible, until the classic age of Greece, to match the exquisitely supple modeling of the two human statuettes from Harappa. . . . In the religion of the Indus peoples there is much of course, that might be paralleled in other countries. This is true of every prehistoric and most historic religions as well. But, taken as a whole, their religion is so characteristically Indian as hardly to be distinguishable from still living Hinduism or at least from that aspect of it which is bound up with animism and the cults of Siva and the Mother Goddess—still the two most potent forces in popular worship. Among the many revelations that Mohenjodaro and Harappa have had in store for us, none perhaps is more remarkable than this discovery that Saivism has a history going back to the Chalcolithic Age or perhaps even further still, and that it thus takes its place as the most ancient living faith in the world (Marshall 1931: vol. I; vi–vii)

He further goes on to write:

One thing that stands out clear and unmistakable both at Mohenjodaro and Harappa, is that the civilization hitherto revealed at these two places is not an incipient civilization, but one already age-old and stereotyped on Indian soil, with many millennia of human endeavour behind it. Thus India must henceforth be recognized, along with Persia, Mesopotamia and Egypt, as one of the most important areas where the civilizing processes of society were initiated and developed. I do not mean to imply by this that India can claim to be regarded as the cradle of civilization; nor do I think on the evidence at present available that that claim can be made on behalf of any one country in particular. . . . In each of these river valleys, on the banks of the Nile and the Euphrates as on those of the Karun, the Helmand or the Indus, mankind may be assumed to have had equal chances of development, and it is natural to suppose that progress in one direction or another was being made in all these regions simultaneously and doubtless in many others besides. If this view, which is surely the most rational one, be accepted, if we regard this wide-flung civilization of the Afrasian belt as focussed in various centres and developed by the mutual efforts of different peoples, we shall better understand how, despite its general homogeneity, it nevertheless comprised many widely differing branches, each of which, in its own sphere, was able to maintain its local and individual character (Marshall 1931: vol. I; viii).

It is interesting to note that virtually the same sentiment was expressed by V. Gordon Childe. The civilization, according to him,

represents a very perfect adjustment of human life to a specific environment, that can only have resulted from years of patient effort. And, it has endured; it is already specifically Indian and forms the basis of modern Indian culture. In architecture and industry, still more in dress and religion, Mohenjodaro reveals features that have always been characteristic of historical India (Childe 1952: 183–4).

I consider it important to draw attention to these definitive statements made by Marshall and Childe on the distinctive and Indian character of the Indus civilization as a *civilization* (not as a tradition or culture) because this is exactly what is missing in the writings of many subsequent scholars. In their quest for its separate components and regional diversities they very often lose sight of the totality of this Bronze Age civilization which, despite being much larger than any of its contemporaries, is, because of the undeciphered status of its writing, the most ill-understood of them all. The continuity of cultural development and the elements of regional diversity are no doubt important in the study of archaeological records but the status of these issues need not make us oblivious of the homogeneity and sheer splendour of this civilization which Marshall's statements so strongly evoke. In the preceding chapter I emphasized my support for the view that the presence of literati as proved by the existence of a writing system should be considered the ultimate dividing line between the pre-civilized and civilized or non-urban and urban contexts anywhere. From this point of view the nearest Bronze Age civilization to the west of the Indus was Elam or southwestern Iran with Susa as its centre. From this point of view again, there was no contemporary *civilization* in the Oxus valley or to the north of the Hindukush. From my point of view the Indus civilization formed a large, literate oasis in an unrelieved landscape of non-literate and hence 'barbarian' groups.

Even before Marshall's opinion that the Indus civilization 'must have had a long and antecedent history on the soil of India' (Marshall 1931: 106) was published, one of his own officers, Nani Gopal Majumdar, discovered, in the course of his prehistoric explorations in Sind (1929–31), evidence of at least a part of this 'antecedent history' at the site of Amri. On the basis of his excavations at the site Majumdar showed clear stratigraphic evidence to argue that the Amri pottery 'should be looked upon as representing an earlier phase of the chalcolithic civilization than that represented by Harappa and Mohenjodaro' (Majumdar 1934: 27). Further evidence came from a few other sites, notably Ghazi Shah where the Amri ware belonged to the earliest period of occupation and co-existed for some time with the Indus civilization pottery till only the latter type was used (Majumdar 1934: 85). More than a decade later, Mortimer Wheeler (1947) found some pottery below the 'defences' of the AB mound at Harappa, testifying to the presence of an earlier culture at the site.

In the fifties scholarly opinion on the origin of the Indus civilization varied from Stuart Piggott's sober statement that an origin outside India was 'inherently improbable' (Piggott 1950) to R. Heine-Geldern's reference to 'colonial cities' in the Indus context (Heine-Geldern 1956) or D.H. Gordon's idea of a piecemeal migration from Elam and Mesopotamia (Gordon 1958). In between these two opposing categories of thought was Wheeler's explanation in terms of A.L. Kroeber's concept of 'stimulus diffusion' (Kroeber 1940), which was first put forward in 1953 (Wheeler 1953: 93–4; repeated in two subsequent editions of this work in 1960 and 1968). There is no point in discussing Wheeler's theory in detail now (see Chakrabarti 1984); it will suffice to point out here that there is a contradiction between his premise of the migration of civilization from Mesopotamia to the Indus and his statement that the high-built citadels of Mohenjodaro and Harappa 'seem indeed to be frowning upon their cities with a hint of alien domination'. One must also note that it is from this time that the Indus civilization began to be conceived of as something fertilized by Mesopotamia in particular and West Asia in general. It is also interesting to observe that the Indian and Pakistani scholars of the period have hardly commented on the background of this civilization except for pointing out, as B.B. Lal (1953) has done in his essay on protohistoric investigations in 1953, the gradually growing significance of chronologically earlier chalcolithic finds (cf. W.A. Fairservis' first report on the Quetta valley in 1952) in Baluchistan.

The work of the Indian and Pakistani scholars on this problem came into focus from the mid-fifties onwards. In 1955 and 1957 F.A. Khan of the Pakistan Department of Archaeology excavated the site of Kot Diji near Khairpur in Sind. A substantially thick deposit with evidence of a fortified settlement going back to a time earlier than the beginning of the Indus civilization was found here for the first time. It was further observed that certain ceramic shapes and designs and some miscellaneous elements (cf. terracotta 'cakes') continued from this phase into the phase of the

Indus civilization. However, there was also a burnt level between these two phases. The work soon gained support from the French work at Amri in Sind under J.M.Casal (1959–62) and the Indian work at Kalibangan in the dried up Ghaggar valley under B.B. Lal and B.K. Thapar of the Archaeological Survey of India, which began in 1960. Casal's work at Amri brought to light the ceramic and structural details of the 'Amri culture' at the site. The evidence of a 'transitional' phase between the Amri culture and the Indus civilization was also discovered here. A fortified 'pre-Indus' settlement with different house orientations from those of the succeeding 'Indus' phase occurred at Kalibangan where it was found that the 'pre-Indus' pottery continued alongside 'Indus' pottery for some time. As a result of this work it was now possible to understand the stratigraphic contexts of the ceramic material found by A. Ghosh in 1950–52 at some sites in the Ghaggar valley in Rajasthan. It was realized that the 'pre-Indus' Kalibangan pottery was found for the first time at Sothi (for a more recent note on Sothi, see Dikshit 1984) during Ghosh's explorations.

Thus it is obvious that by the early sixties some meaningful archaeological discussion on the background and origin of the Indus civilization was possible. This was provided by A. Ghosh in a seminar on the prehistory and protohistory of India, which was held at the Deccan College, Pune, from 24 May to 31 May 1964.

Ghosh began by pointing out that the pre-Harappan pottery of Kalibangan was identical with the Sothi pottery identified by him earlier in the Sarasvati-Drishadvati valley of Rajasthan. He further pointed out that this pottery was 'found mixed up with the Harappan pottery on the surface of practically all the Sarasvati-Drishadvati sites'. He also found this pottery to be 'analogous with the pre-defence (Periano-Ghundai) pottery of Harappa and also with that of the earlier (pre-Harappan) period of Kot Diji'. Some of the designs on this pottery were then compared with those on the pottery of the Quetta valley (Kile Gul Mohammad black on red slip; Kechi Beg black-on-buff; Quetta ware and Quetta wet ware), north Baluchistan (Sur Jangal coarse and painted wares), south Baluchistan (Mehi-Nundara) and the lowest excavated level of Mohenjodaro. It was also noted how some of its elements 'continued in the mature Harappa': the fish-scale and the pipal leaf; the pottery with external ribbing; the external cord-impression; basins with deep incisions or shallow combings in the interior; the pre-citadel Harappan ring-stand paralleled by finds at Mohenjodaro; the short-stemmed dish-on-stand of Sothi; and a terracotta cake from the lower levels of Kot Diji. Ghosh came to this conclusion:

The occurrence of the Sothi ware, comparable in some details not only with the Zhob (Periano-Ghundai) but with Quetta and central Baluch industries, in the lowest levels at Harappa and Mohenjodaro, its abundance on practically all Harappan sites on the Sarasvati, the persistence of its traits in the Harappan pottery not only in the Sarasvati region but also at Mohenjodaro and Harappa, the co-existence of the Sothi and Harappan people at Kalibangan (KLB-2) and possibly also at Kot Diji—all this cannot be dismissed as accidental but on the contrary must have a bearing on the Harappan genesis. A firm Sothi substratum is obvious in the make-up of the Harappa—much firmer than that of the other earlier cultures. There is every justification for regarding the Sothi as 'proto-Harappan' (Ghosh 1965).

This is certainly a clearly formulated hypothesis which does Ghosh much credit. Much later this found its full expression in M. Rafiq Mughal's Ph.D. dissertation on 'The Early Harappan Period in the Greater Indus Valley and Northern Baluchistan (*c*. 3000–2400 BC)'.

The second part of Ghosh's argument deals specifically with the mechanism of origin and is linked to Wheeler's theory. The form of the civilization, he argued, was the result of a deliberate choice made by 'a few genius-dictators' who 'borrowed the idea of cities from the contemporary Sumerians' and promoted foreign trade and standardization to gain prosperity. In his own language, he postulated a 'highly artificial birth of the culture'.

George F. Dales in 1965 (Dales 1965) and W.A. Fairservis in 1967 (Fairservis 1967) tried to understand the proto-historic cultural growth in Baluchistan and the Indus system in terms of a few developing 'phases' (Dales) or 'stages' (Fairservis). Dales' Phase C was supposed to herald the first discernible period of settled village life in the area extending from Mundigak in south Afghanistan to the Quetta and Zhob-Loralai areas in north Baluchistan and the Kalat area of central Baluchistan. Both south Baluchistan and the Indus plain supposedly remained untouched. This phase was characterized by metal objects, progressive refinement of stone tools leading to the first parallel-sided blade industry, ground alabaster bowls, crude clay humped bull figurines and the development of a rich pottery industry. Settlements spread in the succeeding Phase D not merely to south Baluchistan (early phase of the Nal complex) but also to the Indus plain and north Rajasthan below and were characterized generally by the gradual elaboration and refinement of the earlier types. Phase E marked the transition from villages to towns with fortified citadels (Kot Diji, also Mundigak in south Afghanistan) while Phase F was taken to represent the Indus civilization itself.

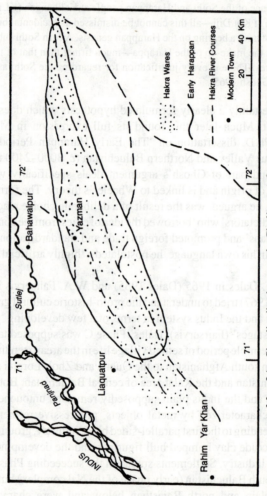

Map 2A: Site distribution area in Cholistan (after Mughal 1992)

Fairservis' Stage III is characterized by a fully developed sedentary village life with regionalization and inter-regional contact. He included in this not merely the relevant sites in Baluchistan (Damb Sadaat II, Sur Jangal III, Rana Ghundai III, Anjira IV, etc.) but also sites like Amri, Kot Diji, Kalibangan and other probable ones in Sind and north Rajasthan. In Fairservis' analysis the agricultural settlements of this period represented an elaborate adjustment with their ecological settings, which was manifest in the developed type of settlements and the presence of various ceramic designs like the humped bulls, cobras, birds, fishes, etc., typically Indian designs in themselves. This stage was followed by the Indus civilization which was Fairservis' Stage IV. The distinctive traits of Stage III were supposed to be large villages, a wide variety of copper-bronze pins, knives, axes (including socketed types), female and other types of terracotta figurines, compartmented seals, an elaborate system of potters' marks, alabaster vessels, diverse painted pottery, open-based immovable bread-ovens and a 'very apparent regionalization'. Of the various regions manifesting these traits, Fairservis chose the one in northern Sind and Kachhi plain to describe as early Harappan (Fairservis 1967: 11). Since this is the first use of the term early Harappan, as opposed to Ghosh's 'proto-Harappan', his line of argument may be cited in detail:

Most significant is the style found in northern Sind, along the southern borders of the plain of Kachhi, and the foothills of the Khirtar Range. Apparently a localized outgrowth of the Kulli-Quetta culture styles of Baluchistan, it is characterized by such features as unpainted terracotta bangles round in cross-section, female and animal figurines with rather gross features, so-called 'cakes' of terracotta, and a pottery corpus closely related to that of Baluchistan. However, the painted designs on the pottery, though derived from Baluchistan, are characteristically composed in over-all patterns in which floral elements have a special place. Unfortunately, no excavator has as yet uncovered these settlements, but surface remains indicate that the villages were probably large and flourishing. The above style characterizes some of the styles of the Harappan civilization and in fact, is known to have existed prior to the mature phase of that civilization at certain sites, including Mohenjodaro. This provides a reason to label it Early Harappan and thus in the direct line to the so-called mature or urbanized phase of that culture (Fairservis 1967: 11).

Apart from trying to define an early Harappan horizon, largely on the basis of surface finds, Fairservis tried to explain the origin of the Indus civilization. His theoretical position in this regard was certainly contradictory. 'The Harappan civilization can be said to have achieved its characteristic style indigenously; its elaboration may be the result of

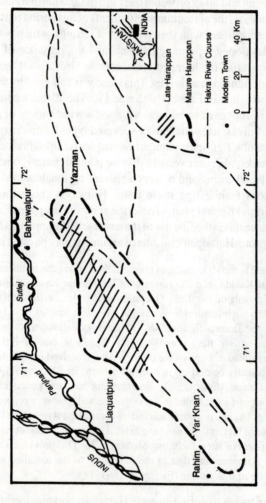

Map 2B: Site distribution area in Cholistan (after Mughal 1992)

Mesopotamian contact' (Fairservis 1967: 15) Although Fairservis (1967: 19) realizes that the 'urban situation in the Indus river valley was a logical development from advanced village farming in an optimum situation', he does not deny what he (Fairservis 1971: 222) calls the 'outside-influence factor'. An 'important diffusionary movement overland from southern Mesopotamia and Khuzistan . . . played a part in the development of the style of the late, if not the early, phase of the Kulli culture and undeniably the Harappan civilization' (Fairservis 1971: 228). This, according to him, was the first factor. The second factor was the 'subcontinental setting', a setting which possessed considerable 'subsistence advantages'. The third factor was called the 'social readiness for civilization'. It is less easy to define, but the basic idea is that the highland villages in the valleys of Baluchistan had already established a socioeconomic, cultural and organizational network of their own. When the transition to the Indus plains took place, this network was 'extended by degrees with consequent shifts of population according to the successful settlement of region after region'. This meant that the links between the different regions were not broken nor did they lose touch with the highland setting as the expansion of settlements in the valley went on. In Fairservis' argument:

. . . the urbanization process so necessary to the definition of a civilization would appear to have come about as the inevitable result of the direction already taken by the villagers of the borderlands. What was lacking in the highlands was the space and the natural resources to stimulate the process. In the Indus both were at hand. With little technological innovation but with an already largely established hierarchical system the organization necessary to handle the problem of settled life in the valley was created (Fairservis 1971: 238).

B. and F.R. Allchin (1968: 123–5) in 1968 agreed broadly with Ghosh in seeing the 'continuity from pre-Harappan to Harappan times' in the Indus valley as 'suggesting that a large if not a major element in the Harappan civilization must derive from the pre-Harappan culture of the Indus valley itself' and as constituting the 'formative stage' which led to the formation of the first Indian cities from villages. They also pointed out many cultural resemblances between the pre-Harappan sites of the Indus valley and suggested that there already was a considerable cultural uniformity in the area. According to them there were three sub-regions of the pre-Harappan culture province: the central, including Kot Diji, Harappa and possibly Mohenjodaro; the southern or Amri with ties with south Baluchistan; and the eastern or Kalibangan, with hypothetical affinities further east.

R. Mughal's dissertation is dated 1970–71 and is influenced in two ways by Fairservis (1967). First, Mughal's use of the term early Harappan goes back to Fairservis' use of the term. Secondly—and perhaps more importantly—like Fairservis before him, Mughal postulates a north Baluchistan-greater Indus valley axis. Unlike Fairservis, however, his analysis of the data is more detailed and his explanation of the origin of the civilization is not dependent on the 'outside-influence factor'. Terminology—the applicability of terms like pre-Harappan, proto-Harappan, early Harappan and early Indus, all of which are known to mean the same age—is not particularly important. But what is important is that there was a cultural continuum with a good deal of shared traits in both north Baluchistan and the greater Indus valley. Mughal systematically considered the mass of data from all the relevant excavated and unexcavated sites and added considerable precision to them in cultural terms. Perhaps the most important part of Mughal's analysis from the point of view of the origin of the Indus civilization is his comparative analysis of early Harappan material remains and their distributional patterns in the greater Indus valley. The items considered are not merely pottery (which he considers in detail, taking into account both the similarities and dissimilarities and defining the different areas of distribution of Amri, Kot Dijan and Sothi or Kalibangan wares) but also every other cultural item—architecture, terracotta, metallurgy, stone tools and technology, graffiti and fauna. In north Baluchistan he first studied the data in terms of internal comparative stratigraphy and then showed how this area was linked externally with south Afghanistan and the associated areas beyond. Comparing the north Baluchistan material with the greater Indus valley early Harappan assemblage, he found close culture inter-relationships between the two regions. The importance of north Baluchistan as a link with the west seemed to have ceased with the beginning of the Indus civilization and this role seemed to have shifted to south Baluchistan. Mughal also pointed out that towards the end of the early Harappan period, there was an increase in population both in north Baluchistan and the greater Indus valley. Mughal's concise summary of the evidence needs a close consideration at this point.

Concerning the evidence of Early Harappan period in the Greater Indus Valley and the questions pertaining to the rise of urbanization, some points require re-emphasis. Permanent occupation is indicated by the use of stone and mud-bricks in successive levels exposed at Kot Diji, Kalibangan I and Amri IB-ID. There is a progressive change from simple domestic structures of one or two rooms to complex buildings of several rooms with elaborations of platforms, drains and soak wells. The stability of settlements through time may also be linked with the availability of favourable means of subsistence. A monumental aspect of architecture is demonstrated by the presence of defence walls, indicating also that important centres—administrative?—had emerged and there was need for defense. There was common knowledge and use of copper, steatite and lapis lazuli, indicating accessibility to the sources of raw materials or availability of means for procuring them. A common technological level is reflected by the uniformity of stone and bone tools. Specialized crafts, like flint-knapping, had emerged indicating possible occupational and/or class stratification. The use of wheeled carts is common as shown by the presence of numerous toy-cart frames and wheels. The carts were probably drawn by bullocks because *Bos indicus* is attested in the faunal remains of the Early Harappan period and by the discovery of many bull figurines modelled in clay. The ceramic groups in different parts of the vast Indus plains, despite some regional differences are marked by many similarities in their forms and decorative designs. Thus, the appearance of permanent settlements, some degree of monumentality in architecture, craft specialization, the use of draft animals, and distribution of identical forms of pottery over an extensive area in the Greater Indus Valley and also in northern Baluchistan is the phenomenon precisely like that in Mesopotamia during the 'Ubaidian' (Ubaid 3 and 4) period of the late fifth and early fourth millenium BC which Braidwood calls the period of 'incipient urbanization'. The similarities of many cultural traits reflected in both the ceramic and non-ceramic materials of the early Harappan cultures represent like the 'Ubaidian' phase in Mesopotamia, the first *oikumene* of the Greater Indus Valley, which subsequently crystallized into an overall homogeneity and standardization of artifactual remains during the Mature Harappan period . . . most of the elements that later characterize the developed stage of the Harappan culture merely represent the intensification and climax of these processes (Mughal 1971: 373–4).

Mughal is on less firm ground when he tries to explain the origin of the civilization. He confesses, 'it does not seem possible to reconstruct the circumstances leading to urbanization in the Indus Valley as clearly as Robert McC. Adams has done in the case of Mesopotamia' (Mughal 1971: 376). As far as I can deduce, he puts emphasis in this regard on two factors. First, he tries to argue that during the mature Harappan period the centre of power shifted from north to south Baluchistan and settlements spread to the coast suggesting intensification of trade with Mesopotamia. Secondly—and this seems to be more important in his scheme of analysis—he tries to infer a population increase during the early Harappan period. However, even in this case he is far from being sure:

It is possible that population increase or its concentration, was the primary causative factor in precipitating the Urban Revolution in the Indus Valley. However, on the present evidence, it is difficult to pinpoint the exact time when the change from the 'incipient' to the full urbanization took place (Mughal 1971: 377).

Mughal's summary of the evidence, which is cited and which highlights the basic significance of the early Harappan level in the make-up of the Harappan civilization, finds an echo in my independent assessment of the evidence in 1972–73:

In an impressionistic view, the pre-Harappan villages may be said to have introduced in the Harappan distribution belt the following technologico-economic features: an extensive use of wheels, a limited but developed knowledge of copper-bronze, a plough-based cultivation along with a knowledge of locally cultivable crops, the use of durable building materials, the laying out of a nucleated settlement within walls, the turning out of a wide variety of terracotta and stone objects, a good deal of regional inter-connection, and undetermined quantum of external trade contacts, etc. (Chakrabarti 1972–73).

The problem of origin still remained. In 1973 Mughal wrote:

On present evidence, the mature Harappan culture at early Indus or Harappan sites arrives with a fully developed mature culture. Does this sudden change mark a major shift in the socio-political structure of the Indus people? If so, what were the circumstances in which such a change occurred? At present, we have no evidence to answer these pertinent questions (Mughal 1973: 15).

The possibility that the process of change from the pre-Harappan rural base to the Harappan civilization was 'basically in the social-institutional sphere, giving the earlier village horizon a new, qualitatively different dimension' has also been suggested by me (Chakrabarti 1972–73: 30).

In 1972 C.C. Lamberg-Karlovsky (1972) brought in the issue of trade as a possible causative factor of Indus urban growth. The important point in Lamberg-Karlovsky's argument is the emphasis he puts on the significance of sites like Tepe Yahya and Shahr-i-Sokhta in southeast Persia which had control over certain natural resources and were either manufacturing or distributing centres of finished products based on these resources (steatite at Tepe Yahya; lapis lazuli and albaster at Shahr-i-Sokhta). The demand and supply relationship which this region had with Mesopotamia must have provided the basic economic base of urban growth at these sites and 'as in a system feedback', contributed to the urban growth process in Mesopotamia also. Because of an established pre-Harappan trade network with the region, the Indus system also could have been influenced by this process like Mesopotamia was. This hypothesis thus focusses attention in the Indian context on the nature of the relationship between the Harappan level and what Lamberg-Karlovsky

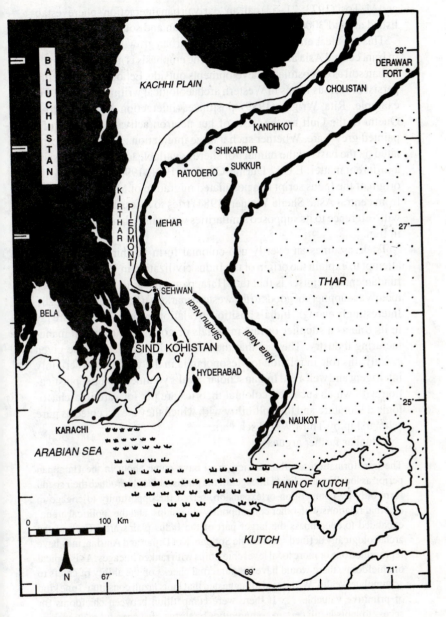

Map 2C: The suggested Indus-Hakra flows during the period of the
Indus civilization (after Flam 1981)

and M. Tosi (1973: 21–53) call an 'early urban interaction sphere' established around 3000 BC in Turkmenia, Seistan and south Afghanistan.

This is a clear attempt to link the Indus urban growth to developments in Iran, central Asia and Afghanistan. The emphasis is not so much on the Indian soil as on postulated developments outside. Echoes of this attempt persist in various forms in Western archaeological writings on India. For example, Rita Wright (1989) postulates interaction stretching from Quetta to the Gulf on the basis of her neutron activation studies of a painted grey ware. Whether such a large interaction zone can be postulated on the basis of the number of sherds available to her for analysis is a different matter. E.C.L. During-Caspers (1991, 1992) tries to link the origin of the Indus script to a postulated migration of Mongoloid people from central Asia. Sheila Weiner (1984) tries to assess Indus art mainly with reference to its supposed similarities with miscellaneous specimens in Iran.

Trade assumes an overtly neo-colonial form in Shireen Ratnagar's attempt to explain the origin of the Indus civilization in 1981. One of her fundamental premises is that the 'Harappans appear to have functioned mainly as suppliers of goods to the western markets' (Ratnagar 1981: 228). Interestingly enough, India's position in relation to the British empire lay in its role as a supplier of raw materials or goods to the British manufacturing industry. The fact that the Indus civilization should be given exactly this role in relation to Mesopotamia in the writing of a certainly intelligent and well-read Indian scholar speaks volumes for the sophistication with which such neo-colonial theories are put forward in archaeological literature and the gullibility with which they are accepted as pure scholarship by Third World scholars.

Ratnagar further argues:

The transformation to urban society may have come about in the Harappan period as locally subordinate lineages of the plains, able to reproduce their social form only by competition or expansion, seized the opportunity to engage in external relations with other contemporary chiefships, and the 'political arena' expanded to encompass the larger part of the Indus plains area. Each of the archaeologically defined spheres, the Sothian, Kot Dijian and Amrian, may have represented one or more local level chiefships with ranked lineages. As is typical of chiefdoms, there would have been internal checks on the ability of chiefs to accumulate wealth. We have also suggested that lapis lazuli constituted one kind of primitive valuable. . . . If there were competition between chiefdoms for access to lapis lazuli certain communities by virtue of successful relationships with mobile pastoralists who perhaps transported this material to the plains, would have an advantage over others. Lapis lazuli and its gifting and countergifting would then acquire a circle of personal dependents (Ratnagar 1981: 245).

Citing the opinion of two Western anthropologists, she argues that 'under such conditions heads of subordinate lineages would be drawn towards the chiefly centres, that local groups of the hinterland would begin to lose their autonomy, and that subsequently dependent clan members would also move towards the centre' (Ratnagar 1981: 245). It is a pity that such a cleverly constructed 'anthropological' argument should collapse with the discovery of lapis lazuli in the Chagai hills and the Zhob valley.

In 1982 B. and F.R. Allchin (1982) used the terms 'Early and Mature Indus stages' and called the early stage 'the formative period, the stage of incipient urbanism'.

The essential basis for the mature urbanism must be seen as the gradual build-up of population, and its spread through the Indus plains . . .; the growth of technology and agricultural know-how; and the establishment of a socio-economic interaction sphere over an enormous area. These things are all to be deduced to have reached their fulfilment during the Early Indus stage (B. and F.R. Allchin 1982: 165).

This formulation does not differ in any way from the formulations made by Chakrabarti (1972–73) and Mughal (1973), among others, but one of their assertions is difficult to explain:

Because . . . Early Indus period corresponds with the Early Dynastic of Mesopotamia and the most affluent period of such Iranian sites as Shahr-i-Sokhta, we may expect, and indeed evidence is forthcoming to confirm these expectations, that there would have been an unprecedented increase in trade with these regions (B. and F.R. Allchin 1982: 163).

It is difficult to agree with this premise because there seems to be no evidence of trade with Mesopotamia during the early Harappan/early Indus period. Moreover, the early Harappan/early Indus stage comes before the early dynastic period in Mesopotamia. What is interesting is that it is somehow difficult for them to think of the origin of the Indus civilization without trying to link the issue in some way with Mesopotamia.

D.P. Agrawal in the same year (Agrawal 1982: 140–1) did not pay much attention to the problem of the origin of the Harappan civilization except for saying that 'the Harappa culture was not a transplant from Sumer'. However he argues that 'the Sumerian civilization . . . was a thousand years earlier than the Indus' and 'so the idea of city-life and its innovations was already in the air to have influenced the pre-Harappans and Harappans too'. It is difficult to understand the basis of his chronology of the early dynastic Mesopotamia or what he calls the Sumerian civilization vis-a-vis the Harappan civilization. As far as the second part of his opinion is concerned, Agrawal merely echoes Wheeler's opinion on this issue.

Mesopotamia and Elam figure prominently in Louis Flam's explanation of the origin of the Harappan civilization (Flam 1984, 1986):

My recent research in Sind has now established clear artifactual correspondence between Kot Dijian ceramics at Nippur in Mesopotamia during the Jemdet Nasr Period (c. 3300–2900 BC) and between the Jamdet Nasr ceramics and the Amrian phase at the site of Ghazi Shah in Sind Kohistan. Lamberg-Karlovsky has also found Amri and Nal ceramics in Eastern Iran and has suggested this area as a possible contact zone between the Indus Region and Mesopotamia during the Jemdet Nasr Period. Thus, the correlations linking Amri-Nal-Kot Diji with Mesopotamia are further magnified by these correspondences between Amri-Nal and Eastern Iran, at a date approximately 600 years earlier than the Harappan civilization. In addition, a clear link can now be established between the site of Kulli in Southern Baluchistan, and the region of eastern Iran, Bahrain and Mesopotamia, dating to the Early Dynastic II period in the Mesopotamian chronology (c. 2700–2400 BC). In a recent paper Tosi has presented an argument in which he has named Eastern Iran 'Outer Elam'. On the basis of the limited but provocative evidence, suggested in this paper this region of 'Outer Elam' may have to be extended at least through Southern Baluchistan and Sind Kohistan at the end of 4th and the beginning of the third millennium BC. The preceding evidence emphasizes the importance of Western Sind and the complex relationships or interactions which developed there which eventually led to the development of the Indus civilization (Flam 1984: 82).

It has been necessary to cite Flam's and others' Mesopotamia/West Asia-centred theories in detail because these unerringly demonstrate how the idea of the origin of the Indus civilization has hardly changed since Wheeler's day, Mughal's and some others' efforts notwithstanding. Flam has simply been more forthright than the rest; he did not even bother to give the details of his Kot Diji ceramics at Nippur and the evidence of a 'clear link' of Kulli with Mesopotamia.

The eighties began with one of the most momentous discoveries in subcontinental archaeology (Jarrige and Meadow 1980). The excavations in the Bolan valley at Mehrgarh in the Kachhi plain are significant not so much for the light they shed on the history of the growth of villages which led to the development of the civilization in the Indus valley and elsewhere as for the fact that they show the importance of this part of South Asia with regard to the cultivation of wheat and barley and the rearing of sheep, goat and cattle. Secondly, by providing a continuous sequence of cultural growth in this area from *c.* 7000 BC they have brought into sharper focus the picture of cultural development elsewhere in Baluchistan in so far as these developments relate to this sequence. However, the question remains as to what extent can the discoveries at Mehrgarh be treated as part of the growth of village settlements in the Indus plain?

The Kachhi plain—about 5310 square miles of alluvium between the MariBugti hills in the east and the Kirthars and central Brahui Range on the other side—is no doubt a projection of the Indus alluvium into what is now administratively Baluchistan, but its geographical conditions, it seems, are different. The area enjoys about three inches of annual rainfall (most of it in July–August) and is subject to scorching heat in summer, the highest temperature in the subcontinent being recorded in Jacobabad. The major rivers of the Kachhi plain—Nari, Bola, Sukleji and Mula and the hill torrents such as the Dhoriri, Lahri and Chhatr—dissipate into countless natural channels on entering Kachhi. These are seasonal courses but during the floods water is raised to the surface by a system of large dams across the beds of these rivers. On the whole, the picture is very different from that obtained in the Indus flood plain, and from this point of view alone, it is difficult to argue that Mehrgarh in the Kachhi plain stands as a milestone in the linear course of development towards the Indus civilization except in a general sense. The immediate context of the Indus civilization is provided by the pre-urban settlements in the plains of the Indus in Sind, the Indus and her tributaries in Panjab and the Ghaggar-Hakra in the Rajasthan/Cholistan desert. One of the major issues in this context is to try to delineate the core-area of this development.

The process began, on Mughal's reckoning (Mughal 1990), in the first half of the fourth millennium BC. By this time the village-farming communities of the Baluchistan hill valleys, Bannu basin, Gomal valley and Las Bela coast had established deep roots, displaying nucleated settlements with mud/mud-brick houses, copper-bronze metallurgy, a wide range of plain and painted wheel-made pottery, terracotta mother goddesses and cattle figurines, regionally available raw materials and some evidence of participation in the trans-regional trade to the west. At this point in time the challenge lay in harnessing the tremendous agricultural potential of the two major river valleys to the east—the valleys of the Indus and the Ghaggar-Hakra.

The most significant cluster of pre-early Harappan sites in this valley region can be seen in the distribution of Mughal's Hakra ware sites in the Cholistan desert in the Ghaggar-Hakra valley or in the ancient Sarasvati system. The diagnostic traits seem to be a pottery with a mud-roughened surface and a red ware with a black slip all over the body. On the Indian side of the Rajasthan/Bahawalpur border only one site has been reported (Dalal 1981); its basic distribution is in the Pakistani segment. The distribution apparently extends to the central Indus valley because the Hakra ware has been reported in the first period at Jalilpur near Multan (Mughal 1974). In fact Jalilpur is the only site where this pottery has been stratigraphically isolated; its wider ramifications, if any, are not yet understood. Mughal reports 99 Hakra ware sites in Cholistan, mostly on mudflats and some on the fossilized sand dunes in the area. These include 52 temporary occupations or camp sites, 45 settlement sites and 2 sites where industrial or craft-related activities are indicated by the presence of kilns. The criteria for these distinctions, specially between the camp sites and settlement sites, are not made clear. What is interesting is that only two of these sites were occupied in the succeeding early Harappan period and only four in the mature Harappan stage. It is difficult to explain why there was such a distinct settlement shift after this period. Mughal (1992) links this to a change in the course of the Hakra, but the point does not come out clearly in his brief discussion of the problem. Apart from pottery the surface finds at the Hakra ware sites comprise terracotta animal figurines with short and joined legs which include representations of cattle, shell and terracotta bangles with triangular/rectangular cross-sections, fragments of grinding stones, bits of copper and a lithic industry including microblades, borers, leaf-shaped arrow heads, scrapers and cores. The Jalilpur I assemblage shows, in addition, gold, coral and semiprecious stone beads. This discovery of varieties of stone, copper, shell, gold and coral objects clearly underlines a pattern of internal trade network. What is of further interest is that Mughal (1992) posits a four-tiered settlement hierarchy for the sites of this period: 0.1–5 ha.: 21; 5.1–10 ha.: 5; 10.1–20 ha.: 7; 20.1–30 ha.: 4. This is an impressive site hierarchy in the context of this period, and on the basis of the available data it is not difficult to postulate the existence of a social and administrative hierarchy, craft specialization and an exchange network. It may also be stressed that the inception of this culture which apparently emerges full-fledged in the region is obscure and one would reckon the excavation of Hakra ware sites in Cholistan an archaeological priority.

The second phase of the Cholistan sequence is represented by a Kot Diji-related horizon or what Mughal calls the early Harappan period. He lists 40 or more early Harappan sites in this area with a slightly different but overlapping distribution with the earlier Hakra ware sites. He offers a size category analysis for 37 of them: 0.1–5 ha.: 19; 5.1–10 ha.: 8; 10.1–20 ha.: 3; 20.1–30 ha.: 2. He further says that only 3 of the early Harappan sites could be called 'camp sites' and that the number of sites with kilns increased from two in the earlier period to fourteen. The four-tiered site hierarchy apparently continued but two of the sites—Gamanwala (27.3 ha.) and Jaiwali (22.5 ha.)—were comparable in size with Rehman Dheri in the Gomal valley in the west and Kalibangan in the east. The distribution of these sites peters out to the east of Gamanwala, i.e. in the direction of Kalibangan.

There is a difference in the site distribution during the mature Harappan period in the area. First, the core distribution area lies further downstream. In fact, to the east of 72-E there are very few mature Harappan sites, Sandhanwala being one of them. The implication is that the sites in Rajasthan fall outside the scope of the Cholistan distribution area. Secondly, the number of sites (174) greatly increases in this period. Mughal offers a size category analysis for 73 of them: 0.1–5 ha.: 44; 5.1–10 ha.: 20; 10.1–20 ha.: 8; over 80 ha.: 1. He further observes that at 79 sites there were areas 'exclusively ear-marked for kilns and mass production of items'. As there is hardly a site in this area where the mature Harappan phase directly overlies the early Harappan one, Mughal (1992) infers that another hydrographic change after the early Harappan period necessitated 'relocation of settlements on new ground'.

If Mughal's work has been our base-line in Cholistan, Louis Flam's work should be our base-line in Sind. Here the demarcation between the Kohistan–Kirthar piedmont and the main Indus valley is clear, and according to Flam's map (Flam 1981), only one site, Kot Diji, is way out in the valley, although not on the valley floor itself but on a hill outlier overlooking it. The rest of the Amri–Kot Diji sites marking the first phase of village-growth in this part is confined to Kohistan and the Kirthar piedmont. As Flam's maps (1981) clearly suggest, there is an overlap between the distribution of Amri and Kot Diji sites, and from this point of view his grouping together of these two categories of sites is a logical exercise. But in the same area he also shows some 'transitional phase' sites which he relates to 'early Kulli' of southern Baluchistan. The main interest in Flam's work lies in the fact that he refers to a division between an acropolis and a lower town in the pre-Harappan settlements of this region. It is relevant to cite Flam in detail on this crucial point:

The most conspicuous prehistoric settlement type in Sind Kohistan consists in part of an artificially built, conically-shaped hill which rises to an average height of 25 metres above its surrounding plain. These conically-shaped hills . . . vary in circumference, but each one exhibits the remains of a series (2–4) of encircling, terraced stone walls on its slopes, and remnants of inclined stairways or ramps ascend its southern side. Below these conically-shaped hills lie the remains of numerous stone foundation walls indicative of domestic structures. I refer to this settlement type as *acro-sanctum/lower-towns* to emphasize its highly elevated *(acro-)* conically-shaped configuration and to infer that the high hill, vis-a-vis the lower habitation area, was certainly a private place if not sacred *(sanctum)*. . . . Excavation on top of the acro-sanctums is necessary to ascertain their exact nature, but their spatial exclusiveness from the lower town is clear from unexcavated surface remains.

Of the 13 prehistoric sites located in the Kirthar region, one site displays the acro-sanctum/lower-town settlement pattern. The pattern appears in 13 of the 40 known sites in the Sind Kohistan region. The earliest of these acro-sanctum/lower-town settlements can be dated by ceramic parallels to the Amri phase in Sind Kohistan. Other sites with the settlement pattern can be assigned to a linked Amri-Transitional phase, still others to the Transitional phase . . . although Kot Dijian ceramics do not predominate on the surface of the acro-sanctum/lower-town sites, some typical examples are commonly found on the sites of Amri or Amri-Transitional date (Flam 1986: 74–5).

Another important part of Flam's analysis is that he points out the mutually exclusive character of the Amri and Kot Diji-related sites. In contrast to the dense distribution of 'early Harappan' Kot Diji sites in Cholistan, the Kirthar and Kohistan regions have the densest distribution of Amrian sites. 'Thus, two major cultural spheres, or ecosystems, can be delineated with linked interaction between the two indicated by the Kot Dijian sites in the Kirthar and Kohistan regions' (Flam 1986: 80).

Regarding the distribution of Kot Diji sites in the lower Indus region Flam's testimony is important. He demonstrated that barring the three Kot Dijian sites, two of which are located in Sind Kohistan and another in the Kirthar piedmont, and the site of Kot Diji itself which, although technically in the lower Indus valley, is on the top of an outlier, there is no Kot Dijian site in the valley itself. Flam discusses the reasons of Kot Diji–Amri interaction as evinced by the presence of Kot Diji sites in Kirthar–Kohistan but he also points out the ecological difference between the floodplain and Kirthar–Kohistan:

Without a large-scale canal irrigation system, *sailabi* (inundation) irrigation could only produce a single *rabi* crop. In Sind Kohistan and the Kirthar region perennial spring water for agricultural purposes permit double cropping, i.e. a *rabi* as well as a *kharif* crop. In the latter regions, however, soils are generally poor, shallow, and not widely available; with large grazing areas and plentiful year-round water supplies, pastoralism flourishes. In the Lower Indus Basin, rich soils are plentiful, and the problem lies in the seasonality of the floods (Flam 1986: 80).

Among the excavated sites of this region, both Amri and Kot Diji, beginning around the middle of the fourth millennium BC, show a fair amount of semi-precious stone beads including those of lapis lazuli, and shell and copper objects, demonstrating the regional exchange network. The evidence from Kot Diji is more elaborate. Of the twenty-one occupational layers at Kot Diji the top four layers (up to 3A) are Harappan; the next layer is a burnt one and the lower sixteen belong to the 'Kot Diji' culture. The settlement at this level seems to have been divided into two parts, one of which was encompassed by a wall, and has been called the citadel area. This surrounding wall was massive and solid, of mud resting on an undressed stone-block substructure, and supported at places on the outer side by a mud brick revetment. The wall was also strengthened externally with bastions. The bastion at the north-eastern corner measured 32 ft by 20 ft (9.75 m by 6.09 m). The stone and mud houses inside were very close to the surrounding wall, occasionally even using it as one of their own walls. The floors of the houses were paved with mudbricks and perhaps they were flat-roofed. The evidence of house remains outside the 'citadel area' is disturbed. The broad features of the Kot Diji pottery remain the same throughout but in its style of decoration and partly in texture and form there seem to be two main stages of development. In the earlier stage the texture is thinner and the shape is mostly a squat, globular, rimless and neckless form. The decoration is almost exclusively confined to a characteristic neckband. In the later stage the shapes and designs both become more diverse. The designs include such motifs as fish-scales, pipal leaves, etc. and the shapes comprise dish-on-stands, beakers, globular vases, etc. One of the paintings represents what has been called a 'horned deity'. The tool-types in stone consist of blades, scrapers, micro-blades, leaf-shaped arrowheads, etc. Copper does not seem to have been reported from Kot Diji but the use of copper must have been known at the site. Terracotta objects include toys, plain and painted bangles, cakes, cones and beads. There is also a finely modelled terracotta bull with a well-developed body, stout muzzle and short pointed horns. Other minor antiquities are limited to a few objects of shell and bones (for Amri, Casal 1964a: 8–20, 1964b: 57–65; for Flam's work at Ghazi Shah, Mughal 1991; for Kot Diji, Khan 1964, 1965). Broadly, the 'Kot Diji' level at Kot Diji falls in the first half of the third millennium BC. Mughal

(1990) points out that the published information from the site of Kot Diji is very selective, and on the basis of his own study of the stratified material he writes:

The occurrence of different categories of materials in both Kot Dijian and Harappan levels clearly demonstrates continuity throughout . . . the only significant difference is the absence in the Kot Dijian levels of mother goddess, of the type and form so familiar to us from the mature Harappan sites. . . . Another conclusion . . . is the presence of terracotta 'cakes', cones, cart-frames and cart wheels in the Early Harappan level at Kot Diji, confirming the evidence . . . from the pottery types. These objects, pottery such as offering stands, and painted designs of fish scales and intersecting circles were usually associated with the (Mature) Harappan culture only (Mughal 1990: 186).

The third area where the Kot Diji-related horizon is prominent and early is the Gomal valley. The early Harappan level at the site of Gumla (Dani 1970–71) in this region rests on two earlier levels, of which the first one is aceramic and the second one has wheel-made painted pottery, copper-bronze tools and beads, terracotta human and animal figurines, bird whistles, cart frames and bangles, stone pestles, grinders and pounders, and microblades and other types of microliths. The Kot Dijian pottery appears in Period III which has also semi-precious stone beads, terracotta beads, bangles and hooded female figurines with the lower parts of their bodies shown flat and bent at right angles, and 'true Harappan style parallel-sided blades'. This period at the site is dated soon after 3000 BC. Period IV is mature Harappan.

The evidence from Rehman Dheri (Duranni 1988) in the same region is more detailed. It is a large site (1700 ft by 1500 ft by 15 ft or 518.16 m by 457.2 m by 4.572 m) and, like Gumla, is located on an old terrace of the Indus. The area has about 10 inches of annual rainfall; the vegetation is sparse and dry, and cultivation depends on what is locally called the 'barani dagar' method of irrigation. This is a method by which, during the period of heavy rains, fields covering a wide area are embanked on the lower sides with the upper sides kept open. Water can thus flow in, and when the surface is dry, the land can be ploughed, sown with crops and levelled with the help of a wooden plank. This levelling leads to the sealing of the capillary line of the soil and thus preserves soil moisture and quick evaporation.

Since its earliest occupation (Period IA) the large site of Rehman Dheri was surrounded by a 4 ft (1.2192 m) wide wall resting on a 6 ft (1.8288 m) wide foundation or support wall, both made of packed mud, brick-shaped clay slabs and dressed clay blocks. The rooms show centrally kept mud-built and mud-plastered grain silos of varying diameter (2 ft 5 inches to 4 ft 5/6 inches or 73.66 cm to 1.3462/1.3716 m). There are also circular ovens and/or rectangular hearths or fireplaces. Pottery was almost exclusively wheel-made, of thin fabric and with floral and geometric motifs including pipal leaves painted on a predominantly red/red-buff surface. The silos have yielded mostly wheat and some barley as well. The bones of buffalo, cattle, sheep, goat and fish have been identified. Period IB is dated around 3000 BC and among the new features one may mention the Kot Diji type of rimless and neckless ovoid jars and an ivory seal (3 by 2.7 by 0.2 cm) depicting two mountain goats with wavy horns and a few symbols on one side, and two scorpions, one frog and one symbol on the other. Period II shows more frequent 'typical Kot Dijian type jars and Kot Diji-Sothi-type specimens', apart from an increasing number of incised/painted graffiti on pottery. Peacock and pipal leaf motifs increase and fish-scale motifs in black/red make their appearance. In the next two periods (III A and III B) 'the ceramics are reminiscent of evolved Kot Dijian types, with some comparable to typically Harappan examples'.

This large site has been subjected to only limited excavations (Durrani 1988: 133). One cannot yet say if the settlement was laid out on a grid plan or not. What is worth considering is that the settlement was from its very beginning a rectangular area enclosed by a wide mud wall and that the periods have been demarcated mainly on the basis of changes in the frequency of certain pottery types.

In the Bannu basin, apart from Sheri Khan Tarakai (Khan, Knox and Thomas 1991) which goes back to a neolithic level of the mid-fifth millennium or earlier, the reported village sites all belong to the Kot Diji-related period. Site sizes vary from 0.6 to 10 ha. The excavated sites of this period—Lewan (Allchin et al. 1986) and Tarakai Qila (Allchin and Knox 1981)—have yielded, in addition to mud-brick structures, wheat, barley, field-pea and lentil, a large number of stone objects such as ring stones, hammers, pounders, grinders, axes, etc. and a microlithic industry including microdrills for bead-making. Lapis and turquoise have also been reported. The dates fall in the last part of the second half of the third millennium BC and later.

Kot Diji-related occupations in the Taxila valley date around the middle of the third millennium BC and later. There is an immediately earlier neolithic level (Saraikhola I) in the area but Mughal (1990: 183) has pointed out that in this area there was only rain-dependent agriculture, and it is possible that proto-historic occupations could not strike deep roots. He points out the cases of Hathial and Jhang where the Kot Dijian occupation is found between sterile layers, and the sites were reoccupied after long abandonment.

There is some geographical problem in understanding the distribution of sites with the early Harappan level in Panjab, Rajasthan and Haryana. First, as we have seen, according to Mughal's assessment of the situation, the Kot Diji-related horizon in the Taxila valley/Potwar plateau could not strike deep roots because of the limitations of local agriculture. Secondly, east of the Potwar plateau, i.e. in the doabs of western Panjab (in Pakistan) only one site, Khadinwala, has been reported (cited by Mughal 1990), but the site seems to be on the western bank of the Ravi. The point is that the Panjab doab region in Pakistan, especially the region to the west of the Ravi, is said to be harsh and arid. Despite Mughal's protestation that the presence of Khadin-wala is a 'clear indication of the presence of many more sites in the Punjab waiting to be documented', I consider this a little unlikely. The early Harappan sites are concentrated in the region to the east of the Ravi and in the Indo-Gangetic divide between the Sutlej and the Yamuna. The Ghaggar and Chautang valleys or the ancient Sarasvati-Drishadvati valleys are a part of the Indo-Gangetic divide and form the major foci of early Harappan site distribution in the region. But, how does one geographically understand the location of Harappa on the Ravi? Was it a part of the distribution straight from the Jalilpur/Multan area of the central Indus valley along the Ravi? Or was it a part of the spread along the upper course of the Ghaggar and the course of the Chautang till it meets the Ghaggar? I do not think there are clear answers to these geographical queries at present.

Recent excavations at Harappa on the eastern bank of an old course of the Ravi have thrown a lot of light on the early Harappan occupation in the area, although as early as in 1946 Wheeler found its ceramic evidence below the mature Harappan defence wall around the western mound of AB at the site (Wheeler 1947). The early Harappan period is now taken to stand for two periods: Period I marked by initial settlement on the natural plain surface with ceramics and other materials related to the Kot Dijian tradition. According to G.F. Dales (1992), Period II is 'characterized by the construction of massive mudbrick revetments or retaining walls at the periphery of the mound as revealed so far at the northwestern corner of Mound E. The ceramics are basically those of Period I but with the addition of new forms that represent a transition to Period III'. J.M.Kenoyer (1991) sums up the data available up to the 1990–91 field-season. To begin with, he infers that the original surface on which the early Harappan settlers first settled was 'undoubtedly a terraced river plain with ox-bow lakes and scattered dry river channels'. The northwestern edge of Mound E has shown, all over it, Period I hearths, miscellaneous cultural debris and traces of mudbrick walls. The cultural debris include Kot Diji-related pottery, grey fired clay bangles, blades of greyish-black chert, a stone celt, beads of lapis lazuli, steatite and carnelian, and terracotta human figurines. The initial settlement was confined to the northwestern corner of Mound E with possible hamlets scattered over the plain. In Period II which is a continuation of Period I, massive perimeter walls made of large mudbricks and with 5–6 different building phases were constructed ('in a single episode') at the northwestern corner of Mound E. It appears that these walls, the exterior faces of which are eroded and the interior ones are pristine, functioned as retaining or revetment walls. Kenoyer (1991) observes: 'Overall, these walls represent a relatively massive scale of architecture that would have involved the large scale mobilization of labour both in wall construction and the manufacture of bricks from numerous clay sources.'

A systematic lay-out of habitation areas with house walls oriented in the cardinal directions and located along a major north-south street (defined by north-south oriented cart tracts cutting into the natural soil) is found along the southern edge of the mound. Kenoyer (1991) further points out that the categories of artifacts which continue to be used in the succeeding mature Harappan period or Period III of the site include specific ceramic types, animal figurines, triangular terracotta cakes, terracotta toys and terracotta bangles. Tan-brown chert from the Rorhi hills and shell bangles made of the marine shell *Turbinella pyrum* appear in the late levels of Period II, and this could mean 'an extension of trade to the south, as far as Rorhi and possibly even the coast'. Except for a single example from Period I where the date falls in the calibrated range between 3300 + and about 3200 BC, even the calibrated dates of Period II hover between 2500 and 2300 BC.

In the Indo-Gangetic divide, i.e. the area between the Sutlej and the Yamuna on the one hand and between the Simla foothills and the Ghaggar course in Rajasthan on the other, the major distributional study of pre-/Harappan, Harappan and late Harappan sites is by J.P. Joshi, Madhu Bala and Jassu Ram (1984). I will take up the issue of the distribution of pre-early Harappan sites in this region later, but I would like to reiterate my belief that the sites in this region belong to a different cluster than the cluster of early Harappan sites in Cholistan. In the comprehensive map of the period published by J.P. Joshi and his associates there are only three early Harappan sites between 73 E and 74–30 E in Rajasthan. The early Harappan sites form a dense cluster only in Sangrur-Bhatinda in Indian Panjab and Jind-Hissar-Karnal-Gurgaon in Haryana. The major excavated data come from Kalibangan in Rajasthan, Banawali and Kunal in Haryana and Mahorana in Panjab. The other excavated sites such as Siswal, Mitathal, Balu, etc. provide only the ceramic details and underline the stratigraphic position of this level in the regional archaeological sequence.

The early Harappan settlement at Kalibangan located on the southern bank of a bend of the dried-up course of the Ghaggar was within a parallelogrammatic fortified enclosure (western arm/240 m; eastern arm/ 250 m; southern arm/170 m; northern arm/not a straight line, with the main entrance to the enclosure being located in its northwestern section) in two structural phases. The average width of the mudbrick fortification/enclosing wall was 1.90 m in the first phase whereas in the second phase it was increased to 3–4 m. A 1.5 m wide lane was identified in the southeastern section of the early Harappan settlement. Five structural sub-periods marked the house-remains which showed mud mixed with chaff as plastering material and rooms centred around courtyards. The use of burnt bricks has been attested to by their use in a drain. Both underground and overground ovens or *tandoors* of a type which is still used in the local countryside have been found in the courtyards along with stone saddle querns for grinding foodgrains and limeplastered cylindrical pits or silos for storing them. One of the most interesting discoveries in this level is that of an agricultural field with some mutually intersecting east and north-south furrow-marks still intact. The east-west furrows were interspaced at a distance of 30 cm whereas the north-south ones were interspaced at a distance of 1.90 m. B.B. Lal (1979) has pointed out that horse-gram was sown in the short-distanced furrows, with mustard sown in the long-distanced ones. Backed and serrated small blades of chalcedony and agate have been found along with copper axes and a type of implement, *parasu*, still used in Rajasthan for cutting scrubby bushes after being hafted at the end of a wooden rod. Copper, shell and terracotta bangles have been found. Beads were made of shell, copper, agate, carnelian, etc. The division of the Kalibangan pottery of this period into six fabrics has been criticised by Mughal (1990: 184) because a particular vessel form may occur in more than one fabric. However, on the basis of his study of the Kalibangan pre-/early Harappan pottery Mughal writes:

Fabric C contains diagnostic short-necked Kot Dijian globular vessels with a wide painted band on the neck. A similar type is also included in Fabric A. Fabric

D includes Kot Dijian grooved ware, and 'E' cups and dishes on stands. Fabric B includes specimens of Kot Dijian forms but the external surface is plain and sand-slipped ('rusticated') and is also treated with multiple wavy lines in relief, otherwise known as 'Periano Wet' in Baluchistan. In the assemblage are certain types which have precise parallels with those from the Early Harappan sites in Cholistan, Jalilpur, Harappa and the Gomal valley (Mughal 1990: 184–5).

According to R.S. Bisht, who excavated Banawali on a dried-up course of the Ghaggar/Sarasvati in the Hissar district of Haryana, the excavated material from the pre-/early Harappan level (3 m thick) of the site 'bears an overall likeness to that from Kalibangan I' (Bisht 1982: 115). Although no direct evidence is forthcoming, he infers that this settlement had a surrounding wall, now possibly encased within the surrounding wall of the succeeding mature Harappan phase settlement. A 2 m wide brick-on-edge pathway belonging to the early Harappan level runs along the inner side of the defensive wall of the Indus citadel, delimiting the pre-Indus settlement on the north. Thus, the Indus wall may be found 'to conceal within it the enclosure wall of the antecedent period, as is the case in places at Kalibangan'. Further, although there is no direct evidence of early Harappan town planning, 'some system seems to have been followed since the structures are oriented to cardinal directions'. Both mud and burnt bricks were used, conforming generally to a standard ratio of length, breadth and width. Most of the houses possessed single-brick thin walls and were thus possibly single storied, low and squat with light thatched roofs. Some houses possessed thick multi-brick walls. A partially uncovered house complex showed burnt earthen floors and several hearths, ovens and fire-pits, suggesting a metalsmith's workshop. The presence of large and small thickly plastered circular pits in courtyards underlines their use as storage pits. The pottery comprises all Kalibangan early Harappan types. Copper is said to be scarce at the site. Bone points and awls are supposedly numerous. A solitary microblade of chalcedony represents the lithic industry. Beads were made of gold, semi-precious stones, steatite, faience, shell, bone and clay. There were bangles of terracotta, shell, faience and copper. Terracotta animal figurines, stone pebbles, clay pellets, etc. were among the miscellaneous finds. Perhaps the most interesting small find is a sherd depicting a canopied cart with spoked wheels. Graffiti marks on pottery have been mentioned and there is also reference to a stone weight, weighing 87.855 gm and supposedly closely approximating 'a sum of a hundred times the supposed Indus unit weight of 0.857 gm'. Bisht also hints at the presence of a transitional phase between the early and mature Harappan levels, pointing out the existence of 'a thin deposit of only about 50 cm'. Apparently this has been isolated in 'small segments of two quadrants'. He adds, 'the buff and light red fabrics of the pre-Indus ceramic tend to be more matted and pinkish red or buff in colour and heavier and thicker in texture in these areas' (Bisht 1982: 116).

The early Harappan level at Kunal (IAR 1985–86: 23–5) on the bank of a dried-up course of the Ghaggar/Sarasvati in the Hissar district of Haryana shows, in addition to 'all the six known pre-Harappan fabrics of Kalibangan', a black-and-red ware and a bichrome buff ware on which geometric designs were painted in tan or chocolate colour on a buff surface. The black-and-red ware was not painted. The mudbrick conformed to a standard ratio of length, breadth and width (1:2:3) and there were large storage pits with plastered walls. However, some small pits of the same type were found to contain burnt animal bones, ash and charcoal. There were steatite, carnelian, agate, lapis lazuli and terracotta beads and there were bangles of terracotta, faience and shell. A steatite seal was found to contain a geometrical design. The other finds included chalcedony micro-blades, bone points, copper arrowheads, antlers, grinding stones, etc.

Other excavated early Harappan levels in Haryana include those at Siswal (Bhan 1973), Balu (IAR 1983–84), etc. but apart from the ceramic details there is hardly anything interesting at these sites. In eastern Panjab, Mahorana in the Sangrur district shows in its early Harappan phase (Bala 1992: 38 ff) some Kalibangan early Harappan type of pottery, traces of mud platforms, *tandoor* ovens, terracotta bangles, beads, cakes and cartframes, and steatite and faience beads. Rohira in the same district seems to be another site in Panjab where some early Harappan remains have been excavated (Bala 1992: 40 ff). It may further be noted that in the Mansa taluk/tehsil of the Bhatinda district in Panjab, 'eight pre-Harappan and Harappan sites located at Gurnikalan, Hassanpur, Gurna, Baglianda-theh, Lakhmirwala, Naiwala Theh and Dhalewan are huge in dimensions' (Bala 1992: 28 ff).

A date from this level at Bara is around the middle of the second millennium BC but there are three earlier dates as well, roughly between 2100 and 1800 BC. The early Harappan dates from Kalibangan are not particularly consistent. Out of ten such dates, two are plainly out of context (TF-439: uncalibrated 4750 +/~130 BC; TF-957: uncalibrated 475 +/~205 BC); there are three dates with initial points around 2900/2800 BC calibrated, but the other dates are in the second half of the third millennium, some being as low as 2200/2100 BC.

The issue of a pre-Harappan phase in Gujarat has been kept alive since S.R. Rao (cf. 1963) clearly reported a micaceous red ware of the Harappan context in the region. M.K. Dhavalikar and G.L. Possehl (1992) have discussed the evidence from Nagwada in the Rupen estuary, Dholavira in the Great Rann of Kutch and Prabhas Patan (Somnath) on the west coast of the Saurashtra peninsula. To begin with, no separate and pre-Harappan micaceous ware level could be isolated. Secondly, even at Nagwada, although some pottery from a burial site is supposed to have possessed affinities with the Amri pottery in Sind, the premise of an Amri connection in pre-Harappan Gujarat is certainly not beyond dispute. Again, the two early radiocarbon dates from the earliest level at Prabhas Patan (2800/2900 BC calibrated) are no doubt interesting, but one notes that as late as in 1984 Dhavalikar (1984) was arguing that a pre-2000 BC (uncalibrated) date for this level was unlikely. The only solid evidence in this regard has emerged from Dholavira where R.S. Bisht (1991) has stratigraphically isolated a pre-Harappan culture (60–70 cm thick) which shows wheel-made red and comb-incised/reserved slip wares. The occasional addition of white to otherwise dark-coloured painting has been considered by Dhavalikar and Possehl (1992) interesting because 'painting in white is one of the hallmarks of the Early Harappan, occurring in the Amri/Nal, Kot Diji and Sothi complexes'. Bisht reports a good knowledge of the uses of copper. The clear nature of this evidence leaves no doubt as to the extension of the early Harappan in Gujarat.

Having reviewed the basic available evidence, its chronological aspects should be brought into sharper focus. In the Cholistan area, from where our review of the evidence began, the base-line is the Hakra ware horizon of which there are 99 sites belonging to a four-tiered settlement hierarchy and constituting a well-defined occupation area in the valley of the Ghaggar-Hakra. I need not comment on its origin but in view of the fact that nothing archaeological has come out of the botanical premise of the presence of *cerealia* pollens coupled with signs of burning in the pollen profiles of the Salt Lakes of Rajasthan, the origin of the Hakra ware complex may be viewed as having something to do with a mixture of the local 'mesolithic' hunter-gatherers identified in the Indian section of the desert with a still undefined 'neolithic' impulse from the hills of the northwestern frontier. It is interesting to note here that a major ceramic type of the fifth–fourth millennium BC site of Sheri Khan Tarakai in the Banu basin is said to be identical with the Hakra ware, although it must be pointed out that there is only one more recorded site of this type in the Bannu basin (personal information from J.R. Knox). Mughal (1990: 106) writes that this complex could have begun in the first half of the fourth millennium BC.

This, incidentally, makes it as early as, if not earlier than, the period IA at Amri in southwest Sind where the focus is really on the Kirthar piedmont and Kohistan, because, as has been pointed out by a number of scholars (cf. B. and F.R. Allchin 1982: 141; the location of Amri at the edge of the Indus floodplain), no site at this period is located in the Indus floodplain proper. Although the Kot Diji level has been typified at the site of Kot Diji around a rocky outcrop near Khairpur, the densest concentration of Kot Diji-related/early Harappan sites is in Cholistan where, as Mughal (1900) points out, there is a four-tiered hierarchy of settlements with at least two sites falling in the 20.1–30 ha. size bracket. Chronologically this falls in the second half of the fourth millennium.

The third area is typified by the early Harappan level at Harappa. There are geographical queries in this regard, but on the whole it is not an improbability that the early Harappan presence in the Harappa area was a part of the general distribution of similar sites in the upper reaches of the Ghaggar-Hakra. In the west these sites reach out as far as the Ravi, and even in the Ravi belt the number of sites is strictly limited. On the other hand, the distribution of sites greatly increases in the direction of Ferozepur, Bhatinda, Kapurthala, etc. So there is a possibility that the growth of villages in the Ravi stretch of Panjab was a part of the general eastward spread of the early Harappan horizon along the Ghaggar system. In any case, as I have already mentioned, the calibrated dates of Period II, which is considered transitional between the early Harappan and mature Harappan levels at the site, hover between 2500 and 2300 BC, with only a single date from the earlier period going back to 3300/ 3200 BC. It is unlikely that the early Harappan horizon in the Harappa area begins before—or at least significantly before—3000 BC. In fact, the chronological spread of the early Harappan level at Harappa seems to be something like the chronological situation of this level at Kalibangan where at least there are three relevant dates with initial points around 2900/2800 BC. In modern Haryana which is further upstream along the Ghaggar system there is no radiocarbon date from the early Harappan level, but in view of the mature Harappan dates from Banawali, the early Harappan level of the region is likely to belong to the first half of the third millennium. The situation in Gujarat, as typified at Dholavira, is still uncertain. The Gomal valley near its junction with the Indus, where the early sites are in fact located on an old terrace of the Indus, shows a clear priority in the growth of village settlements in the sense that here the Kot Diji-related horizon dates from *c*. 3000 BC with two earlier village levels in the area.

To what conclusion does this resume of dates in various areas bring us? Only in three of the areas which I have considered relevant to the growth of the Indus/Harappan civilization is there a clear sequence of village-growth: the Kirthar piedmont and Kohistan to the west-southwest of the Indus floodplain in Sind; the Cholistan area; and the Gomal valley where the ancient sites are located not so much on the banks of the Gomal as on an old terrace of the Indus. Of these three areas only Cholistan can boast of a dense and well-integrated distribution of the early Harappan sites to be followed by more dense and equally integrated mature Harappan sites (174 in number, as compared to 138 in Rajasthan-Haryana-Panjab and 101 in Gujarat). There is more than an even chance that it was in the Ghaggar-Hakra system in Cholistan that the transition from the early Harappan 'culture' to the mature Harappan 'civilization' was achieved.

Before examining the possible causative factors behind this transition, i.e. before offering explanations of the origin of the Indus civilization, it is important to examine whether the geographical premise just offered fits in with what is known of the prehistoric physical geography of the Indus and the Ghaggar-Hakra plains. In the context of Sind the details of the hydrographic setting during the prehistoric period have been worked out by Flam (1981):

The writings of Arab geographers and historians have related that the Indus river adopted the present course through the limestone hills near Sukkur sometime between the tenth and thirteenth centuries AD. Therefore, the present course of the Indus river and its associated landforms are less than one thousand years old. Thus the present location of the river could not have been the prehistoric location. The evidence derived from aerial photo-composites and ground surveys indicates that two rivers flowed through the Lower Indus Basin during the fourth and third millennium. One, in the western part of the region I have chosen to name the Sindhu Nadi, and the second, in the eastern region the Nara Nadi.

The Sindhu Nadi had its origin in the Lower Indus Basin near the present day town of Kandhkot. A short distance west of Kandhkot, the river's course turned southwest, passing west of Shikarpur and Rotodero, through Warrah and west of Mehar. South of Mehar the course continued in a southerly direction down the western flank (or Sind Hollow) of the Lower Indus Basin, passing through or just north of the present-day Manchar Lake area. The course subsequently followed an easterly path past Sehwan. To the east of Sehwan landforms of the Sindhu Nadi have been obliterated by the present-day course of the Indus river. The southernmost course of the Sindhu Nadi can be traced on the aerial photographs southeast of Nawabshah. In this area the river followed a southeasterly course through the town of Samaro and joined the course of the Nara Nadi south of Naukot.

In the eastern portion of the Lower Indus Basin the Nara Nadi was a perennial river whose course is known by different names along its length. From Fort Abbas to Fort Derawar it is known as the Hakra river, and is marked by a depression which is clearly visible on the aerial photographs of the region. Southwest of Fort Derawar, the course of the Hakra becomes increasingly unclear and intermittently becomes 'lost' beneath sanddunes which have encroached upon the area. Remnants of the river's course emerge where dunes are less numerous and thus can be aligned with the Raini and Vahinda channels. South of these latter two channels, the Nara Nadi can be clearly traced as a depression southward along the eastern edge of the Lower Indus Basin, where it was eventually joined by the Sindhu Nadi.

There can be little doubt that the coastline of the Lower Indus Basin during the fourth and third millennia was located a good distance north of the present-day location. Present research suggests that the delta of the Sindhu-Nara Nadi was located in the southeastern portion of the Lower Indus Basin. Through the centuries the delta slowly moved to the west and southwest, pushing the coastline to the south. During the prehistoric period the central and western portion of the Lower Indus Basin was probably a bay, with the coastline located somewhere north of Tatta and south of Hyderabad. Terrestrial Kutch probably consisted of an island or islands, and can be considered part of the Lower Indus Basin.

The major ecological resources of the Lower Indus Basin were its perennial rivers with seasonally high, overbank floods and fertile alluvial soils (Flam 1981: 52–3).

In the light of what is stated above it is hardly a matter of surprise that the number of mature Harappan sites in the floodplain of the Indus-Nara interfluve in Sind proper should only be fourteen–fifteen (Flam 1981: map) whereas an equal number, if not more, of these sites have been found in the Kirthar piedmont and Kohistan. In Flam's map the combined stream of the Indus and the Nara flows into the Rann of Kutch and thus the mature Harappan sites in all the three areas of Gujarat, the peninsulas of Kutch and Kathiawar and the mainland Gujarat, form a part of the dissemination of the mature Harappan sites along the Nara/Hakra into Kutch first and then into Gujarat as a whole, and it is also natural that an early Harappan level should be isolated in Kutch as has been the case at Dholavira. If one were to comment on the location of Mohenjodaro at this stage, one would point out that Mohenjodaro is located half way between Sikarpur at the mouth of the Kachhi plain and Sehwan and thus, apart from being located in the most fertile part of Sind, was centrally positioned in relation to the resources of the Kirthar piedmont and Kohistan and beyond on the one hand, and the goods coming down the Bolan and reaching the Indus through the Kachhi plain on the other. The whole area constitutes a clear and distinct economic zone of the Indus civilization and no doubt of its formative stage as well. However, as I have argued, the primary and earlier zone lay in Cholistan.

Regarding the course of the Hakra I have cited Flam in the context of Sind. Further up, its course is reasonably clear up to the Panjab foothills and so is the outline of its tributary system which incorporates the ancient Drishadvati or the modern Chautang. On the Indian side of the border the dried-up course of the Ghaggar is several kilometers wide. Does it mean that during the protohistoric period the river was flowing in a single sheet, carrying a tremendous and uncontrollable volume of water as the major rivers of Bangladesh delta do today? The issue is not easy to settle, but there are some indications. On the basis of the presence of gazelle bones at Jalilpur, Mughal (1990) has inferred the prevalence of an arid climate in the protohistoric context of that area, and this seems to be the opinion of H.P. Francfort (1992) in the case of the Haryana region as well. The basis of Francfort's opinion is the geological stratigraphy of the Ghaggar system area in Haryana, as reconstructed by M.A.Courty:

1. Composition of layers more than 10 m deep; grey non-stratified micaceous sand corresponding to the constant flow of rivers rising in the Himalayas probably supplied by the melting of ice, active upto around 20000 BP.

2. Six to 8 m deep; aeolian sand deposited during the period of maximum aridity (20000–12500 BP/maximum period 18000 BP) corresponding to the reworking of fluviatile sands by strong wind in an arid climate.

3. Fine stratified micaceous sand; corresponding to the reactivation of a hydrographic system rising from the Himalayas and supplied by the melting of ice at around 12500 BP.

4. Alluvium from flooding mixed with aeolian sand; fine sediment deposited by a piedmont hydrographic system supplied by important precipitation in the course of the last maximum humid climate phase (10000–7000 BP); the region was covered at that time by a multitude of river channels which forced their way between the dunes; these intermittent deposits of alluvium date from the same time as the slight reworking of the earth by wind.

5. Silty sand partially reworked by wind corresponding to the evolution of flood plains from the prehistoric period to the present day; progressive decrease in the regime of floods, gradual filling in of depressions by the combination of wind and local changes. This infilling of depressions and drop in riverine activity during the protohistoric period coincides with neither fluvial activity

nor a rainy phase, which refutes two of the most widely accepted hypotheses. However it still provides no clue as to the spatial distribution of sites at the regional scale (Francfort 1992: 95, 97).

We can visualize the situation in the following manner:

Within the 8 km broad limits there was a channel which, although basically dry in the summer months, carried a lot of water during the rains in the mountains, as the defunct channel does so partly, and up to the vicinity of Hanumangarh in Rajasthan, even now. It was this water which must have been tapped by the canals postulated by Francfort.Otherwise, in the dry months of the year, the braided shallow channels of the Ghaggar-Hakra flow or ancient Sarasvati formed lakes/lagoons at various places and it is possible that such areas were distinctly preferred by the protohistoric inhabitants of the area. The snow-fed Indus has always been a very difficult river to control; in the Indian tradition it is a *nad*, the masculine form of the term *nadi* which is feminine and used to denote the general range of rivers in the subcontinent. On the contrary, the potential of the shallow, braided channels of the ancient Sarasvati was much easier to utilize, just as the neolithic settlers of Mehrgarh decided to settle in a zone where the hill streams, once they entered the Kachhi plain, got dissipated into numberless courses. This postulated environmental setting may also explain the concentration of protohistoric sites in Cholistan, Rajasthan, Haryana and Panjab in a few pockets (cf. maps of the area in Mughal 1990; Joshi, Bala and Ram 1984; Francfort 1992).

ORIGIN

While discussing the origin of the Indus civilization, one may begin with two points, one positive and the other negative. The positive point is that the Kot Diji-related horizon or what Mughal insists on calling early Harappan is indeed the most immediate foundation or basis of the Indus civilization. I accept in its essentials Mughal's arguments in his 'Discussion of the early Harappan' in 1990 (Mughal 1990). Firstly, I agree with Mughal that the settlement pattern during the early Harappan phase in Cholistan shows a four-tiered hierarchy (0.1–5 ha., 5.1–10 ha., and 20–0.1–30 ha.) which was not 'undifferentiated'. Secondly, on the basis of the data available from Rehman Dheri, Kalibangan, Banawali, sites in Kohistan, etc. I believe that the architectural range and pattern of the mature Harappan settlements was very much within the technical competence acquired by the early Harappan phase in this regard. I agree with Mughal's statement (Mughal 1990) that 'there is no marked difference between the industrial specialization at Chanhudaro, Lothal or

Mohenjodaro and any Early Harappan site'. The absence of an 'elite population' and of writing should not be an issue in the early Harappan context because these are among the crucial traits which one associates with 'civilization' which the mature Harappan context undoubtedly was. In fact, although the concept of an 'elite population' is not a very clear one, the problem is not that these features are absent in the early Harappan phase. The problem is rather to know how these features came into sharp focus with the emergence of the Indus civilization. I also support Mughal's premise that the character of the distribution of Kot Diji sites in Cholistan underlines its status as 'a unified, organized, integrated social and economic system', although I feel reluctant to visualize it as a stage of 'early urbanism', as Mughal does, because of the absence of direct/ indirect evidence of writing in the archaeological records of this phase.

My negative point in this context is about the role of external trade as a causative factor of Indus urbanism. Mughal (1990) argues that at the beginning of the mature Harappan phase there was a shift in settlements towards the Gujarat and Makran coasts. He further believes that this 'significant' shift 'brings up the role of trade in the cultural processes leading to full urbanization of the Indus civilization'. However, he is cautious enough to add that, 'this line of argument may have to be reconsidered if the Kutch region also produces evidence of Amri or Kot Diji-related settlement'. Now that an early Harappan level has been isolated at Dholavira in Kutch, this part of Mughal's argument is obviously no longer valid.

Possehl (1990) apparently sets great store by the value of external trade as one of the two causative factors of the Indus civilization which have been suggested by him:

Trade, broadly defined, focussing to some degree on the Mesopotamian contact with ancient India (known to them as Meluhha) may have played a significant role in the century of paroxysmal change that seems to have led to the development of Indus urbanization (Possehl 1990: 276–7).

Meluhha need not have meant India alone, and I have to stress what I pointed out in 1990:

Can we really date the beginning of the Mesopotamian Meluhha trade? Secondly, it is possible to argue that the long-distance external trade of the Indus civilization was a concomitant of the Indus civilization. This trade did not antedate it. Mesopotamia and the Gulf were outside the Early Harappan orbit, and so was a very large part of Iran. The only area where there was an external trade network during the Early Harappan stage was the area between the Indus and the Oxus, but the data do not suggest an intensification before the beginning of the mature Harappan period. We, in fact, find it difficult to suggest a causal link between the Indus external trade and the genesis of the Indus urbanism (Chakrabarti 1990: 169).

I would like to stress further that the tendency to invoke external trade as a causative factor of change in the context of ancient India without going into the quantum, chronology and various other related historical aspects of this trade is, to interpret it most charitably, just another way of invoking diffusion/foreign influence as the divine instrument of change in this context. Such attempts are also intended to relate the development of the Indus civilization in some way to the Mesopotamian situation.

The second factor suggested by Possehl (1990) is certainly more interesting:

Strong lines of continuity notwithstanding the peoples who made and used the material culture we associate with the Harappan Civilization created a distinctive set of signs and symbols that can easily be differentiated both from what came before it and from the material culture of the contemporary peoples in adjacent regions. It is conceivable that this set of distinctive signs and symbols could ultimately be traced back to a set of precepts that form some kind of Harappan 'ideology' involved in the revolution of change . . . (Possehl 1990: 279).

This is a perceptive point, but the problem is that unless the Indus textual sources can be read with satisfaction, this probable role of ideology will have to remain uncertain. I also do not believe that there is any purpose in speculating, as Possehl (1990) does, as to whether the transition to the Indus civilization was achieved slowly or in a 'paroxysm of change'. It is not at all a relevant issue. I admit that there is a qualitative change between the pre-civilized stage and the stage of civilization, but it may be impossible to pinpoint when the transition (or 'leap', if one prefers) occurred, when 'quantity' passed over into 'quality'.

I have so far only expressed my agreement or disagreement with some of the ideas put forward to account for the origin of the Indus civilization. But leaving aside the issue of the ideology of the related social-institutional framework of which there is no proper comprehension at present, what are the variables to which particular significance would be attached in this context? Before discussing this, however, I may reiterate my opinion that the transformation from the pre-civilized early Harappan stage to the civilized mature Harappan stage took place in Cholistan, i.e. in the Ghaggar-Hakra valley where the process of desiccation, if H.P. Francfort's opinion based on M.A. Courty's analysis is true, had already begun and the river was flowing through shallow braided channels creating ox-bow lakes in places. The Indus was flowing to its west but also through a semi-arid environment which could not be far removed from what it is today in this area. The Ghaggar-Hakra flow eventually joined the Indus and the combined flow went into the Rann of Kutch. Upstream in Haryana the Ghaggar-Hakra course has a large concentration of early Harappan sites, and although this concentration dates later than that in Cholistan, the Ghaggar-Hakra course as a whole may be assumed to have belonged to the more or less same environmental setting.

In the context of the Indus valley the decisive step in its settlement history was the growth of human occupation in the floodplain itself. The early Harappan settlements were located in the Kirthar piedmont and Kohistan; it is only during the mature Harappan 'civilized' phase that we find settlements, one of which was Mohenjodaro, in the floodplain. This decisive step in the settlement history of Sind needs an explanation for which one has to take into consideration the basic geographical setting of the Indus valley before the introduction of modern irrigation canals. A detailed research on the pre-modern agricultural geography of Sind is possible on the basis of the records of such pre-modern Sind rulers as the Nawabs of Talpur and the accounts left behind by the first British administrators of the province, but pending this kind of research one may turn to the description of the valley in *The Imperial Gazetteer of India* (vol. 23) published at the beginning of this century (1908). The plain is clearly described:

The Indus brings down from the turbid hill torrents a greater quantity of detritus than can be carried forward by its diminished velocity in the plain; and hence a constant accumulation of silt takes place along its various beds, raising their level above that of the surrounding country, and incidentally affording an easy means of irrigation, on which the agricultural prosperity of Sind entirely depends, by side channels drawn from the central river.

The importance of irrigation has been strongly emphasized in the gazetteer(p. 414):

The dry character of the soil and the almost absence of rain render irrigation a matter of prime importance. Sometimes, indeed, for two or three years in succession, no rain whatever falls in the province. Under these circumstances the Indus is to Sind what the Nile is to Egypt. When the province was annexed in 1843, numerous irrigation canals existed which derived their supply direct from the river. These canals are carried away from the river bank in the direction the water can most easily flow to reach the fields that are to be irrigated. None of them has its head where the bank is really permanent, and they can draw off water only during the inundation season. The river must consequently rise several feet before the canals will fill. Many of these canals are but old deltaic channels, reopened and extended, and all have the appearance of rivers rather than artificial cuts.

The gazetteer (pp. 393–4) also contains information about the climate and pre-modern agriculture in the valley:

Owing to its prevalent aridity, and the absence of the monsoons, the climate of Sind ranks among the hottest and most variable in India. . . . No other part of India has so long a continuance of excessively hot weather, owing to the deficiency of rain. . . . On the verge of two monsoons, Sind is unrefreshed by either. The south-west monsoon stops at Lakhpat, in Cutch, in the south-east; the north-east monsoon passes no further than Karachi in the extreme south-west. The rainfall of Sind is thus scanty and irregular, and it averages only about 8 inches. The record of series of rainless seasons is occasionally broken by a sudden excessive fall.

The gazetteer (p. 412) stated the agricultural regime of the province to be:

The soil of Sind is plastic clay, deposited by the Indus. With water, it develops into a rich mould; without water, it degenerates into a desert. There are two principle harvests—the spring or *rabi*, sown in September, October, or November, and reaped in February, March, or April; and in autumn or *kharif*, sown during the floods of the river from May to August, and reaped from October to December. The *rabi* harvest consists of wheat, barley, gram, vetches, oilseeds, and vegetables. The *kharif* includes the millets known as *bajra* and *jowar*, the two chief foodgrains in Sind; rice, indigo, *san* hemp, pulses, and cotton.

In 1988, I (Chakrabarti 1988a: 96) suggested the possibility of millet being an 'integral part of the Harappan crop-system'. In view of the pre-modern agricultural geography of Sind, it is a logical inference, and the reason for millets not being found in the mature Harappan assemblage in Sind may simply be due to the fact that these have not been looked for in the relevant excavations.

The premise of the invention of an irrigation system before the early Harappans could move to the floodplains cannot, regrettably, be corroborated by the data from Cholistan because the details of the river channels and site distributions are still unpublished, but some indications have emerged from Francfort's work at Haryana (1992).

Francfort's summation of the geological stratigraphy of this area has been cited. Here his observations on the postulated canal system are given:

These genuine, natural, hydrographic fossil systems, which are much smaller than the great Ghaggar, and almost invisible on the surface and are not represented on maps can be examined by means of trial-pits. The canals are slightly carbonated depressions about 1 m deep and 300–500 m wide. They mark the courses of ancient natural waterways which were used and perhaps, in some places, rerouted by man. These traces of small river channels . . . appear to have reached all of the archaeological sites. . . . Not only did they supply with water but at the same time they made the surrounding area more fertile than the natural plain. . . . The picture we are left with is that of a small-scale system, less impressive than the great hydraulic works of Mesopotamia or Central Asia during the same period. But here, as well as there, the spatial unit is the network, or the branch, or the cluster of networks which mark the ground and define the irrigable areas for farming (Francfort 1992: 98–100).

I would also like to draw attention to the increasing level of craft-specialization from the early to the mature Harappan levels. The issue has been touched upon in a perceptive piece of analysis by J.M. Kenoyer (1992). He was able to isolate a ceramic production area on the north-eastern slope of Mound E at Harappa, where he found pottery manufacturing kilns at both early and mature Harappan levels. The area was used for ceramic production right from the time the site was inhabited. Although this does not suggest control of the production of pottery by any external authority, the evidence suggests that this particular area was being used as a specialized production area because 'the potters were involved in producing specific types of vessels'.

Moreover, in the context of craft-specialization at least three things stand out unmistakably. First, there is hardly any major change in the types of raw materials used between the early and mature Harappan contexts except jade in the latter context at Mohenjodaro and Harappa. Secondly, the sources of all these raw materials are not located at a great distance from the distribution area of early and mature Harappan sites. Even jade could come as jadeite from Kashmir (or from central Asia through Shortughai in the Oxus valley). This may also serve the purpose of emphasizing that the mature Harappan long-distance trade was not a crucial factor in the sustenance and/or survival of the Indus civilization. Thirdly, although the pattern of use of raw materials does not change from the early to the mature Harappan levels, the degree of use increases manifold. Nayanjot Lahiri's work (Lahiri 1992) clearly demonstrates these points. The increased use of raw materials could be another variable leading to the emergence of civilization in this context. In the same context, there is some ground to infer that the discovery of extraordinarily rich copper objects belonging to the Ganeshwar culture in a copper-rich area of the Aravallis in northeast Rajasthan underlines in some way this increased use of raw materials. This culture certainly belongs to the first half of the third millennium BC. Among other things, the Ganeshwar-type of artifacts has been found in the early Harappan assemblage at Kalibangan and at the mesolithic level at Bagor in southeast Rajasthan. The point is that this small site in Rajasthan yielded more than a thousand copper artifacts and there are forty-six Ganeshwar-type sites in the list prepared by J.P. Joshi, Madhu Bala and J. Ram (1994). The presence of reserved-slip ware at these sites strongly suggests a Harappan link, and I infer that, beginning with the early Harappan level, this area of Rajasthan was a highly flourishing centre for copper metallurgy and that its relationship with the early Harappan level at Kalibangan and probably beyond, as far as Cholistan, supports my assumption of craft-specialization as a distinct variable leading to the emergence of the Indus civilization.

Thus, it is postulated that within the framework of an ideology which cannot yet be defined in concrete social and institutional terms, an irrigation system, however simple, to cope with the problem of settling down in the riverine plains, and increased craft-specialization as seen by the presence of a large number of raw material types in the early Harappan level and the copper metallurgical area of the contemporary Ganeshwar culture, were two key variables in the emergence of the Indus civilization. If one accepts Fekri Hassan's argument that 'the key variables in the emergence of civilization consist of the large size of agricultural communities, their sedentariness, and the increase in the number of consumers relative to foodproducers' (Hassan 1981: 257), one has perhaps offered here an arguable case in the context of the Indus. But then one should also humbly admit that 'interpretative theories for the rise of civilization remain in the form of plausible stories—logical, but not objectively confirmed' (Redman 1978: 346).

Chapter Three

Harappan Settlements

The small plain of Shortughai (Francfort 1984, 1989) is near the confluence of the Oxus (Amu Dariya) river and one of her tributaries, the Kokcha. This river comes down the Badakhshan hills famous for their lapis lazuli and ruby mines (for the presence of ruby mines: 'for which Badakhshan has long been famous', IGI, vol. 6, 1908, p. 176). The lone Harappan settlement in this plain, which is about 5 km away from the Oxus and about 25 km away from the Kokcha, is the earliest of the seven recorded Bronze Age sites in the region. The evidence of both dry-farming (suggested by the discovery of a ploughed field covered with flax seeds) and agriculture based on canal irrigation has been found in the context of this period. The Harappan occupational deposit in Shortughai covered only 2.5 hectares (ha.) and was 50 cm thick in its Period I but its assemblage of pottery, terracotta, metal objects, raw materials such as lapis lazuli, agate, carnelian, turquoise and steatite, sea shell bangles, mudbrick architecture with bricks of the Harappan size (32 by 16 by 8 cm), square seals with pictographs, graffiti, etc. was identical with that of any mature Harappan site (Francfort 1989). The identity extended even to 'the modest field of firing techniques which are well-known in the subcontinent but not recorded in Central Asia: burnt cracked pebbles have been flung on hearths to maintain heat for any domestic or artisanal use' (Francfort 1984: 303). There are enough radiocarbon dates from this level to indicate that it began in the second quarter of the third millennium BC. The undoubted physical presence of the Harappans near Badakhshan in the Oxus valley raises more questions than it answers, especially when there is no other comparable site beyond the limits of the subcontinent, but this certainly indicates, as I have pointed out before (Chakrabarti 1990: 129), that 'the Harappans were using one of the Panjshir valley passes with their orientation towards Kabul'.

A marginal area between the central Asian plateau and the Indus plains, Baluchistan, is essentially mountainous, with its peaks occasionally

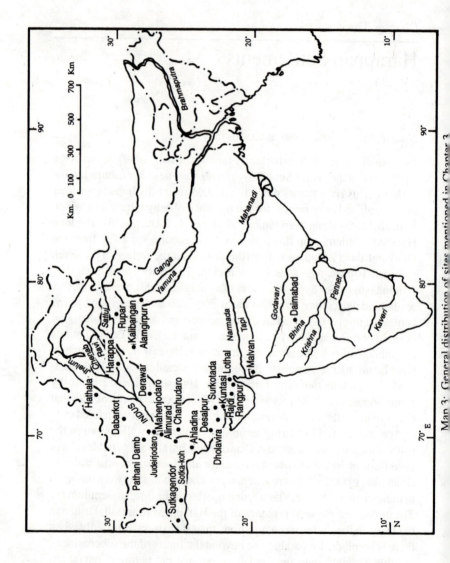

Map 3: General distribution of sites mentioned in Chapter 3

touching the 11000 ft (3352.8 m) level. In Fairservis' analogy (Fairservis 1956: 183) Baluchistan is like surf on the sea-shore, the shore being the Indus valley and the high waves being represented by the high mountain ranges of central Asia. Northeast Baluchistan, with Quetta at the head of the Bolan pass as the central node and Marri-Bugti country to its southeast, lies between the arcs of the Sulaiman range in the south and the Toba and Kakar ranges in the north. The Zhob, Loralai and Beji are the principal rivers which drain this area. Beyond Quetta the Afghanistan border is marked by the Khwaja Amran range, with the Pishin Lora flowing below. The Kachhi plain is below the Bolan pass and to the southeast of Quetta are the territories of Kharan, Sarawan, Jhalawan and Las Bela which include the Kalat plateau and are all ensconced in a number of major (roughly) northeast–southwest ranges which are known as the Ras Koh, Central Bruhui, Pab and Kirthar ranges. The Nari drains the Kachhi plain whereas the Hab and the Mula flow across the Kirthars. The Purali flows into the Sonmiani bay in Las Bela. To the north of Ras Koh is the Chagai hill on the Afghanistan-Seistan border, with two desert depressions (Hamun-i-Lora and Hamun-i-Mashkel) in the area, while to its south are the Makran ranges including the Makran Coastal Range parallel to the coast. The Hingol and the Dasht carry the main drainage of Makran, with the Rakshan as the major river to its north. There is a difference in rainfall between the highlands (about 10 inches annually) and the plains (annual rainfall 5 inches, decreasing to 3 in some areas), and Baluchistan on the whole is a singularly arid area, although 'this is redeemed in places by level valleys of considerable size, in which irrigation enables much cultivation to be carried on and rich crops of all kinds to be raised' (IGI, vol. 6, p. 267). Or again:

Within the mountains lie narrow glens, whose rippling watercourses are fringed in early summer by the brilliant green of carefully terraced fields. Rows of willows, with interlacing festoons of vines, border the clear water, while groups of ruddy children and comely Italian-faced women in indigo-blue or scarlet shifts and cotton shawls complete a peaceful picture of beauty and fertility. Few places are more beautiful than Quetta on a bright frosty morning when all the lofty peaks are capped with glistening snow, while the date-groves, which encircle the thriving settlements of Makran, are full of picturesque attraction. The frowning rifts and gorges in the upper plateau make a fierce contrast to the smile of the valleys (IGI, vol. 6, p. 267).

Whether the region enjoyed a wetter climate during the prehistoric period, as suggested by Aurel Stein (1931, cf. p. 2), is far from clear, but a case was made out against it by R.L. Raikes and R. Dyson (1961).

In the uplands of Baluchistan the Harappan sites are understandably limited in number, and such sites as exist have been primarily interpreted as trading settlements, a logical enough hypothesis to account for their specific geographical locations. For example, Dabarkot (Stein 1929: 55–64) in north Baluchistan, where extensive Harappan deposits are visible atop a mound with a basal diameter of 1200 ft (365.76 m), 'lies on an ancient trade route from the Indus valley in the direction of Kandahar' (Wheeler 1968: 62). One is not, however, sure if the major Indus sites in the Kachhi alluvium such as Nausharo and Judeirjodaro can be interpreted only as trading settlements because even in the early part of this century Kachhi was producing three crops a year and some Kachhi bullocks had a market in Panjab. The Harappan settlement at Nausharo (Jarrige 1989) showed evidence of building blocks separated by parallel streets, bathrooms connected by terracotta pipes with soakage jars outside, huge mudbrick platforms, etc. It has further been argued by Jarrige (1989) that there was at Nausharo 'a monumental canal' or a large water-tank 'into which had been set . . . a baked-brick spillway for water, comparable with the spillway of the so-called dockyard of Lothal'. Another interesting feature at Nausharo was the use of wooden beams blocked with pebbles and clay at the foundations, the use of pebbles being a new feature here. Judeirjodaro is another major Harappan site in the Kachhi plain. About 18 miles northwest of Jacobabad, it occupied 'an important position along the highway long used to connect the lower Indus basin with Baluchistan and Afghanistan' (Pakistan Archaeology 1: 11–12). Apart from the main mound where rainwater gullies may indicate ancient streets, there is a row of five mounds, slightly isolated from the main one, and all the mounds cover a total area of 600 by 400 yards (548.64 by 363.76 m). Pathani Damb is at the mouth of the Mula pass on the Baluchistan side and 'consists of a series of continuous ridges and hillocks covering a vast area and including a higher central mound. . . . Its location suggests that this town may rank with Mohenjodaro and Harappa as a metropolitan centre of importance in the civilization of the Indus valley' (Pakistan Archaeology 1: 28). In the Khurkera alluvial plain on the northeastern side of the Las Bela and the Sonmiani bay the site of Balakot (Dales 1976) which measures 180 by 144 m (about 2.80 ha./6.94 acres) and is divided into a high western mound and a lower eastern one, showed in its Harappan level a wide east-west lane bifurcating the area at right angles to which there are two smaller lanes. Mudbrick is generally used but burnt bricks have been used in some drains. There is a thin plastering of the floor in some rooms. The floor of one room is ornately paved with burnt square tiles decorated with impressed intersecting circle designs. Another floor, presumably a courtyard, is lime-plastered with a circular depression in the centre, which contains the remains of a wooden column. A wooden threshold has been noticed in some cases, and at least there is one complete example of a bathroom with a ceramic tub (with intersecting circle designs on the inner side of the bottom), a hearth, a buried storage jar and a drain made from a broken pot. One room measures 2.20 by 3.20 m. There is no positive evidence of an enclosing wall but a large Harappan kiln has been traced along with smaller ovens for baking animal figurines. There is a painted jar of possibly Persian Gulf origin in the Harappan level at Balakot, fitting in with the emphasis during this period on the use of estuarine and marine sources like fish and shell. Of the latter there was obviously a flourishing industry.

The hilly terrain to the north of Bela which is cut by the Porali, Hingol and Hab rivers has some major Kulli-related settlements with clear evidence of Harappan contact. The better known sites of this area are Niai Buthi (Fairservis 1971: 189–94), Nindowari (Casal 1966) and Edith Shahr (Fairservis 1971: 195–205). Among these, Nindowari may serve as an example. Large stone-built platforms rising in receding stages to the platform on top, which possibly contained stone or rubble structures seem to be the key feature of Nindowari possessing a single radiocarbon (calibrated) date around the middle of the third millennium BC. In the 'Edith Shahr complex' Fairservis (1971) reported some usual settlement remains which indicate that during the period of the Indus civilization the southern part of Jhalawan and the northern section of Las Bela contained major habitations of which I am not fully aware except that they were somehow associated with the Kulli culture. It is also interesting that these places are all located in the copper-bearing areas of Las Bela (Lahiri 1992: 23).

The evidence of Harappan settlements is explicit in the Makran coast. From the coastal strip of Makran to inland Baluchistan there are two main routes along the valleys of the Dasht Kaur and Shadi Kaur, and each of them had a fortified post—Sutkagendor and Sotka-Koh.

The site of Sutkagendor (Mockler 1877, Stein 1931: 60–71, Dales 1962) now lies about 30 miles away from the sea, at the eastern edge of the Dasht valley. As early as in 1877 Major Mockler recorded a local Baluchi tradition that the sea once reached as far up as Sutkagendor which was then a port. But to Mockler that was only 'the Baluchi way of accounting for the shells and other marine deposits belonging to the geological formation' (Mocker 1877: 126). Stein was equally sceptical but he took care to point out that the site occupied a position which was the converging point of a number of routes from small fishing harbours in the area and could have the same significance in the protohistoric period. Dales has argued that 'a slight lowering of the coast-line level and the removal of 4000 years of alluvium and wave deposited land would probably allow the waters of the Arabian sea to extend up the Dasht valley, at least as far as Sutkagendor. Even under present conditions, small boats can navigate almost 15 miles up the river from the sea' (Dales 1962). The argument was also subsequently put forward but the issue is still uncertain; Dales (1979) himself does not infer any coastal change in the context of Las Bela which is located next to the Makran coast in the east.

The nucleus of the Harappan settlement at Sutkagendor is an irregular walled enclosure measuring about 197 yards (180.13 m) from north to south and 113 yards (103.32 m) from east to west. Its northern and southern sides are natural, formed by two ridge lines. These are joined at their ends by two north-south walls made of large slabs set in clay mortar and 'oriented within one degree of the magnetic compass' (Dales 1962: 89). The thickness of the eastern wall at the point of Dales' operation B is 7.45 m. There were perhaps mudbrick structures on its flat top, about 3 m wide at this point. Inside the enclosing walls there was a 3 m thick Harappan occupational deposit with a few jerry-built walls of a later date. Here Dales (1962) distinguished three phases.

The enclosing stone walls belong to Phase I and 'at the same time, a large mudbrick platform about 2.5 m thick was built against the inner face of the stone wall' (Dales 1962: 88). The second phase consisted of a floor of packed earth laid on a 30–45 cm thick stone filling above Phase I. Parallel rows of stone foundations characterized the final Phase III. One of these 'stopped about 1.75 m before reaching the citadel wall platform, probably to provide a passage way. This passage way was later blocked, however, by a secondary wall of less carefully laid stones' (Dales 1962: 88). At the southwestern corner of the enclosure Stein noticed that 'very massive foundations of what may have been two towers clearly mark a gate' (Stein 1931: 62). Besides this, Dales' plan shows at least two other possible salients or bastions. 'At the base of the citadel, around its northern and eastern sides, are the fragmentary remains of a small or outer town' (Dales 1962: 88). There are surface indications of structures, etc. but the stratigraphy of 'the lower town' in Dales' operation is '4.5 m of sterile silt and sandy deposit' (Dales 1962: 88).

The position of Sotka-Koh (Dales 1962: 91) is somewhat like Sutkagendor. On the top of a natural rock formation, the site is still unexcavated but the 'remains of a large stone-wall, at least 500 m long, were clearly visible along the east edge of the site. There were no clear indications however that the walls continued around to form an irregular enclosure as that at Sutkagendor'.

Another site of this type has been added to the list by Snead (1967: 560) at Khairia Kot on the west side of the Las Bela valley. This site, the details of which are not published, is 25 miles from the coast line but has been interpreted by Snead as a possible 'Harappan port'.

SIND

The lower Indus valley or the modern province of Sind is low but sharply defined between the Kirthars and the Thar. The province of Sind as a whole has a number of physiographic units (Pithawala 1936, 1959): western highlands—Kirthars and Kohistan; lower Indus valley—western valley section, eastern valley section, and the delta; desert—Pat and Thar. With an average altitude of about 5200 ft (1524 m) and rising in places to a height of about 7000 ft (2133.6 m), the Kirthars, a part of the Indian extra-peninsular mountain system, have a high relief (except in the south where it sinks to the Pab hills) and are marked by a number of transverse torrents which run down its eastern flank into the valley below and whose transverse lines of drainage act as pathways from Sind into adjacent Baluchistan. An offshoot of the Kirthars, known as the Lakhi range, extends eastward in the direction of Karachi. There are a few insignificant limestone ranges intersecting the Indus valley and among them may be mentioned the Ganjo hills (with an elevation of about 30 m) on which the Talpur capital of Hyderabad stands, and the hills of Sukkur and Rorhi. East and southeast of the Kirthars is Kohistan or 'mountain country' spreading as far south as the sea. In between its low, often parallel ridges are broad undulating plains with a number of thermal springs and rivers, the more important of which join the sea near Karachi. Kohistan continues almost up to lake Manchar, a huge freshwater deposit connected with the Indus by the reversible flow of the Aral. Beyond it, flanked by the Kirthar-Sulaiman line on the north and west and by the Indus on the east is the older alluvium of the western valley section whose main watercourse, besides the Indus, is the western Nara, possibly an old course of the Indus itself but now flowing into the Manchar. The eastern valley section lies between the Indus and the eastern Nara which, following Flam, I have earlier envisaged to be a living river joining the Indus and flowing as a combined stream into the Rann of Kutch. Of recent growth, the Indus delta is an inhospitable stretch of mudbanks, sand dunes, swamps or lagoons while among the desert areas, Pat lies between Sibi and Jacobabad in the north (i.e. the Kachhi plain), and Thar abuts the eastern Nara and the delta on the east.

In his map of the distribution of Harappan sites in 1968 Wheeler (1968: 4) shows about 20 sites in Sind, a number which may not be exhaustive (see Lambrick 1964: note 2). In fact, many of these sites shown by Wheeler seem to be in the lower Indus basin itself: 'the number of sites in the lower Indus basin increases from 3 during the Amri-Kot Diji phase to 20 during the Harappan phase' (Flam 1981: 55). Flam's map (1981: 57) shows at least 13 Harappan sites in the interfluve between the Indus ('Sindhu Nadi') and the eastern Nara ('Nara Nadi'). This makes sense. 'A large part of the belt of land between the Indus and the Nara (i.e. the Eastern Nara)—the doab, 70–80 miles wide—is very fertile. . . . The types of soil found in the Western Valley section . . . are also found in this portion of the basin' (Pithawala 1936: 304). Secondly, the location of sites in this area which is supposed to have been thoroughly disturbed by shifting river courses (Lambrick 1964: the map facing p. 36, suggesting some probable ancient courses of the Indus) suggests that ideas regarding the frequency of changes in the Indus river course may be exaggerated.

Heat and aridity are well-known climatic features of Sind ('no other part of India has so long a continuance of excessively hot weather, owing to the deficiency of rain': IGI 22: 303) with summer temperatures shooting up to 120°F and average annual rainfall limited to 8 inches. However, this fact does not support by itself Marshall's hypothesis of a wetter protohistoric climate in Sind on the basis of the prevalence of burnt bricks at Mohenjodaro, the extensive drainage system and the representation of a fauna preferring humid climate on her seals (cf. rhinoceros, tiger, elephant and buffalo). Modern scientific research also is hardly conclusive on this point (for Marshall's opinion, see Marshall 1931: 2–5; for a more recent opinion, see the section on 'weather systems and prehistoric climate' in Kenoyer 1991; for an endorsement of the idea of climatic change, see D.P. Agrawal 1992, which will be discussed later) but one point can safely be assumed: biotic interference must have led to a general lessening of the rainfall since then. Even in the early part of this century there were rich forests of principally *babul (acacia arabica)* skirting the reaches of the river for miles together, and the alluvial strip which borders either bank of the Indus for a distance of 12 miles is considered superior to every other part of Sind in soil and productiveness.

Mohenjodaro

The Larkana area of Sind, where Mohenjodaro is located, was described in 1908 as 'perhaps the finest tract in the whole of the province' (IGI 16: 144) which yielded, even before the advent of modern irrigation, three crops a year. It was one of the most important grain marts of Sind, producing the finest rice in the province along with wheat, largely on the river banks.

Centuries of denudation have reduced Mohenjodaro to what it is today: a sprawling mass of weather-bitten mounds which on the site-plan tend to form a pattern showing a higher western mound and a lower but larger eastern mound, with a marked depression in between. Michael Jansen (1989: 252, note 2) puts the visible urban space at 95 ha. (234.74 acres). The precise limits of the ancient periphery are hardly established. Marshall (1931: 9) wrote that early potsherds might be picked up for about half-a-mile on the east and to a lesser extent on the west and south, but it is doubtful if this extended area was within the city proper and did not constitute its 'extra-mural suburbs'. Jansen (1987) provides a very important piece of information: 'archaeological remains seem to continue for almost 2 kilometers, at least to the east of the site. Their uppermost strata are below the present surface of the plain at a slightly varying height of 44–6 m a.m.s.l. They represent the (Late?) urban phase. Some tests east of area B show no deposits for some distance'. The total built-up area of the city could be more than 200 ha. or about 500 acres. The point is that the original estimate of Marshall that Mohenjodaro covered 240–50 acres could be a gross underestimate. As early as in 1965 J.P. Plenderleith (1965) pointed out that Mohenjodaro covered an area at least twice the size that had been supposed. Mortimer Wheeler (1968: 26) estimated the area to be one mile square or 'upwards of three miles in circuit', erring obviously on the conservative side.

The Indus now flows about three miles to the east of the site. There is no positive evidence that it once flowed close by. R.D. Banerjee (cited in Marshall 1931: 8) suggested that the depression between the western and eastern groups of mounds might be an ancient river-bed or a part of it. Although Banerjee's hypothesis was considered probable by Ernest Mackay (1938: 4), Marshall (1931: 8) called the depression 'the most important thoroughfare of the city'. In 1965 (Dales 1965: 148) Dales accepted the possibility that it was originally a canal or a branch of the river. However, Jansen (1991) has conclusively shown that there was nothing in this open space.

Before discussing the general morphological features of Mohenjodaro, a few current issues regarding the history of this settlement must be made clear. Our understanding of these issues has been to some extent impaired by the early excavators' preference to record all excavated objects including structures in relation to a fixed bench-level on the top of the mound (for a criticism of the method, see Wheeler 1947: 144–7; for a vindication of the early stratigraphic reconstruction of Mohenjodaro, see Lambrick 1971). However, the early excavators of the site had been eminently successful in doing what they had tried to do, i.e. reveal the total patterns—morphological and otherwise—of the long-buried Indus civilization (for a similar observation, see Wheeler 1950). As the state of publication of many modern 'scientific' excavators is not beyond reproach, it is this total pattern reconstructed by the early excavators which still demands primary attention.

What is the sequence of the Indus civilization site of Mohenjodaro and how was it constructed? The answers to these two questions are interlinked. One may begin with the current estimate of the level of the original floodplain of Mohenjodaro. Today it is about 48 m 'above mean sea level' (a.m.s.l.), with the following a.m.s.l. heights for some major points of the ancient city: average height of the lower city—52–3 m; the level of the Great Bath on the citadel—54–5 m; the highest points of the citadel—59–60 m. The estimate of the level of the original floodplain on which Mohenjodaro stood varies from Jansen's 41 m to M. Cucarzi's 33 m (Jansen 1987). In this context Jansen argues that these probable levels of the original floodplain do not suggest that the city was subjected to heavy floods during its occupation. Jansen (1987) further observes that 'the sedimental material identified within the architecture as "flood-deposits" is not in primary but in secondary position'. So the issue of floods at Mohenjodaro seems to have lost its relevance now. Secondly, the stratification which was proposed earlier for Mohenjodaro (Marshall 1931; Mackay 1938: xiv–xv) postulated the existence of seven successive cities, with the provision for two more cities below the level up to which the digging could be conducted: Early III, Intermediate I, II, III, and Late Ia, Ib, II and III. Although the idea of seven or more cities laid horizontally in succession is discarded now, there is yet no clear alternative framework to understand the history of Mohenjodaro. A revised stratification, at least for the DK-G area, is being prepared by Jansen. I now come to two further points in this context. First, as Jansen (1987) argues, there is no evidence at all of the existence of an early Harappan level at Mohenjodaro. In fact, as noticed earlier, the existence of a Kot Diji-related early Harappan level in the Indus floodplain proper is rather improbable. Secondly, it has been suggested that the finds of cultural remains deep down in different boreholes in the perimeter of the city do not necessarily imply that there were regular settlements much lower than the level reached by the excavators. As Jansen (1987: 13) argues:

If we calculate the amount of clay and sediments for the construction of two platforms, one for the 'citadel' and one for the 'lower town', based on an average height of 5 m, we receive a figure of about 4 million cubic metres (about 400,000 cubic metres for the citadel) without counting the millions of bricks. The pits dug for the clay were most probably located close to the platform, and might have surrounded them. This amount taken into consideration, both platforms could theoretically have been surrounded by a ditch at least 5 metres deep and more than 100 metres wide which, once filled with water, became a sort of moat, and together with the platform served as fortification similar to the early historical cities in the Ganges plain. . . . This would explain why no one has ever found fortification walls, and also why pottery fragments and brick-pieces were found at a greater depth. They would represent a secondary position, rubbish which was thrown into the ditches.

More work will obviously be needed but this explanation offered by Jansen makes sense, especially because it is known that the structures of Mohenjodaro stood on mud/mudbrick platforms.

Meanwhile, the idea that Mohenjodaro was planned as 'a gridiron system of main streets running north-south and east-west, dividing the area into blocks of roughly equal size and approximately rectangular, 800 ft east to west and 1200 ft north to south' (Piggott 1950: 165) has to be modified now, because, for one thing, the space between the citadel and the lower city has been found devoid of structures, and secondly, there is now a different understanding of the orientation of streets in the lower city. Again it is Jansen's research which has brought about this change in understanding.

Apart from one north-south thoroughfare (First Street), there are indications of two more, both equidistant (180 m) from the First Street. No definite traces of an east-west thoroughfare have as yet been found. It has been argued that

. . . not only the orientation system might have shifted in time towards north-northwest but also that in the case of special architectural structures like the Great

Bath a single major orientation system with a dependent subsidiary orthogonal system was not followed, but that the orientation was based rather on two independent systems not necessarily coinciding at right angles. This might indicate a north-south orientation by a star and an east-west orientation by the sun, thus following the cosmic principle of day and night. Besides these observations on orientation there are several other indications that suggest that Mohenjodaro (and probably the other Harappan cities as well) was a city built according to a highly sophisticated planning concept most probably based on cosmological principles. If this was so, who were these city planners who worked out, developed and executed this planning concept?

Recent discoveries at Mohenjodaro may go some way towards providing answers to these and other questions. We now know that at least the 'citadel' was constructed on a gigantic man-made platform measuring approximately 400 by 200 m and attaining a final height of approximately 7 m after twice being further enlarged. The platform consisted of a mudbrick retaining wall over 6 m thick enclosing an inner filling composed of sedimentary material, including sand and silt, from the surrounding plain. The material for the mudbricks must have come from pits dug nearby which gradually filled up with water and were used as rubbish dumps. Using this platform as foundation, further platforms were built on top in order to elevate structures of special significance such as those now lying beneath the Buddhist remains, including the 'granary', Great Bath and even the 'assembly hall'. All these monumental structures rest on huge mudbrick substructures which in turn are built on the foundation platform of the 'citadel'. Some of the buildings, such as the Great Bath . . . were surrounded by walkways both inside and outside. The highest raised buildings must have stood more than 20 m above the surrounding plain and were visible from afar. Similar elevations were also observed in some parts of the 'Lower City', even house units had small raised platforms generally associated with bathrooms (Jansen 1991: 77–8).

It has been necessary to cite Jansen in such detail because in recent years he has been the most serious student of the manifold aspects of the site of Mohenjodaro, and his ideas in this regard deserve careful consideration. In the context of his idea that cosmological principles were involved in the planning of Mohenjodaro and possibly other Harappan cities, all that one can say is that its proof will depend on whether or not ancient Indian cosmological texts contain descriptions of, or allusions to, such planning.

I. The Basic Structural Evidence

The five volumes of excavation reports published in the thirties (Marshall 1931, Mackay 1938) are still the primary source, although some important supplementary details have emerged from the works of Wheeler

(1968) and Dales (1965). Jansen's work in aimed primarily at the re-documentation of the already excavated remains. According to him (Jansen 1979: 405) the plans published by Marshall and Mackay 'are partly incorrect or at least not quite comprehensible. The technique of cross section was unknown at that time, and prospects of walls were not documented scientifically. Beside these problems, the specific location of artifacts had not been accurately reported'. This criticism by Jansen notwithstanding, the basic image of the city has not significantly changed since the early days of excavations at the site.

II. The Western Mound

Excavated first under Marshall and Mackay the western mound or the 'stupa mound' was brought into sharper focus by Wheeler in 1950. The mound is roughly parallelogrammatic in shape and slopes from about 40 ft (12.192 m) to about 20 ft (6.095 m). The highest point lies at the northeast corner where it is surrounded by a Buddhist stupa of the early centuries AD (Verardi 1987). In 1950 Wheeler (1950: 39, fig. 7) showed that around the western complex as a whole there was a mudbrick circuit wall with traces of salients on the southeast and west. Besides, there was a mud and mudbrick artificial platform all over the area. In the stupa area, i.e. at the northeast corner of the site, Marshall found definite traces of this platform. The intervening space between his 6th and 7th strata was 'occupied almost entirely by crude brick or alluvial mud heaped up artificially so as to form an immense platform over the whole of the stupa area as well as over a big expanse of ground to the north' (Marshall 1931, I: 125). Dating from the 'optimum phase of the city's development' (Wheeler 1950: 39) or the 'intermediate' period of the early excavators, this platform was contemporary with the buildings on its top.

On the southeast, the earliest of the towers along the circuit-wall which was contemporary with the platform stood on a burnt-brick foundation and was reinforced by horizontal timber work, the slots of which still survive.

In the stupa area Marshall laid three trenches inside the courtyard, one of which was 40 ft deep from beneath the Buddhist pavement.

My main object in making these deep cuttings was to lay bare the succession of prehistoric strata from the top to the bottom of the mound; for I judged that this mound, being the loftiest and most conspicuous on the site, would be likely to yield specially instructive evidence on the question of stratification. In view, too, of the proximity of the Great Bath and other imposing structures on the west, I was hopeful that the remains concealed here would prove to be those of some religious or other edifice of more than ordinary interest. The latter hope was not to be fulfilled (Marshall 1931, I: 124).

It was in this deep trench that Marshall proved the existence of the artificial platform mentioned earlier and also realized that 'for the support of this platform stout retaining walls would be indispensable'. Portions of such walls were traced to the east and west.

Mackay (1938:16) excavated immediately to the northwest of the stupa area (Block 10) and found the remains of a great open court with massive southern and western walls. It was only partially exposed.

The position of this court in relation to the supposed temple beneath the Buddhist stupa unavoidably recalls to mind the similar great court at Ur between the quays and the House of Nannar. In that great Khan-like court of Ur, it is thought, payments in kind were collected for the temple revenues. The same might well be true of the great enclosure in this part of Mohenjodaro (Mackay 1938: 16).

To the west of the stupa area is Mackay's Divinity Street (north-south) which widens from 6 ft 9 ins (2.0574 m) to 10 ft 4 ins (about 3.15 m) in the south. A covered drain with a channel averaging 10 ins (254 mm) in width and 20 ins (500 mm) in depth runs along its eastern side for a while and then moves to the west.

Across the street are the ruins of a structural complex which despite its obscure architectural history, seems to be important. With an early core (Mackay's Intermediate I, cf. Mackay 1938: 11) this was much rebuilt and the plan we have in Mackay (1938, II: pl. 7) is essentially that of the Late period. The main entrances were from the east and one of them led to a hall which opened into a corridored courtyard on the right. Towards the end of occupation this courtyard was cluttered with poorly built walls. There was a series of self-contained and isolated rooms across the entrance-hall, perhaps with an upper storey. The southern part of the building was divided into three blocks by parallel passages opening out westwards from a corridor on the east.

According to Mackay (1938: 100) this was 'a building of unusual character' and hence of 'exceptional importance'. He emphasizes the thick outer wall and its size (230.7 ft/70.31 m by 78.5 ft/23.92 m) and composition as a single architectural unit. The proximity of this building to a presumed sacred shrine beneath the Stupa and its fenestrated wall recalling that of the Great Wall made him believe that this was 'once the residence of a very high official, possibly the high priests' (Mackay 1938, I: 10). He names it the 'collegiate building' and even suggests that the entrances to the southern blocks were 'students' entrances'.

Mackay's 'Main Street' runs along the western wall of the collegiate building and narrows from 14 ft 8 ins (4.47 m) in the north to 12 ft 3 ins (3.73 m) in the south. In the Late period this displays two interesting features. In the northern sector a part of the road was filled by rubble with a newly built parallel partition wall as support. Mackay's guess is that it was intended 'to serve as a make-shift protective wall perhaps in place of a section of the city wall that may have been washed away' (Mackay 1938, I: 15). In the northern sector again, entirely blocking the road, was a brick-construction with ten shallow pits in two parallel rows of five. The pits might hold timber upright across which there might be rails and thus the entire thing might imply, according to Mackay (1938, I: 14), an 'octroi post'. To the north of the collegiate building there is an east-west lane and beyond this lane is an open court, the southern and western walls of which are some 6 ft 9 ins (2.05 m) thick. I have already drawn attention to this court which Mackay compares to a court at Ur.

Another 'remarkable building, whose counterpart has not been un-earthed in any ancient city . . . lay to the west of the Main Street at its northern end. Though large (185 by 82 ft or 56.38 by 24.99 m), it is cluttered with late constructions. The central focus is a . . . series of rooms in two rows of four separated by a narrow passage down whose centre is a remarkably well-built drain'. The rooms are generally alike in size and shape and possibly served as ablution places. Stairs led to an upper storey. If the Great Bath was for the general public, this was, according to Mackay (1938, I: 18–20), for the select priesthood 'to which they descended at stated hours to perform the prescribed washing'.

Beyond this to the north across another east-west lane, there are three other clusters of excavated buildings—Mackay's Blocks 7, 8 and 9, only partially cleared and hardly making clear sense.

Perhaps the most famous of all the structures in Mohenjodaro is what is known as the Great Bath lying to the west-southwest of the collegiate building. Its basic plan is simple: the rectangular pool whose western, eastern, southern and northern sides measure 39 ft 4 ins (14.52 m), 39 ft 3 ins (14.5 m), 22 ft 11 ins (6.98 m) and 23 ft 4.5 ins (7.12 m) respectively, lies in the midst of an open paved courtyard, itself encircled by different gallaries and rooms. From the north and south bricksteps with a wooden cover set in bitumen or asphalt lead to the floor of the pool sunk 8 ft (2.43 m) below the level of the paving of the courtyard. At the base of the northern staircase is a low platform and a small further step. At the southeastern corner an outlet is connected with a corbelled drain which goes down the western slope of the mound. The precise method of filling up the pool is uncertain but there is a well in one of the enclosing rooms and that may have supplied the necessary water. The general masonry of the entire construction is careful. The bricks are set on edge and covered with gypsum mortar. To make the bath water-tight, a thin layer of bitumen is applied around the outer wall. This wall itself lies within another surrounding wall and the intervening space between the two is rammed with mud.

Marshall constantly describes this bath-complex as a 'hydropathic establishment' (Marshall 1931, I: 24). The term 'hydropathy' carries the sense of the treatment of a disease by water, and thus the description is perhaps inappropriate. D.D. Kosambi has suggested that this might be a ceremonial *Pushkar* or the ritual tank of a Hindu temple.

This curious building, situated apart from the city on the citadel-ziggurat mound, could be expanded to fill the tank with water. There is no imagery or decoration of any sort but the tank is surrounded by rooms which may have been used by living representatives, companions or servants of the goddess, the *apsaras* of the day; the water need not have been so labouriously drawn unless for water deities to whom it was essential. The range of seemingly unconnected meanings for the word *Pushkara* is highly suggestive: the root *Push* from which it is derived, like the very close *Pushkala*, denotes fertility, nourishment, plenty . . . one may note further that one of the holiest of places of pilgrimage is a *tirtha* named *Pushkar*, identified with one of that name in Rajasthan, but presumably representing earlier artificial tanks of the sort. The *Pushkar* is a necessary adjunct to every Hindu temple not actually by a river, even in well-watered regions (Kosambi 1962: 71–2).

Jansen (1989) points out that the Great Bath stands on older foundations, has a street (up to 5 m wide) on all sides and may be 'the only known single freestanding structure in Mohenjodaro which could be walked around outside'.

To the immediate southwest of the Great Bath Marshall excavated a few rectangular blocks of masonry, some with vertical chases and divided by criss-cross passages running between them. He suggested that these were remnants of a *hammam* or hot-air bath (Marshall 1931, I: 26). In 1950 Wheeler worked on the complex and inferred it to be the podium of a granary. The rectangular blocks which are twenty-seven in number measure in total 150 ft (45.72 m) from east to west and 75 ft (22.86 m) from north to south. To the north, integral with the main complex, is a brick-loading platform with an alcove at its eastern end. The podium with its massive battered outer wall held a wooden superstructure and the vertical chases and crisscross passages might be for wooden ramps and for the circulation of air, respectively. It has been argued that the podium was veneered by a 5-inch timbering, the decay of which led to local collapses and subsequent patches of brick-work (Wheeler 1968: 43). The construction in its original form antedates the Great Bath as its corbelled passage cuts across the eastern end of the loading platform.

Marcia Fentress (1984) points out that there is no clear explanation of how the suggested wooden superstructure was fitted into the main brick structure. 'Either the timber fitted into postholes in the ground surrounding the base of the walls, or sockets were provided in the brickwork itself. Since the latter is not clear, proof of a timber superstructure should have been sought at the foundation level.Since there is no actual evidence for this type of superstructure, one can suggest that there was no space for grain storage' (Fentress 1984: 93).

Across the street (11 ft/3.35 m wide) to the south of the Bath is a massive battered wall of the 'Intermediate' period, the purpose of which is uncertain. Associated with it is a cluster of disjointed walls, both of the Intermediate and Late periods.

To the south of the stupa area there are eight blocks of houses, marked off from one another by streets and lanes. The street at the northwest corner is about 14 ft (4.26 m) high. Nothing seems to be of particular significance here except the usual assemblage of bathrooms, walls and drains.

To the south of the stupa area and separated from it by a distance of about 92 ft (28.04 m), the L area exposes eleven blocks of houses. Among them there is at least one particularly interesting building.

Though the walls of different periods are mixed up together on the published plan, it is quite clear that in the Late phase of the city's life this area declined considerably in standard and became congested. The spaces which were once open were partitioned off and that too rather poorly. Otherwise the usual cluster of buildings and a few ill-exposed streets and lanes do not deserve any particular attention.

The pillared hall in the northern part of this area is, however, important in itself. Approximately square, this has twenty rectangular brick-piers arranged in four rows of five each, which divide the hall from east to west into five aisles or corridors. Unpaved strips of about 3.5 ft (1.06 m) run between the aisles and their purpose is probably to hold raised benches. On the analogy of the 'Durbar hall' at Kanheri, a Buddhist rock-cut cave site near Bombay, Marshall (1931, I: 23) conceives this to be a place for assembly. Mackay is 'more inclined to the view that it was intended for a large market hall with lines of permanent stalls along the aisles' (Mackay 1948: 45).

III. The Eastern Mound

Till 1964–65 there was almost no evidence to suggest that the eastern group of mounds, like its western counterpart, was surrounded by a wall. Marshall (1931, I: 9) pointed out that the surrounding wall, if any, stood on the level of the contemporary plain and must have gone under the subsoil water since then. On the western edge of the mound in the north Mackay (1938, I: 5) found a portion of a very thick wall (about 30 ft/ 9.14 m thick) and also a 'fortress-like structure' with a 'ghat-like' stair-case outside, but this find was not something on the basis of which a generalization could be made. Dales' find in 1964–65 was that of a 'massive construction composed mainly of huge solid mudbrick embankments with baked brick retaining walls' at the mound.

IV. HR Area

This area occupies roughly the southwest corner of the eastern mounds. Outside the western edge of the HR where the mudbrick embankments and their burnt brick retaining walls were discovered, Dales' excavations on the top of the mound ran through a squatter type of occupation on the top and the remains of the Late and Intermediate periods below. The bottom was not reached because of subsoil water. More detailed evidence comes from the early excavations.

A north-south street, 30–5 ft (9.14–10.66 m) wide and designated as the First Street in the reports, divides the entire excavated area in this sector into two. There are two cess-pits in the entire excavated area in this sector 'with a brick-drain between them to carry off surplus water from the northern to the southern pit which is provided with a series of brick-steps on one side, so that a man could climb down when necessary to clear away the solid sediment' (Marshall 1931, I: 188). There are also burnt-brick drains along both sides of this street.

The houses in the eastern sector are arranged around three lanes. Two of these—the 'High Lane' and the 'Deadman Lane'—open out from the First Street and then take a turn to the south. On the western side of its junction with the 'South Lane' there is a brick-built enclosure (8 ft by 4 ft or 2.43 m by 1.21 m), presumably a dust-bin. The South Lane goes east but takes a slight bend to the south at its eastern excavated end. During the Late phase of the city, the Deadman Lane went out of use; there are structures built over it.

The houses in this eastern sector of the HR area belong to the Intermediate period, though there are traces of Late wallings. In some cases, the remains of staircases suggest more than one storey.

The main focus of the houses is in most cases a couryard either fully open or covered with only a light matting of thatch and reed. The rooms, their number depending on the size of the house, crowd around this courtyard. Well-paved bathrooms, connecting drains, wells and occasional latrines are among the other distinctive features.

One of the houses in this sector, which has been designated as House I, has drawn the attention of both Mackay (Marshall 1931, I: 176–8) and Wheeler (1968: 52–3). It is bounded on the north by South Lane and on the west by Deadman Lane. The basic plan shows a large structure (32 ft by 40 ft or 9.75 m by 12.19 m) with more than 4 ft (1.21 m) thick walls, access to which was provided by two stairs on the south. This was approached by a 'monumental double gateway' between two irregular blocks of buildings. A ring of brickwork (4 ft/1.21 m internal diameter) in the inner couryard is taken to indicate a protective enclosure around a sacred(?) tree. A 6.9 ins (0.17 m) high bearded human head in white limestone was found inside a room adjacent to the gateway, and a seated/ squatting human figure (16.5 ins/0.41 m high) with his hands resting on his knees was found in broken pieces in the vicinity. The arrangement of the stairs, the double gateway and the thick outer walls do not suggest ordinary domestic or industrial functions for this building, and the discovery of two iconic specimens in the precincts led Wheeler to argue that the structure could represent a temple. Jansen (1985) offers a detailed analysis of the plan, stratigraphy and finds related to this house and supports Wheeler's inference.

Two streets roughly parallel to the First Street and ten adjoining alleys criss-cross the western section of the HR area. These streets and lanes do not have any uniformity in width. A reference to Streets 2 and 3 on the plan shows that the variation is sometimes considerable. The lanes turn frequently, and their corners are right-angled. The groups of houses around these vary in size, some blocks, especially Blocks 2 and 5, being considerably larger than the rest. Block 2 was perhaps one building, later divided into different units. In the northwestern corner of Block 5, a house has been inferred by Mackay (in Marshall 1931, I: 204) to be 'of exceptional character, probably sacred'. The walls are up to 4.5 ft (1.37 m) in thickness and rise to a height of 8–10 ft (2.43–3.04 m), enclosing solid podia of mudbrick. These are likely to constitute the foundation walls of a monumental superstructure.

To the west of this is a double row of sixteen houses having in most cases 'a single room in front with one or two smaller rooms at the back'. Some had a paved bath corner with a drain or a narrow passage at one end. These have been interpreted as shops or retainers' quarters by Mackay (in Marshall 1931, I: 204) and as 'coolie-lines' by Piggott (1950: 169).

V. VS Area

The VS area lies across a broad depression to the north of the HR area. This depression was surmised by Marshall (1931, I: 214) to represent 'one of the principle streets of the ancient city'. However, the existence of such an east-west thoroughfare has not yet been found. At its eastern limit the VS area is crossed by the First Street which continues from the HR area.

A small part lies to the east (Section B) but the main part (Section A) lies to the west. Besides the First Street there are five lanes in this area and a number of narrow alleys. The lanes are often tortuous and seldom uniform in width. Section A or the western section has seven blocks or thirty-eight buildings. There are only two blocks or three buildings in the eastern sector or Section B. The buildings vary in size but the usual arrangement of courtyards, bathrooms, wells, drains, flights of steps, etc. does not differ. The individual features, however, are not negligible. House I in Block I is 144 ft (43.88 m) from east to west and is much larger than the average private dwellings. House VIII in the same block is a long rectangular structure (195 ft by 32 ft or 32.004 m by 9.75 m). A wayside room in this house possesses a well which is connected by a drain with a street drain outside. House II (86 ft 5 ins or 26.46 m by 19.62 m) has, in one of its rooms overlooking First Street, 'five conical pits or holes sunk in the floor and lined with wedge-shaped bricks, apparently meant to hold the pointed bases of large jars'. A flight of steps connects the room with the street outside and in one corner there is a narrow well. The adjacent rooms with which it is connected are paved neatly with bricks on edge. This could be a sweetmeat shop or a place to keep dyeing vats.

VI. DK Area

The DK area has five sections or excavated parts in all. Of these, Sections A, B and C occupy the eastern edge of the mound while E and G are in the north.

Section A has about four blocks divided by a street with a drain into parts. There are about twenty-seven chambers in the area. The northern most one, because of its location on a higher ground than the rest, thick-built walls and careful laying of bricks, is supposed to be a shrine (Marshall 1931, I: 235). Section E is interesting as almost all of it shows Late period masonry work. Architecturally it has nothing to recommend; the walls are thin and badly built.

The bricks were placed in the queerest position, some on edge, others showing their flats; points gape and have been left unbroken in many places. This kind of masonry illustrates the great deterioration that had taken place in the art of building since the preceding period; the difference in style of the two periods is at once evident to the casual eye (Marshall 1931, I: 236).

There are four blocks in this area. A wide street separates Block 1 at the extreme south from the rest. Block 2 is apparently made up of two or more buildings separated by a drain which probably once lay below an east-west lane. A 7 ft (2.13 m) wide street skirts Block 3 on its east side. Block 4 does not seem to have anything distinctive.

Section C covers a wide area and has sixteen blocks. The most important feature of the northern portion of this area is a wide street (29 ft or 8.83 m wide) moving from east to west and provided with drains and soakpits. To the north of this street are four blocks, divided into two by a lane with a drain opening out from the main street itself. Opposite its junction with the main street is a soakpit. The earlier walls were sometimes filled up with mud to support the late buildings. Block 3 is marked by a huge courtyard which has been supposed by Mackay (in Marshall 1931, I: 244) to be a temple.

Blocks 5–9 constitute a separate cluster. A rather badly aligned street separates it from Block 10 on the south. Two narrow lanes, both with drains, connect this with the wider street on the north. At the extreme south, Block 11 is separated from Block 12 by another lane which is 5 ft 10 ins (1.78 m) wide. A small alley issues from its eastern end. The remaining blocks consist merely of scraps of wallings.

Mackay's DK area, Section G, covers a considerable stretch of ground as the northwestern edge of the eastern group of mounds. The First Street continues along the eastern limit of the excavated area and bifurcates into two. Mackay (1938, I: 32) believes that this was the main entrance to the city from a gate in the northwest, perhaps overlooking the river and the quays. Roughly parallel with the First Street and meeting the Central Street before the latter turns northwest is another street ('West Street') cutting across the northern area from north to south. A lane runs parallel with the West Street to its west and another issues from it to its north.

What has been revealed by excavations in this area belongs essentially to the Late period.

To the west of this West Street is a cluster of blocks comprising the numbers 13–17 and 29. That a marked deterioration took place in the town planning during the Late phase of the city is clear from the irregular alignment of the lane between the Blocks 14 and 15. The lane (3 ft 10 ins or 1.16 m wide) was properly aligned in the north, gradually becoming wider and irregular towards the south.

Of the two houses in Block 29, only one is complete, the other one being completely destroyed. Block 13 has two houses but neither of them is well-preserved or interesting. Block 14 is relatively compact and has a number of houses, one of which at least (Room 18, House III) possesses a privy. Between the badly aligned lane on the west and the West Street on the east is a long row of fragmentary houses denoting Block 15. Its northern limit was marked by an alley 4 ft 8 ins (1.42 m) wide. The same alley formed the northern end of Block 16 also. It is damaged and seems to have three houses.

Of Block 17 to the north of that alley, Building 4 deserves special mention. Apart from its annexe, this is 48 ft 6 ins (14.78 m) long (north-south) and 23 ft 4 ins (7.11 m) wide (east-west). A remarkably steep stairway (3 ft 6 ins or 1.06 m wide) with very narrow treads (11 ins or 0.27 m high and 7 ins or 0.17 m broad) leads upward from one of its rooms at the base. According to Mackay, 'this stairway would have been most awkward for domestic purposes and it strongly suggests the ascent to a watch tower' (Mackay 1938, I: 147). Mackay also thinks that the original structure must have been 'a watch-tower which in such a situation would have commanded the down-river approach to the city, as well as two important entrances, namely the gateway of First and Central Streets' (Mackay 1938, I: 148).

Block 18 to the east of the West Street is massive. It includes possibly Block 19 also in the north and the entire structure erected on a mudbrick platform is thus 242 ft 6 ins (73.91 m) long. Of the remaining blocks in this area (Blocks 20–8) Block 20 is built on mudbrick foundations. The massive battered outer walls of Block 11 again indicate its importance. Little remains of the rest.

At least five lanes ('Low', 'Loop', 'Fare'; 'Crooked' and 'Long' lanes) cut across the area which has been called the DK area, Section G, South. Among them, only Low Lane is roughly parallel with First Street, the rest following a zig-zag course. Mackay (1938, I: 25) thinks that at the south end of First Street there was another street, surely as wide as, if not wider than, Central Street with which it should be parallel.

It is in this area that an attempt was made to work out the architectural history of the numerous buildings from the Intermediate III period, whatever that might mean. Deep digging showed that there was no break in cultural continuity. It was also quite impossible to determine the use of a building from the nature of antiquities found in them. Of its twelve blocks with subdivisions not all deserve notice, most of them being a cluster of ordinary dwelling houses.

Much emphasis has been given by Mackay (1938, I: 46) on what he thinks was the palace of a prince or governor. There is nothing except its size (about 180 ft by 70 ft or 54.86 m by 21.33 m) which marks it apart from the usual run of houses at Mohenjodaro, although it must be admitted that the size is not altogether uncommon. Kosambi (1956: 50) believes that this was 'merely a merchant's house . . . only a little larger than the other merchants' houses which surround it'. The essential features of its planning are two courtyards separated by a wide passage with a double turn and no door on either side. The entrances were from the north and south. The complex of rooms suggests diverse functions.

Block 8A also suggests something out of the ordinary. There is an L-shaped structure with buttresses at intervals along the walls which probably carried roof-beams or was an open gallery giving access to small rooms around it. According to Mackay (1938, I: 92) this was a hostel for pilgrims. In any case this does not seem to be a common building.

Interestingly enough, Mackay (1938, I: 119) calls one particular house 'khan' or a place of rest for the caravans coming into the city. The lower floor does not contain many rooms but at the immediate entrance a stair runs upwards. Even in a modern khan it is the upper floor which is important as the sleeping apartments, and if one accepts Mackay's argument that the river-side gateway of the city was nearby, the place may have been suitable for a caravan-serai. As elsewhere in Mohenjodaro, this part of the city deteriorated considerably during the Late phase of its life.

VII. Moneer Site

This site, excavated principally by Q.M. Moneer in 1933–34 and located about 200 m to the east of the VS area has been described by Jansen (1984) and Th. Urban (1987). The substantial remains excavated were numbered according to blocks which comprised clusters of detached house units along with a number of streets. One such street is on the east-west axis, and is about 2 m wide. This has been traced for 66 m. The present excavated area is dominated by a house complex which covers about 890 sq. m and has walls about 2 m thick. Jansen (1984) has broken down this complex 'structurally into 6 zones according to their relation to the interior system of intercommunicating access routes'.

Chanhudaro

The site of Chanhudaro was discovered by Majumdar (1934: 35–44) and more elaborately excavated by Mackay(1943), although not up to virgin soil because of the presence of subsoil water. It is now about 12 miles (19.30 km) away from the left bank of the Indus, but it stood on or near the river-bank. Mackay (1943: v) points out that about 37 miles (59.53 km) away there is a gap across the Kirthars, which is still fre-quented by caravans. This geographical element might have given the site an added importance. The site itself, which was once a complete whole, is now a cluster of three mounds, marked I, II and III and 950 ft (289.56 m), 1060 ft (323.08 m) and 450 ft (137.16 m), respectively. Both Majumdar and Mackay concentrated on Mound II which showed three Harappan and two later occupational phases. The scheme of cultural succession at the site from the bottom upwards, as enumerated by Mackay, is: Harappa III, II, I; Jhukar and Jhangar. Piggot (1950: 222) has reclassified them as: Chanhudaro Ia, Ib, Ic (Harappa culture), Chanhudaro II (Jhukar culture) and Chanhudaro III (Jhangar culture). The three Harappan phases at Mound II are separated by two debris layers and bear no structural relationship whatsoever.

What one gets in Harappa III of Mackay in Mound II is essentially a few chambers and fragmentary walls. Mackay sums them up by saying that these 'represent three, if not four separate houses, all of them quite small but evidently the houses of fairly well-to-do people' (Mackay 1943: 15). The upper part of a mudbrick platform, about 13.5 ft (4.08 m) wide, is traced above flood-level.

The remains of the succeeding phase (Harappa II) are more elaborate. A street runs from northwest to southeast with a width of 15 ft 6 ins (5.68 m). Two covered drains run on either side of it. Another street crosses this main street at right angles while yet another opens up to the west from its southwestern end. Parallel to it is a lane, roughly 3 ft 10 ins (1.16 m) wide. The most important excavated structure in the main street is what Mackay (1943: 41) calls a bead factory with a furnace, lying on its eastern side. The principal part of the building is 33 ft (10.05 m) long and 13 ft 6 ins (3.81 m) wide. The direct entrance from the street is into a small chamber, No. 215 in Mackay's Plan IV. In an adjacent room to its north is a brick floor which is compartmented by thin brick walls and has a criss-cross of flues underneath. The abundance of finished and unfinished beads in the building suggests that the wall with flues was meant for glazing them but the absence of ash, etc. indicates that it may never have been used. The other buildings of this level do not seem to be of any particular significance. A noteworthy feature is a number of solid mud-brick platforms, the upper portions of which have been exposed and which evidently raised the houses above flood-level.

The occupation level of Harappa I is too denuded to suggest an intelligible plan. At the edge of Mound II was discovered a long (traced for about 80 ft or 24.38 m) and wide (4 ft 9 ins/1.44 m–5 ft 4.5 ins/ 1.73 m) wall which took a right-angled turn to the west at its eastern end. 'The fact that the interior face of the wall was rough showed that the surviving fragment had revetted an internal platform, such as that which carried the granaries at Harappa. The scale and excellence of the work indicates an important structure worthy of further exploration' (Wheeler 1968: 57).

To the southwest of Mound II is Mound I, the remains of which suggest at least two streets and a lane with effective drains and at least one cesspit. The houses are mostly dilapidated but some of them are of substantial build.

Ali Murad

Ali Murad (Majumdar 1934: 89–91) seems to have been an extensive settlement, the larger of the two mounds covering an area of 1100 ft (335.28 m) by 1000 ft (304.8). Majumdar traced a 'long rampart wall of irregularly dressed stone blocks' for 170 ft (51.865 m) on the southeast of the mound and partially on the north and east also. To the south there is a definite gap in the wall but whether or not that is an opening for a gate is undecided. The houses on the inner side of the wall or the enclosure have not been properly excavated but there are 'visible traces of innumerable stone walls' and at least one well.

Kot Diji

F.A. Khan (1965: 17) refers to a 16.5 ft (5.02 m) thick cultural deposit of the Harappan level at the site. He further refers to rooms with stone foundations, mudbrick paved floors and mud-plastered reed-mats of

2–3.5 ft (4.41 m by 3.50 m). 'A well-regulated town-plan' has been inferred on the basis of a lane and 'a spacious street running from north to south between two blocks of houses'.

Ahladino

The mound of Ahladino (Fairservis 1982), with a diameter of about 100 m, is near the junction of the Malir river and its tributary. It is a single culture site and contains at its central and highest part, an open court (20 by 8 m) with a stone-built well (roughly 60 cm by 90 cm) which has a 'Harappan intersecting circle bath tub' attached to its southern side. The court is entered by passageways through surrounding buildings, one of which contains a stone-lined bathroom with covered drains and outlets. No enclosing wall could be traced around the site.

CHOLISTAN

The former princely state of Bahawalpur (IGI, vol. I: 6, 1908, pp. 194–204) was divided lengthwise into three great strips. Of these the first is a part of the Great Indian Desert and is known as the Rohi or Cholistan. The central portion also is chiefly desert and resembles the Bar or Pat uplands of western Panjab. It is only along the Sutlej which flows past the town of Bahawalpur before combining with the flow of the Chenab that the tract of the area is fertile. Our concern here is with the course of the Hakra which separates the Cholistan desert from the central part of Bahawalpur. The Cholistan desert thus lies to the south and east of the Hakra depression. Following Flam, I outlined in the previous chapter the course of the Hakra lower down till it joins the Indus and flows into, or in the vicinity of, the Rann of Cutch. On the Indian side the river is known as the Ghaggar and is identified with Sarasvati of early literature. This extinct river retains some water in its upper course during the monsoon but this does not extend beyond the modern town of Hanumangarh, medieval Bhatner. Starting from the Panjab foothills it touches the plains near Ambala, flows past Thaneshwar, Karnal and Patiala, and enters Bikaner beyond Sirsa. It may be remembered that for a while in the upper reaches the Sarsuti (derived from Sarasvati) and Ghaggar are two separate rivers with a few minor streams inbetween, but this does not affect the issue of identification. In Bikaner it continues along the small *tehsil* towns of Hanumangarh, Suratgarh and Anupgarh, and then crosses over to adjoining Bahawalpur as the Hakra. We have already seen how Flam has traced the course of his Nara Nadi flowing into the Indus. The sea then was further north, with Kutch constituting perhaps an island (or islands) and forming a part of the lower Indus basin. While the Ghaggar was alive it might have had a number of tributaries. The course of one of them, also originating in the Panjab foothills, is easily traceable and archaeologically important. It is Chautang or the Vedic Drishadvati, joining the master-stream near Suratgarh.

The problem of the desiccation of the Ghaggar plain is interesting and has drawn considerable geographical attention. S.M. Ali (1941) points out that the Ghaggar has been a non-perennial river from historical times. He, however, does not believe in the hypothesis of a basic climatic change to account for this desiccation. 'The diminution of water in this river has been due to: (1) direct causes, for instance (a) the diversion of a few of its feeders to the Jumna or the Sutlej, (b) canalization and increasing cultivation in the area; and (2) indirect causes as (a) deforestation and erosion in the hills in which lie the headwaters of the streams of the divide, (b) the erosion in the plains due to overcultivation and excessive pasturage' (Ali 1941: 177). R.L. Raikes (1968) has postulated that the Ghaggar catchment has alternated between the Ganges and the Indus systems and its final eastward diversion to the Ganges in about AD 500 may have led to its death as a river.

The issue, however, is far from clear. It does not rest only with the problem of desiccation; dating is equally important, at least from the archaeological point of view. The complicated nature of the issue may be understood from the contradiction between Francfort's and D.P. Agrawal's premises. According to Francfort (1992), when the protohistoric people settled in the modern Haryana segment of its course, 'no large perennial river had flowed there for a long time'. This contrasts with Agrawal's contention that 'as far as the archaeological evidence is concerned, the presence of the Early and Mature Harappan sites on the Ghaggar channels shows that the river was alive during the period of Third and Second millennia BC' (Agrawal 1992: 240). Basically the debate centres around the date of the beginning of the desiccation process. According to Agrawal, this process began by the Painted Gray Ware period whereas according to Francfort, it began much earlier. Incidentally, Agrawal argues that an understanding of both the Sutlej and Ghaggar systems is necessary in this context. According to him, the present confluence of the Sutlej with the Indus does not appear to be an old feature. A distinct palaeochannel suggests that the Sutlej 'flowed through the Nara directly into the Rann of Kutch'. Regarding the Ghaggar system, Agrawal writes:

1. The ancient bed of the Ghaggar has an almost constant width of 6–8 km from Shatrana in Punjab to Marot in Pakistan.
2. There is a clear palaeochannel southeast of the river Markanda which joins the ancient bed of the Ghaggar near Shatrana.
3. Another channel which corresponds to the present Chautang seems to join the Ghaggar near Suratgarh.
4. Near Anupgarh, the ancient Ghaggar bed seems to bifurcate and both the channels come to an abrupt end. These two terminal channels of the Ghaggar seem to disappear into a depression near Marot. There is no indication of any palaeochannel connecting the ancient Ghaggar with the Indus or the Luni rivers.
5. The palaeochannels of the ancient Yamuna show that it changed its loyalty in the past, three times. The first channel flowed into the old bed of the Ghaggar; the second channel flowed through a channel which includes the present day Chautang (ancient Drishadvati) and met the Ghaggar near Suratgarh; the third time it went southward and joined the Ganga through the Chambal.

    . . . To conclude, basically the Ghaggar is a descendant of the original Sarasvati. Due to neotectonic upheavals, its two main tributaries—the palaeo-Satluj and the palaeo-Yamuna—were pirated by the Indus and the Ganga respectively, leaving the Sarasvati (the present day Ghaggar) high and dry. This drying up of the major river of the Indo-Ganga divide, had catastrophic consequences for the human settlements, as one can see by the sticking of the early man to the changing courses of these channels (Agrawal 1992: 240–1).

It must also be stressed that, according to Agrawal, 'the evidence of climatic change in Rajasthan is now incontrovertibly established and is supported by a variety of data, supplemented by the data from the Arabian sea' (Agrawal 1992: 243). Apart from G. Singh's pollen profile which shows a wet condition coinciding (4000–2000 BP) with the 'pre-Harappan and Harappan' presence, the salinity curve of the Didwana salt lake shows that 6000 to 4000 years ago the water in the lake varied from being deep fresh water to moderately fresh water. There have been two brief arid phases in the past 4000 years. According to Agrawal this fits in with the evidence provided by the work on the Arabian sea which marks out early Holocene (8000 years ago) as a period characterized by humid tropical conditions. However, after this phase was over, there was a fluctuating regime with an apparently gradual lessening of rainfall.

Apart from the work of L.P. Tessitori (1919), the first systematic archaeological investigation of the Ghaggar-Hakra basin was undertaken by Aurel Stein (1942). He explored along the Ghaggar from above Hanumangarh in Bikaner to the lands below Derawar in Bahawalpur.

From below Derawar to Fort Marot his sketch map shows a cluster of mounds 'with prehistoric (chalcolithic) pottery'. From Fort Marot to some miles below Suratgarh are mounds 'with sherds decorated with impressed patterns'. The rest up to Hanumangarh is all shown to be historical, meaning thereby an occupation phase within the early centuries AD. The number of prehistoric mounds on Stein's map is forty-two, including Sandhanwala near the Bahawalpur-Bikaner border. Of these at least twelve, according to his map, are Harappan. The cultural character of the second set of mounds is not known but he prefers to place them between the Harappan and historical periods.

The subsequent exploration by A. Ghosh (1952) considerably changed the picture on the Indian side of the border. The number of ancient sites discovered by him in the Bikaner portion of the Sarasvat-Drishadvati valley is about a hundred, of which twenty-five are Harappan. In Bahawalpur, Henry Field (cited in Pakistan Archaeology 1: 35–6) recorded seven new sites which belong to the Harappan and Cemetery H categories.

In Cholistan or Bahawalpur the most important work is by Mughal but the details are still to be published. Out of a total of 414 sites discovered by him along 300 miles of the Hakra river bed 174 are mature Harappan ('Mohenjodaro and Harappa related'). Mughal observes:

The most striking aspects of the Mature Harappan Period in Cholistan are: (1) a general shift of sites from the northeast to the southwest, around and beyond Derawar Fort, (2) an increase in the number . . . size and height of settlement sites, among which at least one. . . . Ganwerwala at 81.5 hectares (201.3865 acres) in size, is essentially the same size as Mohenjodaro, and a profusion of industrial sites . . . and their clear separation from habitation areas. However, sites combining both residential and industrial functions . . . also occur (Mughal 1992: 92).

Mughal's map clearly establishes the fact that towards the Indian border in the east, the distribution of the mature Harappan sites is distinctly thinner, and thus the mature Harappan sites in Rajasthan and beyond may be considered to belong to a separate distribution area. Mughal argues that the shift in the concentration of settlements from the northeastern part of Cholistan to the southeast was dictated by hydrographic changes 'necessitating relocation of settlements on new grounds' (Mughal 1992). Elsewhere Mughal (1991) enumerates the size-categories of seventy-three mature Harappan sites in this area: 0–5 ha./44 sites; 5.1–1 ha./20 sites; 10.1–20 ha./8 sites and over 80 ha./1 site.

WESTERN PANJAB

Panjab or the upper Indus valley is literally 'the land of the five rivers', the country enclosed and watered by the Jhelum, Chenab, Ravi, Beas and Sutlej. The 'daman-i-koh' or 'skirts of the hills', the Siwaliks and the Indus provide a more or less clear boundary line for the broad doabs or interfluves of Panjab except in the east where they seem to merge imperceptibly in the broader alluvium of the Ganges-Yamuna tract. The doabs are five: the Sindsagar between the Indus and the Jhelum, the Jech between the Jhelum and the Chenab, the Rechna between the Chenab and the Ravi, the Bari between the Ravi and the Sutlej and the Bist between the Sutlej and the Beas. Outside the Himalayan submontane the topography, except that of the Aravalli outliers of the Kirana and Sangala hills, is one of unrelieved monotony. West of the Ravi the country is arid and sandy; the central portion of the Sindsagar doab, the Thar, 'approaches true desert conditions'. The aridity is also marked in the southwest where Panjab merges on the northeastern fringe of the Thar while it is less so in the Indo-Gangetic divide between the Sutlej and the Yamuna.

The geographical distribution of the Harappan civilization in western Panjab is not clear. Whether it is due to lack of intensive exploration or not, Harappa, the type-site of civilization on the Ravi, seems to mark the westernmost limit here. In its immediate periphery there is only one other reported site—Chak Purvane Syal. Another site, Vainiwal, has been discovered on the right bank of a dried-up course of the Beas.

Harappa

The Ravi now flows about six miles to the north of the site (basic sources: Vats 1940, Wheeler 1947; for further excavations of the cemetery R 37, see Pakistan Archaeology 5, 1967, 63–8; for more recent work, see Dales and Kenoyer 1989, 1992, Kenoyer 1991a, 1991b) which is situated beside the confluence of the two dried-up beds of this river, one of which is clearly shown on the site-map. Before the advent of modern canal irrigation the Ravi doab, on the western part of which Harappa lies, was an inhospitable wasteland. The writer of the Montgomery district gazetteer in 1900 described it as a 'howling wilderness' (Fagan 1900: 3). The area is likely to have been greener when Harappa was alive; the cause of subsequent desiccation is not known. Marcia Fentress (1982: 248) traces 'almost 6600 square kilometres of immediately available farm land for Harappa thus precluding any necessity for dependence on a wide-ranging network of agricultural villages for its food needs'. Shireen Ratnagar (1982) argues that Harappa was more of a redistributive centre rather than a manufacturing one. The fallacy of this argument has been pointed out by Lahiri (1992).

It is almost impossible to define the precise boundary of the city with any accuracy. Brick-robbing by neighbouring villagers and contractors of the Lahore-Multan railway reduced Harappa long ago to mere shambles (Piggott 1950: 13–14).

On the site-plan the most imposing mound is what is termed AB (roughly 1450 ft/441.96 m by 800 ft/243.84 m). Its contour marks show an ascent of 40–50 ft (12.19–15.24 m) from the level of the surrounding plain. Between this and the dried-up Ravi is the less high (20 ft/6.09 m) Mound F (970 ft/295.65 m by 980 ft/298,70 m) while to its south are Mounds D.J. and H. As it is a cemetery Mound H should perhaps be located outside the city-limit. The area extends considerably to the east to include Mound B and a smaller one, Mound G, to its south. The modern village of Harappa also was within its periphery. The total circuit should be about 3.5 miles. Mackay (1948: 6) thought that Harappa was larger in area than Mohenjodaro, but this does not seem to be the case. Dales and Kenoyer (1989) have written on the basis of the surface surveys, test pits and systematic borings made in 1987 and 1988 that the site is much larger than previously supposed. They put it at 150 ha. (370.65 acres). Some interesting light on the contemporary or near-contemporary environment is shed by the soil-scientists working with archaeologists in the area. 'The basic conclusions are that the carbon isotope ratios of pedogenic carbonate in inner portions of nodules forming at Harappa reflect an arid climate with a very low soil respiration rate' (Dales and Kenoyer 1989: 150).

I. Mound AB

The striking feature of this mound is a fortifiction system around its periphery. On the plan this has roughly the shape of a parallelogram. Only on the west side does it take a sharp inward bend for a while. The lowermost portion of the defences is a mud and mudbrick 'bund' or rampart built right over the alluvial soil and carried up to a height of 10 ft (3.04 m). Its purpose was to protect the site against floods. It also acted as the base of the defence wall itself.

This wall was is not of uniform width. In Wheeler's cutting, HP XXX, it is 39.5 ft (12.03 m) wide at the base while in another cutting (HP XLV) its width is 51 ft/15.54 m. It is battered both externally and internally, the angle to the vertical varying between 13 and 20 degrees. On the outer face of the wall is a burnt-brick revetment, also battered. Its thickness varies from point to point and phase to phase.

Intermittently along the wall are bastions or salients. The salient which guarded the inward bend of the wall on the west projects 23 ft (7.01 m) at its northwestern and 15 ft (4.57 m) at its southeastern ends. The salient at the northwestern corner shows three phases of construction. Wheeler's cuttings, HP XL, XLVI and XXXVIII, reveal three other salients. In the north a marked inlet along the wall suggests an entrance but this is still unexplored. In the west the evidence is more clear. The continuous line of defences is interrupted at this point by two lateral walls of mudbrick and burnt brick and 'between the flanking walls a filling of mud, with at one place a transverse mudbrick retaining wall, may be presumed to have carried the ramp or stair' (Wheeler 1947: 71).

The wall to the north of this entrance is fronted by terraces showing three constructional phases and is approached through outer gates. Seemingly these were not for normal needs of defence. Wheeler suggests that 'the plan was designed to conform with the needs of some sort of ceremony—religious or secular or both—in which the terrace or terraces played a dominant role and to which processional access was required' (Wheeler 1946: 74).

Behind the rampart and integral with it is a platform of mud and mudbrick which is 33 ft (10.05 m) high and 'designed to carry the internal buildings of the citadel' (Wheeler 1947: 65). These buildings, however, are too ravaged to show any meaningful pattern. Both Vats and Wheeler noted that there were six structural phases (Vats 1940, I: 137–44). In recent excavations a well (1.2 m internal diameter) built of specially made wedge-shaped bricks has been found in the east-central portion of this mound.

II. Mound F

On the river bank Mound F reveals three interesting structural complexes, all under the shadow of the high Mound AB.

One is the 'Great Granary'. It stood on the river bank and has two blocks (150 ft/45.72 m by 56 ft/17 m each), eastern and western, with a 23 ft (7.01 m) wide open aisle in between. Each of the blocks dissolved into a series of six halls (51 ft 9 ins/15.77 m by 17 ft 6 ins/5.33 m) alternated by five corridors of similar length but narrower width. The timbering of the floors in each hall rested on three sleeper-like walls, the space underneath being meant for the circulation of air which flowed in through air-holes at the end. These air-holes were later additions to facilitate the flow of air, after the ground-level outside rose. The whole of the southern and parts of the eastern and western sides stood on a battered retaining wall. The absence of this in the north suggests that the approach was from the north, i.e. the riverside. This also suggests the use of water-transport for carrying grains to the granary.

The idea that the structure was a granary was first formulated by Marshall (cited in Vats 1940, I: 137–44) on the analogy of the granaries of Roman Britain where too the air ducts formed a necessary feature to prevent the grain from getting mildewed. There is another point which has some bearing on its being a granary. The end-portions (for a length of 7 ft/2.13 m) of the sleeper walls in each hall were wider than the remaining portion. This implies that the superstructure along both ends was considerably heavy. A granary of this type was excavated in 1965–66 at Telul Eth-Thalathat in Iraq (near Mosul) dated to the Nineveh V period (*c.* 2900 BC; Egami and Sono 1970). The existence of grain pounding platforms in the vicinity of this structure does not leave much room for doubt (cf. Fentress 1984) about its function as a granary. However, the structures unearthed in the immediate vicinity of this granary are a fragmentary heap and do not add up to a significant pattern.

A few hundred feet to the south, however, there is a row of circular platforms which deserve notice. Vats unearthed seventeen such platforms and Wheeler added one more. Almost all of them are equidistant from one another, the distance varying between 20–1 ft (6.09–6.4 m) from centre to centre. 'Each platform is 11 feet in diameter and consists of a single course of four continuous concentric rings of bricks on edge masonry with a hollow at the centre equal to the length of three bricks. The mortar used in them is mud but the pointing is of gypsum' (Vats 1940, I: 74). Vats was uncertain of their purpose but burnt wheat and husked barley were found in the hollow of Platform 8 and the shape resembles the platform for pounding grains with a pestle in many parts of India. In all probability they were used for husking grains.

Between these husking platforms and Mound AB there is an assemblage of fourteen small houses grouped symmetrically along three east-west lanes intersected by six narrower alleys at right angles. They stood within an enclosure wall, the traces of which still survive. The rows are incomplete at both ends; the number of houses may have been more. Each of these little (56 by 24 ft/17.06 by 7.31 m) detached houses was accessed through an oblique passage to ensure privacy, and had about two rooms with partially brick-paved floors. At a higher level, near these houses, were found sixteen pear-shaped furnaces. Their major axis varied from 3 ft 4 ins/1.01 m to 6 ft 2 ins/1.87 m in length. A crucible for melting copper found in one of these furnaces is suggestive of their purpose.

The proper Harappan cemetery, Cemetery R37, lies to the south of

Mound AB. Mound E, the counterpart of the eastern mounds of Mohen-jodaro, lies to the east and has been excavated only recently.

III. Mound E

The excavations which have been conducted at the site since 1986 under Dales and Kenoyer have, apart from the cemetery area, concentrated on the excavations at Mound E, i.e. the mound overlain by the modern Harappa village. On the top of the northwestern corner of this mound were found intact architectural remains including small streets, drains and soak pits. On the slope of this sector of the mound a series of mudbrick platforms with burnt-brick retaining walls was found. A large as well as a small pottery kiln was also found associated with this level in this sector. The major burnt brick wall here is 2.5 m thick. A major north-south street is located on the southern slope of Mound E, with the evidence of a house along its eastern edge. One of the houses was found built on a mudbrick platform in which there are three postholes indicating pillars for roof-support. Perhaps the most important architectural discovery is indicated by the following:

The southern end of this street leads toward an impressive east-west mudbrick wall system of Period III. Two superimposed stages of the wall have been revealed. The later stage ranges from 5.4 to 6.5 metres in width and has been traced so far for more than 73 metres. Piercing the wall system is what appears to be a major gateway with an opening of 2.6 metres. The associated wall at the gateway is 9 metres wide. Traces of a fired brick facing were found bonded to the mudbrick wall on the southern side of the gateway. The discovery of this free standing wall system provides an unexpected contrast to the massive facing walls, revetments and platforms that characterise the northwestern corner of Mound E (Dales 1992: 31).

RAJASTHAN, HARYANA, EAST PANJAB AND U.P.

The area as a whole lies between the Sutlej and the Yamuna and between the Panjab Siwaliks and the course of the Ghaggar in the former Bikaner state of Rajasthan. That Harappan sites occur in this area have long been known. We have already referred to A. Ghosh's work in the Bikaner area. Vats' report on Harappa contains a reference to Kotla Nihang Khan near Rupar in the upper Sutlej valley. Rupar was excavated in the early fifties. Alamgirpur, still the easternmost Harappan site near Meerat, was identified in 1958–59. Since then an enormous amount of work has been done in this area beginning with excavations at Kalibangan on the dried-up course of the Ghaggar in 1960–61. This continued till the early seventies and was followed by Suraj Bhan's explorations and excavations which culminated in a Ph.D. thesis submitted to the University of Baroda in 1972 (Bhan 1972). Bhan located 97 protohistoric sites in this area: 17 in the Sarasvati valley, 40 in the Drishadvati valley, 24 in the Yamuna valley and 16 in the Ghaggar and other valleys. A detailed list of sites appears in Bhan's dissertation; their distribution is shown in a map published by him in 1973 (Bhan 1973). His sites cover the entire spectrum from the pre-/early Harappan to the late Harappan phases, and he excavated the sites of Siswal and Mitathal in the lower part and Daulatpur in the upper part of the Drishadvati system. Siswal represents the early/pre-Harappan culture of Kalibangan I whereas Mitathal I is supposed to represent its late phase. Mitathal II is mature Harappan whereas Daulatpur I is late Harappan. Thus a stratigraphic and associated ceramic index was built up for this area, and on behalf of Kurukshetra University, Suraj Bhan and his colleague, U.V. Singh, organized surveys by their Ph.D. students in a large number of districts of Haryana. They also did limited excavations at Balu. Bhan and Shaffer (1978) did some further explorations in the late seventies. Another person who was active in this area is R.S. Bisht who began his work on behalf of the Haryana state department of archaeology and followed it up by prolonged excavations at the site of Banawal in the Ghaggar/Sarasvati. At this place it may be noted that there is still a river course in the area which is locally known as Sarsuti, joining the course of the Ghaggar. The work of the Panjab state department of archaeology seems to be limited principally to the excavations of late Harappan sites. A very significant piece of exploratory work was done by J.P. Joshi and his associates in this area in the eighties, and in the upper Yamuna system in western U.P., field-research on the Harappans culminated in K.N. Dikshit's excavations at Hulas in the Saharanpur district. The distribution of sites belonging to the pre-/early, mature and late Harappan phases in this area as a whole has been published in three detailed maps prepared by J.P. Joshi, Madhu Bala and J.Ram (1984). More recently, there has been some work in the Haryana sector of this area by the Indo-French project led by H.P. Francfort whose aim was to prove the existence of irrigational canals in this area during the Harappan period and earlier. The idea that there could be canal-based irrigation dating from this period in this area was clearly propounded by R.S.Bisht (1982) on the basis of his own fieldwork.

In the course of his extensive exploration in North and Central Haryana, and in some parts of Northeast Punjab (India) the present author has observed that the

Sarasvati and its tributaries had probably been extensively harnessed. Protohistoric man apparently dug canals for irrigating fields and storing water in large ponds. The existence of a network of abandoned canals and river beds, dotted with numerous chalcolithic and Early Iron Age sites, in the Sarasvati valley in Haryana bears testimony to this (Bisht 1982: 114).

Francfort postulated the same thing about a decade later through the extensive use of remote-sensing techniques, and he came to the conclusion that 'archaeological sites are located not only on the banks of former natural waterways, but also at a distance from them, sometimes far away, and even in the middle of the supposed large river beds'. He points out that the location of a proto-Harappan (early) site on a dune in the middle of the Chautang (Drishadvati) river bed proved that it was 'established after a dry period of a certain time and that no major silting had disturbed it in 4000 years'. The logic of this type of distribution can be explained by the presence of artificial canal networks.

At this juncture it is interesting to point out a contradiction between Francfort's understanding of the location of a major site known as Rakhigarhi away from any river course and Bhan's report (Bhan 1972: 49) that this site seems to have been located on the right bank of the Drishadvati.

The data on the size-estimates of Harappan sites in this area are not available and one can only draw attention to the listed major sites. Bhan (1973: 257) mentions three 'metropolitan centres'—Mitathal, Rakhigarhi, Banawali—'dominating respectively the Yamuna, Drishadvati and Sarasvati valleys'. It is difficult to place Mitathal in the Yamuna valley unless the line of the western Yamuna canal to the east of the modern flow of the Yamuna extends further to the southeast and represents an old course of the river. Bhan argues that this indeed was the case. The twin mounds of this site have a 20 m wide gap between them and measure 150 m by 130 m and 300 m by 175 m. The total area is thus 72,000 sq. m or roughly a little more than 7 ha. Banawali is about 1 km to the south of the village of the same name lying above the floodplain of the dried-up Sarasvati (locally called Rangoi) on its right bank. This site, according to Bhan (1972), measures 100 m by 80 m, whereas, according to its excavator, R.S. Bisht, it measures 400 m by 400 m (160000 sq. m or roughly 16 ha.) and constitutes a single mound. According to Bhan (1972) Rakhigarhi near Jind measures 600 m by 400 m (240000 sq. m or about 24 ha.), whereas, according to Francfort (1992), the site is as large as Harappa.

J.P. Joshi (1991) has discussed the distribution of sites of this period in the Mansa *taluk* of the Bhatinda district of Panjab, situated along the

modern Sirhind rivulet which is now a tributary of the Ghaggar. Out of
a total of twenty-five sites the measurement of five (pre-Harappan and
Harappan) sites exceeds 100,0000 sq. m:

1. Dhalewan—1500 m by 1000 m—150,0000 sq. m (roughly 150 ha.).
2. Gurni Kalan I—1200 m by 1200 m—1440000 sq. m (roughly
   144 ha.).
3. Hasanpur II—1000 m 1000 m—100,0000 sq. m (roughly 100 ha.).
4. Lakhmirwala—1500 m by 1500 m—2250000 sq. m (roughly
   225 ha.).
5. Baglian Da Theh—1000 m by 1000 m—100,0000 sq. m (roughly
   100 ha.).

In addition to these sites there are four sites measuring 500 m by
500 m each (250000 sq. m/roughly 25 ha.) and six sites measuring
400 m by 400 m (160000 sq. m/16 ha.). The reason why so many large
sites are concentrated in this small section will need further detailed
research.

No data are available on the size of the Harappan settlements in western U.P. except in the case of Hulas which is said to measure 330 m by
172 m (56760 sq. m or about 5.5 ha.).

Kalibangan

Although the site was visited by Stein (1942: 179), its Harappan significance was first understood by A. Ghosh (1952: 40). For about a decade
from 1960–61 it had been excavated by B.B. Lal and B.K. Thapar (for a
comprehensive discussion, see Lal 1979, but otherwise the report is
unpublished).

The site lies on the south bank of the dried-up Ghaggar and covers a
total area of about 'a square kilometre' (IAR 1960–61: 31). According to
R.L. Raikes (1968: 286), the size approaches that of Judeirjodaro. There
are two distinctly separated mounds, both rising immediately from the
river bank. The western mound is the smaller one, though it is the higher
of the two, the maximum height being about 12 m from the level of the
surrounding plain. There is no habitational deposit in the gap between the
two mounds. It may be pointed out that the site was apparently deserted
for some time, 'as evidenced by the erosion of the then mound (KLB-I)
at several places and by the accumulation of blown sand in some of the
depressions, before the reoccupation of the site (by the Harappans)' (Lal
1979: 75).

I. The Western Mound

On the plan the western mound is roughly parallelogrammatic, divisible into two almost equal but separately patterned parts, both fortified. A rhomboid on the plan, each side measured 120 m and thus the overall fortified enclosure measured 240 m by 120 m. The fortification wall was of mudbrick, 3–7 m wide, and had two structural phases, the earlier one using larger bricks (40 cm by 20 cm by 10 cm) than the latter (30 cm by 15 cm by 7.5 cm). The general outline of the wall, broken at intervals by rectangular salients and towers, is clear, although in places, particularly in the western and eastern sides, it is much damaged. It has not been possible in all cases to obtain the exact measurements of the salients and towers because of their damaged condition but to take only one example, the central salient on the southern side projected 9.35 m from the main wall face, was 17 m wide and 'rose imposingly with a battered extension' (IAR 1963–64: 30). The walls, salients and towers were all mud-plastered.

The entrance to the southern sector of the fortified enclosures was from the north and the south. The available structural details of the southern entrance are not adequate but apparently it consisted of steps fronting the fortification wall, across which a passage was provided. The northern entrance was primarily in the form of a stairway running up the wall between two centrally located salients. On the basis of the total plan Lal and Thapar (1967: 84) suggest that the southern entrance was meant for the people from the eastern part of the settlement while the northern one was for the residential elite.

The dominant constructional feature inside the southern fortified enclosure seems to have been five or six differently sized mud and mudbrick platforms which were not integrated with the surrounding wall and had passages of varying width between them. Access to the top or the work-floor of these platforms was by means of a series of steps from the level of the passages. The passages fronting the steps were paved. Systematic brick-robbing may have destroyed the details of the buildings which could have existed on the top of these platforms but it appears that no major buildings ever stood on these platforms. The discovery of fire-altars—burnt-brick-lined rectangular pits, in one case with definite remains of an offering (bovine bones and an antler)—is significant and suggests a religious use for the top level of these platforms. Inside the enclosure one also notices a well and a few burnt-brick drains. Lal's analysis of this sector may best be described in his own words:

The southern rhomb contained several mud-brick platforms, oriented along the cardinal directions, on each of which stood a special structure. Although in most cases the details of these structures have disappeared owing to subsequent spoilation, there is reasonable evidence about their likely use. Thus, atop one of the platforms there lay a series of seven 'fire-altars' in a row. Behind these fire-altars ran a wall in a north-south direction, which shows that people had to face the east while performing rituals at these altars. The altars were oblong on plan, sunk into the ground and lined with clay. They contained ash and charcoal, besides a cylindrical and faceted clay (burnt or unburnt) stele standing up near the centre. Though in the series under discussion only fragments of what are called 'terracotta cakes' were obtained, elsewhere these were found in sufficient numbers showing that they formed some kind of an 'offering'. To the west of these fire-altars lay embedded the lower half of a jar. It contained ash and charcoal and was evidently connected with the use of fire-altars. Within a few metres of these altars were a well and a few bath-pavements suggesting ablutions before the performance of a ritual—a tradition still in vogue in India amongst the Hindus (Lal 1979: 77–8).

The northern sector of the fortified enclosure might have contained the dwellings of the elite but little is known about them except that the houseblocks were separated from the dividing or bipartite wall by a wide passage paved with bricks on edge (Lal and Thapar 1967: 84).

II. The Eastern Mound

Across the depression the eastern mound comprises the general habitational area where deep digging has revealed nine phases of construction. A mudbrick fortification wall has been traced for a considerable length on its western and eastern sides, and it is obvious that this wall once ran around the whole of the eastern mound. Its general available width is 3 m to 3.9 m and the number of maximum available courses is fifteen. In the northern section the wall on the west was built in a box-pattern with mud-filling inside. A 3 m to 7 m wide gateway, connected with an east-west lane, has been inferred on the west. A room situated in the interior of the southern flank of this gateway may be a guard-room. The east-west length of the occupational area is about 240 m. The precise north-south length is undetermined but it should be more than 360 m.

There are at least five north-south arterial streets and many lanes, the width of which vary between 1.80 and 7.20 m. In addition to the entrance gateway identified on the west, there was another entrance in the northwestern corner. The north-south streets tend to become wider in the south. At some street-corners there is evidence of 'fender-posts', protect ing the houses from vehicular traffic. Except in the last phase when terracotta nodules were used, the streets were largely unpaved. There is no evidence of a regular system of street-drainage but soakage jars were occasionally placed on the streets outside to receive waste water from the house-drains made of wood (U-shaped section) or brick. Except for the occasional small mudbrick platforms in front of the houses there was no encroachment on the streets.

Of the many house-blocks formed by the intersecting streets and lanes the plan of one may be typical of the rest (IAR 1967–68: 42–5). It had a street each on the eastern and western sides and a lane on the southern side to link the streets. The block had more houses than one. The entrance to one of them was from a lane. The entrance led to a corridor, itself opening into a courtyard. There is no evidence of an entrance from the corridor into the side-rooms. The rooms varied in dimension from 3 m by 2 m to 2 m by 1 m, and as the presence of a single socket on the sill suggests, were interconnected by single-leaf doors, about 70–5 cm wide.

The floors were usually of rammed clay with a soling of terracotta nodules interspersed with large bits of charcoal to make them damp-proof, a practice still prevalent in the area. In one case at least, the floor was paved with tiles decorated with intersecting circles. Most of the houses had a 'fire-altar', a scooped-up shallow oval or rectangular pit with a cylindrical or rectangular block fixed in the centre. It is rare to find wells in the houses at Kalibangan. Oblong troughs of mudbricks in courtyards may suggest how fodder was served to the cattle following an age-old custom. In one of the houses a partly preserved staircase suggests an upper storey or perhaps merely an access to the roof which was likely to be flat and mud-plastered. To the east of the eastern mound, outside the fortification wall, a structure containing five fire-altars have been found. There is no other structure in its vicinity. It is possible that this structure had a religious function.

A Harappan cemetery lies outside the city area, about 300 m west-southwest of the western mound.

Banawali

R.S. Bisht (1982: 114) points out that Banawali is located on the bank of the dried-up course of the Sarasvati river in Haryana. As he is familiar with the dried water-courses of the region, which are still a problematic issue, his observations in this context are summed up. In their upper reaches the Ghaggar and the Sarasvati are two separate rivers, the

Ghaggar being the more westerly of them. The Sarasvati has its traditional source at Adi Badri in the Siwaliks. It flows through Kapalmochan, Bhagwanpura, Thaneshwar and Pehoa till it is captured by the flow of the Ghaggar at Bahar. The old course of the Sarasvati, now known as the Sottar valley and about 2–4 km wide, runs through the districts of Jind, Hissar and Sirsa in Haryana before it apparently joins the Ghaggar near the Haryana-Rajasthan border. Bisht points out that there are mounds on both its banks, the excavated site of Banawali being one such mound on the northern bank.

The Harappan settlement of Banawali lay within a rectangular (plan in Bisht 1984: 92) enclosure which measured not less than 300 by 150 m. There was no separate citadel mound; what appears to represent the citadel complex was built on 'the accumulation of pre-Indus debris' and occupied the southwestern and partly the southeastern portions of the settlement. A 5.40–7 m wide wall 'segregates the citadel from the rest of the town' with which it appears to have a common wall on the south and west sides. Two entrances to the citadel from the town-side could be located. One was in the form of a 1.5 m wide gap associated with a burnt-brick-built drain in the northeastern corner of the exposed division wall, and the second one was in the form of a ramp from the town side in the northern sector of this wall. At both these places the presence of a bastion has been suggested. Another bastion has been postulated in its southern sector.

As far as the general inner planning is concerned, a good reference point is the presence of two streets on either side of the division wall. Street 1, 5.5–5.6 m wide, is on its inner side, whereas Street 2, 9.1 m wide, is on the town side. These two streets are joined by lanes at the two gates— the 'drain gate' and the 'ramp gate'—mentioned earlier. Lane 1 (1.5 m wide) has been traced with its house-blocks on the 'citadel' side of the division wall. A house with a small chamber and unusually thick (1.20 m) walls was traced here. In another house of the same area there was 'a square fire-place with an earthen cone standing in the centre'.

In the town sector the alignment of seven streets (Streets 2 to 8) and two lanes have been traced. They run in different directions and crisscross each other at different angles. Street 2 is 9.10 m wide while Street 3 (5.5–6 m wide) runs obliquely to meet Street 5 (4.20 m wide). Street 4 runs along the inner side of the outer fortification on the east. Streets 6, 7 and 8 have been traced in the northeastern sector of the excavated area where a more or less complete house-plan has been obtained. It measures 52 m by 46 m and is entered from a lane. The plan with several rooms, a large courtyard, a bath with traces of a soakage jar and a burnt-brick-built drain is self-explanatory, but there are two interesting features of this house. First, five small cubicles (1 m by 1 m; in one case 2 m by 1 m) were located in the thickness of the walls, possibly as blind vaults or storage cells, and secondly, a room in the northern part of the house was found to contain a platform built against the brick wall and some fireplaces (one with a terraced cone standing in the centre) before it. There was a lot of ash and charcoal in the room. Bisht (1984: 95) thinks that this room was used for household rituals.

Another major house complex has been excavated near what Bisht calls the 'drain gate' between the citadel and the town.

It contained several rooms, probably a courtyard and a corridor, a large room having many earthen jars half embedded in the house floor, a sitting room paved with bricks, a worship room with a fire-place, and a kitchen with several hearths—both on an elevated ground and the ground level—a toilet fitted with a wash-basin emptying its sullage through a pucca drain into a soakage jar placed outside the major street, and a roadside platform constructed against the building complex and just outside the room of the pottery jars mentioned above. .... A prominent merchant might have been the owner of this house since it has given a rich harvest of seals, weights, beads, including those of gold, lapis and etched cornelian, besides the deluxe pottery of the age (Bisht 1984: 96).

It is interesting to note that there is no evidence of a public drainage system here, as at Kalibangan. In both cases there must have been a system of municipal scavenging. Bisht (1982: 118) notes that there is very little household refuse in the composition of road materials.

The minor excavated Harappan or Harappan-related sites of the region have been surveyed by Y.D. Sharma (1982), K.N. Dikshit (1982) and J.G. Shaffer (1986), among others. None of them is a major settlement, and detailed structural evidence has not been obtained from any of them.

KUTCH, KATHIAWAR AND MAINLAND GUJARAT

The almost quadrilateral peninsula of Kathiawar juts out into the sea between the Gulf of Kutch and the Gulf of Cambay. A tidal channel once joined the little Rann, southwest of Kutch, with the Gulf of Cambay. Though silted up since then by mainland rivers like the Sabarmati, Luni, Banas and Rupen, the course of the old channel is still marked by the lakes and marshes of the Nal depression.

Inland Kathiawar beyond the coastal strip breaks into a series of hills, northeastern and southwestern, lined by a narrow and sinuous ridge. This hilly central tract is the watershed of the peninsula. The rivers which flow

out are the Bhadar, Shatrunji, Machu, Aji, Bhogava, Sukha Bhadar, etc.
The drainage pattern is almost radial.

Coastal Kathiawar, beyond the muddy foreshore, mangrove swamps
and the windblown hills of the coast itself is a fertile stretch of alluvium;
the south and southwest are particularly fertile, the strip of the country
called Nagher being very fertile and well-watered. This belt of alluvium
widens in the northeast, i.e. in the lower basin of the Sabarmati, which is
called Bhal in the local language.

Between the Rann and the Gulf of Cambay, Kutch is not unlike
Kathiawar in topographical detail—a knot of central hills with outlying
narrow alluvial basins except in the north where the Rann intervenes. The
peninsular Kutch and Kathiawar shade off into the latitudinal mainland
strip of Gujarat under the shadow of the western Ghats and the Aravallis.
In between the swampy coastal waste and the alluvial piedmont between
the highland and the plain is 'the great shelf of firm alluvium, some
250 miles long and up to 60 wide' (Spate 1967: 650) and drained by the
lower reaches of the Sabarmati, Mahi, Narmada and Tapti.

Sindhi Harappan and Sorath Harappan?

Before I discuss the relevant archaeological data from Gujarat I would
like to state that I find it difficult to attach any significance to the proposed
distinction between 'Sindhi Harappan' and 'Sorath Harappan'. A clear
statement of this distinction, initially proposed by G.L. Possehl and M.H.
Raval (1989: 15) and subsequently restated by Possehl and his associates
(Possehl and Rissman 1992), comes from K.K. Bhan (1992):

The first category of settlements, . . . designated as 'Sindhi Harappan', share
material inventory of Harappan sites of Sind as well as reflect the variable impact
of local 'non-Harappan' and 'early/pre-Harappan' ceramic types. This group is
represented by 20 settlements such as Desalpur, Surkotada, Dholavira and
perhaps all the listed Mature Harappan sites of Kutch as well as Nageswar and
Lothal in Saurashtra, and Nagwada I and IV in north Gujarat. This category of
settlements appears to have developed to facilitate administration, trade and
access to raw material. The other category, designated as 'Sorath' Harappan is
represented by 152 small simple rural settlements. Most of these have an average
size of 5.3 hectares except Rojdi, which is approximately seven hectares, having
structures with stone foundations and a stone wall encircling the settlement.
These settlements have simple architectural features such as remains of round
huts as at Zekhada, Kanewal, Nesadi and Vagad, and have thus been interpreted
as small villages and dry season pastoral camps engaged in millet cultivation
(Bhan 1992: 174–5).

I shall leave out Bhan's 'functional interpretation' of these two

supposed categories of Harappan settlements; the archaeological literature on the Harappans in Gujarat has in recent years become as esoteric
as the literature on south Indian megaliths. I shall restrict my comments
to the proposed distinction between 'Sindhi' and 'Sorath' Harappan.
First, why should the first category be designated as 'Sindhi Harappan'
and not as 'Panjab Harappan', 'Haryana Harappan', and so on? What is
the special 'Sindhi' stamp on the twenty Kutch sites and the few other sites
in Saurashtra, which Bhan has mentioned? Secondly, why should the
peninsula of Saurashtra alone have a very large number of a functionally
separate class of mature Harappan settlements? Why should the peninsula of Kutch in Gujarat not have them, or for that matter, mainland
Gujarat? If there is a special geographical reason for this situation, I am
not yet aware of it. Thirdly, when the stratigraphic evidence is in conflict
with the radiocarbon dates, do I accept the radiocarbon dates and ignore
stratigraphy which is the main basis of archaeology itself? Fourthly, how
do I handle radiocarbon dates? Do I ignore the calibrated range altogether
and accept only a mean point in that range?

The primary basis of the postulated distinction between 'Sindhi' and
'Sorath' Harappans is provided by the radiocarbon dates from Rojdi
(Possehl and Rissman 1992) and Vagad (as Bhan 1992 argues):

The material inventory of Rojdi initially suggested that the history of the site was
to be found within the post-urban phase, with a possibility that the settlement was
founded in the later part of the Harappan Urban Phase. However, new radiocarbon dates place most of the occupation within the time period of the Urban Phase
Harappan (Possehl and Rissman 1992: 434).

The stratigraphy established by Possehl and Raval (1989) is not easily
understood, but it is known from Steven Weber (1991) who apparently
worked at the site that 'Prabhas Ware' occurs at all levels of the site and
'Lustrous Red Ware' is present too except in the earliest level. On the
basis of the latter evidence, the earliest level of Rojdi can be equated with
Rangpur IIB. Regarding the Prabhas Ware it may be noted that this
pottery occurs in the early levels of Phase V or the late Harappan level
at Lothal. As far as the general understanding goes, the occupational span
of Rojdi should be equated with Rangpur IIB, IIC and III (this is also the
opinion of R.S. Bisht with whom I discussed the issue in 1992).

As far as the implication of the use of terms such as 'Sorath Harappan'
is concerned, Mughal (1990 b) has already described it as an example of
'archaeo-political frenzy'. It is palpably a part of recent attempts to seek
ethnicity in Indian protohistoric archaeological records. These attempts

regretfully choose to ignore the fact that 'ethnicity' has a history too; modern ethnic groups are usually based on language-identities. For instance, the Bengalis of modern India may claim themselves to be an ethnic group, but this identity is based almost wholly on the Bengali language and literature which has evolved only over the last thousand years or so, with a great admixture from various quarters. Secondly, large ethnic groups may split into sub-groups because of different historical situations, and in time, these sub-groups may become major ethnic groups in their own rights. The point is that ethnicity in south Asia is not a rigidly defined historical entity with its own archaeological record. Attempts to seek ethnicity in archaeological records are about as valid as attempts to establish the racial basis of a particular culture. Biological heterogeneity of population and the ideas of race and ethnicity are not the same in archaeological records.

Lothal

Among the excavated Harappan settlements in Gujarat it is Lothal, discovered by S.R. Rao in 1954 and excavated by him between 1955–62 (with a season's break in 1960–61?), which still commands primary atten- tion. The site lies in the rich wheat and cotton growing area of Gujarat, the Bhal, between the Bhogavo and the Sabarmati. This area is low-lying, with sheet-floods as one of its annual features. For about three months in a year the villages of the area, which are located on artificial earthen mounds, 'look like small islands in a vast sea' (Rao 1979: 19). Rao ob- serves that the sheet-flooding of this low-lying area 'must have necessi- tated construction of irrigation works such as dams and canals'. *Acacia* and *Tamarisk*, found during excavations, suggest a dry deciduous type of vegetation, suggesting in turn no change in vegetation and climate since Harappan times except an increased aridity caused by biotic interference (Rao 1979: 20).

The enclosed area of Lothal does not seem to measure more than 240 m by 210 m, but Rao (1979: 20) argues that Harappan potsherds and bricks are also found considerably to the south of this enclosed portion. The nearest point to the sea is at present 10–12 miles away but there is a strong local belief that the sea was once much nearer, a likely enough hypothesis in view of the high siltation rate of the Sabarmati delta.

A little more than 8.5 m thick occupational deposit at Lothal has two main periods—mature and degenerate or late Harappan—and five con- structional phases, the first four of which belong to the mature Harappan period. A layer of flood-borne debris is supposed to intervene between each structural phase. In the first phase Lothal was a small village with mudbrick houses and a peripheral mud wall. In its early levels non-Harappan wares such as micaceous red ware, black-and-red ware and coarse grey ware occurred more frequently than the Harappan wares which increased in greater quantities only in the late levels. The typical Harappan city is that of Phase II: the peripheral wall was strengthened and enlarged with mudbricks on all sides except in the north where burnt bricks were used. The peripheral wall with an entrance opening on the southern arm had a width which varied from 42 ft (12.8 m) in the south to 72 ft (21.94 m) in the east. It was about 6–8 ft (1.82 m–2.43 m) high in the south and about 8 ft (2.43 m) high in the east. The houses were built on artificially raised mud and mudbrick platforms whereas at the southern end of the settlement a separate complex, designated by the excavator as the 'acropolis' of the site, stood higher on a 14 ft (4.26 m) high platform and enclosed three blocks, one of which was a 'warehouse' for storing cargo unloaded in the 'dock' area to its west. The settlement of this phase has a regular lay-out with both underground and surface drains, cesspools and soakage jars. After a flood of 'considerable magnitude', which ushered in Phase III, the habitational area was extended and the houses built on higher platforms. This phase came to an end due to 'a flood of great intensity and duration' leading to 'successive layers of flood-borne debris, silt and sand accumulating to a thickness of 4 to 5 ft over the ruined buildings' (Rao 1979: 31). There were Harappan settlers afterwards, in Phase IV, but without the earlier level of accomplishment. In any case, there was another 'great flood' at the end of this phase. In Phase V which has been correlated to Rangpur IIB and IIC (minus the lustrous red ware of these levels at Rangpur) the settlement had only 'jerry-built houses of mud and reeds' (Rao 1979: 34). The classic Harappan settlement plan of Lothal can thus be understood only from the remains of Phases II and III.

The overall planning seems to have been based on rectangular houseblocks, seven of which were traced in the excavations. The size of these blocks varied from 375 ft by 75 ft (114.3 m by 22.86 m) to 160 ft by 135 ft (48.78 m by 41.14 m), and the individual platforms on which the houses stood varied in height from 4 ft to 12 ft (1.21 m and 3.65 m). Block A lying to the north of the 'acropolis' has been interpreted as constituting the 'bazaar part of the Lower Town'. A street, designated as Street 1, divides the block into two sectors, eastern and western. It is not very clear as to why this has been considered a market area but perhaps the location of a copper smithy in its northern part has something to do with it. It is also in this sector that a house has been identified as 'that of a merchant engaged in foreign trade'. This identification is based on the finds of reserved slip ware, 2 steatite seals, 3 carnelian beads and 8 gold pendants with axial tubes in some of its rooms. The size of the house is 47 ft by 23.5 ft (14.32 m by 7.16 m) and this had, behind a 40 ft (12.19 m) wide verandah, a number of rooms of three sizes (8 ft by 9 ft or 2.43 m by 2.74 m; 10 ft by 5 ft or 3.04 m by 1.52 m; and 6 ft or 1.82 m square). A soakage jar, 'the rim of which was skirted by burnt bricks' was placed within a mudbrick semi-circular enclosure projecting from the plinth and there was another mudbrick projection for the steps to the varandah. Most of the houses had well-arranged bathrooms/ablution places connected with the drains/soakage jars outside. The houses were generally made of mudbricks. Some houses possessed sacrificial altars/enclosures of bricks and clay, containing ashes, triangular terracotta cakes and oval terracotta balls. Two houses have been identified as bead factories. An interesting feature found associated with the copper smithy is the provision of a niche in the outer face of the western wall on the roadside. Rao (1979: 95) suggests that oil lamps were kept in such niches and similar niches meant for lamps in the outer walls of present-day houses at Gundi and Saragwala may be survivals of an ancient tradition.

Nine streets and 12 lanes have been traced at this site. They were all paved with mudbricks and covered by a layer of *kankar* (gravel). The width of the streets varied from between 12 ft and 18 ft (3.65 m and 5.48 m), the lanes being narrower, between 6 ft and 9 ft (1.82 m and 2.74 m). The internal width of the street drains is quite impressive, 4 ft (1.21 m) to 2 ft and 1–1/2 ins (0.64 m). Their gradients are steep enough to 'carry sewage disposal as well as storm water'. There is even provision for screens at the mouth of the drains to collect solid waste matter before they debouched into cess-pools, one of which measures 4.5 ft (1.31 m) square and was about 5 ft (1.52 m) deep.

At least two important structural complexes have been unearthed at the Lothal 'acropolis'. One of them is the 'warehouse', a plan of which has been published by Rao (1979: 112). The mudbrick podium on which the complex stands has a maximum height of 13.5 ft (4.11 m) on the northern side, approximately measures 160 ft by 135 ft (48.76 m by 41.14 m) and is further protected by an outer platform. Originally 12 solid blocks of partially burnt mudbricks separated by 4 ft wide criss-cross passages and measuring 12 ft (3.65 m) square and 3 ft (0.91 m) high stood on this podium. As many as 65 terracotta sealings have been found which bear impressions of packing material such as reed, woven fibre and matting, and of twisted cords tied into knots on the reverse and Indus seals on the obverse. As Rao (1979: 113) observes, 'one can easily deduce from the data that wet labels of clay were affixed on packages of goods secured by cords and were sealed with one or more seals for authenticating the contents'. Rao identifies this as a 'large warehouse wherein packages of goods were examined and stored. The mudbrick bases had a roof of some perishable material over them to protect goods from rain and sun'.

Another important structural group in the 'acropolis' has been excavated in Block B (Rao 1979: plate LVIII). The complex as a whole is centred around two major streets, a few lanes and two public drains, draining both the northern and southern sectors. It is the southern sector which is more interesting and shows a row of 12 houses, each 25–8 ft (7.62 m–8.53 m) long and 18 ft (5.48 m) wide, with their 'ablution pavements' built in the rear portions and connected with the main drain at the back.

The entire eastern sector of Lothal is taken up by the 'dock' which is roughly trapezoidal in shape (western embankment wall: 716 ft/ 218.23 m; eastern embankment wall: 705.5 ft/215.03 m; southern embankment wall: 117 ft/35.66 m; northern embankment wall: 123 ft/ 37.49 m) and enclosed by a strictly vertical, four-course wide and continuous burnt brick wall with no access to the bottom. The maximum existing depth seems to be about 14 ft/4.26 m. The basic constructional features which seem to mark this out as a 'dock' are three: two inlets (one each in the northern and the southernmost portions of the eastern side) and a spill-channel in the form of a narrow brick-built water-passage leading off from the southern arm. Through the inlet channels a ship could enter at high tide and by sluicing off water through the spill-channels a regular level of water could be maintained inside the enclosure at all times.

The spill-channel and the eastern inlet are described in some detail in the reports. A 23 ft (7.01 m) gap in the eastern wall led to a channel outside, also of the same width and cut into the natural soil. This channel linked the eastern inlet with the second stage of the ancient river-bed. Moreover, 'a dwarf wall at the inlet gap retained water at low tide within the docks to enable the ships to move about' (Rao 1961: 302). At the mouth of the spill-channel 'could be seen two grooves for a sliding door. Narrow steps at the end, and grooves at regular intervals in the side-walls of the channel suggested that a door could have been made to rest against wooden logs at desired places to maintain the required level of water' (IAR 1958–59: 14).

The gap in the northern embankment, i.e. the northern inlet, is said to be about 40 ft (12.21 m) wide, connected with a channel leading to the first stage of the ancient river-bed. According to Rao the 'dock' which was built in Phase II of the site and continued to be in use in Phases III and IV, had two stages. In the first stage 'the ships reached Lothal from the Gulf of Cambay through the estuary of a river flowing along the western margin of the town and entered the dock through the gulley running east-west on the northern margin' (Rao 1965: 32). This explains the northern inlet.

The eastern inlet, according to him, was created in Phase IV when the flow-channel of the river was silted up 'due to an unprecedented flood' (Rao 1965: 32) leading to the shifting of the river to the eastern margin of the city instead of to the western one. In the history of the 'dock' this marks the second stage. Rao points out that because of a comparatively narrow width of the eastern inlet (23 ft) and the somewhat restricted depth (2 m–2.5 m) of the connected channel, large ships could not have entered the dock in the second stage. 'But, originally, the dock was designed to sluice ships of 18 to 20 m in length and 4 to 6 m in width through the 12.21 m wide inlet in the northern embankment. At least two ships could pass through the inlet simultaneously' (Rao 1965: 33). On the analogy of the coast of modern Gujarat he further calculates that 'it is reasonable to suppose that ships with a draught of 2 to 2.5 m could enter the dock at high tide through the inlet in the eastern embankment (second stage)' (Rao 1965: 35).

To substantiate the general idea of a dock, Rao has also referred to the discovery of a few 'anchor-stones', mostly large spheroidal perforated stones, and the evidence of external maritime contact of the site as a whole. The postulate of a dock at Lothal has been questioned a number of times in archaeological literature (cf. Shah 1960, Leshnik 1968). Rao (1991) has cited the opinions of various maritime authorities of India, who are professionally familiar with the Gujarat coast, and it appears that there cannot be any theoretical objection to accepting this complex as a dock. What is equally important is that no better explanation has been offered. Leshnik's assumption that the enclosed excavated basin could have served as an irrigation tank falls through because one cannot really think of a settlement of Lothal's size with such a large irrigation tank even in modern Gujarat. Moreover, the ethnographic support produced by Rao in the form of a local goddess worshipped by sailors makes the idea of a dock more plausible.

The features of the city beyond the 'dock' take the form of a 'wharf' which is basically a mudbrick platform, 800 ft (243.84 m) long and 42 ft (12.80 m) wide, adjoining the western embankment, and supposedly the place built for loading and unloading goods. The dockyard workers probably lived in small houses built on a clay platform adjoining the northern embankment. The Lothal cemetery lies to the northwest of the settlement and a street is supposed to have led to the place.

Rangpur, Surkotada and Dholavira

Among the other excavated mature Harappan settlements in the Kathiawar peninsula Rangpur may be mentioned (Rao 1963) where in Period IIA one encounters houses on mudbrick platforms, burnt brick drains connected with bathrooms, and also a 3 ft (0.91 m) deep public drain. Not much structural evidence has been obtained from sites such as Kuntasi and Padri.

The Kutch peninsula has recently emerged as an important focus of mature Harappan settlements in Gujarat. K.V. Soundara Rajan's earlier excavations at Desalpur (IAR 1963–64) showed a mature Harappan settlement with a fortified complex built of rubble and stone (Soundara Rajan 1984), but a proper study of Kutch from this point of view had to wait till J.P. Joshi's survey of sites in the area and excavations at Surkotada (J.P. Joshi 1979, 1990). Of the three phases of Surkotada, the last phase, IC, may be put in the late Harappan category. The earlier two phases (IA and IB) clearly reveal the nature of the mature Harappan settlement at the site. The focus is on a citadel and its residential annexe but no 'lower town' complex has been unearthed here. To the northwest of the fortified enclosure is the cemetery where pot-burials (with or without bones) and the practice of keeping a large stone slab on the top of the pit or making a stone cairn over the pit or placing a vertical stone slab in the western section of the pit are novel discoveries in the Harappan context. Before the citadel and its residential annexe were constructed the ground level was raised by earth deposits by about 1.5 m in the citadel area and 0.5 m in the residential area. The dimension of the residential complex could not be properly determined but the citadel section roughly measured 60 m square. The basal width of the mud and mudbrick rampart in the citadel area was 7 m. It had a rubble veneer on the outside and mud-plaster on the inside. A buttress of mudbrick with rubble cushioning was provided at a later stage on the eastern side. The major entrance was on the southern side, but there was another entrance on the eastern side for communicating with the residential annexe. The wall around the residential sector was 3.25 m wide. Three phases of rubble-built houses were traced, and although no complete house-plan could be obtained there was evidence of a drain, bathroom and soakage jar. The plan did not significantly change in Period IB.

R.S. Bisht's work in Kutch has further highlighted the significance of the region in the Harappan scheme. Although adequate surveys of the southern and western sections are not complete, Bisht (1989) can refer to the discovery of sixty sites, of which about eleven 'have shown evidence of fortification while many others provide strong suggestive indication of the same'. Another significant point is that '70% of the total sites had their beginning during the early mature phases while the remaining came up during the late phase only'.

Although Kutch has a meagre annual rainfall (300–400 mm), it has a good reserve of underground water which is sweet and potable in the central and northeastern areas. Before the advent of irrigation the emphasis was on summer crops such as bajra, jowar, pulses, cotton, other fibrous plants, wheat, sesamum and other oilseeds, etc. The winter crops accounted for only 4 per cent of the cultivated area. It may be noted that there is evidence of the damming of streams in and around the Harappan site of Dholavira. One cannot also ignore the fact that Kutch offers good grazing land, and people find livestock farming more profitable to offset the usual agricultural deficit. Moreover, there is a good distribution of different rocky materials, and Bisht points out that a Harappan mound, Khandaria, was meant for extracting chert, carnelian, agate and jasper which were possibly available at the site itself.

We have referred to the postulate that the combined stream of the Indus and the Nara used to flow into the sea in the area of the Rann of Kutch. If so, the present-day Kutch may be visualized as an island at the mouth of the Indus-Nara delta. The present-day Rann is a desolate salty waste subject to seasonal innundation by sea-water, although it remains more or less dry between November and March. However, communication across the Rann does not pose any problem even during the period of innundation because this water is generally less than a metre deep. Thus, the Rann is always 'crossable on foot, in carts or riding a camel, a horse or an ass' (Bisht 1989). Whether the Rann was once an arm of the sea or not is a difficult point to settle because even in recorded memory the area has been subject to tectonic changes due to earthquakes.

The most important Harappan site in Kutch is Dholavira which has been excavated in recent years (Bisht 1991). The site lies in the northeastern corner of Khadir *bet*, an island in the mid-portion of the Rann. Except for the presence of potable subsoil water, the area has nothing to recommend it agriculturally because the suitable soil, although a fertile sandy loam, has a limited distribution and lies in any case in an area of very limited annual rainfall (262 mm). The failure of monsoon rains over a period of 3–5 years is said to be frequent and causes people to migrate from the area. As Bisht (1991: 71) puts it, '. . . the land has almost an incongenial environment for human occupation and the situation might not have been much different in the past. In such circumstances, location of such a large city as Dholavira, indeed poses an engima and as such a challenge to archaeologists for a satisfactory solution'.

The site, or at least the portion lying within the outer fortification or enclosing wall, lies between two seasonal rivulets—the Mandsar in the north-northwest and the Manhar in the south. The Mandsar is totally beyond the city wall but the Manhar flows through the southeastern section of the enclosure. These two rivulets join each other about 1.5 km downstream. The inside measurement of the enclosure is 767.6 m (east–west) by 614.15 m (north–south). The excavator refers to a series of small mounds and built-up area 'far and wide to west and northwest of the main site' and interprets them as 'suburban establishments'. The overall area, according to him, is more than 100 ha. The outer wall which is apparently built of mudbricks with a veneer provided by dressed stones has not survived through its entire length. For instance, it has not survived in the eastern section where it ran close to the built-up area. The nature of the wall has been understood from the excavations of its southern segment. It was 8.40 m wide at this point, mud-plastered on the inner face and stone-covered on the outer face. It seems that the stone veneer was added later when its initial width was also increased. Traces of bastions have been found at some points. In the east the wall has worn down to the rock-bed which itself is higher than the level of the built-up area on that side. Bisht points out that there are raised pathways on either side of the wall 'for an easy walk of the patrolling guards round the fortification'.

Apart from the well-defined outlines of open spaces which were almost all over the areas adjacent to the outer fortification except in the east and had a plaster of calcareous clay (light-deep pink, and offwhite in colour), the built-up areas of the settlement had three distinct foci—the 'lower town' which was not separately enclosed and lay to the east, the 'middle town' which had its own enclosure walls, and the 'acropolis' which had two subdivisions, the western 'bailey' and the eastern 'castle'.

The two divisions of the 'acropolis' were each fortified, also sharing a common dividing wall. The occupational deposit in the eastern section is about 14 m. The western section which is also the lower one was never used for regular living, according to the excavator. The occupational deposit here is 7 m thick.

It is the eastern section which has been better studied. Its original 'massive mudbrick fortification' was, on its inner side, first widened and then provided with a revetment before undergoing, on the outer side, substantial reconstructions after a 'devastating natural calamity'. Its total extant height and width (excluding the revetment) are 9 m and 15.5 m respectively and it possesses a steep batter. It further appears that there are centrally located gates on all sides, two of which, those on the east and the north, have been excavated. Within the thickness (12.30 m) of the defensive wall the eastern gateway is provided with a staircase, a sunken passageway and an elevated chamber, with the whole complex having a high terrace in front. The front edge of the chamber apparently possessed a row of pillar supports or foundations—neatly cut and highly polished limestone blocks and *damaru*-shaped pillar-bases, some examples of which have been found in the excavations. A 31 cm long and 3 cm deep groove in each of the discovered stone blocks was possibly meant to hold 'a square pilaster made of stone or wood'. The front terrace on the inner side, in front of the north gate, was 6 m high from the ground level and projected 12 m into the space in front. Its east-west length was more than 19 m.

What is called the 'middle town' lies to the north of the 'acropolis'. This was enclosed too, but whereas the eastern, western and northern walls were made of mudbricks and had stone-facings, the one in the south had three parallel stone walls with their interstices filled up by each. This may be a late construction. The western wall is 4.20 m wide.

No specific evidence seems to have yet emerged from the 'lower town' in the east. Its east-west measurement is 300 m. The measurements of the 'middle town' are 335 m (east-west) and 181 m (north-south), although on the west it measures 200 m. If the built-up area to its south is taken into consideration it will measure 230 m from the north to the south. The eastern section of the 'acropolis' is 114 m by 94 m while the western section is about 123 m square. These measurements which have been taken internally are not very specific.

In addition to having open space on the inner side along the walls of the outer fortification, there was a vacant space (about 55 m wide) between the 'acropolis' and the 'middle town'. Another noteworthy point is that there was a 'massive wall' which emanated from near the east gate of the 'acropolis' and met the outlying enclosure wall in the south, after running in an irregular fashion.

ASPECTS OF HARAPPAN URBANISM

Some Features of Distribution and Size

The previous sections contained the basic settlement data from the major excavated Harappan settlements in different areas. Although the general distributional aspects of these settlements were referred to, they are discussed more specifically at this stage.

The presence of the mature Harappan settlement of Shortughai in the Oxus plain in northeast Afghanistan is still problematic in a way. It is a small (2.5 ha./10125 sq. m) and isolated site. However, Gardin's premise that the Harappans were responsible for introducing a system of canal-based irrigation in this part of the Oxus valley implies that the Harappan occupation in the region was more deep-rooted than the available data would suggest. All that one can infer now is that Shortughai was a Harappan trading colony. Trade in this context could be based, on the Harappan side, on the lapis lazuli and rubies of Badakhshan and tin of central Asia and Afghanistan. Although the discovery of lapis lazuli in the Chagai hills has considerably devalued Badakhshan as a source of Harappan lapis, still the location of Shortughai suggests that the Harappans were getting a part of their lapis supply from that region. Central Asian raw materials such as jade could also come through Shortughai.

The two or three Harappan sites on the Makran coast—Sutkagendor, Sotka-koh and Khairia Kot—have been generally interpreted as ports in the maritime links with the Gulf and Mesopotamia, and with the discovery of an Omani sherd at Surkotada (Chakrabarti 1990) the hypothesis has gained strength. At the same time, this may not have been the only or the primary function of these settlements. First, basic communication between the Makran coast and Sind could perhaps be more easily maintained by sea; one understands that different manufactured items including pottery used to be shipped from Sind to the Makran coast till very recently, and there is no reason to believe that the situation would have been significantly different in protohistory. Both Sutkagendor and Sotka-Koh are located in areas which facilitated the movement of such goods to the interior. Secondly, the famous dates of the Panjgur oasis to the north of the coast were perhaps among the goods shipped to Sind from these two and possibly other entrepots on this coast. The Harappan level at Balakot in the estuary of the Windar river in Las Bela may have a trading component too, as is indicated by Dales' report of a 'painted jar of possible Persian Gulf origin' (Dales 1979: 266). All these sites are small in size. The fortified enclosure of Sutkagendor measures 15000 sq. m or less than 4 acres (less than 2 ha.). The general mound of Balakot is said to be 28080 sq. m or roughly 7 acres (less than 3 ha.). This size contrasts sharply with the size of a site like Nindowari in the copper-rich section of Las Bela. Nindowari reputedly measures 80 ha., which may be a gross exaggeration, considering that it is basically a kind of ceremonial site with a huge platform, etc. The hills of south Baluchistan do not seem to contain evidence of distinct Harappan settlements, although there is evidence of Harappan contact at some Kulli-Mehi sites in this area. Elsewhere in Baluchistan, Dabarkot (180000 sq. m, Jansen 1979: 260) in north Baluchistan seems to possess a distinct Harappan level, along with an extensive Harappan presence at another mound in the same region, Duki. Considering the accessibility of Afghanistan from this area, Dabarkot may be a trading or resource-procuring settlement. It seems that the Thal river plain in which Dabarkot is situated was an area of some importance for the Harappans.

As N.G. Majumdar (1934) pointed out years ago, the Harappan sites in Sind Kohistan and the Kirthar piedmont are generally near the local perennial springs and probably served the dual purpose of agriculture and resource-procurement. Irrigation was achieved either by damming the torrents when there was a rush of water from the hills during the rains or by carrying off water from the springs by means of channels. The region also features as a raw material procurement area because Majumdar frequently refers to the scatters of chert blades and flakes here. The sites in the Lake Manchhar area deserve special mention. The Manchhar Lake in Majumdar's time was about 8–10 miles in length and breadth, 'swelling enormously in innundation time' with water from the Indus on the one hand and the rainwater from the hills on the other. Majumdar argues that settlements (cf. Lal Chhatto) near this lake must have been heavily dependent on fishing, and if one may suggest, also on the cultivation of lands which got dry in winter. Majumdar further refers to the top of the Tharro hill as a centre of the flint knapping industry, something like the recent discovery of the Harappan presence in the Sukkur-Rorhi hills indicates (Biagi and Cremashi 1990).

Being located in the Larkana area of Sind, Mohenjodaro undoubtedly enjoys an agricultural advantage, but did it also serve, in the protohistoric period, a role similar to the town of Shikarpur, located more or less in the same broad region, as the main mercantile centre in relation to the overland trade stretching across to Iran and central Asia in the nineteenth century? Further, the riverine route was naturally important, although, while voyaging upstream against strong currents, the goods were carried for short stretches by camels before being embarked again on the Indus (Lahiri 1992: 116 ff). Lahiri has moreover pointed out that 'there were several overland routes connecting southern Sind to the northern regions. An old trade route went north from Karachi to Thano Bula Khan and entered Larkana district north of the Laki range. This route was undoubtedly significant in this period, considering the cluster of sites all along it from Karachi district, where there was a concentration of sites around Ahladino, to Karachi, Amri, Ghazi Shah, Ali Murad, Lohumjodaro to Mohenjodaro in the Larkana district' (Lahiri 1992: 116). In fact, the special craft-activity areas of Mohenjodaro hint at the possibility of its role as a manufacturing and redistributive centre linked to both caravan trade in the western regions and riverine trade with other inland areas. Lahiri points out the occurrence of a plethora of raw materials and indications of a large number of manufacturing activities at Chanhudaro, and quotes Mackay's opinion that the ancient city was very favourably located for trade. Ferry crossing points across the Indus, the importance of which has been emphasized by the early twentieth-century writers on Sind, might also have played a part in the location of settlements such as Chanhundaro. Another point which may be noted about the distribution of Harappan settlements in Sind is that, even if we adhere to the earlier estimate of 240–50 acres for Mohenjodaro, it is about three times the size of the nearest large Harappan settlement in Sind, which is Naru Waro Dharo (roughly 86 acres). Chanhudaro is on the smaller side—about 16 acres—whereas the bottom end of the scale is indicated by sites like Ahladino which is not much more than 2 acres

In Cholistan, out of 174 mature Harappan sites, Mughal (1900) offers size category data for 73 sites: 0.1–5 ha.: 44 sites; 5.1–10 ha.: 20 sites; 10.1–20 ha.: 8 sites; over 80 ha.: 1 site. What is perhaps more interesting was the 'emergence of the areas exclusively earmarked for kilns and mass production of items that are recognized at 79 sites' (Mughal 1992: m108). Some of these sites were involved in copper-smelting; the occurrence of slag has been reported to be a frequent feature. As Cholistan is out of the way of any resource distribution area but is easily accessible from Rajasthan (for the specific routes between Bahawalpur and Bikaner—Jaipur, Lahiri 1992: 120), the Rajasthan copper must have been among the primary metals smelted in this area. In this connection Lahiri (1992: 119) writes:

Bahawalpur was of great significance in the trade and trade route net-work . . . connecting the Indus plains with the Punjab and Rajasthan and further south, with Gujarat. In fact, the region, at the end of the nineteenth century, used to enjoy commercial transactions with Karachi, Lahore, Bombay and Calcutta. . . . The chief centres of commerce were Bahawalpur, Ahmadpur east, Allahabad, Khanpur and Hasilpur, and part of the commerce used to go to Afghanistan and Turkestan.

Beyond Cholistan the Harappan sites spread out, first comparatively thinly and then densely, in the northeastern direction towards Rajasthan, Haryana, Panjab and the upper part of the Ganga Yamuna Doab in U.P. The drainage lines control the distribution, and as one proceeds towards the Siwaliks from the lower side, the drainage lines fan out. This is reflected in the pattern of site distribution in the maps prepared by J.P. Joshi et al. (1984). It is possible that the irrigation canals of the period, the existence of which has been strongly argued for by Francfort on the basis of scientific studies, tended to follow the alignment of some older drainage lines, which, in fact, has very often been the case in India.

Except for some occasional outliers of the Aravallis the entire region is alluvial, and the Harappan settlements of this region must have had agriculture as the mainstay of their economy. The relevant data are not always published, but it appears that the average size of settlements here was not more than a few acres, going up for Banawali and Rakhigarhi to about 39/40 acres (about 16/17 ha.) and 60 acres (about 25 ha.) respect-ively. The height of the mound of Rakhigarhi, which Francfort for some reason refers to as being as large as Harappa, was put by Suraj Bhan (1972) at 30 m, and this fact in itself suggests the existence of a huge mud and mudbrick structural complex at the site.

A great complexity has been added to the Harappan distribution situation in this region by the report of twenty-one sites in an area of approximately 50 by 25 km (Joshi et al. 1984). Five of these sites, all with 'pre-and-mature Harappan' pottery on the surface, are supposed to measure the following:

Site Name	Measurement	Area
Dhalewan	1500 m by 1000 m	1500000 sq m/about 150 ha.
Gurni Kalan I	1200 m by 1200 m	1440000 sq m/about 143 ha.
Hasanpur II	1000 m by 1000 m	1000000 sq m/about 100 ha.
Lakhmirwala	1500 m by 1500 m	2250000 sq m/about 225 ha.
Baglian Da Theh	1000 m by 1000 m	1000000 sq m/about 100 ha.

These sites are said to be situated at a distance of 3–5 km from each other. Again, some of these mounds are reported as being 8–10 m high. So they cannot be said to be sites with marginal occupational deposits. They have to be admitted as being regular, massive settlements, with four of them being in the category of Harappa (150 ha., Dales and Kenoyer 1992) and one of them being as large as Mohenjodaro, even in the light of the current estimate of the size of Mohenjodaro.

Harappa, as Lahiri's (1990) analysis clearly indicates, was a major manufacturing centre. She lists evidence of the use of the following raw materials: steatite, alabaster, ivory, shell, coral, carnelian, agate, jasper, chalcedony, jade, lapis lazuli, silver, gold, lead, chert, sandstone, limestone, yellow Jaisalmere stone, flint, haematite, quartzite, basalt, *sang-i-abri*, marble, calcite, serpentine, feldspar, hornblende, slate and granite. As far as the sites in the Siwalik piedmont of Panjab are concerned, Kotla Nihang Khan near Rupar measures about 2.60 ha. whereas a site like Dher Majra is less than a hectare in area. The extensive or large sites are said to be absent in the Doab region, and Dikshit (1984) reports their average size as being 200 m by 150 m or about 3 ha. These sites mostly occupy the small tributary valleys of the Yamuna in Saharanpur and Meerat districts.

In the light of the assumption that the combined flow of the Indus and the Hakra moved into the sea either in the Rann of Kutch itself or in its neighbourhood, the modern Rann area may be considered as an arm of the sea, and from this point of view the modern peninsula of Kutch was an island. The first point to be remembered about the Harappan settlements in Kutch is an opinion expressed by Bisht: 'the Harappans brought here their full-blown culture and lived almost a full life before their culture declined and fragmented causing large scale migration from Kutch to the hinterland of Gujarat and also perhaps Saurashtra'. He further mentions that the Harappan sites in Kutch were unlikely to have been based only on agriculture because, with only 10–15 inches of annual rainfall and a poor soil cover, Kutch is by no means agriculturally prosperous. But at the same time Kutch has potential for the cultivation of cotton and possesses in any case good grazing land. As Bisht (1989: 267) puts it:

People find the livestock farming much profitable in order to offset the usual agricultural deficit. It is why the livestock are one-and-a-half times the human population. The Kutchi cattle was held in esteem even in the time of Panini. Its horses and camels were highly prized in the medieval times. Herds of the cattle, buffaloes, camels, sheep and goat make a common sight everywhere in Kutch. Study of archaeological remains from excavations may produce revealing information in this regard.

There is no firm evidence of Harappan trading activities on the Kutch seaboard (till the summer of 1992 Bisht found nothing at Dholavira which could be interpreted as evidence of a long-distance trading contact). However, Kutch could be an area of resource procurement, in addition to being a major area of animal breeding and cotton cultivation. I have already noted that at Khandaria, Bisht (1990: 267) found evidence of the extraction of chert, carnelian, agate and jasper.

Although they are semi-arid areas like Kutch, the Saurashtra peninsula and mainland Gujarat have a much better soil cover and more flowing streams, in addition to having a better rainfall and some major raw materials—semi-precious stones, marine shells, copper, steatite, ivory, amazonite, gold, different types of ordinary stones, etc. (Lahiri 1992: 81, 106 ff). Besides, Gujarat has good potential for the cultivation of cotton. It has been argued that cattle-farming was a major component of the region's Harappan economy. That some of the Harappan sites in the region were geared to the procurement of raw materials has been documented at such sites as Nageshwar which was apparently devoted to the collection of those varieties of shell which were used for bangles, conch-shells, etc. Another site, Nagwada, has been interpreted as a major manufacturing centre of semi-precious stone objects. Although the discovery of a Persian Gulf seal at Lothal and a seal with a whorl motif at Dwaraka suggests maritime contact with the Gulf region, the evidence is not in any way widespread.

On the whole, it is clearly indicated that the basic character of these settlements was conditioned by factors such as local agricultural geography, distribution of raw materials and the alignment of inland trade routes. A detailed study of the location of Harappan settlements from these points of view may be a fruitful exercise.

Chronology

The first attempt at establishing a Harappan chronology came from John Marshall (1931, I: 102–7) who placed Mohenjodaro between 3250 and 2750 BC and suggested a considerable margin on the earlier side to account for the growth of the civilization itself. I have earlier pointed out that at Mohenjodaro, on the basis of his excavations between 1922 and 1927, Marshall distinguished, besides an earlier unexcavated deposit, seven occupational levels or what he called 'strata', phased into Early, Intermediate and Late, and estimated to be of a duration of five hundred years after an allocation of 'two generations apiece'. To put these five hundred years within an absolute chronological bracket he referred to two Indian-type seals from Mesopotamia, supposedly found in the pre-Sargonic contexts of Ur and Kish and dated in the light of the contemporary Mesopotamian chronology as pre-2800 BC. In view of the lack of any specific evidence these seals were attributed to the Mohenjodaro 'Intermediate Strata' on the Indian side and it was on the basis of this cross-dating that the Mohenjodaro excavated deposits were placed between 3250 and 2750 BC.

In 1938 Mackay (vol. I: 6–7) put the duration of Mohenjodaro between 2800 and 2500 BC, a meagre three hundred years for his nine excavated 'strata' (with two sub-periods for the topmost one) which, he thought, was possible because of the rapidly crumbling nature of the Mohenjodaro bricks. He based his determination of the upper limit on the occurrence of a cylinder seal 'obviously of Indian workmanship' with its elephant, rhinoceros and fish-eating crocodile, in the Sargonic or Akkadian context, dated by him around 2500 BC, of the Mesopotamian site of Tell Asmar. Correspondingly he noted that the cylinder seals occurred rarely at Mohenjodaro and that too only in its upper levels. To suggest the earlier limit he referred to the find of a greenish chlorite-schist vessel in an early context (28.1 ft below datum) at Mohenjodaro. The vessel had on it a carved matting pattern which could be duplicated at Susa II in Flam, tentatively dated around 2800 BC.

To sum up, these two data-schemes of Marshall and Mackay were based on an arbitrary estimate of the duration of Mohenjodaro which varied from Marshall's 500 to Mackay's 300 years, an explicit belief in the pre-Sargonic Indus valley–Mesopotamia contact and the adoption of a Mesopotamian chronology which has since then been brought down. For instance, to Marshall (1931, I: 104) the pre-Sargonic period meant pre-2800 BC whereas the date of Sargon of Akkad is now generally considered to be 2371 BC.

A date-scheme for the Harappan civilization as a whole, *c.* 2500–1500 BC was proposed by Wheeler (1947: 78–83) and was the point of departure for any discussion on the Harappan chronology for many years. In the mass of evidence suggesting the contact of the Indus valley with Mesopotamia, Wheeler could find nothing that could be securely dated before the Sargonic period, itself brought down from Marshall's 2800 BC or Mackay's 2500 BC to 2350 BC. This, however, did not suggest that the Harappan civilization was non-existent before the Sargonic period. This only implied that by the Sargonic period the civilization was mature enough to come in contact with Mesopotamia by way of trade or otherwise. Allowing about 150 years for its period of gestation Wheeler dated its beginning around 2500 BC. The end-point of his estimate, 1500 BC, was based on two assumptions: (1) the destruction of the Harappan civilization by the Aryans, a hypothesis based primarily on the Rigvedic references to the fort-destroying activities of the war-lord Indra and the evidence of some amount of insecurity in the late Harappan phase itself, and (2) the conventional date of 1500 BC as that of the coming of the Aryans to India. The first of these assumptions was borrowed by Wheeler, without specific acknowledgement, from R.P. Chanda's monograph on the survival of the Indus civilization (Chanda 1929).

In the early sixties the newly obtained radiocarbon dates were first assessed by D.P. Agrawal (1964). On the basis of the dates obtained from the Harappan levels of Kalibangan, Lothal, Rojdi, the late period Mohenjodaro, and those of the relevant levels of Damb Sadaat, Niai Buthi and Kot Diji, he put the chronological range of this civilization between 2300 and 1700 BC. Two major developments have taken place since then. First, one has to take into consideration the factor of calibration. For instance, an uncorrected radiocarbon date of about 2300 BC offers a calibrated date-range of 2900–2600 BC, based on a single plus-minus variation. If the variation estimate is doubled, one certainly gets a far more probable range, but at the same time, the range becomes very wide. One is not sure if the selection of a mean fixed point in this range by following a particular computer programme or calibration method is a desirable or even acceptable exercise from the archaeological point of view. There is no reason to believe that this increases the probability range of the calibrated dates (for an example of such an exercise in the Harappan context, see Possehl 1991; for a list of the Indian dates in general, see Possehl 1989, 1992, Shaffer 1992). Moreover, there has been a great increase in the number of dates from the Harappan and related sites and it is important to examine these dates to see if they are internally consistent in the light of the established archaeological sequence of all these sites. It has also become imperative to judge if the available dates cover the representative areas and levels of this civilization. On the whole, it appears that the archaeological interpretation of the radiocarbon dates is almost as important as the laboratory procedure to obtain them.

Secondly, the issue of cross-dating with Mesopotamia is much clearer now. There is virtually no doubt at all that two distinct Indus bead types in carnelian were reaching Mesopotamia in Early Dynastic IIIA, i.e. around 2600 BC (Crawford 1991: 446–7). These beads were not manufactured before the beginning of the mature Harappan period. There are also other categories of data showing Indus–Mesopotamia contact in the pre-Sargonic period (Chakrabarti 1990). There cannot really be any doubt that by *c.* 2600 BC the Indus civilization was already in existence. One may, thus, put the date of its very beginning around *c.* 2700 BC, if not earlier. This simple historical argument based on cross-dating with Mesopotamia does not leave much scope for jugglery with radiocarbon dates. In fact, the MASCA calibration of dates led J.H. Brunswig (1975) to argue that the mature Indus civilization had its first stage around 2800 BC. One of the reasons why this argument has put off some scholars in the field is the fact that this will put the beginnings of the Early Dynastic Civilization of Mesopotamia and the Indus civilization of south Asia on the same chronological level. To these scholars it is not at all an attractive proposition.

One fixed point in the radiocarbon chronology of the Indus civilization is provided by the five radiocarbon dates from the upper levels of Mohenjodaro. When calibrated, all of them point to 2200 BC for these levels. So, by *c.* 2200 BC. Mohenjodaro was on the decline. How long should one estimate its earlier duration to be ? Even accepting Jansen's idea that Mohenjodaro was conceived and built within a comparatively short period, as the deliberate construction of high mud and mudbrick platforms all over the habitation area may indicate, there is no special reason to infer that the city outlived its utility and went into decline soon after it came into existence. It may be useful to remember at this point that there is a piece of direct evidence showing contact between Mohenjodaro and Early Dynastic Mesopotamia in the form of an intercultural style chlorite vase fragment associated with the lower levels of Mohenjodaro (Chakrabarti 1990: 110 ff).

The other end of the scale is provided by the finds of Indus seals in the Kassite contexts at Nippur and Failaka, bringing down the evidence of Indus contact with Mesopotamia and the Gulf to *c.* 1400 BC and later (Chakrabarti 1990: 112). A number of radiocarbon dates also suggest the continuation of the Indus civilization till about the middle of the second millennium BC and later. The Indus civilization, thus, covered not merely a large geographical territory but also a large segment of time.

As far as I have been able to understand it, the Indus civilization had its origin in the Cholistan tract on the bank of the Ghaggar-Hakra course. A short time after this took place, the civilization spread across the Hakra-Indus doab towards Mohenjodaro and other places in Sind. I am not sure when the spread towards Harappa along the Ravi took place; my inference based on the bulk of the radiocarbon evidence is that this took place sometime after 2500 BC. It is interesting to observe that the general range of calibrated dates from the level of the Indus civilization at Harappa is roughly 2400/2300 BC and 2100/2000 BC (Dales 1992). I suggest that this expansion, and also the expansion towards Rajasthan, Haryana and Panjab took place after the phase of expansion towards the lower Sind. The dates from Kalibangan show a similar radiocarbon dating spread. Along with the movement towards the lower Sind there was in all probability another movement towards Kutch which was then likely to have been an island and lay virtually at the mouth of the combined Hakra-Indus flow. In fact, if one takes into consideration the Rajasthan-Panjab-Haryana sites, the distribution of the Indus civilization sites shows the most dense concentration along the Ghaggar-Hakra course at three points—in Cholistan, along the Sirhind *nala* which is a part of the Ghaggar-Sarasvati system in the Bhatinda area, and in Kutch in the estuary of the combined Ghaggar/Hakra-Indus flow. The movement towards the Saurashtra peninsula and mainland Gujarat took place from Kutch, possibly in a somewhat later period. The long chronology of the Indus civilization becomes meaningful in the light of the geographical hypothesis suggested above.

Elements of Planning

Among the hypothesis thrown out of gear by modern research on the Indus civilization is the premise that its cities are based on chess-board patterns. The roads do not always move straight, nor do they criss-cross at right angles. At the same time there is clear evidence of centralized planning at all the major excavated sites. This is clear from the physical configurations of the individual settlements: the way in which the two separate and separately enclosed mounds stand in relation to one another, the way in which the fortifications and/or enclosure walls were laid out with bastions, corner towers and entrances, etc. The available basic settlement types suggest a detailed concept of typology for them. First, there are settlements like Mohenjodaro, Harappa and Kalibangan where the twin mounds are separately enclosed and suggest a clear division between the public administrative-cum-ritual-cum-residential western sector and the more or less private residential sector. The western mound at Harappa is no doubt heavily disturbed but it has some major public constructions in its shadow outside, between the northern fortification wall and the river. At Mohenjodaro there is no structural complex in the shadow of the citadel wall, whereas at Kalibangan the western mound has two separate walled sectors, one apparently kept apart for a number of ritual platforms and the other presumably meant for administrative buildings and the dwellings of the elite. Secondly, there are places like Surkotada which is a replica of the western sector at Kalibangan. Third, there is Lothal which shows a single enclosed complex with public buildings and ordinary residential structures including craftsmen's workshops. Fourth, although within a single enclosure wall, a place like Banawali had two internal and walled subdivisions, but the alignment of the dividing wall between Banawali's 'acropolis' and the 'lower town' gave the acropolis an arch-shaped assymmetrical form. Fifth, Dholavira constitutes a category of its own because its open spaces and triple divisions between the lower town, middle town and the citadel have not yet been matched at any other settlement. Sixth, there must be some small but presumably urban settlements (cf. Ahladino, Hulas?) which had no internal divisions and no enclosing wall. Finally, there are places like Zekada in Gujarat which are presumably short-lived and seasonal habitations.

Another fact which needs consideration at the outset is that there is no direct correlation between the planning of the Indus settlements and their size-categories. A convenient example is the contrast between Lothal and Mohenjodaro. In the light of the data I cited in 1979 Mohenjodaro is about 18 times the size of Lothal, but Lothal shares with it the features of burnt brick houses, regularly aligned streets, burnt brick drains, etc. On the other hand, Kalibangan is more than twice the size of Lothal but is much poorer in comparison. At Kalibangan there is very limited use of burnt bricks, civic drainage and wells, among other things. So, mere size in the Indus context does not indicate whether the site was rich or poor, properly planned or unplanned. Thus, on the whole, the distinction between a village, a town and a city is to some extent blurred among the Harappan settlements. In the same context it has to be emphasized that not all major Harappan settlements have a number of smaller settlements around them. Both Mohenjodaro and Harappa are classic examples. There is no concentration of lesser settlements in their neighbourhood. On the other hand, we have the curious phenomenon of a large number of sites of all sizes being concentrated in some pockets. One simply does not know what to make of the singularly unusual concentration of five sites, each apparently as large as Mohenjodaro and Harappa, in the Mansa area of Bhatinda.

A number of estimates have been made regarding the population density of the Harappan cities. On the basis of his estimate of the quantity of grain stored in the granaries, which, he thought, was only for general civic consumption, Jatindra Mohan Datta (1962) calculated that the density of population per acre at Mohenjodaro and Harappa was 52 and 73 respectively, giving a total population of 33469 for Mohenjodaro and 37155 for Harappa. But the idea that the stored grain was meant only for civic consumption may be wrong; it may have also served as some kind of capital. Allowing a ratio of 800 square feet per person, Fairservis (1967) puts the total population of Mohenjodaro at 41250 persons on a conservative estimate. On the basis of nineteenth-century statistics figures for Shikarpur in northwest Sind, which, according to him, 'in dimensions and lay-out may be reckoned as approaching the conditions of Mohenjodaro as nearly as possible', Lambrick (1964) estimates the population of Mohenjodaro to be 35000 and feels that the same figure should be true of Harappa as well. If one accepts that the size of Mohenjodaro is double the size of what can be seen today or that Harappa measures 150 ha. in area, the population estimates should also go up accordingly.

Another issue related to Harappan planning is to decide if the walls which enclose in some cases the 'citadel complex' and the 'lower town' separately and the settlement as a whole in others are regular defence walls or merely serve the purpose of demarcating urban territories by peripheral walls. Whereas, after his excavations at the citadel mound of Harappa, Wheeler had no doubt at all about their being components of a military system—and his work at Mohenjodaro in 1950 only reinforced his belief—some doubt has been expressed about this in recent years (cf. Kesarwani 1984, Kenoyer 1991). The basis of this doubt is two-fold. First, as A. Kesarwani (1984) has argued, the entrances to the Harappan 'fortified' enclosures were not at all elaborate and contrasted sharply with the gateway complexes of an ancient Mesopotamian city.

The fortified Harappan towns were of two kinds; some had simple entrances, while others had guard-rooms also, but the guard-rooms were invariably very small, to accommodate only one person. Some of the Harappan 'citadels', such as those at Surkotada and Kalibangan, had partition walls which also had simple entrances, sometimes with steps, but apparently without guard-rooms. . . . The fortifications, therefore, served two major purposes, as protection against floods, and as the hall-mark of social authority over the area they commanded (Kesarwani 1984: 72–3).

Secondly, such walls came up, at least in the case of the western mound at Mohenjodaro, as the retaining wall of the huge artificial mud and mudbrick platform, on the top of which individual buildings, both public and private, stood on their own substructures. This has also been argued in the context of the eastern mound at Harappa; 'while some parts of the walls may have been free-standing and associated with an entrance, other parts served as massive revetments raised up to 3 m against the edge of the mound' (Kenoyer 1991: 352). At the same time I feel that no useful purpose is served by completely running down the defensive character of these walls. When the bastions, corner-towers and gateways are envisaged together, the 'defensive' character of such complexes becomes very hard to deny. Moreover, as Jansen has argued, there is also an element of a moat associated with it. The clay necessary for the raising of the huge platforms, substructures and the retaining wall was likely to have been collected from the same area and this must have given rise to a ditch around the peripheral wall. In a sense this is reminiscent of early historic cities where a fortification and a moat were common features.

Unless the distribution of artifacts is detailed house by house and room by room it is unlikely that positive clues will be found as to the use of excavated house units at any Harappan site (Jansen 1984, for a statement of this issue), but by mainly studying the position of the courtyard in relation to the other rooms Anna Sarcina (1979) proposed five basic models for the house-units of Mohenjodaro, which she illustrated by using different colours: yellow model—courtyard always to the north; red model—courtyard in one corner surrounded by rooms on two sides; green model—a central plan with the courtyard surrounded by rooms on four sides; brown model—courtyard occupies about half the area, with the rest divided into several rooms; blue model—courtyard surrounded by rooms on three sides. Each of these has been assigned various sub-categories, but what is important in Sacrcina's scheme is the following: yellow model for residential purpose; red model with a residential purpose but with an artisanal dimension as well; brown model for artisans; green model also with functions other than residential ones; blue model for an uncertain purpose.

Jansen's (1984) classification envisages three broad categories at Mohenjodaro; the units oriented towards a central space and with a blocked-out view of the entrance from a street or lane; large houses surrounded by smaller units; and large public structures such as the Great Bath, Granary, etc.

Among the streets the main ones at least were of considerable width. The north-south First Street in the HR area at Mohenjodaro was 30–5 ft (9.14–10.66 m) wide and as Mackay (1948: 19) points out, 'could easily have accommodated several lines of wheeled traffic'. Among the lesser ones a width of around 13 ft (3.96 m) is supposed to be common. At Kalibangan the average width of the major streets has been calculated to be around 7.20 m and the width of the smaller ones is generally supposed to be half of this. At Lothal this varied between 12 and 18 ft (3.65 and 5.48 m). The lanes were considerably narrower. At Mohenjodaro their width ranged from between 3 ft 8 ins (1.11 m) and 7 ft (2.13 m). At Kalibangan their average width is 1.8 m, though in some cases it is so narrow that one can easily stride across them. At Lothal they were between 6 and 9 ft (1.82 and 2.74 m).

The streets are not constant in their width. A careful glance at the published plans should show this but to take one example, one of the major streets (the second one from the left) in the lower town of Kalibangan is about 6.15 m wide at its northern end while at the southern end its width is about 8.20 m. These variations in width notwithstanding, the streets ran remarkably straight; the eye moves down from one end to another in one sweep. The variations have been generally attributed to a lack of precise measurements rather than to carelessness, but this seems somewhat improbable as the differences involved are far too large in some cases. The inner lanes, as the plans show, seldom ran straight but often twisted and turned. But even then the bends were not rounded but right-angled. The Harappan planners seem to have been preoccupied with straight lines and sharp corners. Curiously enough, such well laid-out streets and lanes were invariably unpaved (except for a stretch of the First Street in the DK area, Mohenjodaro, and the evidence of terracotta nodules on the streets in the upper levels of Kalibangan).

The most distinctive feature of the Harappan streets and lanes is perhaps the number of burnt-brick drains associated with them. The drainage system seems to have been quite extensive, at least at Mohenjodaro and Lothal. At Mohenjodaro where the evidence is fully published, there are drains in all the larger streets and more often than not in the smaller lanes also. They were primarily intended to carry off the waste household water and connected as such in most cases through a water chute with the smaller drains of the houses. The idea that they were intended to cope with the rainwater is doubtful. In the context of Mohenjodaro, Raikes and Dyson (1961: 277) show how 'the drainage system is inadequate to carry off the storm water from an average present day short period storm'.

The width and depth of the drains varied. At Mohenjodaro the general width might be around 9 ins (about 228 mm) while the usual depth was between 18 and 24 ins (0.45 m, 0.60 m). From the regular deposits of little heaps of sand beside them Mackay (1948: 36) infers that they were subjected to regular cleaning. Stone slabs or bricks were put as covers over them in such a way that they could easily be removed for the purpose of cleaning. The general masonry of the drains was careful and the bends were carefully rounded so that the general flow of water was not impeded at any point. Besides, brick culverts, 'some as large as two and a half feet wide and between four and five feet high' (Mackay 1948: 37) and meant for the discharge of the collected water from the city-drains, have been reported from the outskirts of Mohenjodaro.

For the sewarage there were not only drains but also soak or sediment pits in places. Sometimes they were mere pottery jars placed at the mouth of the water chutes coming out of the houses. Usually there was a hole at the bottom of the jars to let the water sink into the earth. The proper sediment pits, of which a number of examples come from Mohenjodaro, were brick-built and even had steps leading inside, allowing access for cleaning. Drains, soakage jars and cess pits are also said to be the normal features of the streets at Lothal. In the context of a public drain at Lothal it has been said that 'to ensure a quick flow of water in the drains, drops were provided at regular intervals on its brick floor. Another interesting feature was the provision of a sluice gate at the mouth of the drain, where a wooden door could be slided in grooves' (IAR 1958–59: 14).

A point which may be of some interest is that there is no system of street drainage at Kalibangan, though soakage jars were occasionally placed outside to hold water from the house drains of wood or brick. In view of this it is tempting to link the Harappan system of drainage with the general material standard of the city. Kalibangan, if its uniformly mudbrick-built houses and comparative paucity of finds are any indication, seems to be a poorer city than Lothal or Mohenjodaro.

A large number of burnt brick-built wells seem to have been another organic feature of Harappan civic planning. It is from Mohenjodaro that one gets the most extensive evidence. Of course, as Mackay (1938, I: 165) points out, 'not every house had its own well, for instance, there were none in certain houses cleared in Block 2, 3 and 5 in the southern portion of the DK area, G section, nor in several blocks in the northern portion'. The inside diamter of the wells varied between 2 ft and 7 ft 6 ins (0.60 m, 2.28 m). Mackay notes that the usual size is 2 ft 2 ins (0.66 m). In some cases this is as low as a little more than 1 ft (0.30 m). Usually round, the wells were sometimes elliptical. The well in Block 6, SD area (Mohenjodaro) is one such instance. In most cases the wells lay within the house but occasionally they were placed between two houses. The latter was probably intended for public use; in fact, the paved portion around them contains many low circular impressions, apparently due to the regular placing of many jars. 'In two instances brick benches were built around the well for the use of people awaiting their turn to draw water' (Marshall

1931 I: 270). Or, as Mackay (1948: 38) writes, '. . . the sight of a knot of people gathered round a well waiting their turn to draw water and exchanging gossip meanwhile must have been as common in Mohenjodaro as it is in the East today'. As their steening was raised from time to time, the wells seldom went into disuse. The wells occur at other sites also but they are rare in the eastern mound of Kalibangan where the river lapping the site in the north must have been the main source of water supply.

Jansen (1989) adds that the wells were made of specially designed, wedge-shaped bricks.

From the technical point of view, the cylindrical well shafts are an impressive feat of engineering as they bear out the fact that the circular form is statically best suited to withstanding the lateral pressure bearing on wells 20 m or more deep . . . an average catchment radius of a mere 25 m per well has been estimated for Mohenjodaro on the strength of the available data. . . . Mohenjodaro must have been serviced by at least 700 wells, with an average frequency of one in every third house. Needless to say, a water supply network on this scale within the actual city itself was unheard of at this period. Contemporary Egyptians and Mesopotamians, for instance, had to make do with fetching water bucket-by-bucket from the river and then storing in tanks at home in the city until needed (Jansen 1989).

Like the streets, drains and wells the Harappan houses also impress one first with their general uniformity. Wood must have been used extensively along with brick; in the 1964–65 excavations at Mohenjodaro, 'considerable evidence was found . . . for the combined use of baked brick and wooden architecture. Wooden beams, sockets, recesses in brick wall faces for wooden beams and a series of regularly spaced vertical slots in the outer surface wall of one building point to the use of wooden architectural components on a scale much more extensive than had hitherto been realized' (Dales 1965). Remains of staircases, usually steep and narrow, suggest in some cases an upper storey. The roofing was of mud-plastered reed matting supported by timber. The plastering was normally of clay, occasionally burnt patches of which still survive. The mortar used was also clay though the use of gypsum and lime was not unknown. The paving inside was either of beaten earth or bricks, both burnt and unburnt. Only the floor of one room at Kalibangan was found paved with tiles decorated with intersecting circle designs. Two more examples of this type of decoration come from Bala Kot and Ahladino. The doorways were simple, probably wooden and closed against jambs. Mackay (1948: 28) gives the usual width of a doorway at Mohenjodaro as 3 ft 4 ins (1.06 m). Their sizes are generally mentioned: 3 ft 3 ins

(0.90 m), 3 ft 6–3/4 ins (1.09 m) and 3 ft 10 ins (1.16 m). At least one doorway in the HR area was as wide as 7 ft 6 ins (2.28 m). This one was corbelled though the normal method was to top the doorway by a wooden lintel. Door sockets were of hollowed-out stone and brick. The entrance doors usually opened into the side-lanes and alleys and rarely into the main streets. The windows are noticeably rare; 'even in some of the better-preserved blocks (of Mohenjodaro) they can be counted on the fingers of one hand' (Marshall 1931 I: 275). They must also have been placed high up in the walls. The primary source of light inside the house must have been the inner open courtyard.

A distinctive feature of the houses is bathrooms and privies. The bathrooms, carefully paved, sometimes with bricks on edge and with a waterchute or drain (in the cases of bathrooms upstairs, pottery pipes) to carry off the waste water, were almost an invariable feature of the Mohenjodaro houses. On the other hand, the privies—two bricks placed sideways with a hole in between—were less common. A general hypothesis (Marshall 1931 I: 282) is that the large number of bathrooms at Mohenjodaro suggest almost a ritualistic value for ablution. This may be true but in view of their rarity at Kalibangan one might contend that the bathrooms may well be mere reflections of the richness of the city and the general habit of cleanliness of the citizens.

Finally, following Jansen (1991), one may point out a major implication of the constructional feature of the western mound at Mohenjodaro. This entire sector covering more than 80000 sq. m was laid out on a 7 m high artificial mud and mudbrick platform, and according to Jansen (1991), this 'huge substructure could have been erected in two winter seasons by approximately 20000 people'.

Social Framework

The Harappan settlements functioned within the political and administrative framework of a state. There is no clear formulation of the problem in the earlier reports of Marshall, Mackay and Vats, though they all seem to have accepted the existence of priests, merchants and artisans among the people who lived in these cities. Gordon Childe (1952: 207–8) wondered about the 'nucleus round which accumulated the social surplus wealth of capital involved in the conversion of the village into the city' and wrote in this context of 'a democratic bourgeois economy as in Crete'. Wheeler, on the basis of his discovery of the fortification around the mound AB at Harappa, wrote the following: 'Whatever the source of their

authority—and a dominant religious element may fairly be assumed—
the lords of Harappa administered their city in a fashion not remote from
that of the priest-kings or governors of Sumer and Akkad' (Wheeler 1947:
76). An Egyptian or Mesopotamian type of kingship need not be
envisaged in the Indus context. In later Indian history, the king, despite
the occasional use of grandiloquent titles, was a much more humble figure
without the tell-tale archaeological evidence of his existence. For one
thing, he does not strut around in sculptural reliefs towering above
ordinary mortals and cutting the heads of his enemies, and for another, he
functioned within the well-formulated concept of the royal duty of looking after the well-being of his subjects. Has any palace been indisputably
identified in the excavations of the later cities of India? The answer is in
the negative. The point I am trying to make is that it is futile to look for
the remains of a royal palace in the ruins of Mohenjodaro and elsewhere
for the simple reason that there will not be any way of identifying it, going
by the later Indian examples. Priesthood is far more sharply visible in the
Mohenjodaro archaeological record. The concept of a *yogin*, one who sits
in meditation, is writ large over the famous Mohenjodaro limestone head
and a few miscellaneous pieces of human sculpture from the same site.
Remains, such as those of fire-altars on the tops of platforms at Kalibangan,
and similar remains elsewhere, though without the association of high
platforms, unmistakably imply the services of priests—priests of a type
that a practising Hindu would engage for performing his household rituals
even today. Many laboured hypotheses have been offered to explain the
components of the Indus religion, but John Marshall's explanation of the
Indus religion has not yet been bettered, mainly because Marshall with
his roots firmly in the ground had no necessity to suggest pointless and
laboured hypotheses. Merchants must have played a major role in the
social and economic life because the overwhelming evidence of raw
material procurement all over the Harappan distribution area leaves no
room for doubt on this score. This is true of artisans, and one need not be
surprised if both the merchants and artisans had their 'guilds' as early as
in this period.

Chapter Four

Prelude to Early Historic Urban Growth

DECLINE OF HARAPPAN CIVILIZATION

The first systematic discussion on the decline of the Harappan civilization was made by Wheeler (1947) who depended, on the archaeological side, primarily on the fortification wall around the western mound at Harappa. In its Phase III, the last period of Harappan occupation, one of the two entrances of its western gate system was blocked completely and the other was partially closed by a screen wall. In the same phase an additional salient was added to its northwestern corner tower. These archaeological indications were interpreted as signs of the Harappans being on the defensive and thus, on the decline. The Rigveda provided the literary data with its wealth of references to the fortified strongholds of the non-Aryans and the tale of their destruction by the war-lord Indra. On the basis of Marshall's (1931, I: 110–11) postulate of the non-and pre-Aryan character of the Harappan civilization and the discovery of a fortified stronghold at Harappa it was not difficult to imagine that the Rigvedic section of the destruction of fortified settlements contains a reference to the destruction of the Harappan cities by the Aryans. The hypothesis seemed to fit in with an additional piece of evidence from Mohenjodaro: the scattered skeletons of men, women and children in the upper levels of the site, which were interpreted as signs of a massacre, a likely enough phenomenon in case of an Aryan attack. If these Aryans needed any specific archaeological identity, it was provided by the 'Cemetery H' people at Harappa, who built jerry-built walls on top of the Harappan occupation at the citadel and seemed generally to linger at the site after the passing of the Harappans.

The theme continues in Stuart Piggott's *Prehistoric India* (Piggott 1950: 214–41). He suggests, in addition, a 'time of trouble' and a post-Harappan infiltration from the West into Baluchistan, Sind and the North-west Frontier, deducible from a motley of archaeological evidence: the

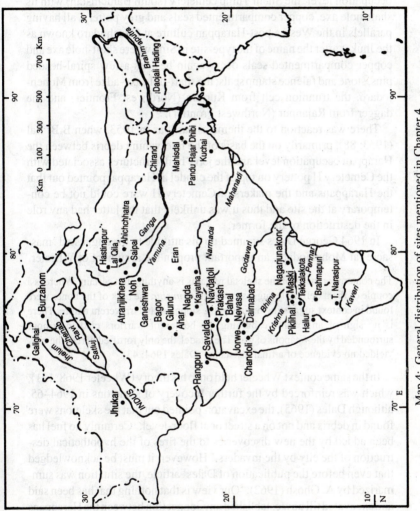

Map 4: General distribution of sites mentioned in Chapter 4

burnt-out deposits over Rana Ghundai IIIC (north Baluchistan) marking a complete break with the previous settlement, at Nal over the Nal cultural deposit and at Dabarkot (north Baluchistan) over the Harappan occupation level; the Shahi Tump cemetery (south Baluchistan) with its shaft-hole axe, copper compartmented seals and grey pottery, all having parallels in the West; a post-Harappan culture at Chanhudaro known as the Jhukar after the name of the type-site in Sind where shaft-hole axe and copper compartmented seals occur again besides a few spiral-headed pins, stone and faience stamp seals; the shaft-hole axe-adze from Mohenjodaro, the trunnion celt from Kurram (Northwest Frontier) and the dagger from Rajanpur (Northwest Frontier).

There was reaction to the theme as early as in 1953, when B.B. Lal (1953: 88), primarily on the basis of the intervening debris between the Harappan occupation level and the jerry built structures associated with the Cemetery H pottery on top of the citadel at Harappa, pointed out that the Harappans and the makers of Cemetery H ware could not be contemporary at the site and thus it was unlikely that the latter had any role in the destruction of the former.

In 1964 George Dales summed up his attitude to the suggested 'massacre' at Mohenjodaro, an important prop in the argument of Wheeler.

The contemporaneity of the skeletal remains is anything but certain. Whereas a couple of them definitely suggest a slaughter *in situ*, the bulk of the bones were found in context suggesting burials of the sloppiest and irreverent nature. There is no sign of an extensive burning, no bodies of warriors clad in armour surrounded by the weapons of war. The citadel, the only fortified part of the city, yielded no evidence of a final resistance (Dales 1964: 43).

In the same context Wheeler held on to his theory (Wheeler 1968: 131), which was reinforced by the further recovery of skeletons in 1964–65, although Dales (1965), the excavator, pointed out that the skeletons were found in debris and not on a street or at floor-level. 'Certainly no fuel has been added by the new discoveries to the fires of the hypothetical destruction of the city by the invaders.' However, it must be acknowledged that even before the publication of Dales' article, the situation was summarized by A. Ghosh (1962): 'Our view is that nothing that has been said and excavated till now established any connection between the Harappans and the Aryans at any stage.' As late as in 1968, B. and F.R. Allchin (1968) wrote: '. . . the numerous groups of hastily buried or unburied corpses left in the streets of its final occupation, and the buried hoards of jewellery and copper objects seem testimony enough of the proximity of foreign barbarians.' The idea of 'foreign barbarians' putting to sword a civilization in its last stage seems to be too appealing to be abandoned.

Meanwhile, in the context of Sind a new line of enquiry was put forward by M.R. Sahni (1956). In connection with his geological fieldwork in 1940–41 he noted the presence of thick bedded alluvium on Budh Takkar and another hillock near Thirak, south of Hyderabad in Sind. The bedded character of the alluvium containing freshwater shells like *Planorbis, Viviparus, Symnaea*, besides *Unionids* suggested a prolonged submerged condition, sometime between the Harappan and post-Harappan phases as indicated by a thick cover of alluvium over at least two Harappan sites noted by him in the vicinity.

The floods may have been due to earthquakes causing elevation, perhaps at more than one point, which dammed the Indus course, or to simultaneous floods in the Punjab rivers which ultimately pour into the Indus. Attention is drawn to the "Allah Bund" or Mound of God', a barrier 50 miles long, 20 miles wide and 10–26 feet high, formed in Kutch as the result of an earthquake in 1918 when an area of 2000 sq. miles was submerged for a period of two years. Furthermore, in 1826, the Indus burst every dam in its course, covering for itself a passage through the old channel discharging into the Koree Creek and overflowed the Sind desert. The author suggests that there were earlier episodes on a vaster scale in the destructive history of the Indus, the cradle of early Indian civilization.

Primarily two categories of evidence led Raikes to the same line of enquiry in his first publication on the subject in 1963:

For a long time the author has found it difficult to accept the explanation that the nine rebuildings of Mohenjodaro and the several rebuildings of Chanhudaro were occasioned by floods in the ordinarily accepted sense of the word. The greatest depth of 'flood-silt' shown in the early available, perhaps the only published stratigraphy of Mohenjodaro is too great to be easily accounted for by an exceptional annual Indus flood . . . in some places reconstruction on top of the existing wall has started some six feet above the previous floor level (Raikes 1963: 657).

Secondly, evidence of a major coastal uplift was forthcoming from Makran with the suggestion that it was on too vast a scale to be restricted merely to the Makran strip and to not have affected the flow of the Indus.

Although put in a more elaborate form in 1964 (Raikes 1964), Raikes' ideas assumed a clearer focus only after his field-study was aided by boring in 1964–65 (Raikes 1965). The total accumulated depth of the silt was some 70 feet (*c*. 21 m), about 10 m above the plain and another 12 m below, as the borings revealed. The content was found to be 'silty-clay', the result of deposition under still-water condition. Raikes considered it improbable that such a vast accumulation of silt could be explained by the normal flood regime of the Indus. He suggests that the still-water condition necessary for the deposition of silty-clay could be possible only due to the emergence of a lake south and downstream of Mohenjodaro. A dam athwart the Indus to account for the formation of such a lake could come up due to a sudden tectonic disturbance throwing up an effective mud barrier. The inherent probability of such a dam with a tectonic disturbance in the background might be supported by a reference to the Allah Bund which Sahni cited and to the eruption of two mud islands off the coast of Sind in the Arabian sea as late as in 1945. 'It seems inescapable that an event or a series of events such as that of Allah Bund, and probably due to intruded volcanic mud, dammed the Indus' (Raikes 1967: 182).

Such a dam for which suitable geological formations are said to exist near Sehwan, some ninety miles downstream of Mohenjodaro, would have been permeable in character because the erupted volcanic mud would also have thrown up the original fine sand with a thin alluvial sandy clay cover of the original flood-plain. This permeability would have entailed that while the dammed-up water could gradually seep through, the whole of the sediment load would have got deposited at the bottom. From the point of view of the human inhabitants of the area it would have meant a gradual engulfment of their settlements in mud. The people of Mohenjodaro would have tried at the outset to raise their houses higher and higher on mudbrick platforms till at one point the endeavour would have seemed useless enough to warrant the desertion of the city. Eventually the water accumulating behind the dam would have spilled over it and thus initiated a process of headwater erosion, which in turn would have exposed the part of Mohenjodaro visible above the flood-plain today (the entire cycle illustrated by a diagram in Dales, 1966).

Apart from the different ramifications of Wheeler's idea (Wheeler 1968: 113) that 'Mohenjodaro was wearing out its landscape' by over-exploitation, the first major criticism of the 'dam-and-lake' theory came from H.T. Lambrick (1967a, 1967b). He maintains that the present flood-plain of the Indus is the result of the unimpeded alluvial action of the river in its natural condition with its characteristic change of course over several thousands of years. He questions the validity of Raikes' estimate of the existing slope of the flood plain at 1 in 7000 and of the slope during the pre-Harappan time at 1 in 3500. He also has doubts about both the factors supposedly behind Raikes' reasoning: the presence of the sea near Amri and the flow of the Indus through the Sukkur gorge in a similarly early period. Regarding the latter he says that it is a comparatively recent phenomenon, a fact suggested not merely by the general configuration of the contours but also by the absence of any literary reference to it earlier than the thirteenth century AD. Regarding the ancient shore-line of 3000 BC his guess is that it was about 60 miles inland from the present coast-line, 'not far short of one-hundred miles below Amri'. Finally, Lambrick suggests that 'the wind, periodically whipping sand, silt and dust off the surface of the grey-white plain' could have deposited it everywhere in the mound, and melted by rain, it would have been very much like the silty clay that Raikes wrote about. He points out that many village-sites have been obliterated like this in Sind.

His positive explanation is that the Indus drifted away from Mohenjo-daro, leaving it out of reach of the annual floods. A change in course was prima facie possible. Besides, classical geographers like Strabo and Aristobulus have referred to the manner in which a change in the river-course brought about the ruin of some areas in Sind. Referring to Sahni's observation, Lambrick argues that the 'silt' on Budh Takkar was a mere debris of man-made mudbrick buildings while on the hillock near Thirak no specific evidence was available. A debate ensued (Dales and Raikes 1968, Raikes 1967a, 1967b) which continued till recently.

In the case of the desertion of sites along the Ghaggar-Hakra course, specifically Kalibangan, Raikes' idea (Raikes 1968), based on the borings at the site and relevant geomorphological and archaeological studies, is that the river Yamuna oscillated, at least from the Harappan age onward, between the Indus and the Ganges river systems. When the Yamuna was within the orbit of the Indus the Ghaggar was perennial and this coincided with the presence of human settlements in the area while the inclusion of the Yamuna in the Ganges system would have meant her drying up and thus, the abandonment of settlements. The Harappan habitation along the Ghaggar dried out when the Yamuna made her eastward diversion to the Ganges after a spell as part of the Indus.

I shall offer an explanation, for whatever it is worth, of the end of the Indus civilization in a later section. The foregoing review may have shown how the problem has been viewed in archaeological literature.

The Late Harappans

I. Development of the Idea

The idea that there is a stratigraphically demonstrable and widespread 'Late' phase of the Indus civilization as opposed to the 'Late' phase of a particular site was first expressed by N.G. Majumdar (1934: 154):

A degenerate and therefore, a Late phase of Indus is illustrated by potteries discovered at the upper levels of Jhukar and Luhumjodaro. The old black-on-red technique continued but in a modified style, and a number of new patterns were also evolved. A noteworthy feature is the reappearance of the bichrome style, although this new pottery differs widely from the earlier fabric in type as well as design. It is either of terracotta or pale buff colour representing a coarse ware, on which the decoration is altogether poor and the number of designs extremely limited. The style can be further studied at the lake-site of Trihni, in its characteristic schematized rosettes. Here, the black-on-red pottery is totally absent, although there are other links connecting this phase with Indus. Side by side with this painted ware there was prevalent a type of pots with incised strokes at the shoulder, some examples of which come also from the latest levels of Mohenjodaro.

Majumdar pointed out ceramic changes, whereas Mackay pointed out the structural data from the late levels of Mohenjodaro.

The masonry of the Late Period . . . is mostly poor as compared with that of the Intermediate Period. . . . Towards the end of the Late Period, the whole of the southern portion of the G section of the DK mound became an artisan's quarter, many of whose inhabitants were potters, for no less than six kilns, including one in the middle of Central Street, were found in this comparatively small area. . . . This quarter of Mohenjodaro, if not the whole of the city, must by this time have declined greatly in social standing and organization, for it is difficult to imagine that the city authorities . . . would have allowed potters to practise their craft within the confines of the city. . . . We have indeed, come upon a striking example of the decay of an once honourable city, the cause of which we suspect to be the vagaries of the Indus rather than pressure by invaders, of whose existence we have, in fact, little positive evidence (Mackay 1938: 6).

There are seven dates from the upper levels of Mohenjodaro, the calibrated versions of which fall comfortably between *c*. 2500 and *c*. 2100 BC. This spread also serves the purpose of demonstrating that at Mohenjodaro the Indus civilization could have come to an end at least a couple of centuries earlier than 2000 BC. The evidence of post-Harappan occupation in Sind came from Jhukar and Chanhudaro where the Jhukar culture as a post-Harappan culture was identified. In Panjab the post-Harappan occupation was seen limited to the Cemetery H ware culture identified at Harappa.

The idea that there was a continuing tradition from the earlier 'mature' urban Harappan level to the late level has been strengthened by a large number of discoveries. First, S.R. Rao's survey and excavations at Rangpur and Lothal in Gujarat established the continuity of occupation from the mature Harappan Rangpur IIA to the lustrous red ware phase of Rangpur III through Rangpur IIB and IIC. Phase V of Lothal was equated with Rangpur IIB and IIC. When calibrated, two 'post-Harappan' dates from Lothal (TF-23, TF-19) show points before *c.* 2000 BC. Surkotada IB and Desalpur IB, both in Kutch, were interpreted as 'modified Harappan'. This evidence was also encountered in an earlier excavation at Rojdi or Shrinathgarh where the Prabhas ware (after the name of Prabhas Patan or Somnath) and the lustrous red ware were found together. Meanwhile, the new excavations at Amri in Sind showed the post-Harappan Jhukar occupation as being one in which no sharp break with the urban Harappan was noticeable. Mughal's subsequent work at Jhukar further focussed on the issue. In the Cholistan area about fifty sites with the Cemetery H-related material were found along with locations in the very same area where mature Harappan sites were found. Towards the east, in the extensive area between the Ghaggar and the Yamuna and between the Himalayan foothills and the area around Kalibangan the 'late Harappan' stage was first identified at Mitathal in Haryana (Mitathal IIB) and this was related to Bara, a site excavated earlier in Panjab. Attempts have since been made in this area to establish links between the late Harappan stage and the subsequent cultures of the region. In Maharashtra the Daimabad excavations led to the identification of a late Harappan level in that region. It is thus more or less clear that the 'late Harappans' have come to occupy a distinct place in the archaeological sequence of Sind, Gujarat, Rajasthan, Haryana, east Panjab, the western portion of U.P. and north Deccan. However, there is a fair amount of regional variation, and only two features seem to be common to the entire late Harappan phenomenon: its stratigraphic position immediately after the mature Harappan urban phase with evidence of its links to this level, and the general absence of some of the principal Harappan urban features.

II. Regional Data

The situation in Baluchistan is still obscure. There is apparently no cognizable set of data from north Baluchistan. In the Kachhi plain it has been argued that the tradition of Kechi Beg pottery in the Quetta valley, which was laid down in the second half of the fourth millennium BC, continued till a much later phase at the site of Pirak which has some evidence of Harappan contact in its post-2000 BC level (Shaffer 1992). In south Baluchistan Mughal (1990) believes that the Kulli culture continued into what would be considered the late Harappan phase in Sind. In Sind his stratigraphic work at Jhukar led him to postulate three successive and inter-related phases at the site, which were all associated with the mature Harappan pottery. On the basis of the stratified evidence he designated 'Jhukar' as 'only a pottery style emerging in association with the continuing Mature Harappan tradition without any break or sudden change in cultural continuity'. However, circular stamped seals with bossed backs made their appearance; the typical Indus rectangular specimens became virtually absent and the use of cubical stone weights and stylized female figurines became rare. The script apparently came to occur only on potsherds. In western Panjab and Cholistan the late Harappan phase is marked by sites bearing the Cemetery H pottery which was first identified at Harappa and Chak Purvane Syal as early as during Vats' excavations (Vats 1940). This has been further defined as belonging to Period 5 of the site in recent excavations (Kenoyer 1991) which also suggest a transitional Period 4 between this period and the mature Harappan Period 3. Drains and burnt bricks, both of a smaller size than those of the mature Harappan level, have been reported from the Cemetery H period, but the details are still unpublished. The emphasis is on cultural continuity from the earlier mature Harappan period. The fifty sites of the Cemetery H phase, which have been identified by Mughal in the Cholistan area, include some sites with kilns and pottery firing areas and display a four-tiered settlement hierarchy among the twenty-six sites for which size estimates are available: up to 5 ha.—12 sites; between 5 and 10 ha.—7 sites; between 10 and 20 ha.—6 sites; above 20 ha.—1 site (Kudwala) which measures 38.1 ha. (about 95 acres). Mughal further refers to a change in their locations in relation to the mature Harappan sites. He again lays emphasis on cultural continuity:

The ceramics do indicate changes in certain forms and painted styles but the Harappan cultural tradition persisted for some time and then gradually dwindled to a vague or faint expression in just a few pottery forms until the end of second millennium BC, by which time, the Harappan tradition was lost and forgotten (Mughal 1990: 2).

In the area between the Sutlej and the Yamuna, which covers the modern Indian political units of Panjab, Haryana, U.P., Himachal Pradesh, Delhi and Chandigarh there are 563 late Harappan sites according to the list published by J.P. Joshi and his associates in 1984 (Joshi, Bala and Ram 1984). Certainly more sites have been discovered in this region since then. Size estimates are available only in patches; most of the reported settlements seem to be within five acres in extent. A good number of them possibly measured much less. The ceramic continuity has been adequately worked out but the cultural details are still meagre. Among the excavated sites in Haryana the late Harappan phase of Banawali has provided some non-ceramic evidence: mud houses, faience ornaments (bangles, anklets, rings, beads and pipal leaf shaped ear rings), beads of ·semi-precious stones, some copper, ritualistic clay objects, terracotta toy cart frames, etc. In Panjab mud floors with postholes and hearths, mudbrick structures, storage pits, kilns and a fire altar (divided into two parts containing ash and unbaked and semi-baked mud cakes) were found at Sanghol. At Dadheri the settlement stood over a solid mud platform which acted as the substructure on which mud houses were built. The excavated antiquities of the period include terracotta wheels, beads, copper objects, a painted bull, faience bangles and beads of carnelian and lapis lazuli (for the Panjab sites, Bala 1992, 24 ff). The site of Mohrana in Panjab yielded in this level remains of hulled and naked six-row barley, dwarf wheat, club wheat, lentil and grape pips (*Vitus vinifera* L). Rohira showed, as early as in its pre-Harappan level, barley, dwarf wheat, emmer wheat, lentil, horse gram (*Dolichos biflorus*), sorghum millet, grape pips and date-palm. One may assume that the same crops were known at this site in the late Harappan phase as well (for these crops, IAR 1983–84). At Hulas in the Saharanpur district of the doab in U.P. the most distinctive feature of the late Harappan level is the presence of circular mud and reed houses, copper objects and an impressive variety of crops. These crops include rice, barley, dwarf wheat, bread wheat, club wheat, oats (*Avena sativa*), sorghum/jowar, ragi/finger millet (*Eleusine coracana*), lentil, field pea (*Pisum arvense*), grass pea (*Lathyrus sativa*), Kulthi (*Dolichos biflorus*), green gram/moong (*Vigna radiata*), chick-pea or gram (*Cicer arietinum*), a broken seed cow-pea (*Vigna unguiculata*), cotton (*Gossypium arboreum*), castor (*Ricinus comunis*) and some varieties of fruit and wild grasses. Almond (*Prunus amygdalus*) and walnut (*Juglans regia*) are among other noteworthy finds from this site. These crop-lists clearly suggest that the hundreds of late Harappan sites in the Indo-Gangetic divide were not temporary settlements but settlements with well-developed farming practices (for the crop-list from Hulas, see IAR 1986–87). What is equally remarkable is that the later cultures of the region are found interlocked with the late Harappan levels at a number of sites in the region. The co-occurrence of Painted Grey Ware with the late Harappans at the Panjab sites of Bhagawanpura, Dadheri, Nagar and Katpalon (see Bala 1992) and the roots of Ochre Coloured Pottery in the late Harappan assemblage at the doab sites of Ambkheri, Bargaon, etc. clearly demonstrate, among other things, how the Harappan culture, instead of coming to an abrupt end, merged into the main flow of the Gangetic valley archaeological sequence. Another interesting point is that, although the distribution of pre-/early Harappan and Harappan sites in the region shows a concentration in some pockets, the distribution of the late Harappan sites here seems to be more evenly spread. This simple fact may imply that, contrary to Francfort's hypothesis that the postulated irrigation system of the earlier periods declined during this period and brought about the end of the Harappan civilization in the region, the irrigation system became more broad-based.

For a clear approach to the problem of 'late Harappans' in Gujarat, it may be best to begin with S.R. Rao's statement on the indisputably 'late Harappan' Lothal B or Lothal Phase V (Rao 1979: 33–6). In addition to ceramic changes, there were jerry-built houses of mud and reeds, less use of copper, short blades of jasper and chalcedony in place of long blades, ribbon-like blades of chert, biconical terracotta beads in place of jasper and carnelian beads and 'a gradual replacement of cubical weights of chert and agate by truncated weights of schist and sandstone larger in size than the earlier ones'. The use of rectangular steatite seals with the Indus script continued but during this phase there is no seal with animal motifs.

Some observations on comparative stratigraphy by Rao in this context are important. (1) The Prabhas ware of Prabhas Patan occurs 'in very small quantities' in this phase at Lothal 'with the degenerate Harappan wares', (2) this Prabhas ware also occurs in Rojdi Ia 'along with the straight-sided bowls in a degenerate Harappan fabric', (3) 'Phase V of Lothal, i.e. Period B can be roughly equated to Rangpur IIB and IIC except for the fact that the evolved ceramic types of Lothal B do not bear a lustrous red surface as in Rangpur IIC'. Thus, all the above-mentioned levels, i.e. Lothal B, Rojdi Ia, Rangpur IIB and IIC belong to the late Harappan phase in Gujarat on the basis of the stratigraphic evidence worked out by Rao at Rangpur and Lothal.

The recent claim that Rojdi and all Rangpur IIB and IIC sites in Gujarat should be treated as mature Harappan and not as late Harappan sites (Bhan 1992) has arisen because the radiocarbon dates from Rojdi are on par with those from the mature Harappan phase of Lothal. The claim that there were two mature Harappan traditions in Gujarat, one represented by Lothal and the other by Rojdi, is perhaps both unwarranted and unfortunate. If one notes carefully, the range of calibrated dates from Lothal B is not significantly lower than those from Lothal A. Should one argue on this basis that both Lothal A and Lothal B belong to the same period? Secondly, going by the Rojdi dates and accepting the stratigraphic argument that Rojdi is later than Lothal A, it is also possible to suggest that the mature Harappan phase at Lothal belongs to the first half of the third millennium BC. In other words, the date of the beginning of the Indus civilization is much earlier than the postulated 2500 BC. Then, again, what happens to the Lothal A radiocarbon dates, none of whose calibrated initial points is earlier than 2655 BC? So the situation is more complex than Possehl and his associates would have us believe. Till Lothal and Rangpur sequences and their stratigraphic correlations with other Gujarat sites are shown to be wrong, there is no special reason to assume that sites like Rojdi and many others with Rangpur IIB and IIC affiliations in Gujarat are not late Harappan.

The late Harappan phase in Gujarat is likely to have been characterized by a number of settlement types. These settlements apparently belong to two chronological phases which, pending a clear picture, may simply be expressed as pre-lustrous red ware and lustrous red ware sites. To the first phase should belong the assortment of sites like Lothal B, Rojdi, Babar Kot, Padri, etc. It is not easy to put Kuntasi II in the late Harappan category, as its excavator apparently does (IAR 1987–88: 18), because this phase contains 'typical Harappan painted pottery, long tubular carnelian beads, cubical chert weights, etc.'

I have already referred to the jerry-built mud and reed houses of Lothal B. The main find at Rojdi is that of a stone/rubble wall enclosing the main settlement except on the side of the Bhadar river which flows by the side of the settlement on the east. On the western side this wall was pierced by a gateway. The wall, 1.5 m to 2 m thick, was constructed by putting two parallel lines of large basalt boulders (some weighing more than a metric ton) on shallow foundation trenches and filling up the intervening space with rammed earth and rubble. The double-bastioned gateway was built of the same material and miscellaneous structures constructed with rubble-masonry have been found elsewhere at the site. In addition to the millets (*Eleusine coracana, Echinochloa colonum, Paspalum scrobiculatum, Panicum miliare, Setaria italica* and *Sorghum*) the crop remains at this site include barley (*Hordeum sp.*), mustard (*Brassica*), khesari or *Lathyrus*, lentil, linseed, pea (*Pisum sativum*), vetches/broad bean/field bean, a number of gram varieties (moong, horse gram, etc.), jujube and an assortment of weeds, medicinal plants and grasses which could be used as animal fodder (Weber 1991). The site of Rojdi measures about 7 ha. in extent. Babarkot (Possehl and Raval 1991) measures about 2.7 ha. and shows a fortification wall made of stone blocks and blocks of locally available rock-mixed earth. The crops included millets, gram, etc. Among the metal implements of this phase of the late Harappans in Gujarat, the specimens from Rojdi may be representative of the general character of such finds: axe, bar celt, bangles, rings, a fish-hook, pieces of wire, a pin and a *parasu* (Chitalwala 1989).

Prabhas Patan or Somnath is another site of this genre. Before he joined Possehl (Dhavalikar and Possehl 1992) in extolling the 'pre-Harappan' character of Prabhas I on the basis of a Calib-2 mean of the calibrated range of two radiocarbon dates from this level, Dhavalikar (1984) said that there was 'every possibility' of these dates being contaminated. Incidentally, there is a Calib-2 mean point of 2343 BC from the lustrous red ware level of this site. One wonders if Dhavalikar and his associates would interpret the lustrous red ware as a sub-variant of 'Sorath Harappan'. In any case, Dhavalikar (1984) divides Prabhas II into two sub-periods: Early (without lustrous red ware) and late (with lustrous red ware). S.R. Rao (1990: 153) clearly mentions that late Harappan pottery was in use in the Prabhas culture which is Prabhas II. A stone-built structural complex (stone blocks set in mud mortar) showing a number of small (1.5 m sq.) and large (3.5 m by 1.5 m) rooms has been interpreted as a warehouse. The argument is that these rooms do not have properly plastered floors/postholes/hearths and most of the larger rooms have near their entrance four large stones set in mud mortar to form a sort of platform. Copper, obsidian (available in Gujarat, contrary to Dhavalikar's notion that it came all the way from Turkey), chalcedony, carnelian, agate and gold were among the raw materials used. There are also references to a steatite seal amulet, segmented faience beads and cubical chert weights.

The beginning of occupation at Bet Dwaraka which shows lustrous red ware is apparently later than that at Prabhas Patan, but as a site Bet Dwaraka is certainly very interesting. I cite Rao (1990: 151–2) on this site:

The excavations by the Marine Archaeology Unit (of the National Institute of Oceanography in Goa) from 1984 to 1988 in the sea bed . . . have confirmed the submergence of Dwaraka. The inner and outer fort walls, bastions and a jetty of massive dressed stones have been traced on the right bank as well as the left bank of the submerged channel of the Gomati river. Important finds from the site are stone anchors and the Lustrous Red Ware. . . . The ancient wall of the city in Bet Dwaraka, 500 m long and hexagonal in plan, is exposed in lowest low tide. . . . The island of Bet Dwaraka . . . is noted for a Late Harappan site which was almost wholly submerged under the sea. The ancient city was originally 4 km long and 0.5 km wide. . . . Remnants of fortification are seen in the sea bed at the southern and northern extremities. The western wall in the cliff section of Bet Dwaraka provides convincing proof of a fortified city. Midway between the northern and southern extremities is a massive rectangular stone structure, 580 m long, which served as a fort wall-cum-pier. . . . An Indus seal carved with a 3-headed animal . . . and ceramic wares such as the Lustrous Red Ware, black-and-red ware and the votive jar inscribed in Late Harappan script suggest a 15th century BC date for the ancient city in Bet Dwaraka. Its submergence is attributed to a rise in sea level or subsidence of land or both. A stone mould of coppersmith, shell bangles, etc. are other antiquities from the site.

There is a thermoluminiscent date of 3520 BP or 1570 BC from Bet Dwaraka, agreeing quite well with the archaeological evidence.

In his discussion of late Harappan Gujarat K.K. Bhan draws attention principally to the lustrous red ware sites in the Rupen valley in north Gujarat.

Most of the settlements are situated on the relict sand dunes and are associated with large areas of waste land locally known as *padthar*. Settlements are close to water sources, which develop near the blowout hollows of these sand dunes and accumulate water from the monsoon run-off. They are camping sites for various pastoral communities even today. Usually the settlements are small and contain thin, scattered, ashy patches of cultural material. Most of them are less than 150 by 150 m. . . . However, it should also be noted that settlements at Sai Timbo in Dudkha and Thikariyono Timbo in Khandia villages measure 206 by 263 m and 239 by 116 m, respectively. Both these settlements are associated with larger depressions that retain water for between 7 and 12 months, provided the area receives good monsoon (Bhan 1992: 176).

Among the late Harappan settlements listed by him, Bhan (1992, table 1) provides size measurements for thirty-three sites.

Less than 1 ha.	1–2 ha.	2–3 ha.	3–4 ha.	5 ha.	8–9 ha.
8	11	7	4	2	1

Many of these sites may be cattle-breeders' small seasonal stations, a classic example of which was found in the lustrous red ware context at Oriyo Timbo (Rissman and Chitalwala 1989). However, there are many more sites of this type, as R.N. Mehta (1982, 1984) and K. Momin (1984) clearly demonstrate. The lustrous red ware is apparently absent at some of these sites but at others it is present. However, they represent a distinct late Harappan settlement tradition in Gujarat and were archaeologically identified by R.N. Mehta, a singular achievement for him. Nesadi near Valabhi in the northeastern section of Kathiawar gets flooded during the monsoon and the presence of artifactual scatter over 200 m sq. here has been linked to the seasonal migration of cowherd groups to different parts of western India in different seasons.

In this migration, the cowherds return to the area where they have come before, and thus, the area is repeatedly occupied. This repetitive phenomenon would account for different places of occupation in the Nesadi locality. This phenomenon would also account for the sparse settlement where at any given time, a few cowherd families might live.

The evidence from Kanewal (Momin 1984) in the Kheda district located at the mouth of the Gulf of Cambay is more detailed: circular wattle-and-daub huts with rammed floors, similar to the modern houses of this type (*Kuba*) in the area, oblong and triangular terracotta cakes, terracotta round pellets, carnelian, faience, shell and terracotta beads, terracotta spindle-whorls, net-sinkers, copper and a wide variety of pottery including the lustrous red ware. Regarding the general distribution of these type of sites, Mehta (1982) observes that they are found in a variety of soils and Momin notes that in the Kheda district these sites are 'spread over an area of 30 kilometres, each about 2 to 4 kilometres from the other'. Mehta (1982) clearly mentions that 'ceramics with graffiti of the Indus script from these settlements, especially at Kanewal, indicate some form of literacy'.

The late Harappan situation in Gujarat is, in fact, remarkably interesting and offers a diversity which is not matched elsewhere during this period.

Hypothesis Regarding the End of Harappan Urbanism

The currently available data on the late Harappans suggest that, instead of coming to an abrupt end, the Indus civilization merged into the main flow of Indian cultural development. There is a clear movement of the Harappans from the Indo-Gangetic divide to the Ganga-Yamuna doab and there are also suggestions of their branching out in the directions of Malwa and Maharashtra from Gujarat. However, the form with which the Indus civilization merged in the later pattern of neolithic-chalcolithic growth in inner India was not its urban form. The urban traits could have lingered on at sites such as Rojdi and Bet Dwaraka in Gujarat and Kudwala in Cholistan, but the impression is of a much larger number of smaller settlements with a more diversified agricultural economy. To some extent this impression of a more diversified agricultural system may be due to our incomplete knowledge of the Harappan agricultural system, but at the same time the clustering of a large number of crop types at Hulas, Rohira, Rojdi, etc. tends to give this impression. Along with this, there was a decreased use of raw materials at different sites, and thus correspondingly there is less evidence of interaction between different areas. The external trade must have persisted to some extent, as the finds of Indus seals in the Kassite contexts at Nippur and in Failaka and the occurrence of a seal with a whorl motif at Bet Dwaraka indicate, but on the whole it can be concluded that in the late Harappan context there was a considerable decrease in the volume and intensity of both internal and external trade. There was also much less emphasis on the organization and scale of craft industries during this period. Lahiri (1992: 129 ff) has analysed the general pattern:

. . . in most of the regions, no significant raw materials were being procured over great distances for manufacturing artefacts. . . . The post-Harappan period, in relation to the rich archaeological inventories of the mature urban sites, was admittedly a far poorer cultural horizon. In no region do we find the scale and diversity which marked the mature Harappan phenomenon's archaeological repertoire. Admittedly there were significant continuities—Dehr Majra, near Ropar, continued, at a more extensive scale than before, as a significant bead-manufacturing centre, and Bet Dwaraka marked the continuance in the Jamnagar region of the Harappan tradition of shell-working. But such sites are, relatively speaking, few and rare in this period. What one sees, instead, is a number of smaller sites in different regions broadly following the preceding settlement alignments but with certain areas more closely and extensively populated.

In the ancient context this is likely to mean the demise of an organized structure, centred around one or more units. As we shall see, the binding force of later historic urbanism in India has always been a political force—the chrysalis of a state. There is nothing to argue that the situation would have been totally dissimilar in the Harappan context. Ratnagar (1991) has forcefully argued in favour of a unitary Harappan state over the entire Harappan distribution area (for an earlier argument along this line, see Jacobson 1986). I accept her general idea but add that evidence of the later historical pattern would be corroborated by the postulate of several states in this large area.

In the early historical context the distribution area of the Harappan civilization witnessed political unification only under the Mauryas who, incidentally, did not last even for 150 years. Under the Kushans, the next most powerful political force of the region, Gujarat was probably under the Kshatrapa rule; the area as a whole was not unified. As things stand, one comes across the names of different territorial units for different parts of this area: Sindhu, Sauvira (the area to the east of the Indus), Anarta (a part of the Saurashtra peninsula), Kekaya, Madra (both in Panjab), Brahmavarta (the area between the Sarasvati and the Drishadvati), etc. So, without unduly labouring the point, one may claim that there is an even chance of the Indus civilization being based on a number of kingdoms or organized political units. The political unity is not necessarily suggested by the uniformity of material remains, as the N.B.P.-based early historical culture of northern India from the northwest to the Bay of Bengal did not reflect political unity. In fact, the political unity of this region, which came with the Mauryas, came only towards the end of the overall N.B.P. period between c. 700 and c. 200 BC.

How did the political fabric of the Indus civilization come to be so weak? To a considerable extent the process must have been linked to the hydrographic changes in the Sarasvati-Drishadvati system, leading perhaps to both river course changes and the rapid acceleration of their drying process. But this does not explain the Gujarat situation, nor does it wholly explain the situation in the 'divide' and the doab. A fact which has not been taken into consideration by scholars in this context is that over a very large part of its distribution area, the Harappan civilization did not have a long process of antecedence as it had in its core area, and in a sense, it was imposed on what must have been a basically hunting-gathering economic context. In the entire stretch roughly to the east of the Hakra distribution area in Cholistan, the Harappans cannot be credited with a long antecedence in the sense that the 'early' Harappan level here was probably later than the same level in Cholistan, the Multan area and Sind. In the doab the Harappans did not have any antecedence at all. They were very much in virgin territory. In the Saurashtra peninsula and mainland Gujarat no early Harappan level has yet been identified, the two early dates from the pre-Prabhas ware level at Prabhas Patan notwithstanding. Here, the Indus civilization was imposed on a landscape dominated by microlith-using hunter-gatherers. This must have been very significant in a number of ways, and one can safely predict that many hunting-gathering groups were also absorbed in the Harappan system, but at the same time one has to admit that the Harappans eventually came to be rather thinly stretched on the ground, and the weakening of their political fabric was almost inevitable. They were swallowed up, as it were, by the much less advanced pre-agricultural groups of inner India.

THE NEOLITHIC-CHALCOLITHIC CULTURES
OUTSIDE THE HARAPPAN ORBIT

Whatever the reason or complex of reasons, Harappan urbanism faded away by the middle of the second millennium BC or later (for thermoluminiscent dates from Hulas, see Singhvi et al. 1991). For some centuries, till the beginning of the early historic period in the Gangetic valley and elsewhere in the seventh/sixth century BC, India was, from the archaeological point of view, a land of non-literate village-farming communities.

This section will outline the regional patterns and point out how the basis of later historic India is rooted in them.

Northwest Frontier and Kashmir

We do not have an integrated picture of cultural development in this region which falls into at least three major areas: the area between Swat and Chitral, which is a land of mountain valleys oriented principally towards northeastern Afghanistan and the Kashmir-Pamir axis directly on the way to central Asia; the stretch between Peshawar and Taxila which itself comprises the Peshawar valley and the Potwar plateau, with the Indus acting as the dividing line between them; and finally, the valley of Kashmir which is linked with its neighbouring regions through a large number of routes of varying historical significance. I noted earlier that the neolithic level of Saraikhola in the Potwar plateau gave way to a Kot Diji-related horizon, and in some way this region as a whole was within the trading network of the contemporary Indus plains. In the Swat-Chitral region the large number of sites which have been excavated by Pakistani and Italian scholars show the use of copper-bronze, gold, silver, alabaster, agate, carnelian, jade, lapis lazuli, onyx, chalcedony, quartz, quartzite, schist, limestone, granite, serpentine, shell and ivory, among which shell, coral and ivory were most likely to have reached this region from the Indus plains (Lahiri 1992). The base-line in Swat-Chitral is provided by Period I of the rockshelter site of Ghaligai (Stacul 1969), which perhaps goes back to 3000 BC and shows an assemblage marked by coarse handmade pottery, bone and pebble tools and animal remains which include antler and boar tusks. Period II contains wheelmade pottery which is said to be reminiscent of the Harappan Indus valley and north Baluchistan. In Period III handmade crude pottery with a mat-impressed base and flaked bone and stone tools find a general typological comparison with the first phase of the Kashmir neolithic. Its second phase, with wheelmade pottery and a little copper, has been correlated with Ghaligai IV. Periods V–VII of Ghaligai have been designated as the 'archaic', 'middle' and 'late' phases of the 'protohistoric graveyards' of the region, dated between the second quarter of the second millennium BC and the late centuries BC. The evidence of such graveyards and associated settlements has been categorized by A.H. Dani (1967) as 'Gandhara Grave Culture'; the graves are marked by inflexed burials and urn burials after cremation and belong to a copper stage with rubble stone masonry, wheat, barley, rice and a wide variety of raw materials. Some new ceramic elements and perhaps the use of iron are added to the assemblage in its third period. In view of the geographical position of the region some central Asian and Afghanistan affinities of this culture's pottery and a few miscellaneous artifacts (cf. Jettmar 1967) are only to be expected, but there is no reason to visualize this area and this culture as the springboard of any kind of migration to the interior of the subcontinent. It should also be pointed out that the archaeological evidence from all the explored and excavated sites of this area has not yet been integrated into a coherent picture, the attention of the excavators being directed towards seeking western and central Asiatic ceramic typological parallels.

The beginning of food-production in Kashmir has been linked (Agrawal 1992: 211) to the last palaeosol formation in the valley around 5000 BP. More than thirty neolithic sites have been found scattered in this long and narrow valley but most of them are in the Baramula, Anantnag and Srinagar regions. Whether this suggests uneven exploration or specific geographical preferences of the neolithic settlers is uncertain, but this distribution points out that this was not a culture isolated from the plains. Archaeologically, of course, this fact is well understood because the occurrence of a spiral-headed copper 'hairpin' at Gufkral and a Kot Diji-type 'horned deity design' on a globular pot at Burzahom underline, among other things, the interaction of Kashmir with the Indus plains during this period. The aceramic phase at Gufkral (IAR 1981–82; Sharma 1991), about 400 m by 75 m (roughly 7.4 acres./2.99 ha.), showed large and small dwelling pits with a diameter of 1.5–3.8 m at the top and wider at the bottom. Shallow (20–30 cm deep) and large pits are said to be more common in its earlier phase. These pits as a general rule are surrounded by pits and hearths, with evidence of postholes supporting light struc-tures around their total peripheries. There are examples of pits with two chambers in the later phase. Finished and unfinished stone celts, points, ringstones, pounders, saddle querns, bone/horn tools, terracotta and steatite beads, both domesticated and wild sheep and goat, wild cattles, ibex, red deer (*Cervus elephus*), barley, wheat and lentil were present throughout.

Handmade grey pottery with a mat-impressed base is a distinguishing feature of the ceramic phase of the Kashmir neolithic at both its excavated sites—Gufkral and Burzahom (Pande 1970; Kaw 1979). This has further been divided into two sub-phases. The use of dwelling pits continues, and among other distinguishing traits should be listed a wide range of bone and polished stone tools, a type of pierced rectangular stone 'harvester' with a wide and non-specific distribution pattern in central Asia and China and the addition of common pea (*Pisum arvense*) and domestic cattle and fowl (*Gallus*) to the subsistence base. In the succeeding phase there is further evidence of mud and mudbrick houses, wheelmade pottery, some miscellaneous copper objects including a spiral-headed copper pin and primary and secondary human burials which are occasionally associated with dogs. A rather purposeful burial of animals like the dog, wolf and ibex is another distinctive feature. A stone slab with a stylized hunting scene engraved on it which has been found in this phase might have been derived from the earlier one. This is also the phase which has yielded a horned deity design and about 950 agate and carnelian beads. The neolithic phase in Kashmir merged into a menhir-using megalithic phase around the middle of the second millennium BC (A.K. Sharma 1991).

Northeast Rajasthan

I have already referred to the Ganeshwar culture of this area and its significance as a copper metallurgical centre from the pre-/early Harappan stage onwards. I also argued that the development of such a major metallurgical centre in this area during this period could be one of the factors leading to the intensification of craft industries in the early Harappan context. However, this area maintained its pre-eminence as a centre of copper metallurgy not merely in the subsequent mature and late Harappan stages but also in the neolithic-chalcolithic context outside the Harappan orbit. To begin with, the sites of this culture are concentrated in the Sikar district of northeast Rajasthan, with only two or three reported occurrences in the neighbouring areas of Jhunjhunu and Jaipur. J.P. Joshi, Bala and Ram (1984) listed 48 sites in the Sikar district and plotted them in their map of pre-Harappan sites. Ten more sites, the names of which do not figure in the 1984 list, have been reported in IAR 1981–82 and 25 sites were added to the list of IAR 1987–88, 17 of them in Sikar and

8 of them in Jaipur. These sites are primarily in the Baleshwar and Khetri copper deposit areas which are strewn with traces of old copper workings. There are many reasons to link this area with the Harappan civilization as a major supplier of copper. Harappan pottery has been reported on the surface at two 'Ganeshwar' sites and at the site of Ganeshwar itself there is 'reserved slip ware' of a type which has been found only in the Indus context (for these sherds, see Agrawala and Kumar 1982). Apart from this direct ceramic evidence, Ganeshwar-type arrowheads have been found in the Harappan contexts at Banawali and elsewhere, and equally significant is the fact that double spiral-headed copper pins from Ganeshwar occur at some Harappan sites. It is interesting to observe that the flat and heavy (up to 1.8 kg in weight) pure copper axes that one finds at Nagwada and Surkotada (the analysed specimen from Nagwada has a bevelled cutting edge whereas the Surkotada specimen has a crescentic and sharp cutting edge (cf. Shesadri 1992) are very much like the reported Ganeshwar specimens (Agrawala and Kumar 1982). R.C. Agrawala who first excavated Ganeshwar has traced the copper finds which have apparent links with this area in different parts of Rajasthan, Malwa and the area stretching from Ganeshwar to Haryana and the doab.

Right from the first phase of work at this site by R.C. Agrawala (Agrawala and Kumar 1982) the sheer quantity (about 1000 objects) and variety (arrowheads, spearheads, fish-hooks, celts, spiral-headed pins) were impressive. Another significant aspect was the co-existence of microliths at the site. Both these aspects have been elaborated in the post-Agrawala phases of work in 1981–83, 1983–83 and 1987–88. In 1981–82 three structural phases were reported from this context along with a highly evolved geometric microlithic industry of quartz, chert, jasper, garnet and chalcedony, stone and bone beads, querns, mullers, pestles, and an ochre-coloured pottery with paintings on the rim, neck and shoulder. The copper finds included arrowheads, spearheads, chisels, fishhooks, rings, hairpins and bangles. In 1983–84 almost the same types of metal finds were reported, with the addition of razor blades and antimony rods. A thin dull red pottery with paintings in black and white strokes was considered similar to the pre-/early Harappan Sothi pottery. References were also made to a sturdy red-slipped ware with painting between the rim and the shoulder and to vases fitted with vertical handles. Microliths were found and so were mud platforms with partitions, storage pits, floors with post-holes, and animal bones including those of cattle, fish, fowl, sheep, goat, etc.

The sequence of the site was understood only in 1987–88. The first phase showed a microlithic industry of quartz and chert and animal bones which were found mostly in a charred state and belonged, perhaps exclusively, to wild animals. The second phase witnessed the appearance of copper in a limited quantity (5 arrowheads, 3 fish-hooks, 1 spearhead and 1 awl), structural remains in the form of circular hut outlines and floors paved with pebbles and rock-fragments and 'partly handmade and partly wheelmade' pottery. Microliths and animal bones occurred in good number. The pottery of micaceous clay, with a bright red slip was ill-fired. There is, however, reference to 'a small number of sherds' made of well-levigated clay and well-fired. One is not sure if these sherds were wheel-made or if the pottery forms such as narrow and wide-mouthed jars and small squat 'handis', belonged to the latter type or the earlier one. There was no painted pottery. Period III yielded several hundred copper objects (arrowheads, rings, bangles, spearheads, chisels, balls, celts, etc.), a lesser quantity of microliths and animal bones, and a wide range of pottery (goblets, beakers, tumblers, handled bowls, elliptical vases, cylindrical vases, lids, jars, offering stands, dishes, basins and 'miscellaneous types of pottery of pre-Harappan affinity'. As the excavators, P.L. Chakravarty and Vijay Kumar (IAR 1987–88: 102) put it, 'the evidence of Phase III at Ganeshwar has added a new horizon to the pre-Harappan technology'.

In view of the data furnished above, the significance of northeast Rajasthan as a copper mining and working area should be obvious. Ganeshwar, if one remembers correctly, should not be more than 3/4 acres, and according to the published reports this has already yielded about 2000 copper objects. When one remembers that there are published reports of eighty such sites, the possible scale of this copper mining and working strikes us forcefully. Finally, it is indeed curious that in no report on the excavations at Ganeshwar is there any reference to the actual evidence of copper-smelting in the form of furnaces, crucibles, etc. Much work needs to be done on the archaeology of this region. There are many old copper workings in the Baleshwar valley, and these workings also deserve careful study.

Southeast Rajasthan

Of the chalcolithic group in southeast Rajasthan, a gneissic plain drained by the Banas, Berach and their tributaries, only two sites have been excavated so far—the type-site Ahar (Sankalia et al. 1969; for the earlier work by R.C. Agrawala, see IAR 1954–55: 14–15, IAR 1955–56: 14) and Gilund (IAR 1959–60: 41–6). Sites which belong to the Ahar or Banas culture, which now number more than ninety (Hooja 1988), occur in the districts of Udaipur, Chitorgarh, Bhilwara, Ajmer, Jaipur and Tonk in Rajasthan and Mandasore in Madhya Pradesh. On the basis of a decline in the number of designs on its diagnostic ceramic trait, a black-and-red ware, it has been postulated that the general movement of the culture was from 'southwest to northeast up the course of the Berach and the Banas' (Misra 1967: 148).

Rima Hooja's study shows that the Ahar sites 'were located along rivers, ranged in size from a couple of acres to over 10 acres, were frequently sited within five to ten miles of each other, and pre-empted later period agricultural settlements in their choice of locale' (Hooja 1988: 75). However, it must be admitted that both Ahar and Gilund measured more than 10 ha. The mound at Ahar is 1500 ft by 800 ft (27.5 acres/about 11 ha.) with the possibility of having been considerably eroded previously, while the mound at Gilund measures 800 by 250 yards (*c.* 10.5 ha.).

The bulk of the structural evidence comes from Ahar which has fifteen building phases. The ordinary houses were of mud and stone, 'stone' meaning locally available schist blocks used only as foundation. The walls were strengthened either by bamboo screens or quartz-nodules, and the roofs were probably sloping. The floors were of black clay mixed with yellow silt, occasionally paved with gravel from the river-bed. No complete house-plan is available but at Ahar one house was about 33 ft 10 ins (10.31 m) long, partitioned off by a mud wall. The ovens associated with the houses were multiple-mouthed and represent a type which is still in use in the region. In the earliest structural sub-period at Gilund, a large mudbrick complex, the purpose of which remains uncertain, has an exposed area of 100 ft by 80 ft (30.48 m by 24.38 m). In Gilund-2, sub-period C, five circular or oblong pits, 3 ft to 4 ft 4 ins (0.91 m to 1.32 m) along the major axis, may be storage pits. Another interesting structural evidence comes from the 'middle levels' of Gilund-3 where a burnt-brick wall (36 ft by 1 ft 10 ins or 10.97 m by 0.55 m, incompletely exposed) with bricks of 14 ins (0.35 m) by 6 ins (0.15 m) by 5 ins (0.12 m) were found laid over a stone-rubble foundation.

The diagnostic ceramic trait was a black-and-red ware with a variety of linear and dotted designs in white. Besides this there were cream-slipped, buff, blotchy grey, red-slipped ware and a limited quantity of lustrous red (western India) and Jorwe (north Deccan) wares at Ahar, and plain and painted black burnished grey and red wares at Gilund. At Gilund, there was also a polychrome ware with black, bright red and white paint on a red background.

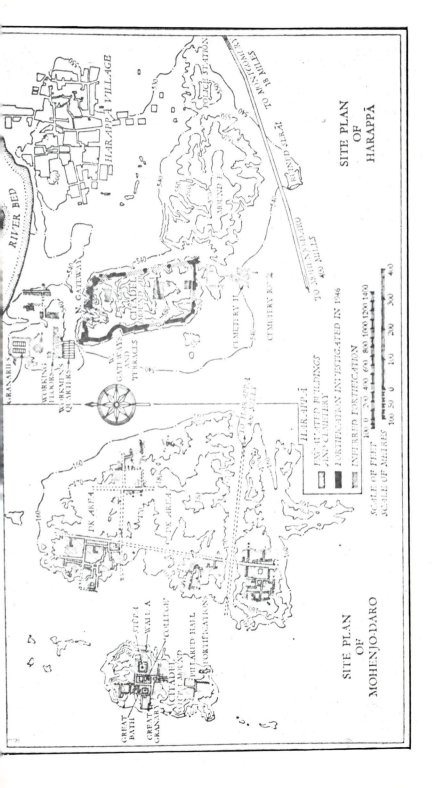

SITE PLAN OF MOHENJO-DARO

GREAT BATH
GREAT GRANARY
STUPA
WALL A
COLLEGE
CITADEL MOUND
PILLARED HALL
FORTIFICATIONS

DK AREA
DK AREA
HR AREA

HAR-402-1
EXCAVATED BUILDINGS AND CEMETERY
FORTIFICATION INVESTIGATED IN 1946
INFERRED FORTIFICATION

SCALE OF FEET
100 50 0 100 200 400 600 800 1000 1200 1400
SCALE OF METRES
100 0 100 200 300 400

SITE PLAN OF HARAPPĀ

RIVER BED

HARAPPĀ VILLAGE

N. GATEWAY
GRANARIES
WORKING FLOORS
WORKMEN'S QUARTERS
GATEWAYS AND TERRACES
CITADEL MOUND
CEMETERY H
CEMETERY R 37
MOUND F

BUND SARĀ

TO MONTGOMERY 18 MILES

TO MULTAN(?) 480 MILES
TO SUKKUR(?) 400 MILES

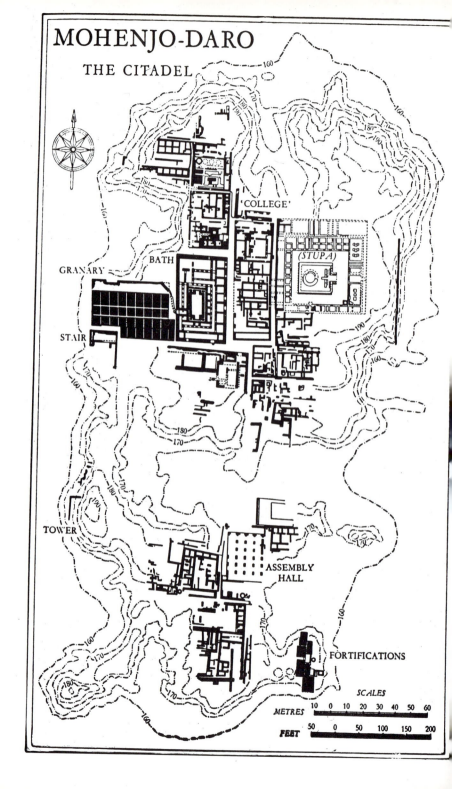

MOHENJO-DARO
THE CITADEL

'COLLEGE'

BATH

GRANARY

STAIR

(STUPA)

TOWER

ASSEMBLY HALL

FORTIFICATIONS

SCALES

METRES 10 0 10 20 30 40 50 60

FEET 50 0 50 100 150 200

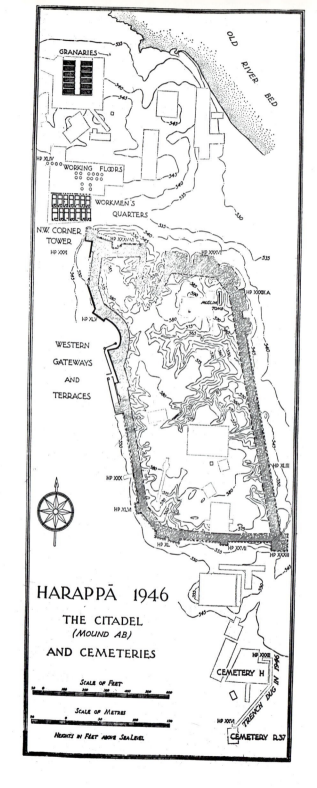

OLD RIVER BED

GRANARIES

HP XLIV

WORKING FLOORS

WORKMEN'S
QUARTERS

N.W. CORNER
TOWER

HP XXXI

HP XXXVII

HP XXXVI

HP XXXIX A

MUSLIM
TOMB

HP XLV

WESTERN

GATEWAYS

AND

TERRACES

HP XLIII

HP XXX

HP XLVI

HP XL

HP XXVII

HP XXXVIII

HARAPPĀ 1946

THE CITADEL
(MOUND AB)

AND CEMETERIES

HP XXXII

CEMETERY H

TRENCH DUG IN 1946

HP XXVI

CEMETERY R.37

SCALE OF FEET

SCALE OF METRES

HEIGHTS IN FEET ABOVE SEA LEVEL

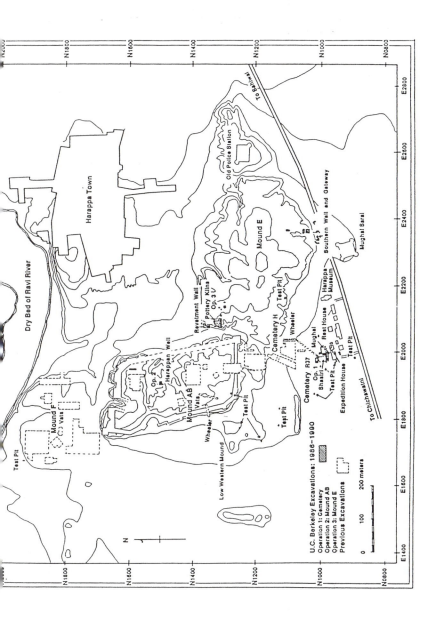

U.C. Berkeley Excavations: 1986–1990
Operation 1: Cemetery
Operation 2: Mound AB
Operation 3: Mound E
Previous Excavations

0   100   200 meters

N

Dry Bed of Ravi River

Harappa Town

Test Pit

Mound F

CJ Vats

Low Western Mound

Wheeler

Test Pit

Test Pit

Mound AB

CJ Vats

Harappan Well

Op. 2

Revetment Wall

Pottery Kilns
Op. 3 V

Mound E

Old Police Station

Cemetery H

Wheeler

Test Pit

Cemetery R37

Op. 1
Bhasin

Mughal

Test Pit

Rest House

Harappa
Museum

Southern Wall and Gateway

Mughal Sarai

Expedition House

Test Pit

To Chichawatni

To Sahiwal

N2000
N1800
N1600
N1400
N1200
N1000
N0800

E1400   E1600   E1800   E2000   E2200   E2400   E2500   E2800

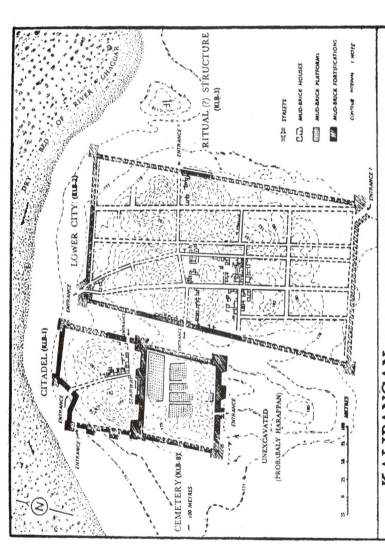

KALIBAŊGAN: HARAPPAN SETTLEMENT, PERIOD II

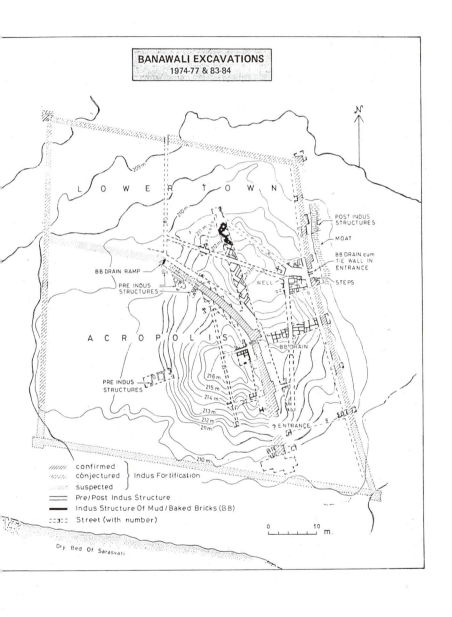

BANAWALI EXCAVATIONS
1974-77 & 83-84

N

L O W E R   T O W N

POST INDUS
STRUCTURES

MOAT

BB DRAIN cum
TIE WALL IN
ENTRANCE

BB DRAIN RAMP

PRE INDUS
STRUCTURES

WELL

STEPS

A C R O P O L I S

BB DRAIN

PRE INDUS
STRUCTURES

216 m
215 m
214 m
213 m
212 m
211 m

? ENTRANCE

210 m

///// confirmed
:::::: conjectured } Indus Fortification
::::: suspected

═══ Pre/Post Indus Structure

━━━ Indus Structure Of Mud / Baked Bricks (BB)

:::::: Street (with number)

0   50
|___|___|___|___| m.

Dry Bed Of Sarasvati

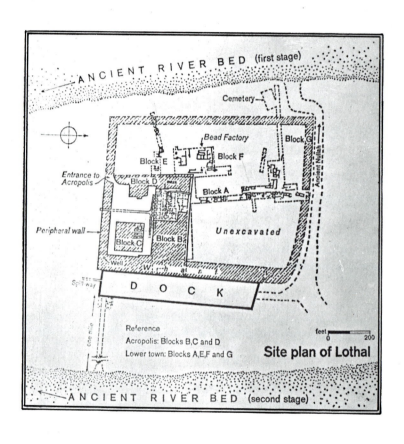

ANCIENT RIVER BED (first stage)

Cemetery

Block G

Bead Factory

Block F

Block E

Entrance to
Acropolis

Block D

Ancient Nullah

Block A

Peripheral wall

Unexcavated

Block C

Block B

Well

Spill way

D O C K

one mile

Reference
Acropolis: Blocks B,C and D
Lower town: Blocks A,E,F and G

feet
0   200

Site plan of Lothal

ANCIENT RIVER BED (second stage)

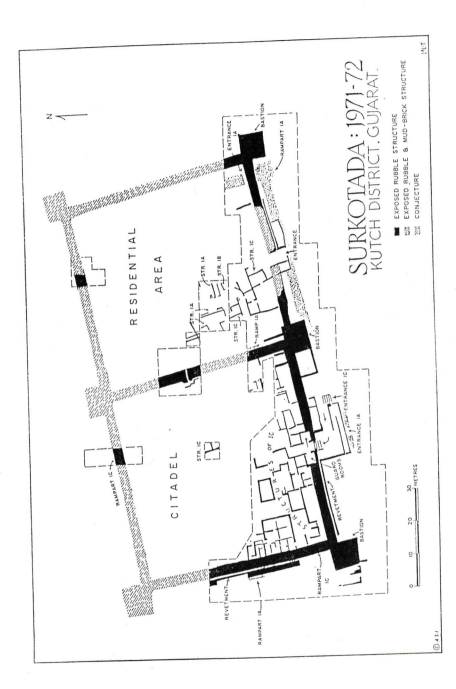

SURKOTADA : 1971-72
KUTCH DISTRICT, GUJARAT.

■ EXPOSED RUBBLE STRUCTURE
▨ EXPOSED RUBBLE & MUD-BRICK STRUCTURE
▨ CONJECTURE

RESIDENTIAL
AREA

CITADEL

STR. IA
STR. IB
STR. IC
RAMP. IA
STR. IC

ENTRANCE
IA
BASTION
RAMPART IA

ENTRANCE

BASTION

RAMPART IC

STR. IC

STRUCTURES OF IC

REVETMENT
GUARD ROOMS
ENTRANCE IC
ENTRANCE IA

BASTION

RAMPART IC
REVETMENT

RAMPART IA
REVETMENT

N

0   10   20   30
METRES

IALT

© ASI

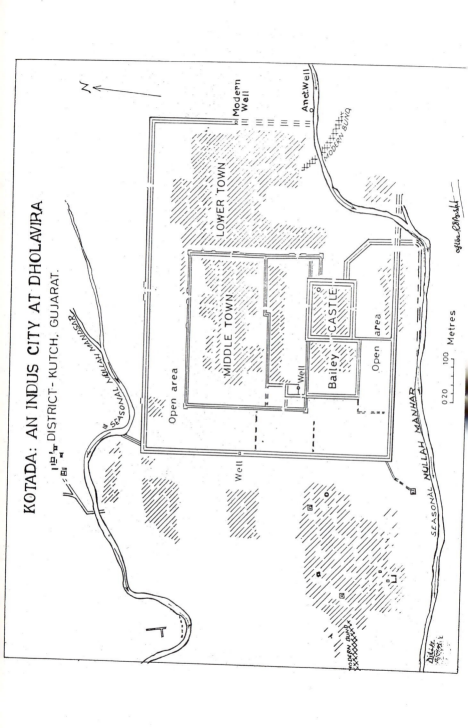

KOTADA: AN INDUS CITY AT DHOLAVIRA
DISTRICT- KUTCH. GUJARAT.

N

SEASONAL NULLAH MANSAR

Modern Well

Anct Well

MODERN BUND

LOWER TOWN

Open area

MIDDLE TOWN

Well

Open area

Bailey CASTLE

Well

SEASONAL NULLAH MANHAR

MODERN BUND

after R.S.Bisht

0 20   100   Metres

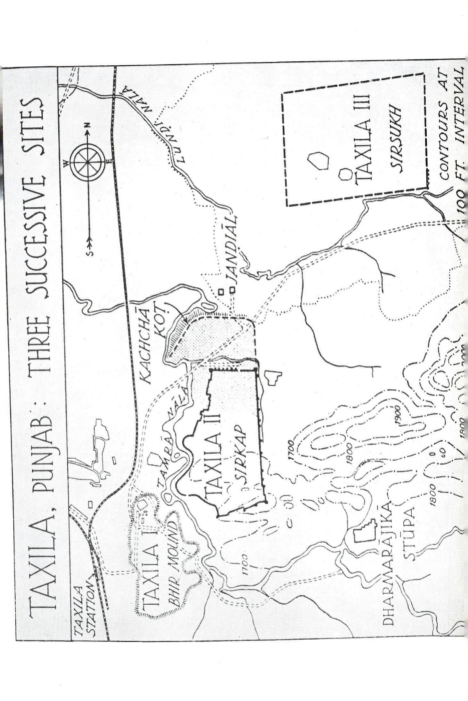

TAXILA, PUNJAB : THREE SUCCESSIVE SITES

N

TAXILA STATION

LUNDI NALA

KACHCHA KOT

JANDIAL

TAXILA I
BHIR MOUND

TAMRA NALA

TAXILA II
SIRKAP

TAXILA III
SIRSUKH

CONTOURS AT 100 FT. INTERVAL

DHARMARAJIKA STUPA

1700
1800
1900
1800
1700
1800

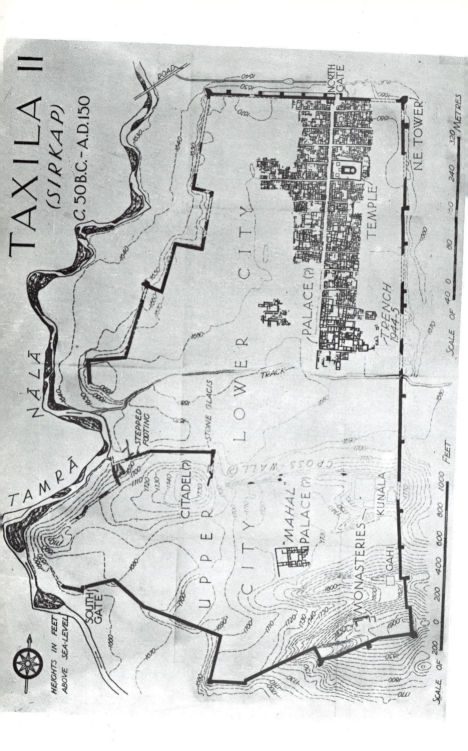

TAXILA II
(SIRKAP)
C.50 B.C. – A.D.150

NĀLĀ

TAMRĀ

ROAD

NORTH GATE

N.E. TOWER

TEMPLE

PALACE (?)

TRENCH 1944-5

LOWER CITY

CITADEL (?)

STEPPED FOOTING

STONE GLACIS

TRACK

CROSS WALL

UPPER CITY

"MAHAL" PALACE (?)

KUNALA

MONASTERIES

GHAI

SOUTH GATE

HEIGHTS IN FEET
ABOVE SEA-LEVEL

SCALE OF 200   0   200   400   600   800   1000 FEET

SCALE OF   40   0   80   160   240   320 Metres

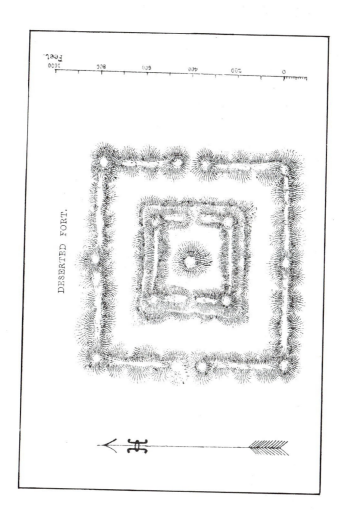

DESERTED FORT.

Feet.
0   200   400   600   800   1000

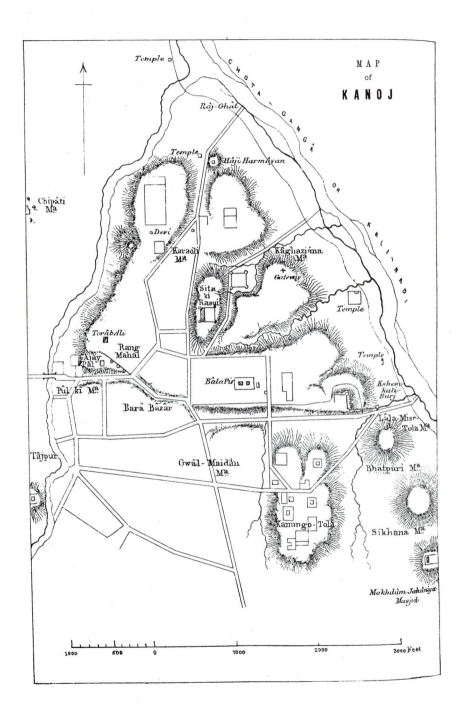

MAP
of
KANOJ

Temple

Râj-Ghât

CHOTA - GANGÂ OR KALI - NADI

Temple

Hâji Harmûyan

Chipâti Mâ

Devi

Karaôli Mâ

Kâghazïana Mâ

Gateway

Sïta ki Rasui

Temple

TorâbÂli

Rang Mahal

Ajay Pâl

Temple

Pûl ki Mâ

Bâla Pïr

Kshem kali Kurï

Barâ Bazar

Lâla Misr Tola Mâ

Tâjpur

Gwâl - Maidân Mâ

Bhatpuri Mâ

Kamungo-Tola

Sikhana Mâ

Mukhdûm Jahâniya Masjid

1000   500   0   1000   2000   3000 Feet

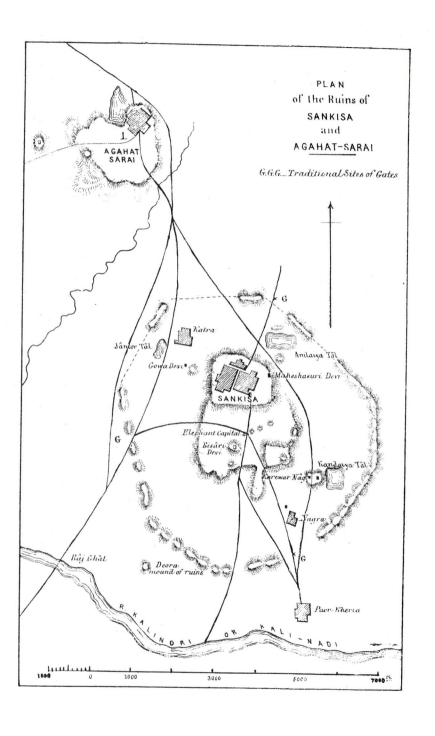

PLAN
of the Ruins of
SANKISA
and
AGAHAT–SARAI

G.G.G._ Traditional Sites of Gates

AGAHAT
SARAI

G

Katra

Jânior Tâl

Gowa Devi

Amlaiya Tâl

Maheshasuri Devi

SANKISA

G

Elephant Capital

Bisâri Devi

Kandaiya Tâl

Karewar Nag

Nagra

G

Râj Ghât

Deora
mound of ruins

Paer-Kheria

R. KALINDRI OR KALI–NADI

1000   0   1000   3000   5000   7000 ft.

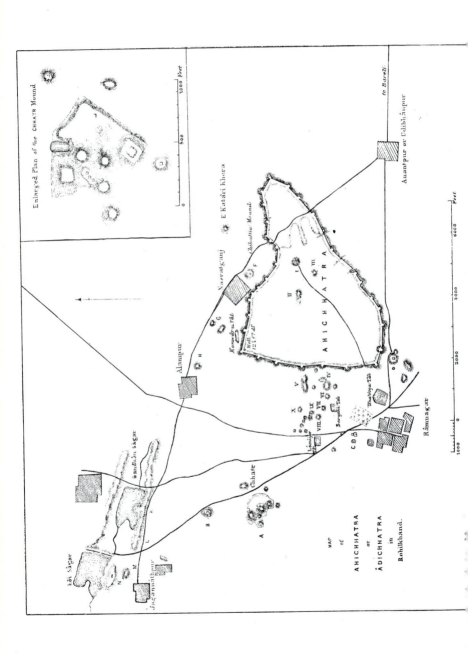

Enlarged Plan of the CHHATR Mound

MAP
of
AHICHHATRA
or
ÂDICHHATRA
in
Rohilkhand.

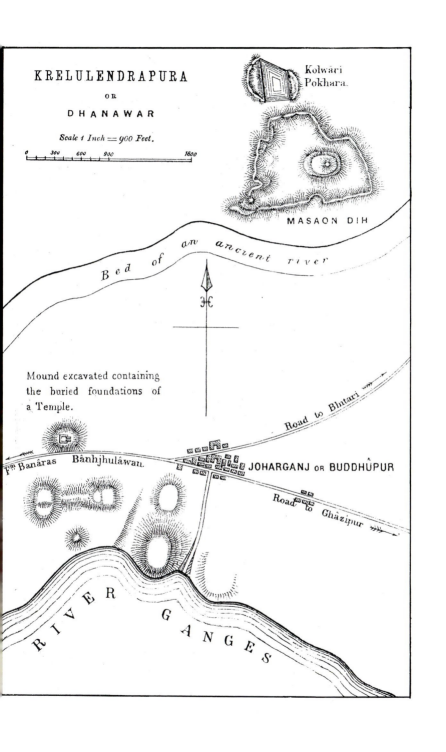

KRELULENDRAPURA

OR

DHANAWAR

Scale 1 Inch = 900 Feet.

0   300   600   900   1600

Kolwari
Pokhara.

MASAON DIH

Bed of an ancient river

Mound excavated containing
the buried foundations of
a Temple.

Fᵐ Banáras   Bánhjhuláwau.

JOHARGANJ OR BUDDHÛPUR

Road to Bhitari

Road to Ghâzipur

RIVER GANGES

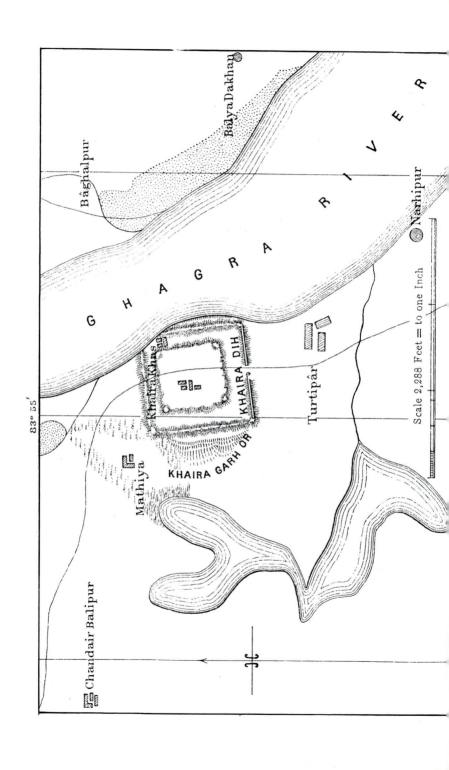

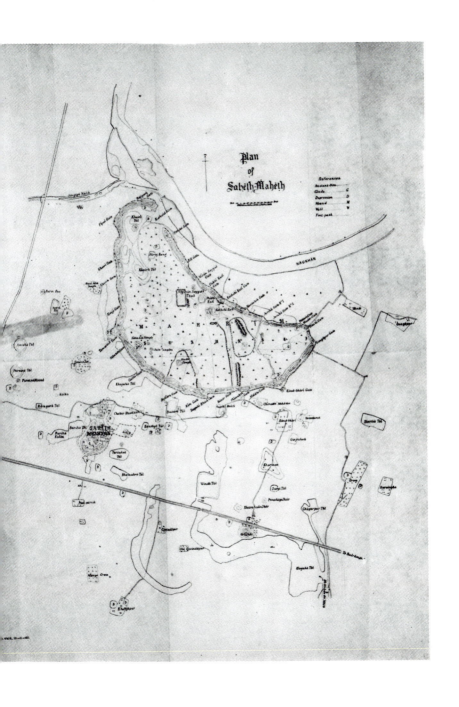

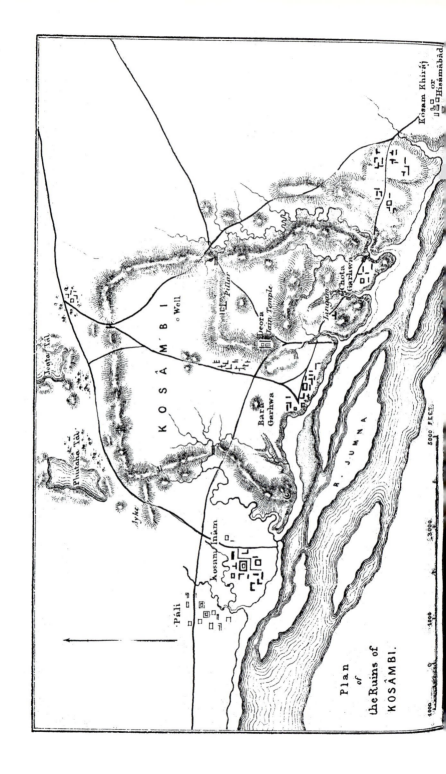

Plan
of
the Ruins of
KOSÁMBI.

Kosam Khiráj
or
Hisámábád

Chota
Garhwa

Jaitham

Well

Pillar

Teora
Jain Temple

Bará
Garhwa

R. JUMNA

Kosam Inám

Páli

Ayke

Pakoha Tál

Tontu Tál

K O S Á M B I

1000   0   1000   2000   5000 FEET

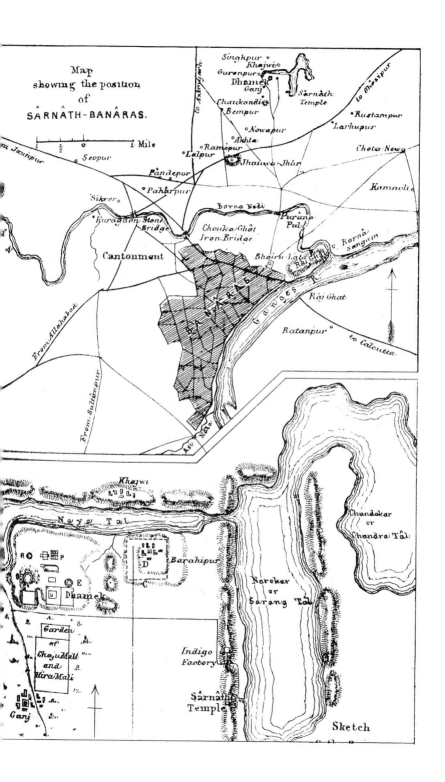

Map
showing the position
of
SÂRNÂTH-BANÂRAS.

½ 0 1 Mile

Singhpur
Khajwi
Guronpur
Dhamek
Ganj
Chaukandi
Bempur
Sârnâth
Temple
Rustampur
Larhupur
Nowapur
Akhta
Ramepur
Chota Newa
Lalpur
Jhaiwa Jhân
Kamauli
Pândepur
Seopur
from Jaunpur
to Azimgarh
to Ghazipur
Sikror
Pahârpur
Barna Nadi
Puruna
Pul
Kuraghon Stone
Bridge
Chouka Ghât
Iron Bridge
c. Barnâ
Sangam
Cantonment
Bhairo La
Raj Ghât
BANÂRAS
Ganges R.
Raj Ghât
From Allahabad
From Sultanpur
Ratanpur
to Calcutta
Asi Nâla

Khajwi
Naya Tal
Chandokar
or
Chandra Tâl
R
P
D
Barahipur
A
E
C
Dhamek
Narokar
or
Sarang Tâl
Garden
of
Chaju Mall
and
Hira Mali
Indigo
Factory
Ganj
Sârnâth
Temple
Sketch

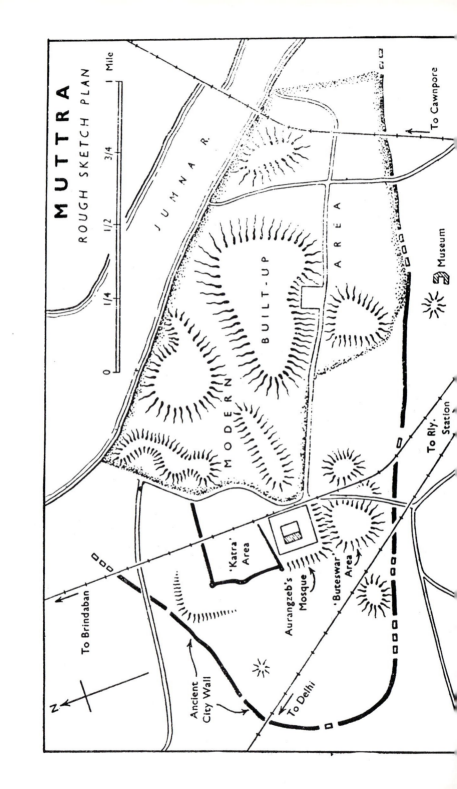

MUTTRA
ROUGH SKETCH PLAN

0   1/4   1/2   3/4   1 Mile

JUMNA R.

BUILT-UP

MODERN

AREA

To Cawnpore

Museum

To Rly. Station

'Katra' Area

Aurangzeb's Mosque

'Buteswar' Area

To Delhi

Ancient City Wall

To Brindaban

N

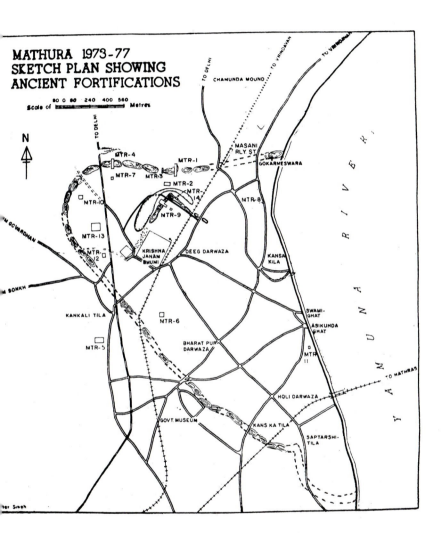

MATHURA 1973-77
SKETCH PLAN SHOWING
ANCIENT FORTIFICATIONS

Scale of [scale bar] Metres
80 0 80 240 400 560

N

TO DELHI
TO VRINDAVAN
TO VRINDAVAN
CHAMUNDA MOUND
TO DELHI
MTR-4
MTR-1
MASANI RLY ST.
GOKARNESWARA
MTR-7
MTR-3
MTR-2
MTR-14
MTR-10
MTR-8
MTR-9
TO GOVARDHAN
MTR-13
R
I
V
E
R.
KRISHNA JANAM BHUMI
DEEG DARWAZA
MTR-12
KANSA KILA
TO SONKH
Y
A
M
U
N
A
KANKALI TILA
MTR-6
SWAMI-GHAT
ASIKUNDA GHAT
MTR-5
BHARAT PUR DARWAZA
MTR-11
TO MATHRAS
HOLI DARWAZA
GOVT. MUSEUM
KANS KA TILA
SAPTARSHI-TILA
Y
A
M
U
N
A
R.

ter Singh

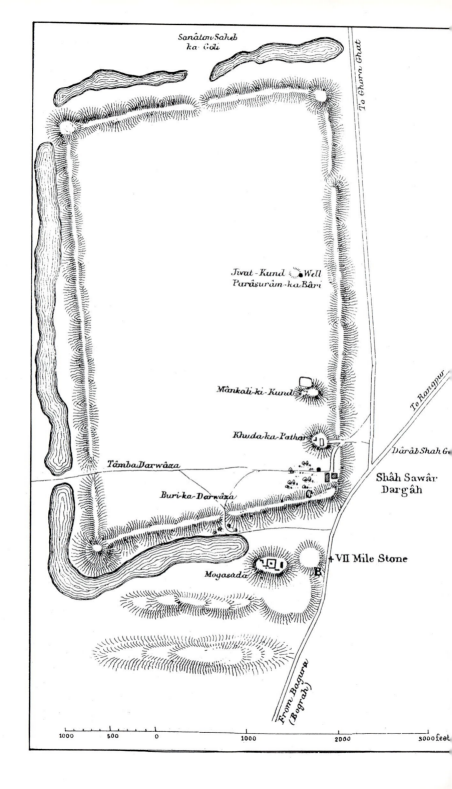

Sanâtan Saheb
ka Gôli

To Ghora Ghat

Jivat - Kund   •Well
Parâsurâm-ka Bâri

To Rangpur

Mânkali-ki-Kund

Khuda-ka-Pathar

Dârâb Shah G.

Tâmba Darwâza

Buri-ka-Darwâza

Shâh Sawâr
Dargâh

C

VII Mile Stone

Mogasada

B

From Bagura
(Bograh)

| 1000 | 500 | 0 | 1000 | 2000 | 3000 feet |

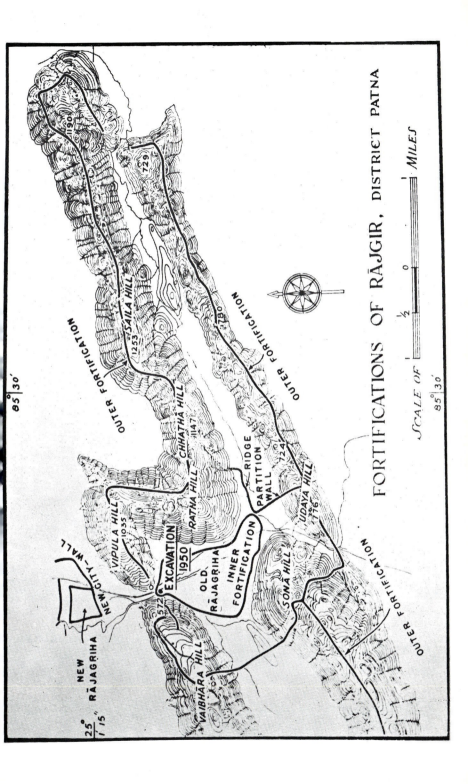

FORTIFICATIONS OF RĀJGIR, DISTRICT PATNA

SCALE OF
½   0   1
                MILES

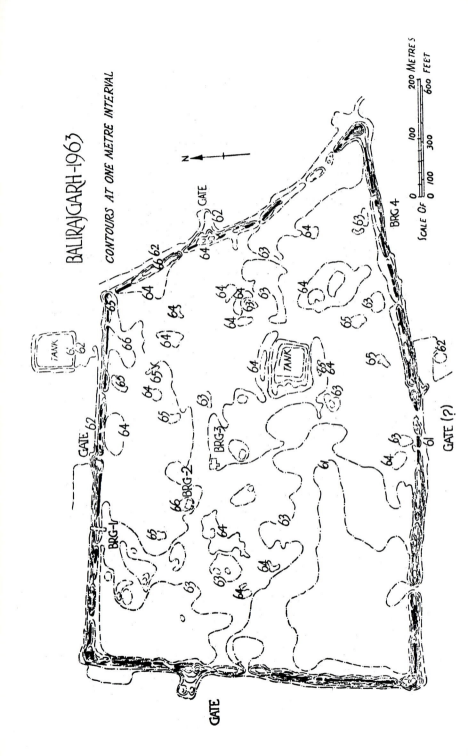

BALIRAJGARH-1963

CONTOURS AT ONE METRE INTERVAL

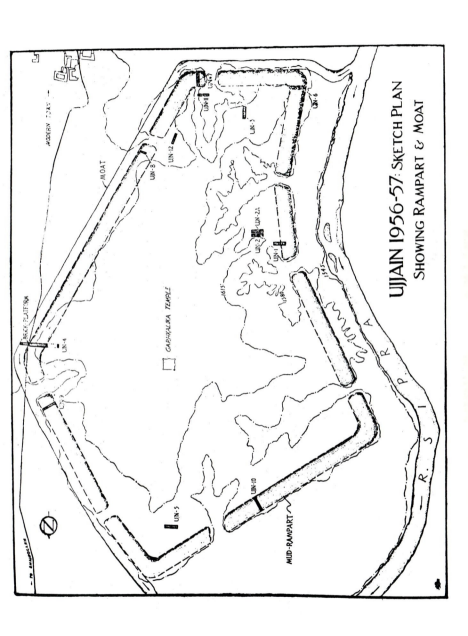

UJJAIN 1956-57: SKETCH PLAN
SHOWING RAMPART & MOAT

MODERN TOWN

MOAT

UJN·7
UJN·11
UJN·3
UJN·6
UJN·8
UJN·12
UJN·2A
UJN·2
UJN·1
1615
1590
BRICK PLATFORM
GARHKALIKA TEMPLE
UJN·4
UJN·10
UJN·5
MUD-RAMPART
K S I P R A
TO BHARTRIHARI

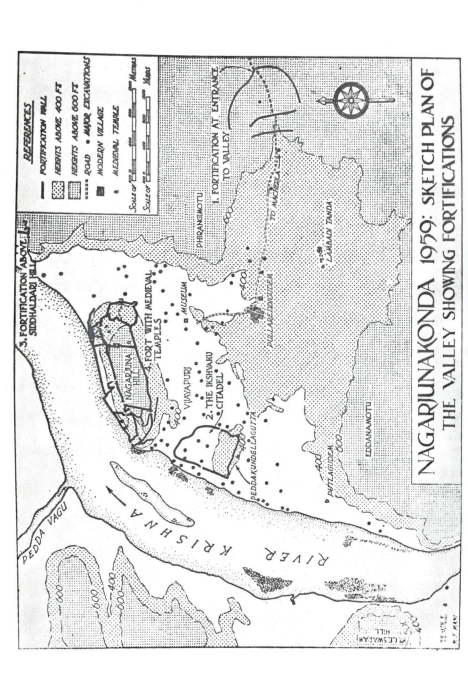

REFERENCES
FORTIFICATION WALL
HEIGHTS ABOVE 400 FT
HEIGHTS ABOVE 600 FT
ROAD ● MAJOR EXCAVATIONS
■ MODERN VILLAGE
♦ MEDIEVAL TEMPLE

Scale of
Scale of

1. FORTIFICATION AT ENTRANCE TO VALLEY

3. FORTIFICATION ABOVE SIDDHALADRI HILL

4. FORT WITH MEDIEVAL TEMPLES

2. THE IKSHVAKU CITADEL

NAGARJUNA HILL

VIJAYAPURI

MUSEUM

PEDDAKUNDELLAGUTTA

PHIRANGIMOTU

PULLAREDDIGUDEM

LAMBADI TANDA

TO MACHERLA

PUTLAGUDEM

EDDANAMOTU

RIVER KRISHNA

PEDDA VAGU

VILLESWARAM HILL

NAGARJUNAKONDA 1959: SKETCH PLAN OF
THE VALLEY SHOWING FORTIFICATIONS

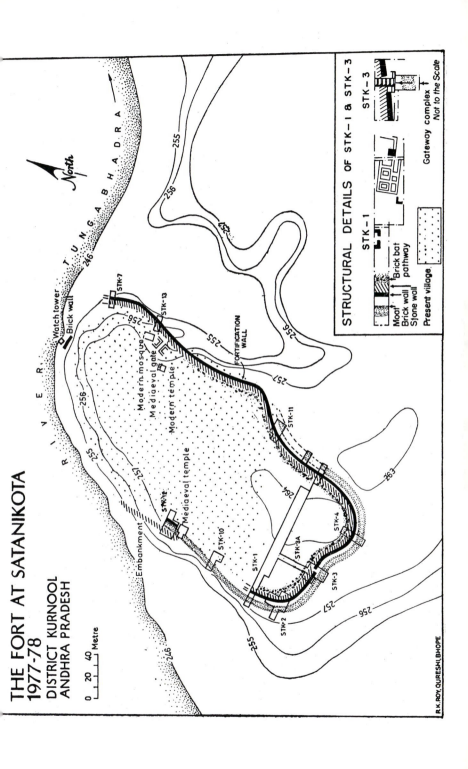

THE FORT AT SATANIKOTA
1977-78

DISTRICT KURNOOL
ANDHRA PRADESH

0 20 40 Metre

North

T U N G A B H A D R A

R I V E R

Watch tower
Brick wall

246

256

255

STK-7

256

STK-13

255

Modern mosque
Mediaeval gate
Modern temple

256

255

255

Mediaeval temple

257

Embankment

STK-12

STK-10

STK-1

STK-2

STK-3

STK-3A

STK-4

STK-11

264

FORTIFICATION
WALL

257

256

255

256

263

257

256

255

STRUCTURAL DETAILS OF STK–1 & STK–3

STK–1

STK–3

Moat
Brick wall
Stone wall

Brick bat
pathway

Present village

Gateway complex

Not to the Scale

R.K.ROY, QURESHI, BHOPE

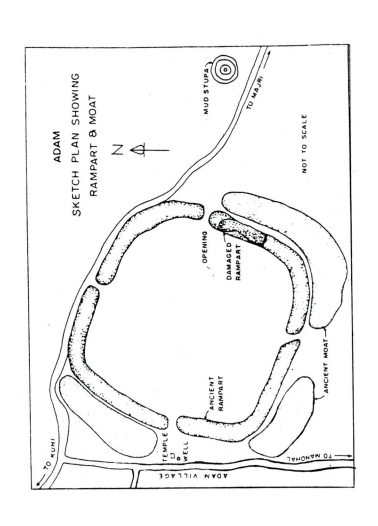

ADAM

SKETCH PLAN SHOWING
RAMPART & MOAT

N

MUD STUPA

TO MAJRI

NOT TO SCALE

OPENING

DAMAGED
RAMPART

ANCIENT MOAT

ANCIENT
RAMPART

TO KUHI

TEMPLE
WELL

ADAM VILLAGE

TO MANDHAL

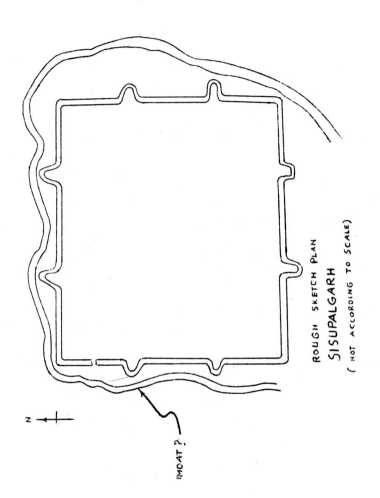

N

ROUGH SKETCH PLAN

SISUPALGARH

(NOT ACCORDING TO SCALE)

MOAT ?

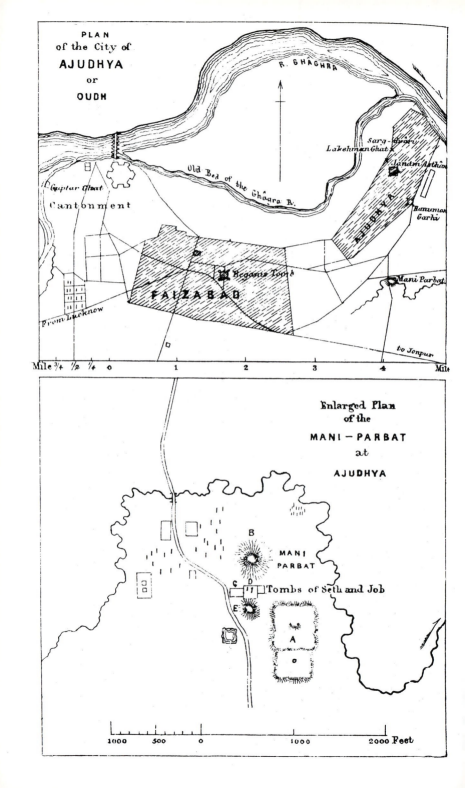

PLAN
of the City of
AJUDHYA
or
OUDH

R. GHAGHRA

Sarg-dwári
Lakshman Ghat
Janam Asthán

AJUDHYA

Old Bed of the Ghágra R.

Guptar Ghat

Cantonment

Hanuman
Garhi

Begams Toomb

Mani Parbat

FAIZABAD

From Lucknow

to Jonpur

Mile ¾ ½ ¼ 0 · · · · · 1 · · · · · 2 · · · · · 3 · · · · · 4 Mile

Enlarged Plan
of the
MANI – PARBAT
at
AJUDHYA

B

MANI
PARBAT

C D
Tombs of Seth and Job

E

A

o

1000 · · · · 500 · · · · 0 · · · · · · · · 1000 · · · · · · · · 2000 Feet

The Ahar excavations in 1961–62 did not yield microliths but the earlier excavations at the site did. Copper was plentiful: rings, bangles, antimony rods, a knife-blade and four socket-less axes. That copper was smelted locally at Ahar has been suggested by the discovery of copper sheet and slag. Gilund yielded both microliths and fragments of copper. Saddle querns and beads of semi-precious stone (including one of lapis lazuli from Ahar) occur at both the sites. There are terracotta beads or spindle-whorls, of biconical or areca-nut shape, with incised decorations at Ahar, and terracotta animal figurines and gamesmen including bulls with prominent humps and long horns at Gilund. Among the crops, rice was definitely grown but it is doubtful whether millet was grown. The animal bones identified at Ahar are those of fish, turtle, fowl, cow, buffalo, goat, sheep, deer and pigs.

There is no radiocarbon date from Gilund but on the basis of the Ahar dates, the beginning of this culture may be placed at around 2500 BC. Perhaps the most significant aspect of the Ahar culture is its effective knowledge of copper metallurgy. It is possible that they were using locally available ores (Majumdar and Rajaguru 1963).

Copper in this area has also been reported from Period II at Bagor on the bank of a small non-perennial river called Kothari in the district of Bhilwara. Period I is microlithic while Period III is iron-bearing. The cultural traits of Period II comprise pottery, mostly handmade but also wheelmade in a limited quantity, circular arrangement of stones, perhaps representing wattle huts protected at the base by stones, microliths which continued to be used from the earlier period but declined numerically towards the end, stone hammers, saddle querns and rubbers besides probable weights for digging sticks, animal bones (usually charred, broken and split open), beads of agate and carnelian, stone pendants and three complete inhumations which have yielded among the burial goods a number of copper objects (one spearhead, three arrowheads and one awl) and one terracotta spindle-whorl. The pottery is said to differ completely from the Ahar ceramic. The contemporaneity of, and interaction between, the settled chalcolithic communities represented by the sites of Ahar and Gilund and the microlith-using hunter-gatherers typified at Bagor have been noted by Hooja.

The raw materials listed at the Ahar culture sites in southeast Rajasthan comprise steatite, shell, agate, jasper, carnelian, lapis lazuli, copper/bronze and ordinary stones. The shell objects were locally manufactured, though the source of shell must have been the Gujarat coast. The occurrence of etched carnelian beads, a single bead of lapis lazuli and the

Rangpur-type lustrous red ware in Ahar IC all underline an element of connection with the Harappans in Gujarat. On the other hand, this culture expanded towards Malwa, with some links as far south as the Deccan (cf. the Jorwe ware of Maharashtra at Ahar). After the reported find of an iron object in the Harappan context at Lothal, the occurrence of iron as early as in Ahar Ib should no longer be in doubt (Chakrabarti 1992: 95).

Malwa

A sort of triangle based on the Vindhyas and drained by the Narmada, Chambal, Sipra, Betwa, Ken, Kali Sindh and others, the plateau of Malwa in central India has been described as 'a vast stretch of undulating plains, interspersed with curiously shaped flat-topped hills and covered with tenacious black soil—a very rich loamy earth possessing unusual power to retain moisture and renowned for its fertility' (Venkatachar 1933: 20). On account of its agricultural prosperity and the role it has played as a passage to west India and the Deccan from the Gangetic valley, Malwa has always been considered a significant region in Indian history.

The earliest phase of the growth of agriculture in the area is reflected at Kayatha (Ansari and Dhavalikar 1975, Wakankar 1982) near Ujjayini, Period I of which may be dated roughly to the second half of the third millennium BC. It possesses three distinct ceramic industries, all wheel-made, a number of copper axes and bangles, microliths including blades, points, crescents, and beads of crystal, agate, carnelian and steatite. Period II is characterized by an Ahar-type black-and-red ware while Period III represents a culture typified not merely at Kayatha but also at Navdatoli (Sankalia et al. 1958, 1971), Nagda (Banerjee 1966), Eran (Khare 1982), Avra (Trivedi 1982), Dangwada (Wakankar 1982, Giriraj Kumar 1982) and a few other comparatively minor sites. Among its excavated sites, Navdatoli, more adequately published than the rest, provides the index. It covers an area roughly 440 yards sq. (*c.* 400 m sq.). As early as in 1967 Wakankar (1982: pl. 25/1) could publish a map of more than 100 chalcolithic sites in Malwa.

The structural character of the chalcolithic settlement at Navdatoli is limited to wattle-and-daub circular and oblong houses. The diameter of the circular houses varied between 3 and 15 ft (*c.* 1 and 4.5 m). Only the larger ones were probably residential while the smaller ones could have served as stores for grain and hay. The rectangular structures were generally 5 to 6 m long. The floors and the walls were plastered with lime. The roofs were perhaps made of some sort of thatch. The evidence suggests that the chalcolithic village of Navdatoli was a nucleated settlement (with a passage between the houses) and by Sankalia's estimate, could have in the earliest phase an average of 200 inhabitants.

A somewhat different picture of the settlement comes from Eran. Surrounded on three sides by the river Bina, the prehistoric village of Eran was defended on the fourth side by a rampart and a ditch. Constructed in the 'middle' of the chalcolithic phase, the rampart had two phases. Its initial basal width of 30.48 m was subsequently increased to 45.82 m. No evidence of a rampart has been obtained at any other Malwa chalcolithic site, although this was once suggested in the case of Nagda.

The dominant pottery type was a black-on-red ware associated with other types like the black-and-red ware, white-slipped ware, etc. The shapes ranged from simple bowls to ornate goblets. Barring a few examples, the painted designs were geometric. The implements used were primarily microlithic blades comprising end-scrapers, long flakes, pen-knife blades, lunates, trapezes, borers, parallel-sided blades (with provisions for hafting in some, and occasionally serrated), etc. Evidence of copper is limited, although Navdatoli possesses copper flat axes, wire-rings, bangles, fishhooks, nail-parers, chisels, thick pins and a fragment of a midrib sword. Eran has yielded a thin gold piece. The miscellaneous objects of stone included saddle querns, rubbers, hammerstones, maceheads or weights for digging sticks, etc. Beads occur profusely and were made of diverse material. At Navdatoli alone they were of agate, amazonite, carnelian, chalcedony, faience, glass, jasper, lapis lazuli, steatite, shell and terracotta. Terracotta spindle whorls, animal figurines, etc. were also a part of the cultural assemblage. A number of crops were grown at Navdatoli: two varieties of wheat, linseed, lentil, black gram, green gram, green peas and khesari or *Lathyrus sativus*. Rice occurs only from Phase II onwards. The Malwa culture, as dated at Navdatoli, falls broadly in the first half of the second millennium BC.

The Malwa culture sites possess the following overall list of raw materials: steatite, shell, coral, ivory, jade, lapis, gold, copper/bronze and ordinary and semi-precious stones. Malwa was, as we have noted, closely linked with Rajasthan on the one hand and the Deccan on the other. But what is equally, if not more, interesting is the presence of the late Harappans in Malwa. Lustrous red ware has been reported at Dangwada (IAR 1981–82: 31–2), and the same issue of IAR draws attention to some late Harappan sites in this region. Much earlier, Wakankar (1982) found in the lowest levels of Manoti 'elongated Harappan jars, dish-on-stand and beaded necked storage jars'. Among the more interesting developments in the study of the chalcolithic cultures in Malwa is the evidence of fire-altars and perhaps temples at Dangwada which has also yielded evidence of bull worship and phallus worship in its chalcolithic stage.

On the fringe of Malwa the Tapti valley is a transitional zone between central India and north Deccan or Maharashtra. Two chalcolithic sites were earlier excavated in this area: Bahal-Tekwada (IAR 1956–57: 16–17) on the Girna and Prakash (Thapar 1964–65) at the confluence of the Tapti and Gomia. The wheelmade, painted black-on-red pottery of Bahal IB is preceded by a predominantly plain grey ware (Bahal IA) recalling the neolithic grey ware of south Deccan. Tekwada on the other side of the Girna yielded three urn-burials and one pit-burial. The first period of Prakash is chalcolithic too on the Bahal model.

Maharashtra

Maharashtra is one of the few areas of the country where the neolithic-chalcolithic context of the region has been worked out in great detail, and one may begin by recalling the first excavations on the Maharashtra chalcolithic at Nasik-Jorwe in 1950–51 (Sankalia and Deo 1955), which were followed by work at Nevasa in 1954–55 (Sankalia et al. 1960). For the present purpose I shall refer primarily to two recent reports, each in its own way invaluable for its comprehensive study: S.A. Sali's *Daimabad* 1976–79 (Sali 1966) and *Excavations at Inamgaon* by M.K. Dhavalikar, H.D. Sankalia and Z.D. Ansari (1988). For a general analytical survey of the total material, Dhavalikar's *The First Farmers of the Deccan* (Dhavalikar 1988) commands attention.

The initial settlement zone, as represented by the distribution of the Savalda culture sites is between the Tapti and the Godavari in north Maharashtra. The date should be around the end of the third and the beginning of the second millennia BC. On the basis of work at Kaothe (Dhavalikar, Shinde, Atre 1990), a 20 ha. site with a 50 cm thick occupation deposit, the Savalda culture has been interpreted as being that of a semi-nomadic community. This interpretation is partially based on the postulated similarity between the excavated house types at the site and those of the local semi-nomadic Dhangar community. In both cases the key element is that a sloping roof of thatch was put over a bunch of sticks which were tied together at the top and rested, in a sloping fashion, around a circular/oval pit-like floor in the case of the Savalda culture but around an ordinary circular, unplastered floor in the case of the Dhangar community. Bone-tools were profusely used at Kaothe, and cattle, buffalo, sheep/goat, pig and dog were domesticated, as well as some wild animals including different types of deer. Beads of shell, opal, carnelian and terracotta deserve notice and so do a variety of millets (*Pennisetum typhoides*) and two varieties of pulses (gram and moong). The ceramic components include a sturdy red ware with both geometric and naturalistic paintings. At Daimabad the area occupied by the Savalda culture measured about 3 ha. but the impression of semi-nomadism, as deduced at Kaothe is offset here by the presence of rectangular mud houses, copper, a microlithic blade industry, miscellaneous bone and stone objects, a limited number of beads of shell, carnelian, steatite and terracotta, a phallus made of agate and a large variety of grains—wheat, barley, pea, lentil, black gram and green gram. The intensity of occupation at the site during this period is indicated by the high phosphorus value of the deposit. In the plan of houses published by Sali (1986: 82) one notes that these houses, some of them as large as 7 m by 5 m and multi-roomed, were open on one side and contained in most cases hearths, storage pits and jars. In some cases they had courtyards in the front, and in one section a lane has been traced. For no apparent reason two houses have been labelled as a 'nobleman's house' and a 'priest's house'. The most prominent feature of the wheel-made Savalda ware is 'the paintings of weapon and tool motifs that have been executed on the surface of mostly thick and crackled slip of the pots' (Sali 1986: 21–2). From Kaothe the primary burials of both children and adults have been reported.

The basic locale of the late Harappans in Maharashtra was in the region occupied by the Savalda culture, i.e. between the Tapti and the Godavari-Pravara valleys. The presence of the Indus script (two terracotta button-shaped seals and four potsherds, all with the Indus script) at Daimabad has clinched the issue of its identification. At Daimabad it appears in the second phase of the site and comes to occupy an area as large as 20 ha. No complete house plan has been recovered from this phase, but one of the houses measured 6.5 m by 4.3 m. The existence of a street has been deduced and the thickness of the mud walls of the houses was 30–50 cm. A grave made of mud-bricks conforming to the standard Harappan ratio of 4:2:1 and containing a primary burial where the extended skeleton was covered by the reeds of a fibrous plant was found within the habitation area. A rich chalcedony and chert blade industry, extensive use of copper, if one takes into consideration the famous Daimabad hoard of copper animals and human figures (Dhavalikar 1982), beads, ivory pendant, fragments of a terracotta measuring scale, a highly weathered terracotta cake, miscellaneous stone objects, wheat, barley, lentil, pea and horse gram were among the other major components of this cultural level at Daimabad. The size of 20 ha. of this settlement at Daimabad contradicts Dhavalikar's statement (Dhavalikar 1988: 14) that the late Harappan settlements in Maharashtra were 'all small villages, each having a population of about 100–200 persons'.

The third period at Daimabad is represented by the 'Daimabad culture' which covered an area of about 20 ha. and had, as its diagnostic trait, ill-fired, black-painted red/buff/cream ware. Three burials of three types (pit burial, symbolic burial and post-cremation pot burial), a rich chalcedony and quartz blade industry, beads of carnelian, opal, agate, fine-grained red basalt, etc., copper slag, miscellaneous terracotta and stone objects, shell-bangles and a number of crops comprising wheat, barley, lentil, grass pea, horse gram, hyacinth bean, green gram and black gram comprised the other excavated materials.

The Malwa cultural phase constitutes the fourth period of the Daimabad sequence. This is also the general period when one notes the beginning of chalcolithic settlements in the Vidarbha region of Maharashtra (cf. the sites of Tuljapur Garhi in the Purna valley, part of the Tapti tributary system; IAR 1984–85: 48–50). Sali's description of the Malwa phase houses at Daimabad classifies them into craftsmen's houses (a coppersmith's house) and religious and residential establishments. A number of 'sacrificial altars' have been found in these mud-walled houses with well-plastered floors. About twenty Malwa houses were exposed at Inamgaon, and although built close together they were separated by a wide space of 1–2 m. 'They were all large rectangular (7 by 5 m) structures with a partition wall . . . a low mud wall and a gable roof. Inside there was a large oval fire pit with raised sides. . . . The grain was stored in deep pit silos (1 m diameter and 1 m deep) and also in bins of wicker work which were placed over circular mud platforms (1.5 m diameter). Some people, however, lived in round huts. . . . Those who were extremely poor lived in pit dwellings' (Dhavalikar 1988: 14). In addition to the lithic blade industry, evidence of copper metallurgy, and semi-precious stone beads, there were the remains of wheat, barley, ragi, lentil, horse gram, beans, hyacinth bean, black gram, green gram, etc. The burials of this phase, of which sixteen have been excavated, were urn burials and pit burials.

The settlement data of the succeeding Jorwe phase in Maharashtra have been closely studied by Dhavalikar (1988). At Daimabad the settlement size increased to 30 ha. Among the 200-odd reported Jorwe settlements, a vast majority were villages ranging from 1 to 3 ha. (population 200–600). Some were very small, 0.5–1 ha. in extent. Some of the small sites, located at a distance of about 2–3 km from the main village site, could be like the present *wadis* of Maharashtra, where, for the convenience of agricultural operations, two or more agriculturist families lived during the agricultural seasons while spending the summer at the main settlement.

The thatched wattle-and-daub houses of the Jorwe phase at Inamgaon vary between 5 m by 3 m and 7 m by 5 m, the larger ones being divided in most cases by partition walls.

Inside the house would be a small oval fire pit, sometimes with high clay walls to serve as a protection from wind, whereas outside in the courtyard invariably we come across a large oval fire pit (1 by 0.5 m) which was probably used for roasting hunted animals. Almost every fire pit has a flat stone in the centre at the bottom, which was daubbed with mud to serve as a support for the cooking vessel. Very often inside, but rarely outside also, there was a pit silo, 1 to 2 m in dia. and equally deep, and lined with lime for storing grain. In addition there was a round mud platform, with 1.5 m dia. and 10 cm high, which served to support a storage bin. The house floor was made of rammed clay with silt and fine sand spread in layers alternately and even the courtyard was well made. The domesticated animals, sheep/goat and cattle, were tethered in the courtyard as indicated by the nitrogen content of the soil (Dhavalikar 1988: 20).

In the late Jorwe phase, which Dhavalikar interprets as belonging to an arid phase, are found more circular houses and clusters of such houses with a common courtyard. What is singularly interesting is that in the early Jorwe phase at Inamgaon there is evidence of an irrigation channel (118 m long, 3.50 m deep and 4 m wide) and an embankment (2.40 m wide and 240 m long) to the west of the main habitation area. Dhavalikar (1988: 27) also suggests that both hand ploughs and seed drills were used in agriculture. Pottery kilns, gold ornaments, copper slag and crucibles, lime kilns, terracotta figurines which can be interpreted as gods and goddesses, some signs of animal and fire worship, extended burials for adults and urn burials for children, etc. complete the picture of chalcolithic village life we have in the Jorwe phase in Maharashtra. This phase is supposed to have come to an end around 1000 BC or later. The ceramic and other artifactual links of the chalcolithic Maharashtra phase have been cogently summarized by Lahiri (1992: 181):

The Maharashtra Plateau had significant contact with central India from the late Harappan through the Malwa phase and in fact, acted as a corridor along which resources from Gujarat and cultural elements percolated through to that region. With Gujarat also, Maharashtra showed an intimate relationship as manifested in the presence of late Harappan/Lustrous Red Ware at a number of sites in the sub-region stretching from Kaothe near the western coast to Tuljapur Garhi in the Amaravati district. By the Jorwe period, however, Maharashtra became more southward oriented with Jorwe ceramic elements found as far as Andhra Pradesh and southern Mysore.

Karnataka, Tamil Nadu and Andhra

This is broadly the area of what is known as the 'southern neolithic culture', with geographical variations in each of the three component 'states'. The Karnataka plateau has two sections—the northern section and the Mysore plateau. The Krishna and the Tungabhadra run through the northern section constituting an interfluve called the Raichur Doab, a sort of corridor from the Maharashtra plateau to the south. Here the terrain is one of rolling plains interspersed with granitic boulders and hills and with a reddish sandy soil supporting a thorny scrub vegetation. Of the Mysore plateau there are two divisions: the Malnad and the Maidan. The Malnad borders on the Western Ghats and is hilly and forested, while the Maidan is an area of rolling plains with low granitic hills. Both parts of the Mysore plateau were peopled by prehistoric villagers and so was the Raichur Doab. The climate at present tends as a whole towards semi-aridity, the rainfall varying from about 25 inches in the north to 30–5 inches in the Mysore plateau. The laboratory analysis of the relevant deposit from the Kupgal ashmound in the Raichur Doab suggests that the climate at the beginning of the neolithic phase in the area was slightly more wet and 'better wooded with thorn and scrub forest interspersed by large areas of grassland . . .' (Majumdar and Rajaguru 1966: 14). The neolithic sites of Tamil Nadu, as studied by B. Narasimhaiah (1980) fall in the plateau region of the northwestern part of the state—mainly North Arcot and Dharampuri districts, although neolithic tools have been found scattered in various parts of the state. Beyond the coastal plain and the Eastern Ghats is mainly the tract of Telengana and Rayalseema.

Neolithic sites abound in the region; around Tekkalakota alone M.S.N. Rao and K.C. Malhotra (1965: 7) report nineteen of them. The flat-topped granitic hills of the region ('castellated hills' of Foote 1914, section VI: 'castellated hills of the Deccan') and the river-banks seem to have provided a suitable occupation ground for the neolithic settlers who have been investigated since the days of Foote and whose principal excavated sites now include Brahmagiri (Wheeler 1947–48), Maski (Thapar 1957), Piklihal (Allchin 1960), Utnur (Allchin 1961), Kupgal (Majumdar and

Rajaguru 1966), T. Narasipur (IAR 1961–62, 1964–65), Hallur (M.S.N. Rao 1971), Nagarjunakonda (Subrahmanyam 1975), Veerapuram (Sastri et al. 1984), Ramapuram (IAR 1981–82, 1982–83), Hemmige (M.S.N. Rao and Nagaraju 1974), Sanganakallu (Subbarao 1948, Ansari and M.S.N. Rao 1969, Sankalia 1969), Palavoy (IAR 1966–67), Paiyampalli (IAR 1964–65, 1967–68), Tekkalakota (M.S.N. Rao and Malhotra 1965), Kodekal (Paddayya 1973), Banahalli (IAR 1985–86, 1986–87), etc. The northern Karnataka neolithic sites have been considered in detail by A. Sundara (1968, 1970). In Andhra Pradesh V. Rami Reddy (1975) has made a useful contribution.

Sites like Sanganakallu and Kupgal provide a background to the growth of the neoliths in the area. Period I at Sanganakallu consists of choppers and chopping tools, scrapers and prepared flakes, all highly patinated and made of trap dyke material. It was succeeded (Period II) by a microlithic industry characterized by quartz flakes, cores and lunates and scrapers. It is only in Sanganakallu III that one finds polished stone axes (at Kupgal there is no separate microlithic horizon between the two as at Sanganakallu) and between these two phases there was a formation of dark brown soil which might indicate a considerable time-gap between the two levels. As far as the neolithic level itself is concerned, an earlier metal-free horizon marked by handmade ware is probable, although by no means positively proved. There were both circular and rectangular wattle-and-daub houses, reinforced in some cases by low walls of granitic blocks. Both the pottery and ground stone industry show considerable variations, although at the base the pottery was either handmade or turned on a slow wheel.

At Piklihal alone the pottery types are five in number with thirteen different forms. At Piklihal, again, Allchin (1960: 85–95) classified the neolithic ground and pecked stone industry into five main types: edge tools, pointed tools, rubbers and grinders, hammers, bored maceheads, etc., each with various sub-types. Paddayya (1973) found 9 main ceramic types with 33 vessel forms, although his classification of neolithic stone tools was divided into 'edge' and 'non-edge' types. Associated with the rich ground stone axe industries is a microlithic blade element comprising flakes, points, borers, etc. Copper/bronze is never profuse, but it occurs at most of the sites. Among other objects should be mentioned beads of steatite, coral and miscellaneous semi-precious stones, terracotta long-horned cattle figurines, terracotta neck-rests, and an elaborate gold ear-ornament from the earliest phase of Tekkalakota. The data on the crop-pattern are meagre, although ragi millet has been found at Hallur. At

Tekkalakota there is horse gram. Extensive remains of cattle, sheep/goat and other animal bones point to the importance of domestic animals in the economy. This importance is also reflected in the variety of interpretations of the neolithic ashmounds found in this region (cf. Allchin 1963). However, it is slowly emerging that these so-called ashmound sites are in fact associated with, or rather are a part of, normal habitational settlements (personal information from Dr Paddayya).

A full-fledged chalcolithic complex occurs in Andhra. Among a large number of sites discovered in the Kurnool area, mostly large open-air settlements, Singanapalli (IAR 1967–68) is a single culture site yielding a profuse quantity of painted pottery—usually black-on-red with channel-spouted bowls as a distinctive shape, stone blades with fluted cores, lime-plastered house-floors, beads of steatite, shell, etc. Another site of this genre, Ramapuram (IAR 1981–82, 1982–83), has been excavated in the same area. The chalcolithic complex of Andhra has been linked to Malwa and Maharashtra, which is possible (discussion in Lahiri 1992: 193–4). The Andhra neolithic element is no doubt part of the same complex in Tamil Nadu and Karnataka, the latter region standing in more close relationship with Maharashtra from where the Jorwe ware came to this region and persisted till a much later period. Chronologically, the large number of radiocarbon dates, when calibrated, show a spread from the first half of the third millennium BC to the second half of the second millennium BC. The Andhra chalcolithic (cf. Ramapuram) possibly emerged around 2000 BC.

Eastern India

Extending over the territorial units of Bengal, Orissa and Assam, physiographically eastern India is not a homogeneous unit. Parts of Bihar and Bengal are dominated by the Ganges but flanking its course on the west is the Chhotanagpur upland. A highland also borders the delta areas of the Mahanadi and Baitarani in Orissa in the north. Assam lies beyond modern Bangladesh, a mesh of ever-shifting rivers, and except for a sixty-mile-wide stretch along the Brahmaputra it consists of a succession of jungle-clad hills.

Neolithic celts have been picked up from the surface from almost the entire area except for the alluvial valleys and deltas. The collection has been large enough to warrant divisions and subdivisions (Krishnaswami 1960). On the basis of the typological studies it has also been possible to speak of two neolithic culture provinces, one comprising Bengal, Bihar and Orissa, and the other Assam, itself with a number of subareas (Dani 1960: 41–7). Each of these provinces is supposed to possess two techno-logical groups. Group I in Bengal-Bihar-Orissa 'consists of typically Indian types' (Dani 1960: 223) and the supposedly later Group II 'shows a mixture with foreign types that are well-known in southeast Asia' (ibid). Group I of the Assam complex includes 'indigenous tool-types almost restricted to the various zones of Assam' (ibid) while Group II consists of 'common types, wholly foreign, identical with some of the types of Yunnan and Burma' (ibid). No chronological difference has been sug-gested between these two groups. E.C. Worman's (1949) postulate of a total cultural affiliation of the eastern Indian neolithic with southeast Asia has been reduced by Dani to one of 'contact and borrowings natural to countries so close to one another' (Dani 1960: 223).

Apart from inferences based on typology, there is little positive evi-dence of the beginning of farming in this wide area. In Orissa, Kuchai (IAR 1961–62: 36) in the Burhabalang valley has yielded very gritty, micaceous, handmade pottery along with a few ground stone axes and some patinated flakes of sandstone. The assemblage is undated but it is preceded by late stone age materials. In Orissa again, the site of Golbai Sasan (B.K. Sinha 1992) in the Puri district has yielded neolithic celts, bone tools (including a small barbed harpoon) in association with a number of wheelmade pottery types. This assemblage is likely to belong to the second millennium BC. To the far east, in the hills of North Cachar in Assam, a site called Daojali Hading (Sharma 1966) has revealed a single-layered cultural deposit where four varieties of sherds (cord-marked, incised, stamped and plain red wares) occur alongside a number of stone axes which comprised shouldered celts, quadrangular adzes, rectangular and oval sectioned small axes and some crudely flaked axes polished only at the cutting edge. The date remains uncertain but regard-ing the affinities of the site it has been said that: 'The cord-marked pot-tery . . . belongs to eastern Asiatic neolithic tradition. The data are not sufficient to comment on the affinity of the plain red pottery, but there is a suggestion that it may be related to the Yang Shao red pottery of the Huang Ho valley, the southern extension of which can be traced as far as Szechuan. It is possible that this pottery reached Assam from that direction' (Sharma 1967). Coarse handmade pottery occurs successively with microliths and stone axes at Selbalgiri-2 in the Garo hills, but the general perspective of the site, as at Daojali Hading, still remains un-certain.

Nothing specific has yet emerged from Manipur also, although the quaternary deposits of the state are gradually coming to our attention (cf. Singh and Singh 1990) T.C. Sharma (personal discussion) claims the presence of a Hoabinhian horizon in Meghalaya, but again, the data have remained unpublished.

It is possible to argue in favour of the existence of an early village level at several sites in West Bengal and Bihar, notably at Pandu Rajar Dhibi (West Bengal), Chirand, Taridih and Senuar (all in Bihar). The relevant cultural material in Period I of Pandu Rajar Dhibi (Ghosh and Chakrabarti 1968, Dasgupta 1965, IAR 1984–85) consists of primarily handmade wares, microlithic blades, house floor levels, fractional burials and husk impressions of rice in the core of pottery. No metal is present. These could probably be dated to the first half of the second millennium BC. Similar but more extensive evidence occurs at Chirand (Narain 1971, 1979; Varma 1971) in the middle Ganges valley in north Bihar. This level at the site has yielded a number of pottery types (red, grey and black wares, some with post-firing paintings), evidence of circular reed-and-mud huts with properly rammed floors, a terracotta industry, a large quantity of antler and bone tools, beads of semi-precious stones and remains of moong, wheat, lentil, barley and rice. Perhaps a limited amount of copper is also present. The date is uncertain but should be in the second half of the third millennium BC. At Senuar in the Kaimur foothills of the Rhotas district, Birendra Pratap Singh (1990) found a 'pure neolithic' level (1.5 m thick deposit) with three principal ceramic types—red ware, burnished red ware and burnished grey ware, all of which are generally wheelmade. A cord-impressed type of pottery, usually associated with the neolithic in the Vindhyas, is also found in a comparatively limited quantity. In addition to a rich microlithic industry of chert, chalcedony, agate, quartz, etc., there are some triangular polished celts, bone tools, semi-precious stone beads and miscellaneous stone objects such as hammerstones, saddle querns, pestles, etc. One also finds house floors, burnt mud chunks with reed impressions, pottery discs and rice, barley, pea, lentil and some millets. Wheat, grass pea, kodon (*Paspa lum scrobiculatum*) and vetch (*Vicis_sativa*) appear in the 'subsequent upper layers'. Rice is said to be the principal crop. The sub-period IB at the site (2.02 m deposit) has been called 'neolithic-chalcolithic' on the basis of the appearance of copper comprising a fish-hook, a piece of wire, a needle and an indeterminate object. A fragmentary rod of lead has also been found. The piece of copper wire has been found to be made of almost pure copper and the lead fragment has been found to contain 'a high amount of silver' (0.20 per cent). There is not much change in the other cultural items but bread-wheat, gram and moong are added to the list of crops. The occurrence of twenty-five faience beads needs attention. The deposit as a whole certainly goes back well into the third millennium BC. Not much is known about the neolithic level at Taradih (IAR 1986–87, 1987–88) except that this has two phases, comprising primarily handmade red pottery in the first phase.

A still earlier phase of the neolithic possibly occurs in the eastern section of the Vindhyas. There are three early (7th, 6th and 5th millennia BC) dates from the site of Koldihawa in the Belan valley in the Allahabad district from a level characterized by a microlithic industry, a plain red ware and an ill-fired, crude black-and-red ware. Doubt is cast on these dates if one remembers that the succeeding phase at this site fits in well with the second millennium BC chalcolithic phase of eastern India. On the other hand the Belan valley and the adjacent Vindhyan country have a well-established and continuous prehistoric sequence culminating in such advanced mesolithic/protoneolithic sites as Chopani Mando showing cattle hoof impressions and wild rice, and when looked at from this point of view the early dates from Koldihawa seem to be quite acceptable. However, the Vindhyan neolithic in the Kunjhun valley goes back only to the 4th millennium BC (when calibrated). There is need for more precise work on this problem in the Belan valley before the chronology of the Vindhyan/Belan neolithic can be objectively assessed. That it was not an isolated phenomenon can easily be deduced from the discovery of neolithic sites in the Kaimur foothills and from the spread of cord-impressed pottery as far south as Taradih at Bodh Gaya.

The chalcolithic phase in the archaeological sequence of eastern India covers a very large number of sites in eastern U.P., Bihar, West Bengal and Orissa. Its hallmark is an assemblage characterized principally by a plain and painted black-and-red ware which is found in association with a number of other ceramic types such as black and black-slipped ware, red and red-slipped ware, a perforated ware, buff ware, etc. Fine painted designs usually occur on the red-slipped ware whereas black-and-red and black-slipped ware, if painted, usually carry short strokes in white. Otherwise this level is found to possess copper, a microlithic industry, bone tools and worked antler pieces, semi-precious stone beads, reed and mud houses, rice as the principal crop, miscellaneous terracotta and stone objects, etc. In Orissa this level has not yet been extensively excavated (for a report, see IAR 1985–86: 62), and in eastern U.P. the number of excavated sites is still limited (cf. Sohgaura in IAR 1961–62; also Chaturvedi 1985), but in Bihar and West Bengal there is a very large number of sites, the number of reported sites in West Bengal alone being more than sixty (Chakrabarti et al. 1993). Their size-range varies from 1 acre or less to about 8–9 acres, with most of them falling in the lower bracket. The distribution of these sites conforms to the distribution of modern village settlements in their respective areas, suggesting a clear continuity of agricultural history from the protohistoric phase onwards. It was also a phase of substantially long occupation; at Chirand the chalcolithic phase (Period II) was about 5.50 m thick at places. There is no doubt that the chalcolithic phase at Chirand goes back to the first quarter of the second millennium BC. The most impressive evidence of crops has occurred in the chalcolithic context at Senuar (B.P. Singh 1991): rice, barley, dwarf wheat, bread wheat, sorghum, millet, chick pea, green gram or moong, field pea, lentil, horse gram, grass pea, sesamum and linseed.

Upper Gangetic Valley

The starting point is a cluster of late Harappan settlements in the upper Doab, evidence of which has been discussed in an earlier chapter. Otherwise, the earliest evidence of village occupation in the upper Gangetic valley is provided by a context which yields an ochre-coloured pottery (OCP). Since B.B. Lal (1951) first identified this in an apparently unassociated context at Rajpur Parsu and Bisauli, it has been found in the basal level of a number of sites spread between the upper Doab (cf. Hastinapur, Atranjikhera) and the lower Doab (cf. Sringaverapura). The most significant range of evidence comes from Saipai and Atranjikhera. Saipai (Lal 1972) has yielded from this level a sword and a harpoon, two type-fossils of the Gangetic valley copper hoards, thus vindicating an earlier hypothesis of Lal (1951). At Atranjikhera this basically red-slipped pottery, which is generally found in originally water-logged deposits and thus in an ochrous condition, was associated with the evidence of wattle-and-daub houses supported by wooden posts of 'babool', 'sissoo', 'sal' and in rare cases 'chir' pine. Evidence of rice, barley, gram, khesari and cattle bones with cut marks indicates the diet of the people. R.C. Gaur (1983: 74) argues that 'the people grew two crops a year—rice in summer and barley along with gram and khesari, both legumes in the winter'. He further points out, 'contrary to the general belief, the Doab at that time perhaps was not covered with dense forests. Its natural vegetation ranged from desert-thorn to ravine-thorn forest with scattered tree, the removal of which was not very difficult'. The next phase at the site is marked by black-and-red ware, cores and waste flakes of semi-precious stones, copper objects, beads of various materials, pottery discs, and wheat, rice and barley. The copper objects comprised a ring and three beads. This phase was followed by the iron-using, painted grey ware culture (PGW). Another contemporary site in the same region is Lal Qila (Gaur 1973) which is found to possess a number of mud floor levels. The use of mud-bricks was usual but burnt bricks were also used in a limited quantity. Unless recovered from a water-logged deposit, the red pottery, the main forms of which include storage jars, vases, bowls with handles, etc. is well-fired, sturdy, fine-slipped and occasionally washed. In the case of the painted specimens the designs are mainly geometric, though natural-istic motifs, including the one which shows an elongated and horned humped bull, are not rare. One notes the occurrence of incised designs also. Some sherds bear graffiti marks which have been classified into ten different types. The copper objects comprise a pendant and a bead, a piece of an arrowhead, a broken part of a celt and an object of indeterminate shape. Besides the usual assortment of wheels, discs, bangles, etc. the terracotta objects include two female figurines. There are also beads of carnelian and soap stone, an agate point, stone querns, net-sinkers, bone arrowheads and points. Barley, rice and pulses have been found in this context. Gaur (1983) dates the OCP phase at Atranjikhera in the first half of the second millennium BC. On the basis of thermoluminiscent dates Lal Qila has been dated between 2030–1730 BC. As far as the general settle-ment pattern is concerned, K.N. Dikshit (1979) has discussed its distri-bution in detail in the upper Doab where an average site is less than 2 ha. What is more important is that the OCP culture may be linked to the late Harappan culture of the area. Dikshit, in his discussion of the problem, writes that the 'Ochre Coloured Pottery types, such as dish-on-stand with drooping rims, basin, hollow lid with central knob and large storage jars noticed in the Upper Doab are having typological similarity with the Harappan assemblage (including Bara) found in this region'. At the same time he points out that there is no other similarity and that 'the pottery types of OCP in Central Doab, on the other hand do not show even this much of typological similarity'. However, he points out that 'the typical compartmented incised designs noticed at Atranjikhera and Lal Qila . . . possess a close resemblance with those found at Bara'. It is probable that this culture is derived in some way from the various late Harappan and related assemblages of Panjab-Haryana and upper Doab.

At Atranjikhera the succeeding phase of black-and-red ware (associa-ted with red and black-slipped wares) is said to be thin but this has yielded the remains of burnt bricks and two hearths in addition to those of copper rings and beads, microlithic waste flakes and cores and teak (*Tectona grandis*) which reputedly had central India as the northern limit of its distribution. In the Kanpur district M. Lal (1984) found nine black-and-red ware settlements (six below 2 ha., and three between 3 and 5 ha.) with an average spacing of 29 km between them. Iron appears in the next phase at Atranjikhera and elsewhere in the upper Gangetic valley.

General Discussion

At a general level the neolithic-chalcolithic data, of which only a very brief outline has been offered above, suggest a few specific points which may be illustrative of the basic pattern of this newly emergent village India of the third and second millennia BC. To begin with, an effective rural-agricultural base was created, all the villages being securely established. The extensive range of their wheelmade pottery, stone tools, occasional but by no means unfamiliar objects of copper, evidence of crops and animal bones (where available), beads of semi-precious stones and other miscellaneous objects including house remains seem to underline this point clearly. More significantly, the entire evidence is suggestive of their having deep roots in the soil. These neolithic-chalcolithic farmers worked out a relationship with their respective areas which persists till today. In all cases, the location of settlements, the house-types and housing-materials used are still current among the villages in the same regions. To take only a few randomly chosen examples, the location of Ahar culture settlements in southeast Rajasthan 'pre-empted later period agricultural settlements in their choice of locale' (Hooja 1988: 75). Also, the Ahar practice of strengthening the mud house walls with quartz nodules finds an exact parallel among the present village houses of the area (Sankalia 1974), while at Tekkalakota the circular huts of the neighbouring Boyas can be matched by excavated specimens (M.S.N. Rao 1965). The Navdatoli evidence of the juxtaposition of oblong and circular houses assumes meaning in the light of the modern Indian practice of building circular houses along with oblong ones for the storage of grain or hay, or for the occupation of low caste groups (Leshnik n.d.). Dhavalikar and others have, as we have seen, emphasized how many settlement situations in modern Maharashtra are rooted in the regional chalcolithic context. A more crucial point in this direction is that the crops which were cultivated by these prehistoric villagers are still being cultivated in their respective regions. Listing the grains from Navdatoli (two varieties of wheat, rice and several varieties of pulses), Sankalia

(1974) points out that the same grains are cultivated in the modern Nimad district of Madhya Pradesh, where Navdatoli is located. The extensive remains of rice from the chalcolithic sites of eastern India suggest that the present primary dependence of this area on rice can be dated as early as its neolithic-chalcolithic period. The eminence of Maharashtra as a silk and cotton growing area finds reflection in the chalcolithic level of the area where both cotton and flax occur. The varieties of millet and pulse of the neolithic south are still grown by the southern farmers. B.P. Sahu (1988) has shown how the importance of cattle which can be easily observed from the animal remains of the neolithic-chalcolithic contexts persists in the early historic levels. Irrespective of the area, the picture is remarkable for its continuity.

It would be wrong to assert that this continuity is true only as regards the material details of village life. It seems that there is an appreciable element of continuity in some aspects of religious life too. We have noticed the presence of 'fire-altars' and 'temples' in the Malwa cultural level at Dangwada. In this connection both Sankalia (1974) and Dhavalikar (1988) have interpreted some terracotta finds of the Maharashtra chalcolithic in terms of a number of still continuing religious beliefs in Maharashtra. The presence of realistic representations of the phallus at some sites is noteworthy.

At this point it may be emphasized that the deep roots which these agriculturists struck should rule out any attempt to explain their origin purely in diffusionary terms.

Secondly, none of these peasant groups developed in complete isolation. On the basis of the use of different types of raw materials by these cultures and their probable source-areas, this aspect of the neolithic-chalcolithic cultures has been worked out in detail by Nayanjot Lahiri (1992), and following her, we may here refer to only a few points. In the late/post-Harappan period there developed lines of movement through Rajasthan, Malwa, Gujarat and Maharashtra. Lustrous red ware, etched carnelian and lapis lazuli beads and marine shell at Ahar could come only from Gujarat, possibly through both Malwa where Ahar sites are found and the more direct line of movement between these areas. Both Malwa and Maharashtra were penetrated from Gujarat, with the Tapti valley providing a crucial passageway in the dissemination of late Harappans and others to the more southern sections of Maharashtra. The Tapti valley also maintained links between Malwa and Maharashtra. According to Lahiri, the Malwa phase coincided with the development of at least three important lines of movement: a route from the coast to Ahmednagar and

Pune, another route towards Aurangabad and the third route towards Vidarbha. From Maharashtra the road to south Deccan or the Karnataka plateau was open in several ways, and in a different direction links between western India and Andhra can be taken back to the Malwa cultural phase, 'whose ceramic elements are found in the Pusalpadu and Patapadu industries'. There were movements across the south Indian peninsula as a whole, and especially in its plateau section. In north India virtually the whole of the Indo-Gangetic plain was thrown open and came to be closely interlinked.

The development of such routes also implies that there was a lot of interchange of raw materials of different types between different areas. Metals no doubt constituted one of the most obvious items of such exchange, along with the various categories of semi-precious stones necessary for bead-making. The material used for the manufacture of beads at Navdatoli alone comprised as many as twelve varieties—agate, amazonite, carnelian, chalcedony, faience, glass, jasper, lapis, sandstone, steatite, shell and terracotta. Usually, as a recent study of the West Bengal chalcolithic context (Chakrabarti et al. 1993) has shown, this trade must have had both local and inter-regional forms. In the case of some metals and some varieties of stones inter-regional trade was necessary; otherwise trade carried on at the local level was enough to take care of the needs of these self-sufficient village-farming communities.

It is not easy in this context to comment on the social institutional framework of the period. A two-tier settlement hierarchy is noticeable everywhere, and one may reasonably postulate the existence of regional centres. Dhavalikar (1988) suggests the emergence of a 'chiefdom' society on the basis of such a settlement hierarchy, and he may well be right. What I find more intriguing is that most of the neolithic-chalcolithic distribution areas conform roughly to the modern geographical entities. This may suggest the emergence of nascent political units.

HYPOTHESIS REGARDING THE ORIGIN OF THE
NEOLITHIC-CHALCOLITHIC CULTURES IN INNER INDIA

The deep roots which the various neolithic-chalcolithic cultures of inner India, i.e. to the east of the Delhi-Aravalli-Cambay axis, show in their respective areas rule out any explanation of their origin in purely diffusionary terms. Here I shall try to put forward a coherent explanation for this. The cultures concerned are those from southeast Rajasthan to south Deccan and Andhra on the one hand and from the Indo-Gangetic divide and the upper Doab to east India on the other. The preliminary points in this connection are as follows:

1. Although some of these cultures could have come into existence in the second half of the third millennium BC—and in the case of the Vindhyan neolithic in the Kunjhun valley this date may even go back to the fourth millennium BC—the rich cultural details which we have perused belong by and large to the second millennium BC. In other words, in the forms in which we primarily know them, they are contemporary only with the late Harappans.

2. So, when the Indus civilization developed around 2700 BC in the Hakra valley in Cholistan, what was the condition in the rest of the subcontinent, especially in the segment to the east of the Aravallis? Or, when the early Harappans and the earlier Hakra ware culture people were in the Cholistan area and the areas to the west, what was the cultural condition like in inner India?

3. The only possible answer to this question is that there were only hunter-gatherers then in inner India (with possibly the exception of the Belan valley and the Vindhyas).

4. The evidence from a number of hunting-gathering sites in inner India indicates that the domestication of animals and incipient food-production/plant utilization were components of this primarily hunting-gathering stage of the economy. Bagor in east Rajasthan, for instance, shows a mesolithic level dating from the fifth millennium BC. The utilization of plant resources is suggested by the presence of querns and rubbing stones and the animals domesticated were cattle, sheep and goat. At Adamgarh in central India near Hoshangabad in the Narmada valley there were domesticated cattle, sheep and goat. The site of Chopani Mando in the Belan valley shows, in its advanced mesolithic stage, wild rice, hoof-marks of cattle, ring-stones, rubbers, mullers, querns, etc. The date of Chopani Mando may fall in the ninth–eighth millennia BC.

5. The agricultural settlers in the greater Indus valley, especially in the Hakra stretch, could not have looked only towards the western hills beyond Sind or the Indus valley for their resources; they were likely to have explored the east too and come into contact with the hunter-gatherers of that region. The fact that they were interacting with the hunter-gatherers is clear from the cultural situation of Ganeshwar, the origin of which antedates the mature Harappan phase. The

Ganeshwar sequence makes clear that it was the local hunting-gathering 'mesolithic' group which took to mining and smelting copper to meet the needs of the pre-/early Harappans.

6. The mature Harappans were also interacting with the Aravalli line in northeast Rajasthan, i.e. with the Ganeshwar area, but they were present in the Indo-Gangetic divide upto Haryana on the one hand and in Gujarat on the other. These very locations open up possibilities of close interaction with inner India, and it is intriguing that etched carnelian beads which are a characteristic mature Harappan bead-type have been found both at Ahar and Atranjikhera. S.R. Rao (1979) has noted the occurrence of teak at Lothal, which possibly came from south India, a region also known for its amazonite and gold.

7. This process of interaction became certainly more obvious in the late Harappan phase when there were many late Harappan settlements in the upper doab and north Maharashtra and certainly some of these settlements were also present in Malwa. The late Harappans, as I have argued before, merged into the main flow of cultural development in inner India.

On the basis of the facts adduced above it can now be argued that the neolithic-chalcolithic cultures of inner India were the results of interaction between the pre-/early Harappan, mature Harappan and late Harappan distribution zones on the one hand and the advanced hunter-gatherers to the east of the Delhi-Aravalli-Cambay line on the other. The full-fledged transition to agriculture among these hunter-gatherers was due to the impetus provided by the late Harappans on the move from the upper doab towards the Gangetic valley, and from Gujarat towards Malwa and Maharashtra. The catalytic factor behind this transition was the contact of the regional hunter-gatherers with the descendants of a highly developed Bronze Age civilization. The specific form this transition took in different areas no doubt calls for further research, but this is a hypothesis which makes the story of India's protohistoric development specifically Indian. This is also a hypothesis which gives the hunter-gatherers of the Indian peninsular block a decidedly positive role in the subcontinent's early history.

The question which confronts us in the end is why the early mesolithic communities of inner India, although familiar with the domestication of cattle, sheep and goat and the utilization of plants, if not with incipient cultivation, failed to expand the latter base of their economy before interacting with the Harappans or perhaps before feeling the impact of the direct presence of the late Harappans in their midst. There can be no offhand answer, but the point worth bearing in mind is that there was simply no pressure on these hunter-gatherers to change their way of life as long as there was no lack of procurable plant and animal food in the forests. Indian forests as a source of food are being anthropologically/ethnobotanically studied (cf. Nagar 1985), and D.D. Kosambi (in Allchin and Chakrabarti eds 1979) gave some thought to it in the context of the Deccan plateau which is by no means 'so rich in vegetation as other parts of India'. Among the semi-wild and less regularly cultivated varieties alone, he could list twenty-six names, and as he puts it, 'in the better-forested regions, many of these minor staples can be gathered wild. The list of edible forest products normally known to the local inhabitants goes to nearly 200 for the Konkan forests. This includes fruit, berries, leaves and mushrooms, but not wild game, honey and the like, nor the coconut upon which the entire west-coast economy depends'. Till recent years there was a marked dependence on wild plant resources in Indian villages and when the grain bins are empty for the poor for two or three months in a year, it is the availability of plant food in the forests which keeps them going till the next crop. A hunting-gathering streak has always run strong through the fabric of Indian subsistence economy and perhaps in various ways through society. At one level the history of India has been the history of the incorporation of the once-endemic hunting-gathering groups into the framework of a higher social and productive organization, the roots of which are traced on the basis of archaeological evidence to the Ghaggar-Hakra stretch.

TOWARDS EARLY HISTORY IN THE GANGETIC VALLEY:
THE IRON AGE

The issue here is not the beginning of the use of iron in India but the distribution and character of Iron Age settlements in different parts of the subcontinent. The data are limited outside the doab. The reason is that in the doab the first iron-using sites are easily distinguishable because of their diagnostic pottery—the painted grey ware, which also occurs extensively further to the west, in the divide. The problem is that in the divide there is an iron-free level of this pottery, and one does not know, by looking at the surface material, which painted grey ware site is iron-free and which is not. This problem has not yet arisen in the context of the doab. In the rest of India, especially in the peninsular block and the middle Gangetic valley, the major protohistoric column is that of black-and-red ware, and it is not possible to determine on the basis of surface assemblages which site is chalcolithic and which one is iron-bearing. The associated wares should give some indication, but one does not suppose that the stratigraphic position of such wares is clearly understood. It will be quite logical at this stage to argue that as far as east India and central India are concerned there is nothing specific to argue that the number of sites during this period became more or that the sites became larger. As far as one can see it, it is the same assemblage of plain and painted black-and-red and associated wares, microliths and some copper and iron. In south India the evidence is a trifle more complex. A number of neolith/megalith overlap levels in the south date the beginning of iron in that part of India sometime before 1000 BC but one does not know, without excavation, whether a particular iron-mixed assemblage is early or not. If one more or less ignores the chronological issue, an excellent study of the different locational aspects of south Indian megaliths (including the ones from Vidarbha) has been published by U.S. Moorti (1991). Out of 1933 reported megalithic sites (the number calculated by Moorti), only some are settlement sites, and out of these sites the size-category data have been cited for 54. While there is a regular hierarchy of settlements ranging from those which are less than 2 ha. in extent to at least one in the 7–7.99 ha. category, 'the position of these settlements in the hierarchy and their role in the regulatory and ritual network, at the moment is not clear'. However, it is pointed out that most of the larger settlements are located on 'the known major trade and communication routes of early historic India'. Secondly, Moorti's study shows that the megaliths are distributed in varied ecozones, some of which form agriculturally fertile areas. Thirdly, one should underline the fact that megalithic monuments 'which on account of their size and complexity, require planning and a labour force' were indeed an integrated part of this society which also shows positive traces of craft activities including metallurgical practices at a number (85) of sites. It has further been recorded that 'out of a total of 1896 burials considered for analysis, 92 burials have yielded weapons in varying quantities. From these 92 burials 285 weapons were recovered. Warfare appears to have increased during this period probably to control resource-rich zones if large aggregations of cemetery in some of these resource-rich zones (e.g. in Wainganga basin, Raichur region, middle Krishna valley, Kolar region and Coimbatore uplands) is any indication'. On the whole Moorti postulates a ranked society during this period. But then, the problem is, 'which period'? Some of Moorti's 1900-odd megalithic sites will no doubt date from 1000 BC but some will date from the early centuries AD too; herein lies the problem.

For the painted grey ware sites in the doab one may depend on M. Lal (1984) and R.C. Gaur (1983). The number of such sites located by M. Lal in the Kanpur district is forty, all of them located on the river banks with the exception of five which are located near low-lying areas. The general distribution of sites is clearly concentrated in the divide and the doab, and one may easily establish a two-tiered settlement hierarchy. The existence of regional centres is probable. Whether some centres like Bukhari in Haryana (9.6 ha.) can be called urban centres or not is a different issue altogether; I do not propose to put the beginning of early historic cities of the 'divide' and the doab in the painted grey ware period, a comprehensive picture of which emerges from the relevant level at Atranjikhera. Wattle-and-daub huts, the cultivation of wheat, rice and barley, miscellaneous terracotta, stone and bone objects, a limited number of semi-precious stone beads, a few glass and shell objects, cattle and other animals including buffalo, and an extensive use of iron seem to give its basic economic and cultural picture.

Those who are willing to give iron technology in the doab more than its due share in the sustenance of agricultural development leading towards the formation of early historic cities in the succeeding NBPW or Northern Black Polished Ware period, beginning around *c.* 700 BC as at Sringaverapura in the central section of the Gangetic valley (for Sringaverapura, see Lal 1992), forget that the village-life and the crop-patterns of the entire subcontinent were laid down in the earlier chalcolithic stage and that not a single major crop was added to the list after iron was introduced. I find no reason to argue that the use of iron had different 'modes', beginning with its use as nails, weapons, etc. and developing into agricultural implements. Nor do I find any reason to believe that the development of iron technology underwent two stages during this period with some significance for the socio-economic development, i.e. in the first stage only wrought iron was known and in the second stage steel was introduced. Given the firm-rooted agricultural base all over the country, especially in the fertile alluvium of the Gangetic valley, the catalytic factor in the early historic urban growth in the region is more likely the formation of clear and powerful regional kingdoms which confront us right in the first phase of our documented political history (Raychaudhuri 1953).

Chapter Five

Early Historical Cities

Between *c.* 700 BC, the date of the advent of the NBPW at Sringaverapura in the central section of the Gangetic valley, and *c.* AD 300, the point immediately preceding the Gupta age maturity, India witnessed the growth of urban centres in all her major geographical regions. Though a well-established village economy always lay in the background, the urban centres themselves did not grow at the same time, nor were they the products of the same type of factors everywhere. Any survey intent on bringing out this regional pattern should be zonal in approach till it is possible to view the entire range of data within the subcontinental framework.

NORTHWEST

Lying between the Hindukush and the Salt Range and divided by the Indus, the submontane Indus region or the Northwest has a number of smaller physiographic subdivisions: the plains of Peshawar, Kohat and Bannu to the west of the Indus and the Potwar plateau to its east. A semicircular lowland of about 2500 square miles and hill-girt except along the Indus, the valley of Peshawar has only 10–15 inches of annual rainfall. It is only along the fans of the perennial streams like the Swat and the Kabul that the region is fertile and conducive to human settlement. The Kohat valley and the plain of Bannu to the southwest of the Peshawar valley enjoy a similar amount of rainfall and are generally noted for agricultural infertility. A general aridity also prevails over the Potwar plateau, which often has a sandy or stony soil and an annual rainfall of about 15–25 inches.

This physiographic note, however brief, should suggest a simple but important point: agriculturally the submontane Indus region is not quite productive. With the help of irrigation the soil could be made to yield a sustenance but it is unlikely that in the area agriculture could by itself lead to urban growth. What this region lacks in agricultural productivity has,

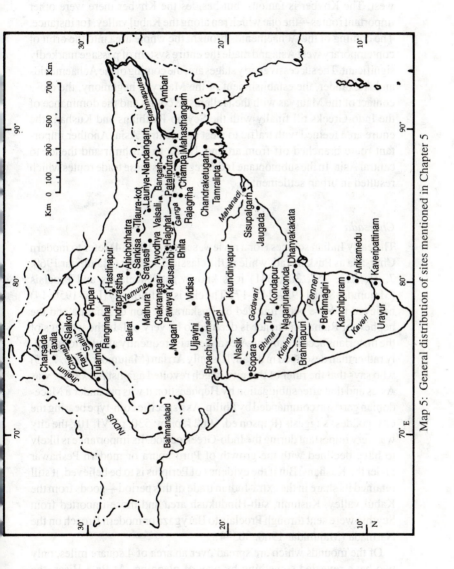

Map 5: General distribution of sites mentioned in Chapter 5

however, been made up by another vitally important factor, i.e. its position at the mouth of one of India's most important openings to the west. The Khyber is famous, but besides the Khyber there were other important routes—the one which ran along the Kabul valley, for instance. The coming of the Achaemenids brought the whole area into the orbit of contemporary west Asia and made the entire system of passage markedly significant. The successive early stages are: the coming of the Achaemenids and Alexander, the establishment of the Mauryan hegemony, the close contact of the Mauryas with the Hellenistic courts and the dominance of the Indo-Greeks till finally with the Scytho-Parthians and Kushans the entire area teemed with traffic to west and central Asia. Another important route branched off from around Taxila to Kashmir and thence to central Asia. In the submontane Indus region it is these trade routes which resulted in urban settlements.

Charsada

The early Indian sources (for a review, see Law 1950: 4) refer to modern Charsada as Puskalavati, while in the classical sources (Majumdar 1960: 7, 15, 215, 257, 303, 341) it is known as Peucelaotis and Proclais (Majumdar Sastri 1927: 115–17). The city is traditionally (Law 1950: 14) believed to have been founded by Puskara, the son of Bharata and the nephew of Rama, and hence is deemed to be very old. In the writings of the historians accompanying Alexander it is frequently alluded to casually rather than described in detail. It is only Arrian (Majumdar 1960: 7, 15) who says that the ruler of this city which revolted against Alexander was Astes and that after subjugation by Hephaestion it was put under a Macedonian garrison commanded by Philip. As a specific coin-type bearing the city-goddess suggests (Rapson ed. 1962 reprint: 530, pl. VI, 10), the city was very important during the Indo-Greek period. Its importance is likely to have declined with the growth of Purusapura or modern Peshawar under the Kushans. But if the evidence of Periplus is to be believed, it still retained its share in the extra-Indian trade of this period—goods from the Kabul valley, Kashmir, sub-Hindukush area and those imported from Scythia were sent through Proclais to Barygaza or modern Broach on the Narmada (Majumdar 1960: 303–4).

Of the mounds which are spread over an area of 4 square miles, only two have revealed something by way of planning. At Bala Hisar, the highest mound at the site, Marshall (1902–3) could unearth little except an assortment of stupas and other buildings. The sequence in the 1956 excavation by Wheeler (1962) began in about the sixth century BC, the date of the Achaemenid annexation of the region. By 327 BC, the date of Hephaestion's seize, the city was strengthened by a ditch and a mud rampart. The occupation also spread outside the enclosed area to the east, across a filled-up river bed. Within the rampart a mudbrick house with five constructional phases has been identified. The ditch was about 15 ft (4.57 m) wide and 10 ft (3.04 m) deep and on a rough estimate based on contours, might have enclosed not less than 15 acres (6.07 ha.). The rampart was about 16 ft (4.8 m) broad. A series of postholes, each a foot in diameter and 1–1.5 in deep (25.4 mm–38.1 mm), indicated a former timber-lined postern and bridge. The passage through the rampart was about 6 ft (1.82 m) wide.

There is more extensive evidence of planning at the neighbouring mound of Shaikhan about 3 furlongs (*c.* 600 m) to the north-northwest and between the arms of two rivulets, the Sambor and Zinde. Air-photography revealed a city in the negatives.

A series of parallel streets—not less than five can be identified—40 yards apart divide the site into blocks in which coherent house-plans can be isolated. One street-interval, slightly larger (50 yards), included the precinct of a massive circular structure which can only have been a stupa or Buddhist (less probably Jaina) shrine. The stupa stood on a slight rise and both by situation and plan dominated the scene. . . . It can be said that the whole site was laid out upon a single coordinated rectangular plan with the temple in its midst (Wheeler 1962: 16–17).

Dani's 1963–64 excavations (Dani 1965–66) have shown that the city was in all probability founded by Menander, the famous Indo-Greek king, in about the middle of the second century BC and that its occupation continued up to the reign of the Kushan king, Vasudeva, at the close of the second century or the middle of the third century AD.

Dani's excavation area was limited and could unearth mostly the structures of the Kushan period. The civic plan laid down by the Indo-Greeks, however, continued unchanged. The excavations identified three parallel streets and a side street crossing at a right angle. The drains, refuse-pits and cess-pools of a wide street all belonged to the Kushan period. The houses of this period were of mudbrick while those of the earlier ones were of diaper-masonry. In a Kushan period room a fire-place was identified, 15 ins square and 'placed in the middle just in the same fashion as we see in modern Pathan houses'. A house of the same period belonged to a Buddhist teacher, Haradakha (identified from a record at the base of a pedestal belonging to a relic casket), and consisted of a central open courtyard with rooms on three sides, the fourth side being closed by a high dividing wall. In the courtyard of the house there was a bathing place connected by a stone-built drain with the street outside. The house underwent a number of constructions, towards the end of which a shrine with the figure of Buddha was installed.

To the west of the Indus Charsada happens to be the only well-known and excavated urban centre. Arrian (Majumdar 1960: 11) refers to a 'great city called Massaga' in the territory of the Assacenoi, a tribe which offered considerable resistance to Alexander. Though identifications have been suggested (Smith 1924: 57, n. 1), the archaeological potentiality of the site is completely unknown. As the literary sources including Hiuen-Tsang (Watters 1961 reprint, vol. I: 201–14) and the stupa at Shar Dheri (Spooner 1908–9) imply, the northern capital of the Kushans—Peshawar or Purusapura—must have been considerably important in the early centuries AD but its precise features have not been investigated archaeologically. In about the same period there was a considerable number of Buddhist settlements, stupas and monasteries, in the Swat valley, all possibly subsisting on the religious generosity of the princes and merchants made wealthy by the teeming west Asian and central Asian traffic. The wealth generated by the same traffic again is likely to have resulted in an increase in the number of urban centres in the area but of their number and character we know almost nothing.

Taxila

To the east of the Indus, Taxila or ancient Taksasila in the Potwar plateau was a trade centre par excellence, owing its importance to its position on the route converging upon Bactria in Afghanistan. A second route connected Taxila to central Asia by way of Kashmir. It may also be emphasized that Taxila gave easy access to the Indus system and thus to the Arabian Sea and thence alternatively to the Red Sea and the Persian Gulf.

The importance of Taxila has been reflected in all categories of Indian literature (Sukthankar 1914–15, Law 1954: 129–31)—Hindu, Buddhist and Jaina—and also in the writings of the Graeco-Roman historians (Majumdar 1960: 113, 257, 276, 371, 386–8, 393, 410, 442). According to the epics, Taxila was established by Taksha at about the same time as Puskalavati and was conquered subsequently by King Janamajeya of Hastinapura who chose to perform his 'great snake sacrifice' there. Taxila finds mention in the Buddhist sources, notably the *Jatakas* where it is primarily known to be a centre of learning (Law 1922). It was also visited by a *Tirthankara* of the Jainas. In the Graeco-Roman testimony the ruling king of Taxila who submitted to Alexander was Taxiles. At Taxila Alexander received envoys from 'Abisaras, king of the mountaineer Indians', offered sacrifices and celebrated gymnastics and equestrian contests (Majumdar 1960: 23). Plutarch refers to some gymnosophists of the city (Majumdar 1960: 200–2). Strabo writes about some of its customs: the custom of auctioning poor girls of marriageable age, of throwing the dead to the vultures and of having more than one wife. He also refers to two Brahmin sophists with disciples, who used to spend some time in the market place and were 'authorized to take as a gift any merchandise they wished' (Majumdar 1960: 276–7).

Archaeologically Taxila is the most extensively excavated city site of the subcontinent. Lured both by its close Greek association and 'something appealingly Greek' (Marshall 1951: preface) in its countryside, Marshall excavated it between 1913 and 1934 while a season's work was added by Wheeler in 1944–45. More recently, the Bhir mound was excavated by S.M. Sharif (1969).

Flanked by the Muree hills and their spurs, one of which, the Hathial, actually divides it into two, the valley of Taxila is watered by the Haro and its tributaries, all hardly more than mere hill rivulets. The northern part of the valley is now well-watered both by streams and modern irrigation canals while the southern part is rocky and the least important except for the Buddhist stupas and monasteries on the knolls and slopes.

The three successive urban settlements of Taxila—Bhir, Sirkap and Sirsukh—grew in the western part of the northern valley within three and a half miles of one another, stretching the history of Taxila from the sixth century BC to the third century AD, from the Achaemenids to the Kushans. Of these, the first two, Bhir and Sirkap, have been extensively excavated while the third, chronologically the last one, Sirsukh, has been merely touched upon.

I. Bhir Mound

The earliest of the three cities in Taxila lies concealed under what is known as the Bhir mound of which a more or less connected plan has been obtained for about three acres in the middle. There are four occupational strata ranging from the fifth–sixth centuries BC (Stratum IV) to the second century BC (Stratum I) and later. The character of the rubble masonry of limestone and *kanjur* (the local name of a soft variety of limestone) is not neat and compact in Stratum II showing a gradual degradation up to Stratum IV. There was a thick internal and external coating of both plain and white-washed mud plaster on the walls of all the strata. The excavated remains are mostly on Stratum II, dated third century BC. So the civic plan of the Bhir mound belongs essentially to the Maurya period.

On plan Mauryan Taxila looks irregular and haphazard. Four streets and five lanes with associated house blocks are clear. With an average width of 22 ft (6.70 m) the First Street, the most important one at the site and dating from its earliest phase, does not run straight but has a distinct northwest-southeast slant. The other streets which vary in width from 9 ft to 17 ft (less than 3 to a little more than 5 m) are more winding with open square spaces along the way. The Second Street in the eastern part of the excavated sector, for instance, has a semi-circular bend in the north, while the Third and Fourth Streets also are equally irregular in alignment. The lanes, though considerably narrower, seem to have a more regular alignment, like Lane I between the Second and First Streets, which is almost straight. According to Marshall 'the lanes giving off the main street rose steeply towards the east and west' (Marshall 1951, I: 91), a normal feature in a settlement where its level was seldom interfered with but that of the lanes and adjacent houses rose with successive buildings.

In Fourth Street and Lane I there are traces of covered surface drains but they do not seem to be connected with any larger drain in the main street. 'The probability . . . seems to be that so far as the main streets are concerned they had to serve as water-courses during the rainy seasons . . .' (Marshall 1951, I: 91).

Despite its irregular streets, narrow lanes and an unsystematic drainage system, Mauryan Taxila was not without some element of civic planning. One notices on the plan round refuse bins set in the open squares and streets and from one of them (in Square S, measuring 9 by 5 ft/2.74 by 1.52 m) came 'bones, broken pottery and such like refuse' (Marshall 1951, I: 91). Marshall suggests that they were regularly cleaned by the town sweepers. There were also rough stone pillars, about 3 ft high (0.91 m) above the ground, acting as wheel-guards, i.e. preventing the corners of the houses from damage by passing carts or chariots.

The houses usually comprised open courtyards surrounded by rooms. The average ground area of a house in the excavated sector which may be taken to be the well-to-do area of the city was about 3600 sq. ft (334.45 sq. m) of which 700 sq. ft (65.1 sq. m) were taken up by the courtyard. On the ground floor the rooms numbered some 15 to 20, and were not more than 150 sq. ft (13.95 sq. m) each, often much less. Some of the ground-floor rooms facing the street might also be shops: 'Room 7 in block D overlooking Second Street . . . was evidently a shell-worker's shop as many pieces of cut shell and mother of pearl were found in it' (Marshall 1951, I: 92). The open courtyards, sometimes two in number in the larger houses, were usually paved with stone. The bathrooms, open passages, etc. were also similarly paved. No traces of any window survive but they may have been placed high up in the walls. For the household sewage there were soakwells, a feature peculiar to the Bhir mound alone in Taxila. To carry off the waste water from the houses there were surface drains built of stone. Smaller drain-pipes were, however, of earthenware and provided with spigot-and-faucet joints. The general appearance of the houses in elevation is uncertain but 'probably they were very much like the houses of modern towns in the Northwest, with their mud-plastered walls, wooden balconies and flat roofs rising to unequal heights' (Marshall 1951, I: 93).

Marshall (1951, I: 98) thinks that one of the excavated houses possesses a religious character. It covers an overall area of about 180 by 70 ft (*c.* 60 by *c.* 23 m) and is divided into two blocks, a larger one to the north and a smaller one to the south. There is a narrow lane with an open square at its western end between these blocks. The northern block possesses two open courtyards, some thirty rooms and a large pillared hall. The religious character of the pillared hall is suggested by the occurrence in the debris of the building as well as among the ruins on the farther side of the lane of a large number of terracotta reliefs representing a male and female deity standing side by side and holding hands, which were possibly made to be sold to the worshippers.

II. Sirkap

In the beginning of the second century BC a new city was laid out in the valley of Taxila, somewhat to the northeast of the Bhir mound. The local name of the site is Sirkap. Unlike the earlier city the new one is characterized by grid-planning, the plan laid out on a chess-board pattern. The site of Sirkap offered certain natural advantages. It could include in the south a portion of the Hathial ridge and thus could not only have the background of the low defensive hill but also an isolated knoll, the last spur of the Hathial, suitable for an acropolis. Besides, the level space in the north could provide a town-planner with a suitable opportunity for planning. The Tamra Nala skirting its western side could also be an effective source of water for the new city.

According to Marshall (1951, I: 118) there are seven occupational strata in Sirkap spanning three or four centuries of occupation. The earliest (Stratum VII) is pre-Indo-Greek; the sixth and fifth date from the Indo-Greek period and the rest belong to the Saka and Parthian domination. The excavated remains of Sirkap are mostly of the second stratum and thus of the Saka-Parthian period.

A new precision was brought to the history of Sirkap by Wheeler's excavations in 1944–45. To the north of the Saka-Parthian Sirkap there are remnants of a mud rampart of the Indo-Greek period, locally known as the Kachcha Kot. Marshall (1951, I: 117) believed that during the Saka-Parthian period when a stone (rubble set in mud) fortification wall was built the perimeter of the city was contracted leaving out the Kachcha Kot area. The 1944–45 excavations have shown that the rebuilding of the Saka-Parthian period did not imply any contraction of the periphery of the Indo-Greek city which included in the north the area of Kachcha Kot, but suggested the shifting of its centre to the south to include for the first time the spurs of the Hathial.

There are thus two successive Sirkaps, essentially distinct from each other: (i) an Indo-Greek city of the second century BC situated entirely on the river-plain and fortified with mud (brick?) defences of which the Kachcha Kot is a fragment; and (ii) a Saka or early Parthian city of the first century BC centred further south in order to comprise the impending ridges of Hathial (Wheeler in A. Ghosh 1948: 84).

Among the modern archaeologists F.R. Allchin (personal discussion) believes that Kachcha Kot is an undated earthen embankment without any archaeological significance.

The periphery of the Saka-Parthian Sirkap was more than 3 miles (4.827 km) long, the entire length being protected by a stone wall. This did not form any rectangle or parallelogram but followed closely the lie of the land. Except in the north and east the wall was never straight. Its thickness varied between 15 ft (4.57 m) and 21 ft 6 ins (6.55 m) and its height might have been between 20 and 30 ft (6.09–9.14 m). On the northern side it was strengthened by a raised beam, about 25 ft (7.62 m) wide, and it had a series of rectangular bastions, possibly more than one storeyed, set at regular intervals along its face. The curtain wall between the bastions also had a beam on the inside for use by defenders and was loopholed above.

Of the gateways only the northern one has been excavated. In all probability there were gateways on the other three sides also. The northern gateway was set slightly to the east of the main street. Marshall (1951, I: 114) suggests two reasons for this particular arrangement: no invader could rush the gateway and the street at the same time and secondly, the rain water coming down the street would meet the city-wall before sliding down the culvert below the gateway. The gateway, a large hall (62 by 35 ft/18.89 by 10.66 m, inside measurement),projected about 20 ft (6.09 m) on both sides of the wall. The outer projection was of a more solid construction, possibly a later addition. The four guardrooms were set against the outer face of the wall. There were two wells here, probably meant for both sentries and wayfarers. The solidity of the construction of the gateway suggests that it had at least one upper storey.

An inner defence separated the acropolis on the Hathial spur from the lower city. Marshall (1951, I: 117) could only suppose its existence but the 1944–45 excavations identified 'the actual remains of the western part of this cross-wall. At one point it is based upon a stone-revetted glacis and at another on a high-stepped foundation' (A. Ghosh 1948: 43).

The excavated portions of Sirkap are limited to a broad strip, which begins at the northern wall and continues along the main street for about 2000 ft (609.6 m). Besides, some work was carried out at a site called Mahal and two stupas (Kunala and G stupas), all within the fortification but situated on the Hathial.

Little is known about Sirkap earlier than the Saka-Parthian period. Though Blocks 1', a', b' and c' in the Indo-Greek level were excavated, the unearthed structures are not of interest. It has, however, been established that the alignment of the outer walls of the houses remained unchanged throughout. The rubble masonry of the sixth stratum (the first Indo-Greek phase) was coarser than that of the fifth stratum (the second Indo-Greek phase) and Marshall infers on this basis that 'in the building of the original city of Sirkap the Greeks were compelled to work in a hurry but that a generation or more later, when they were well settled in Taxila, they improved upon initial efforts' (Marshall 1951, I: 123). A few Indo-Greek structures were revealed in the 1944–45 excavations also.

The Saka-Parthian Sirkap is a compact specimen of grid-planning. The main street is remarkably straight. The side-streets which branch off from it are narrower but seldom less straight (Twelfth Street, however, has a distinct bend). The blocks of houses between them are mostly clusters of private dwellings but a few small stupas (cf. the stupa between the Second and Third Streets) and at least two temples (an apsidal temple between the Fifth and Sixth Streets and the shrine of the double-headed eagle in Block F) are found among them.

Except for a few houses under the city wall which are poor and shoddy, the houses in this part of Sirkap are commodious, with, on an average, 15000 sq. ft (1395 sq. m) of ground each. They represent in all probability the wealthier part of the city, an inference which may be supported by the magnificence of some of the antiquities found here—hoards of jewellery, silver-ware, etc. The house-pattern centred around a courtyard or more than one courtyard with rooms on all sides. A particularly big house is the one marked 1G on the plan, which with its four courts and more than thirty rooms on the ground floor covers an area of 24000 sq. ft (2232 sq. m). The rooms opening on the main street might have served in most cases as shops. Built of rubble-masonry the house-walls were mud-plastered both inside and outside. Occasionally colour was applied to the plaster.

A structural complex in the southeastern extremity of the excavated part has been called a palace by Marshall (1951, I: 171–6). Its over-all area was 250 by 418 ft (106.68 by 127.40 m) and besides the main street to the west it was surrounded by the Twelfth and Thirteenth Streets. Of its three entrances one is from the main street while the two others are from Thirteenth Street. The entrance from the main street led to a court with a raised hall on its southern side, supposed to be the 'court of Private Audience' with an adjunct, something like the Mughal Diwan-i-khas. The entrances from Thirteenth Street led to two other courts, the 'court of the guard' and the 'court of public audience'. From the 'court of public audience' one could go through a door in the north to a few rooms supposedly meant for state-guests while further north lay the 'zenana' or ladies' quarters where a small stupa and a few votive terracotta tanks were meant for the religious rites of the ladies.

It may be emphasized that Marshall's description of this structural complex as a palace rests on three grounds: (1) its similarity with the Khorsabad palace of Sargon ('there is the same great court surrounded by chambers and on one side of it the same court of retainers; on the other, the apartments of the zenana. Here also, the other half of the palace is occupied just as it is at Taxila, by reception and public-rooms') (cf. Marshall 1951, I: 176), (2) its size, far more massive than that of the private houses, and (3) the comment of Philostratus based on Appolonius that there was no great display of buildings in the palace of Taxila and that the men's quarters, the portico and the court were all of a modest, subdued character.

A high ground in the rocky ridges at the extreme western end of the Hathial spur, locally known as the 'mahal' (signifying royal residence) has revealed a complex of buildings which covers an area of 310 by

240 ft (94.48 by 73.15 m). The basic unit consists of a number of open courts which measure between 50 and 60 ft (15.24 and 18.28 m) each way, and the principal rooms around them compare favourably with those in the 'palace'. Its regulated planning is also noteworthy and in marked contrast with the rest of the houses in the lower city. Constructed earlier, the excavated remains of this complex belong to the first century AD (Marshall 1951: I, Chapter 7).

III. *Sirsukh*

In the closing years of the first century AD the Kushans laid out a new city at the site of Sirsukh, about a mile north-northeast of Sirkap across the rivulet of Lundi. What we know about Sirsukh is confined essentially to its fortification wall and a limited area inside. An interesting but unexplored feature of Sirsukh may be the chain of mounds to its north-west.

Somewhat like an irregular rectangle on plan, the Kushan Sirsukh measures some 1500 yards (1371.6 m) along its northern and southern sides and 1100 yards (1005.84 m) along its northern and western sides. An idea of the fortification wall comes from the exposure made near its southeastern corner. It was constructed of rough rubble faced with neatly fitting limestone masonry of the heavy diaper type. In the outer face it had an added roll plinth for the strengthening of the foundation and the prevention of undermining. There were bastions, semi-circular in plan, at regular intervals.

Inside the fortification wall the excavations near what is known on the plan as the Pindora mounds have revealed two open courts with attached chambers, apparently part of a big building.

KASHMIR

Archaeologically it is still not easy to determine when the valley of Kashmir, essentially a mountain-girt narrow strip, about 84 miles long and up to 15 miles wide, gained historical importance. Both at Burzahom and Gufkral the neolithic level is followed by a menhir-building mega-lithic level which at Gufkral has been dated 'from 1550 to 1100 BC'. Three identifiable iron artifacts (2 needles, 1 nail), wheelmade dull red pottery with shapes such as jars with 'shapeless rims', long-necked jars, bowls, basins, a dish-on-stand, a medium-sized globular jar and channel-spouted vessels, and the remains of rice and millet have been found in this level

(A.K. Sharma 1991). The diagnostic early historic pottery—the NBPW—appears in Period II at Semthan in the Anantanag district, its Period I yielding both burnished and plain grey wares, and specimens of wheat, rice and barley. This seems to conform to the megalithic level at Gufkral.

There is no doubt about the wide distribution of early historical sites in Kashmir (cf. IAR 1981–82: 16–19, 1983–84: 35, 1984–85: 23–4, 1985–86: 34–7, 1987–88: 31–2).

The literary sources refer to very early historical beginnings. The classical sources refer to a place designated variously as Kaspapyros, Kaspatyros and Kaspeira, supposedly an ancient city in Kashmir. According to the *Rajatarangini*, Asoka built a city in the valley and in this he was followed by three Kushan kings—Hushka, Jushka and Kanishka—each the founder of a city after his own name—Hushkapura, Jushkapura and Kanishkapura. Attempts have been made to identify these places but there has been no systematic archaeological investigation at any of the proposed sites (see S.C. Ray 1957: 3–10, Chakrabarti 1984). At this point it may be emphasized that the basic geographical importance of Kashmir in the history of India is that it gives access to central Asia through its northern territories of Gilgit and Hunza on the one hand and to Tibet and thus to China through Ladakh on the other. These routes, particularly the one leading to central Asia, became markedly significant under the Kushans in the early centuries AD and it is probable that a systematic growth of urban settlement in Kashmir may be linked to this factor. However, more clear archaeological investigations are needed.

PANJAB PLAINS

The Panjab plains proper lie between the Salt range and the Sutlej. One still is not quite sure when the early historic period began in this area but an investigation of the route of Alexander's campaign and the associated places should provide a convenient starting point. Cunningham (1963 rep.: 130–209) located a number of settlements but his work has not been followed up by excavations except at one place—Tulamba in the valley of the Ravi (Mughal 1967). Tulamba covers a big mound (1630 by 1220 ft or *c.* 530 by 400 m) with the traces of a citadel, and according to the excavator, 'the site may be identified with one of the cities of the Mallois taken not by Alexander himself but by one of the his generals, Peithon' (Mughal 1967: 22). The limited excavated area has, however, belied the assumption of Cunningham (1963 rep.: 189) that the citadel of Tulamba was encircled by a moat during the time of Alexander.

One particular site in the Panjab plains deserves close attention, although no proper archaeological investigation seems to have taken place here. Sakala/Sagala, the capital of the Indo-Greek king, Menander, has been described as a rich and prosperous city laid out on the typical chess-board pattern in a contemporary text, the *Milindapanha*. In the *Mahabharata* this was the capital of Madras, which corresponds to the modern district of Sialkot 'between the Chenab and the Ravi or between the Jhelum and the Ravi' (B.C. Law, 1969). Cunningham confused between Sangala in Alexander's campaign to the west of the Ravi and Sakala lying to its east. He placed the site at Sanganwala Tibba in the Jhang district whereas Sakala is now identified with modern Sialkot. The literary sources further indicate that Sakala was an important early historical trade-centre with connections with the West and the Gangetic valley (for this aspect, see H.P. Chakraborti 1966).

S.M. Ali (1966: 145) has pointed out that 'before the irrigation canals came into existence, the population distribution in the (Panjab) doabs was always concentrated in the northern belt of the doab, i.e., the piedmont zone of the mountains'.

SIND

The early historical archaeology of Sind also remains largely an unknown territory, although the term Sindhu, the ancient name for the modern province of Sind, occurs quite early in Indian literature (Law 1954: 127). The chronology of the classical references is more or less precisely fixed. In 510 BC there was a Persian-inspired voyage under Scylax to explore the course of the Indus beginning from the region of modern Attock. In 326 BC Alexander, while sailing down the Indus, encountered a number of independent Sind tribes and there is a specific reference to the kingdom of Mousikanos whose capital, according to Vincent Smith (1924: 94–110), may be located at Alor or Aror in the Sukkur district. Alexander's chroniclers also refer to a port called Patala in the delta from where Nearchus embarked on his coast-bound journey to the mouth of the Euphrates-Tigris. Despite a suggested identification with Bahmanabad, the place has not been precisely located, nor is there any proof of a settlement of comparable antiquity (except perhaps Brahminabad/Bahmanabad) in the entire province. There is lack of archaeological proof to suggest that in the second century BC the merchants from the Indus delta were travelling as far as the island of Socotra and that Sind during this period was commercially significant enough to find mention in a Chinese source

(B.N. Mukherjee 1970). Sind became undoubtedly significant in the early centuries AD and when it came within the Kushan empire and was an important geographical territory catering to the Indo-Roman trade. Archaeologically even this fact remains largely uncorroborated though 'the many Buddhist stupas which were built in Sind in the early years of the Christian era' (Cousens 1929: 168) point to its increased importance. There have been some investigations at the site of Bahmanabad (Cousens 1929: 52, Pakistan Archaeology, 1, 1964: 49–55) which, although the site of the Arab capital of Sind, Mansurah, seems to have had considerably early beginnings. One detects unmistakable early historic terracotta ringwells and beads 'below the Muhammedan strata' in Cousens' report on this site (for a survey of the 'Buddhist period' in Sind on the basis of the Islamic sources, see Warwick Ball 1989).

INDO-GANGETIC DIVIDE

The Indo-Gangetic divide, the divide between the two great river-systems of India, lies between the Sutlej and the Yamuna and has as its other limits, the Siwaliks on the north, the dried-up course of the Ghaggar in the Rajasthan desert in the south and the Aravalli ridge reaching upto Delhi in the southeast.

O.H.K. Spate (1957: 534) who emphasizes the significance of this area as a physiographical unit calls it a transitional area both physically and culturally:

Commercially and culturally it is the great marchland between Islam and Hindustan: Muslim culture today finds its highest expression in Lahore, while on the other side of the region Muttra is rich in Hindu tradition; between them Delhi is (or was until recently) a Muslim outpost, yet with deep roots in the remoter Hindu Past.

This analysis based on later day Indian history seems to find a significant correspondence with the earlier archaeological aspects of the region. The early archaeological stages are: the Sarasvati-and-Indus-based Harappans who spread over the entire area from Rupar at the foot of the Siwaliks to the sites on the Ghaggar-Hakra; the ochre-coloured pottery which occurs both in the divide and the upper Gangetic valley; the painted grey ware which possesses a similar distribution, and finally the northern black polished ware or the NBPW which heralds the beginning of the historic period in a broad sweep from the lower Gangetic valley to the divide. From then on to AD 300, the entire area was a fermenting point of both Indian and extra-Indian impulses: the growth of the tribal republics of the Yaudheyas and others; and the advent of the Indo-Greeks, Parthians, Scythians and Kushans, all archaeologically reflected in the distribution of their coins and other traits. The Indo-Gangetic divide is, in fact, an indisputable area of cultural transition where influences both from inner India and the west mingled together.

There is no lack of early historical sites in this area (for a general survey, see Y.D. Sharma 1964: 48–9), of which only a few can be mentioned here.

Rupar

At the foot of the Siwaliks, Rupar III, dated *c*. 600–200 BC, yields NBPW, punch-marked and unincised cast copper coins, an inscribed seal in Mauryan Brahmi and other small finds, placing the level on par with the early historical period of the Gangetic valley.

Kankar-stone or river-pebbles set in mud-mortar were used for buildings in this period, although houses of mud and kiln-burnt bricks were by no means rare. A 12-ft wide burnt-brick wall, traced to a length of about 250 ft, proceeds in a curve at the exposed ends and in all likelihood enclosed a tank, since an inlet through the wall was possibly used to feed the reservoir with rain-water. The upper levels of this occupation are characterized by soak-wells lined with terracotta rings (Y.D. Sharma 1964: 48–9).

The next period, marked by a few structural levels of which little has been published, carries the occupation of the site to about AD 600.

Sugh, Sunet, Agroha, Sanghol, Thaneswar and Rangmahal

Excavations at Sugh (IAR 1963–64: 27–8, 1965–66: 35–6) have revealed very little except a broad stratigraphy beginning with the PGW level but the place has been identified with ancient Srughna, mentioned, among others, byHiuen-Tsang (Law 1954: 12–9). The site, according to Cunningham (1963 rep.: 291) is a natural stronghold; it showed evidence of a fortification on the surface and had a circuit of about 4 miles. Sunet (IAR 1983–84: 67–70) or ancient Sunetra in the Ludhiana district, Panjab, showed a sequence beginning with the late Harappans, but the primary structural evidence is from its Period IV (200 BC–AD 300) which revealed a complete houseplan: the main entrance on the northeast, an open courtyard in the middle, traces of stairs, two rooms at the back, a room with an oven (kitchen?), a room with a small water-tank (bathroom?) and a storage room for grains. Built of burnt brick, this house was flanked on three sides by mud huts which have been reported to be servants' quarters. It had an elaborate drainage system and there was a small platform (2.85 by 1.45 m) in front of the main entrance to the house which is supposed to date from the Kushan/late Kushan period. Another interesting aspect of the site is the discovery of a hoard of 30,000 Yaudheya coin moulds and a large number of seals and sealings. Agroha in the Hissar district of Haryana has been excavated for a number of seasons (IAR 1978–79: 68–9, 1979–80: 31, 1980–81: 15–16) showing a sequence back to the NBPW, but little else besides some brick structures of the late-Kushan-Gupta period. Sanghol in the Ludhiana district has been excavated since 1968–69 (IAR 1968–69: 25–6, 1969–70: 31–1, 1970–71: 30–1, 1971–72: 39, 41, 1977–78: 43–4, 1980–81: 46, 1984–85: 62–4), but apart from its late Harappan antecedence the most important feature of the site is the discovery of 117 Mathura sculptural pieces in the context of a spoked and circular stupa of the early centuries AD.

The excavations conducted at modern Thaneshwar near Kurukshetra in Haryana covered principally the mound of Harsh-ka-Tila which, although about 75 ha. in extent, forms only a section of the overall area of ancient occupation (for both literary and archaeological references, see Pande 1990). The report is available for the first season of work (IAR 1987–88: 28–30). Traces of a seventh century AD 'palace' have been said to be obtained. Another related site is Karna-ka-Qila (IAR 1970–71: 15–16) where the NBPW period (Period I) showed both burnt and mud brick structures. There were in all seven structural phases in the early Christian era (Period II). One season's excavation at Rangmahal (Rydh 1959) yielded little by way of planning but that the site was important has been demonstrated by a large collection of terracottas, mostly of the Gupta period, found during excavations.

THE U.P. HIMALAYAN AND SUB-HIMALAYAN BELT

The work by Garhwal University students under K.P. Nautiyal has primarily been instrumental in the discovery of a large number of sites in this region, including apparently protohistoric burials at an altitude of 4000 m near Joshi Math. In addition, the discovery of PGW or PGW-related sites such as Thapli and Jainal-Naula deserve attention. A temple and stupa site has been excavated at Moradhwaj in the Bijnor district (cf. IAR 1982–83: 94–5). Another temple site was excavated by N.C. Ghosh at Virabhadra near Rishikesh (IAR 1973–74: 28–30, 1974–75: 41–2). Kashipur in the Nainital district has a sequence going back to the NBPW period. A structure (24 by 18 m) made of burnt bricks and 'laid in the east-west direction in the shape of a flying Garuda, the head being exactly towards the east and the tail towards the west' (Nautiyal and Khanduri 1990) has been identified as a Vedic brick altar of the second century BC–first century AD at Purola in the Uttarkashi district. No large settlement site has yet been reported from anywhere in the area.

UPPER GANGETIC VALLEY

The downward limit of the upper Gangetic valley has been suggested by Spate (1957: 546) to be a 'line running roughly from the Ganges-Yamuna confluence at Allahabad across the north-northwest–south-southeast section of the Ghaghra'. In terms of modern political units this conforms broadly to the western two-thirds of Uttar Pradesh excluding the montane districts of the north and the districts of Jhansi, Banda and Hamirpur lying on the peninsular foreland. As in the Indo-Gangetic divide, there is no dearth of early historical sites associated with the NBPW in this area. But only a few of them have been properly excavated and have yielded any co-ordinated data regarding urban growth and town-planning. Besides, some sites with an unmistakable urban significance in contemporary literary records have not been excavated at all.

Hastinapur

Hastinapur (ancient name Hastinapura), identified with a place of the same name in the Mawana tehsil of Meerat, now five miles away from the Ganges to the west, had distinct epic, Puranic and Jaina associations. It was the Kuru capital in the Mahabharata till a river-flood led to the transfer of the capital downstream to the ancient city of Kausambi. In Jaina literature it was the dwelling place of Risabha, the first Jaina tirthan-kara and also a place which was often visited by Mahavira, the founder of Jainism (Law 1954: 81). The site was excavated by Lal (B.B. Lal 1955) in 1950–52. He points out that the settlement developed lengthwise along the river and that the original width is impossible to determine. The two main mounds which one now observes at the site formed originally a single unit.

Period III is early historical (600–200 BC) and Period IV has been dated between the early second century BC and the late third century AD. The excavations were not horizontal but whatever evidence there is suggests some amount of planning. In Period III burnt bricks (of three different sizes) came to be in general use for the construction of houses, though mud and mudbricks were also occasionally used. In one cutting there were three structural levels while in another there were six. A burnt brick wall was partially traced for 28 ft and the size of one room was found to be 15 ft (4.15 m) square. Among the burnt brick drains an excavated specimen was 3 ft (0.91 m) deep, possessed a brick-floor and lining and was traced for 24 ft (*c.* 7.5 m). These were perhaps general civic drains while in the case of individual houses several vertically placed long jars with perforations at the bottom generally served as soakage pits. The excavated terracotta ring-wells were of two types: some were shallow, with only a few rings while those of the second type went much deeper. The first type possibly denoted a soakage pit whereas the second type denoted a well in the real sense of the term. The occupational phase of Period III came to an end due to a large-scale fire which is evident from burnt-out remains all over the excavated area. In Period IV there were seven structural sub-periods. Houses were invariably of burnt bricks and squarish bricks were used for the flooring. There is also evidence of regular house-planning with orientations roughly along the cardinal directions.

Indraprastha

Indraprastha in the Purana Qila area of modern Delhi was the Pandava capital in the Mahabharata, also alluded to in other sources (N.L. Dey 1971 rep.: 77–8). Archaeologically, very little is known of the site, though a small excavation in 1954–55 (IAR 1954–55: 13–14) established its cultural succession from the PGW phase to the Kushan period and later. Burnt brick houses and terracotta ring-wells were noted in the early historic period. The subsequent excavations (cf. IAR 1969–70: 4–6, 1970–71: 8–11) did not yield much except the remains of what may be a Gupta temple. A Saka-Kushan house measured 1.80 m square, with a 0.75 m wide doorway. The earlier structures went back to the Maurya period.

Atranjikhera

This large (*c.* 46 ha.) site on the right bank of the Kali Nadi, a tributary of the Ganges, has not yet been satisfactorily identified with any ancient site mentioned in literature, although its excavator, R.C. Gaur (1983), seems to prefer its identification with Vairanja/Veranja of early Buddhist literature (for a differing view point, see A. Ghosh 1989). References have been made to the existence of a mud defence wall, a granary and an apsidal temple in the NBPW phase. Gaur (1983: 254) writes that 'the settlement seems to have grown into a full-fledged town during this period'

Mathura

The literary references to Mathura are copious and of all kinds—Brahmanical, Buddhist, Jaina and classical. In the Mahabharata and the Puranas Mathura has been associated with the Yadava clan, itself divided into a number of septs like the Andhakas and the Vrishnis who later on migrated to Dwaraka in western India. The Milindapanha refers to Mathura as one of the chief cities of India. The numerous inscriptions and *ayagapatas* recovered from the Kankali tila at Mathura testify to the fact that Mathura was an important centre of Jainism from about 200 BC onwards. The Jaina inscriptions are also significant because they refer to various local persons and their professions—caravan-leader, perfumer, banker, metal-worker, treasurer, etc. Mathura was also a noted centre of the Bhagavata and the Naga cults. Among the earlier authors, Patanjali, Panini and Kautilya refer to Mathura. Kautilya refers to its cotton industry while Patanjali speaks of its kettle-drums, garments and karsapanas. Traditionally known as the centre of Surasena country, Mathura also finds reference in Megasthenes as Methora in the country of the Surasenoi. As Methora it has also been mentioned by Pliny and Ptolemy (for the literary and epigraphic references to Mathura, Law 1954: 106–10, Dey 1971 rep.: 127–8, H.P. Chakraborti 1966: 169–73, D.M. Srinivasan 1983).

These literary sources amply testify to the fact that Mathura was both a religious centre and an important entrepot of trade and commerce. The commercial significance obviously sprang from the fact that it lay at the junction of two important Indian trade-routes: the one which travelled from the Gangetic valley to the northwest and the other branching off to west India from Mathura itself. On the political level Mathura was the southern capital of the Kushans. This inclusion in a political unit which had its epi-centre in the northwest and extension up to the west coast must have made Mathura one of the most important commercial centres of the period. Despite intermittent explorations spread over more than a century, primarily aimed at recovering antiquities, Mathura remains among the most inadequately excavated important early historical sites of India, one of the reasons being the location of the modern built-up area over much of the ancient settlement.

A co-ordinated picture of the lay-out of the ancient settlement is hard to come by. In 1862 Cunningham (1966 rep.: 13–46, pl. I) recorded nine separate mounds among which he gave some prominence to the Katra and Kankali tila because of their wealth of stone sculptural and architectural pieces and inscriptions. None of the subsequent explorations and excavations aimed at giving a comprehensive idea of the site as a whole till Stuart Piggott in the early forties (whose fieldwork results have been incorporated in his brief essay on Mathura; Piggott 1945) detected the alignment of a mudbrick fortification wall and also discovered PGW and NBPW from the exposed sections. Evidence of the fortification was also confirmed by subsequent explorations during which a limited area in the Katra mound was also excavated. An exploratory survey 'revealed the existence of two rings of mud-ramparts, the first eliptical in shape and the second quadrangular and comprised within the first, as if signifying a citadel' (IAR 1954–55: 15). M.C. Joshi's excavations at various spots at the site (IAR 1973–74: 31–2, 1974–75: 48–50, 1975–76: 53–5, 1976–77: 54–6) have led to a better understanding of the urban plan of ancient Mathura (M.C. Joshi 1983). Beginning as a small PGW settlement, Mathura became an extensive urban settlement (*c.* 360 ha. or more) fortified by a massive mud wall forming a longish crescent on plan with the Yamuna in the east. Except on the river side, there could be a moat on three of the other sides where regular silt deposits occur immediately outside the fortifications. 'Within this period, houses normally associated with ring-wells, were built on compact mud platforms, probably in clusters, and roofs were supported by mud walls and bamboo or wooden posts. The use of baked bricks was confined to a few structures. In one case, large-sized bricks . . . were used as veneering material on the face of a mud platform serving as a base of a house' (M.C. Joshi 1983). The mud fortification apparently fell into disuse during the next period but there was an increased use of burnt bricks as housing material (the late centuries BC). The next phase continued up to *c.* AD 300.

A significant structural development of this period was the revival and enlargement of the mud fortification around the city. In addition, an inner fortification with possibly semi-circular bastions and a moat on at least the western or northwestern side was also built. Its remains were located in the northern area of the Katra mound. Built of mud, it was externally strengthened by a short retaining wall of broken and overburnt bricks, tiles, clay lumps, etc., and originally had a considerable height. . . . It can be guessed that the inner fortification had roughly a quadrangular shape around the central part of the city (M.C. Joshi 1983).

The mound of Sonkh in the neighbourhood of Mathura (IAR 1966–67: 40–3, 1968–69: 40, 1969–70: 42–3, 1970–71: 39–40, 1971–72: 47–8, 1972–73: 33–5) has hardly revealed anything of structural importance except a Kushan period apsidal complex.

Kampil

Mentioned in both the epics, the Ramayana and the Mahabharata, Kampilya was the capital of South Panchala. Panchala territory corresponds roughly to modern Rohilkhand with the Ganges dividing it into two parts—the northern and southern. There is a reference to it in Panini also (Law 1954: 91–3). Balaram Srivastava (1968: 59–60) points out that Kampilya lay on a route mentioned in the *Satapatha Brahmana*. The place has been identified with the site of modern Kampil, 28 miles southeast of Fategarh in the district of Farrukhabad (N.L. Dey 1971 rep.: 88). Brief excavations (IAR 1975–76: 51–2) have taken the antiquity of the site back to the PGW period.

Sankisa

Modern Sankisa, about 23 miles west of Farrukhabad in U.P. is called Samkasya in the epics and is referred to as the capital of Kusadhvaja, the younger brother of Janaka-Videha, the father of Sita. According to the Ramayana it was on the Ikshumati and was surrounded by ramparts. In the Jatakas it has been referred to as Samkassa. The literary sources leave no doubt that it was an important city (Law 1954: 120, N.L. Dey 1971 rep.: 177). While exploring the ruins at Sankisa, Cunningham (1963 rep.: 311–14) noted the rampart to be more than three and a half miles in circuit. Visual observations of the ruins suggest that the gates were on the northeast, southeast and east sides. In 1927 Hirananda Sastri (1927) unearthed an assortment of structures classified into Blocks A, B, C and D. Among the antiquities there were many clay seals, the earliest of which has been palaeographically dated to *c.* 200 BC.

Kanauj

Kanauj or ancient Kanyakubja, some miles away from modern Kanpur, was primarily important in the post-Gupta period when it was the capital of the Maukharis. But both the epics refer to Kanauj and there is also a reference in the Buddhist *Vinayapitaka* (Law 1954: 9–4). Brief excavations (IAR 1955–56: 19–20) unearthed PGW at the site.

Chakranagar

This site in the Etahwa district of U.P. has been identified as the city of Ekachakra mentioned in the Mahabharata. The finds of a copper coin of Menander and other early historic inscribed material throw some light on the antiquity of this unexcavated place. D.R. Sahni (ann. rep. A.S.I. 1923–24: 59–60) writes:

The ruins consist of a vast *khera* about three miles in circuit and visible from a long way off. In all probability the site was originally occupied by a walled city surrounded by a ditch on three sides, the fourth side being protected by the Jumna river. No portions of the old enclosure walls are now visible anywhere though their position is clearly marked in some places by continuous lines of ruins strewn with brickbats and potsherds. The inner citadel is divided into two portions by a ravine running down to the river on either side. The portion adjoining the river is being gradually cut away by the river. . . . The other portion of the citadel which is standing to a great height appears to be the most promising part of the site for exploration.

(It is surprising that a major site of this type has been overlooked in A. Ghosh 1989.)

Ahichchhatra

This site in the Bareilly district of U.P is known as the capital of North Panchala and has been extensively mentioned in literary and inscriptional sources (Law 1942). By the eleventh century AD the position of Ahichchhatra as the capital of North Panchala was usurped by modern Budaon. A systematic archaeological investigation at the site was initiated in 1940–44 and renewed in 1963–65. The ruins at the site consist of a 'brick fortification of the shape of a rough isosceles triangle with a perimeter of about three miles and a half, enclosing a series of rolling mounds, the highest of which, representing the site of a temple, stands to a height of 75 feet above the level of the cultivated field outside' (Ghosh and Panigrahi 1946: 37–8). The nature of the defence wall around the city was clearly established in 1965–66, though even in the 1940–44 excavations it was found that this wall came to be built not much later than

100 BC and that a long partition wall in the late phase divided the fortified city into two sections—eastern and western—the eastern section being deserted after the construction of a partition wall.

Stratigraphically the defence wall was built in the post-NBPW phase, dated in the early centuries AD, and found to possess four phases. In the first phase it was built of mud and in the second phase was 'reinforced at the apex by the construction of a free-built brick-wall, 4.98 m broad and 2.59 m high running throughout its length. To economise the use of burnt bricks rectangular gaps measuring 2.13 by 1.32 m were left in the brick wall at regular intervals and the openings filled with rubble and clay' (IAR 1963–64). In Phase 3 this brick-wall was given the protection of a mud cover, buttressed by another packing in Phase 4. At a still later stage gaps in the outer wall of mud-packing were filled up by a fragmentary wall of brick and brick-bats till finally a boundary wall in the northeastern corner of the site screened off the insecure area.

Little is known about the structures inside the fortified enclosure but it was noted that burnt bricks came to be used in the NBPW phase and were employed more widely in the succeeding phases. The 1940–44 excavations unearthed two terraced temples, one of which belongs to the early Gupta period. It was also pointed out in the 1940–44 excavations that 'each stratum (of Ahichchhatra) had its own plan and alignment of houses radically different from those of the next stratum' (Ghosh and Panigrahi 1946: 39). This point has not been emphasized in the subsequent report which, on the contrary, says that the houses 'followed the same cardinal alignment throughout the successive level' (IAR 1963–64).

Saketa-Ayodhya

According to A.N. Bose (1961: 205–6) Saketa and Ayodhya, both celebrated in the Buddhist sources and the Ramayana, were the same city, despite an opinion to the contrary. B.B. Lal (in A. Ghosh 1989, II: 31–2) writes that 'the ruins at Ayodhya have a circuit of about 4 to 5 km and rise at places to a height of about 10 m above the surrounding ground-level'. His exploratory trenches show the NBPW in the earliest level with some associated wattle-and-daub and mud house remains. A Jaina figure in grey terracotta (fourth–third century BC) and rouletted ware (*c.* first–second century AD or earlier) are among the noteworthy finds at the site. The sequence in the janma bhumi (birth-place) area begins with the NBPW and this phase continues, with several structural phases up to the third century AD. A massive wall of bricks in this sector before the third century BC has been interpreted as a fortification wall which appears to have had a fairly deep ditch 'almost like a moat' (IAR 1976–77: 52–3).

Hulaskhera

This site in the Lucknow district (IAR 1978–79: 74–5, 1979–80: 77, 1980–81: 71, 1981–82: 71–2, 1982–83: 98–9, 1983–84: 88–9) has, among other things, the remains of a road, a Gupta period citadel and some Kushan structures. The road, traced for about 120 m, had two phases. In the first phase it was 9.8 m wide and was built of burnt bricks 'in double-box pattern with parallel walls on either side and also a wall in the centre. . . . The boxes have been constructed at intervals of 2.30 to 3 m. All the boxes were found filled with compact blackish clay taken from the lake itself. The surface of the road was made of brick-ballast mixed with earth. The double rectangular boxes were intended apparently to hold the dumped clay in position and prevent it from being washed away by water' (IAR 1981–82: 71–2). The road was 5 m wide in its second phase. The northern, western and southern walls of the citadel were 160 m, 157 m and 148 m in length, respectively. A big storage jar found in situ on the floor of a Kushan level house was found to contain some grain. This jar was placed on a specially constructed circular structure of bricks. This used to be a common feature of the houses of the period. There were also some house complexes of the Kushan period, with a space of 75 cm–1 m provided between the complexes (15 by 12 m, 11 by 4.5 m, 13 by 4.5 m) which possessed two or three rooms each. Some of these rooms were brick-paved while some of them had mud-plastered floors.

Kausambi

The references to Kausambi in early literature and epigraphical records have been collated by N.N. Ghosh (1935), Law (1939) and G.R. Sharma (1969). Among the more important references one notes that the *Satapatha Brahmana* refers to a person as Kausambeya, meaning perhaps a resident of Kausambi, a meaning substantiated by the occurrence of the word Kausambeyaka in this sense in one of the Bharhut inscriptions. Kausambi has been referred to in both the epics and according to one testimony the Kuru capital was shifted from Hastinapur to Kausambi by Nichakshu who stood in the direct line of succession from the Pandavas. Usually Kausambi is known as the capital of the Vatsas, Vatsa being one of the sixteen major states or *mahajanapadas* of India on the eve of the birth of the Buddha. Kausambi remained an important political centre in India throughout her history. Some of the references in Buddhist literature are more precisely suggestive of Kausambi's early importance. The *Suttanipata* mentions it as one of the halting places in a journey from Pratisthana (modern Paithan) on the Godavari in the Deccan to Rajagriha in Magadha. Obviously it also lay on the route from the middle Gangetic valley to the northwest. Another pointed reference is that three bankers of Kausambi—Ghosita, Kukkuta and Pavarika, all disciples of the Buddha— built three retreats for him in Kausambi, known respectively as Ghositarama, Kukkutarama and Pavarikambavana. Not merely does Hiuen-Tsang refer to these but also the identity of one, Ghositarama, has indisputably been established by archaeology.

The literary and epigraphic importance of Kausambi has been amply reflected in her present ruins spreading over an area of eight square miles both inside and outside a fortified enclosure. The fortification itself is roughly oblong in shape and possesses a periphery of about 4 miles. The site lies on the left bank of the Yamuna, about 32 miles southwest of modern Allahabad. Cunningham's initial identification (Cunningham 1963 rep.: 330–5) of the place with ancient Kausambi was put beyond all doubt by the discovery and identification of the Ghositarama monastery (G.R. Sharma 1958: 44) and an inscription (dated AD 1565) on an in situ stone pillar at the site which refers to the place as Kausambipuri (Law 1939).

Kausambi has been excavated extensively by G.R. Sharma (1958: 1960, 1969, IAR 1953–54 to 1966–67 with a gap in 1965–66). The 30 ft thick cultural deposit at the site has been divided into four periods. The first two periods antedate the NBPW (Period III) while the last one post-dates it. Period I reveals some pottery among which a black-and red ware seems to be dominant along with some elements which Sharma calls generally 'chalcolithic'. Period II yields PGW. There are twenty-five structural periods in all and except for the first two and the last one they are associated with the four main building stages of the fortification.

Sharma's chronology of the site seems to depend on Periods III–V of the fortification. The sum total of the argument based primarily on a study of coins is that Period III of the fortification should be dated to 'the period of the Mitra kings of Kausambi who, on the grounds of palaeography and other historical considerations, have been assigned to the period from the 2nd to the 1st century BC' (G.R. Sharma 1960: 20). Again, 'on numismatic grounds, Rampart 5 seems to have been built by the Maghas, who made

Kausambi their capital in the second half of the 2nd century AD'. Thus numismatic arguments have also been supplemented by the evidence of inscribed terracotta seals, terracotta figurines and iron arrowheads. The end of the rampart has been placed between AD 510 and 525, the general period of the Huna invasion of the site. On the basis of this duration (from the first half of the second century BC to *c.* AD 585) of Ramparts 3–5 and their associated sub-periods, the average span of a sub-period has been worked out to be seventy years. 'Assuming the same average span of life for the structural sub-periods associated with Ramparts 2 and 1 and also for the two pre-defence periods' (G.R. Sharma 1960: 22) the beginning of the fortification at Kausambi has been dated to 1025 BC and the beginning of occupation of the site itself to 1165 BC. So far as the chronology of the NBPW and the post-NBPW periods are concerned, the foregoing chronological argument should not be in any doubt, and as Sharma (1969, xx–xxiii, chart on p. xxii) demonstrates, the C-14 dates (all obtained from the NBPW phase) substantially support his argument for these phases. His chronology for the first two periods, however, leaves one baffled. The method by which he estimates their dates (assigning an average span of seventy years to all the sub-periods including the earlier ones) has, of course, been utilized earlier in Indian archaeology (cf. Wheeler's dating of the neolithic level of Brahmagiri) but it is never a dependable one. Secondly, Kausambi lies on the southern periphery of the PGW distribution and as such its date in this region is likely to be later than at such classical sites as Hastinapur and Atranjikhera. Moreover, the PGW continued up to the advent of the NBPW around 700/600 BC and is even likely to have coexisted with this for some time. There is not much reason to assume that the PGW at Kausambi dates from its earlier time-bracket and not from the later one. In fact, the probable lateness of the PGW at Kausambi has already been pointed out by some scholars (K.K. Sinha 1973). Moreover, the published section across the Kausambi defences reproduced 'uninscribed rectangular cast coins' in a layer (20) which is depicted as belonging to the phase of the PGW. This should suggest that the PGW at Kausambi belongs to a later period than has been assumed. As long as radiocarbon dates are not obtained for the first two periods of Kausambi, it is not possible to estimate their dates precisely. For the present a general position of their being pre-NBPW should suffice without any precise chronological emphasis.

The most imposing component of the present ruins at Kausambi is formed by her defences. The rampart wall rises to an average height of 35 ft (10.66 m) from the level of the surrounding plain with the individual towers touching the 70–5 ft (21.33–22.86 m) level. There were eleven gateways in all, of which five—two each in the east and the north and one in the west—have been considered to be the principal ones. The road leading to each gate was flanked by two mounds, obviously watch-towers, which lay across a moat encircling the rampart (except, of course, on the river side). About a mile away from this complex, there is another ring of mounds that once might have encircled the city.

The rampart was built initially of mud, the outer side being revetted with burnt bricks. This burnt brick revetment, 9 ft (less than 3 m) wide at the base, had a batter with two different angles. Finally, it was covered by a 2–3 in. (50.8–76.2 mm) thick mud and lime plaster. The earliest moat was dug sometime later and at the same time a mud bund with a basal width of 32 ft (9.75 m) and an approximate height of 18 ft (5.48 m) was built at a distance of about 24 ft (7.31 m) from the revetment of the existing rampart. Still later, in the second main stage of the rampart's history, the rampart was raised and the gap between the original rampart and its subsidiary mud bund was filled up with clay and a new subsidiary mud rampart was laid out at some distance. It was during this period that guardrooms, bastions and a stone corbelled drain were added. The rampart was extended further in its third stage. An interesting discovery which belongs to this stage was that of an altar situated outside the eastern gate at the foot of the defences, shaped like an eagle flying to the southeast and associated with a fire-place, and animal and human bones including a human skull. G.R. Sharma (1960, chapters 8–10) has adduced a mass of literary material to suggest that certain details of the construction of this altar correspond to the fire-altar prescribed for *purusamedha* or human sacrifice in ancient Indian ritualistic texts. Additions and alterations continued to be made to the rampart till its final stage.

The excavations inside the fortification revealed only a limited area of the general residential quarter of the city. Whatever evidence there is suggests that the houses conformed to the usual pattern of having a courtyard as the central focus. An important discovery is that of a road, originally 8 ft (2.43 m) wide but subsequently widened to 16 ft (4.87 m) with a compact surface and regular rut-marks. The drainage system depended both on soak-pits and regular burnt-brick drains. There were also terracotta ring-wells.

A significant discovery is that of a 'palace' occupying an area of 315 by 150 m in the southeastern corner of the fortified area. Built before the beginning of the NBPW phase at the site, the palace had three main phases. In the first phase it was built of rubble, perhaps laid with plaster.

In the second phase a dressed stone facing was provided to the walls while in the last phase the walls were made of burnt bricks but with a facing of dressed stone. The internal plan seems to have consisted of halls flanked by rooms, often interconnected by arched passage-ways. It has been argued (IAR 1960–61: 33–5) that the palace belonged to Udayana, a king of Kausambi who was a contemporary of the Buddha. In any case, the entire palace-complex resembles an inner citadel within the bigger fortification of Kausambi.

The 'Ghositarama' monastery lay inside the fortification, between the eastern gateway and the northern bend of the rampart. The identification has been possible due to the find of a terracotta sealing belonging to the monastic order of 'Ghositarama'. The central plan of the monastery with several building phases comprised a central courtyard with rooms arranged around it. The basic importance of this discovery is that it closely ties up with the life of the Buddha and is thus of immense chronological and historical significance.

Kausambi as a city met its end at the hands of the Hunas in the sixth century AD. It may be mentioned at this point that after G.R. Sharma's death there has been severe criticism (B.B. Lal 1985 a, 1985 b) of the claims of his discoveries of the eagle-shaped altar (syena-chiti) and the palace of Udayana. In the former case it has been argued that this represented nothing more than fallen debris whereas in the second case the whole structural complex has been put in the medieval period. The fact that these criticisms were aired in print only after G.R. Sharma's death has considerably lessened their value. Further, Erdosy (1984) has tried to postulate, on the basis of surface scatters of pottery (especially the NBPW), a developmental sequence of Kausambi. However, surface scatters on a site are remarkably unsure guides to the areas of occupation in different periods.

Bhita

The ruins at Bhita with traces of an oblong fortification pierced by gateways lie about 35 miles downstream of Kausambi. Cunningham ('report', vol. 3) identified the place with the old Bitbhaya-Pattana, a town mentioned in the Jaina text as being contemporary with the founder of Jainism, Mahavira. Marshall (1911–12) identified it with Vichhi or Vichchigrama primarily on the basis of the occurrence of this name in one of the excavated seals. The preliminary work by Cuningham at Bhita was followed by Marshall who excavated it more elaborately and revealed

some part of the town plan. Marshall's excavations were primarily confined to the southeast corner of the site and here he excavated two streets
named High Street and Bastion Street. High Street, marked about 30 ft
(9.14 m) wide, led to a gate, the plan of which could not be reconstructed
but which, Marshall supposed, consisted of two or three gates 'with
guardrooms attached disposed at intervals along the roadway, which ran
between the high flanking walls'.

Bastion Street, somewhat narrower, lay to the northeast of the High
Street. The defences were to its southeast and consisted of an 11 ft 2 ins
(3.40 m) thick wall, raised on an earthen rampart. This possessed a
quadrangular bastion, which projected 15 ft (4.57 m) from the outer curtain of the wall and measured 31 ft (9.44 m). The wall built in the early
Mauryan or pre-Mauryan period originally possessed a gateway at this
point, which was subsequently closed.

A house on High Street, which is supposed to date to the Maurya period
and which Marshall names 'House of the Guild' on the basis of a terracotta
seal (with a mention of the word 'Nigama' or guild) found in one of its
rooms, had twelve rooms arranged around an open rectangular courtyard.
The house perhaps had a second storey and was rebuilt several times.
Several other large houses have been excavated but the general plan was
similar. In most cases, the houses were fronted on the roadside by a row
of rooms which had in front of them a raised platform or verandah, a
feature which may still be seen in Indian bazaars.

The excavated structures and antiquities (quite a few of the seals seem
to bear the names of merchants) suggest that Bhita, whatever its name was
in ancient times, was a prosperous trade centre. As at Kausambi, its occupation also is likely to have come to an end due to invasion by the Hunas.
It may be noted here that Bhita is the only city-site in the Gangetic plain
which has been excavated extensively enough to reveal a coherent picture of urban lay-out.

Sringaverapura

This site, about 1 km long along the eastern bank of the Ganges and of
undetermined width has a strong association with the Ramayana, both as
the seat of Rishyasringa's hermitage and as the place where on his way
to exile Rama crossed the river. B.B. Lal's excavations at the site (1977–
85) have taken the antiquity of the place back to the last quarter of the
second millennium BC (OCP) but were primarily concerned with the
details of a tank complex dated in the late centuries BC (B.B. Lal 1993).

The way in which the water of the Ganges in high flood was channelized into this complex with a total storage capacity of about 2 million litres of water, desilted and stored there for drinking and ritualistic purposes was no doubt a tremendous achievement of the contemporary Indian hydraulic engineers. The neat and careful way in which the total plan of this complex has been archaeologically uncovered over the years and eventually published by Lal and his team (principally from the Archaeological Survey of India) is a significant landmark in the history of Indian archaeology in recent years. However, the other structural details are meagre and the following account of a late Kushan structural complex may be representative:

The complex revealed two units separated by a corridor, having soling with brickbats on the eastern side. The southern unit of the complex was provided with five rooms having four small interconnecting doors. The sizes of the rooms were 2.40 by 2.05 m, 4.25 by 2.05 m, 3.35 by 3.35 m and 3.35 by 2.55 m respectively. The size of one room could not be ascertained. However, in one of the rooms lying on the southwest corner of the complex, a cellar . . . about 2.60 m deep with thirty-eight courses of burnt-brick was encountered. . . . From inside this thin cellar a small copper-bowl and remains of seeds and other pulses were also noticed. The northern unit of the house complex also consisted of five rooms of various sizes (2.40 by 1.95 m, 4.15 by 2.25 m, 3.00 by 3.75 m, 3.20 by 3.20 m), a corridor, a verandah (6.55 by 2.00 m) along with several doors opening towards the courtyard (IAR 1984–85: 85–6).

MIDDLE GANGETIC VALLEY (EASTERN U.P. AND BIHAR)

Rajghat

On the basis of a terracotta sealing bearing the legend '(the seal) of the city administration of Varanasi' inscribed in Gupta characters, ancient Varanasi, a city with extensive early literary references, may be identified with modern Rajghat, 'an extensive table-land rising about 60 ft (18.28 m) above the surrounding ground-level' (IAR 1957–58: 50), in the northeastern outskirts of modern Benares. The site lay between the river Varuna in the north and northeast and the Ganges in the southeast. The result of an accidental discovery in 1940, the site has come to be extensively excavated since 1957–58 (Narain and Roy 1976, 1977, Narain and Singh 1977).

The literary sources, particularly the Jatakas, are unequivocal about its importance as a trade-mart and commercial centre and its connection with such distant places as Taxila. It was, in fact, the meeting point of important trade-routes: on the one hand it was connected by river with all the important centres further downstream and on the other a route went from here to the northwest. A land-route also went to Vaisali and if a reference in a Jataka is correct, there was also a route down the river to the sea and then to Burma (H. Chakraborti 1966: 178–81).

The occupational sequence of the site is found to comprise five or six main periods. Period I, dated 800–200 BC, possesses three sub-periods. Sub-period IA yielded black-and-red, red-slipped and coarse gritty red wares.

Iron occurred from the very beginning. The NBPW was introduced in Sub-period IB which also showed the remains of a burnt clay floor and some pits provided with terracotta rings. There were new ceramic elements in Sub-period IC which had in addition some terracotta ring-wells. Period II, dated between *c.* 200 BC and the beginning of the Christian era, had two structural phases; in the earlier phase was found a house with two rooms, a vestibule, a bath and a well. In the upper levels of this period there were the remains of a brick-foundation and a terracotta ring-well. On the basis of some 'impressive' structures, Period III, dated from the beginning of the Christian era to the end of the third century AD, has been considered to be the most prosperous phase at the site. The extensive structural activity also continued in Period IV dated from *c.* 300 to *c.* AD 700 while Periods V and VI have been found to be medieval.

The most important structural remain of the site is, however, the rampart which has been found to go back to the NBPW phase of the site. This rampart, 'lying almost on the natural soil belongs to the middle, if not the earliest, phase of this period'. This rose to a height of about 10 m with a pronounced slope towards the river. Subsequently, on the north side of the settlement a channel or ditch was dug to connect the Varuna river with the Ganges. 'A series of alternating deposits of sand and silt against the toe of the rampart indicated that it had been breached several times by heavy floods, which also affected some portions of the habitation' (IAR 1960–61: 37). A wooden platform associated with the rampart on the Ganges side has also been reported. It is difficult to fathom its purpose but it is likely to have acted as a reinforcement against the eroding action of the river.

Khairadih

Also written as Kheradih, this site (IAR 1980–81, 1981–82, 1982–83, 1983–84, 1985–86) on the Sarayu river in the Ballia district of eastern U.P. goes back to the pre-NBPW black-slipped and black-and-red ware phase but is known principally as a Kushan period township. At least one major street (of varying width) and some lanes were isolated along with some structures including a two-roomed house with a verandah in front and an attached drain. There is also reference to an underground structure (2.04 by 1.68 m). An interesting discovery is that of a blacksmith's workshop in the NBPW level.

Narhan

The early historic site of Narhan located near the river Ghaghara in the Gorakhpur district is about 10 ha. in extent (Mound I) and begins with a chalcolithic black-and-red ware deposit with iron towards its top(?). Iron certainly features in Period II with black-slipped ware. Possibly NBPW also occurs during this period. Structural evidence is meagre and it is said that the settlement of Mound I was deserted around 450 BC.

Jhusi and Ghosi

Both these sites are unexcavated. The former is near Allahabad, on the opposite bank of the Ganges, and the latter is far to the east in the Azamgarh district and is locally known as Nahush-ka-Tila. The ruins at Jhusi cover several modern villages and the river section along the site is worth observing. Ghosi which has yielded NBPW shows 'a high mud rampart with openings, possibly gateways, on three sides except the east' (A. Ghosh 1989, II: 148).

Saheth-Maheth

Since its initial identification by Cunningham (1963 reprint: 343–8) with ancient Sravasti on the basis of a locally found dedicatory inscription on a Buddha statue, the site of Saheth-Maheth on the border of Gonda and Bahreich districts in U.P. has had a long history of archaeological investigations. Cunningham's identification was doubted by Vincent Smith (1924: 31, n.2) who, mainly on the basis of the itineraries of Fa-Hian and Hiuen-Tsang, placed Sravasti somewhere in the Nepalese territory where the Rapti leaves the hills. The subsequent excavations have, of course, amply vindicated Cunningham's idea. What primarily emerges from a brief review of the literary data (Law 1935) on Sravasti is that it was a 'nerve-centre of the commerce and a number of routes emerged from here, which connected several cities of northern as well as western India. It had routes for Saketa, Rajagriha, Kausambi, Varanasi,

Alavi, Samkasya and Takshasila. It had direct trade-routes for Ujjayini, Mahismati, Pratisthana, Bharukachchha and Surparaka' (B. Srivastava 1968: 76).

The local name of the ancient fortified city-site is Maheth, while Saheth, about 400 m to the west, represents the ancient monastery site of Jetavana celebrated in Buddhist literature as a gift of the merchant Ana-thapindaka to the Buddha. On plan, the city-site of Maheth is 'an almost semi-circular crescent with a diameter of one mile and a third in length, curved inward and facing the northeast along the old bank of the Rapti river' (Vogel 1907–8: 83). The total circuit of the enclosing rampart, occasionally rising to 40 ft (*c.* 13 m) above the surrounding ground-level, is slightly more than 5 miles (*c.* 8 km). There are remains of ancient habitation outside the fortified enclosure also.

A number of gateways are clearly visible on plan and Vogel argues that what is locally known as the Tamarind Gate on the western arm of the rampart 'has distinctly the aspect of a main entrance to the ancient city' (Vogel 1907–8: 82). This remains unexcavated. The excavated gateway is locally known as the Nausahra Gate on the eastern arm of the rampart and is described as 'one of the main gates of the city'. The city wall at this point is about 9 ft (less than 3 m) wide and is built on the top of an earthen rampart. On both sides of the gate the city walls 'curve inwards so as to form two bastions leaving a space of 60 ft in width in between'. Immediately south of this there are two rooms which may have been guard-rooms.

The stratification of the rampart has been made clear by the 1958–59 excavations. It was built in Period II of the site, Period I belonging to the PGW.

In the earliest sub-period, the rampart had a basal width of 95 ft. The highest available point wherefrom it sloped on either side was noted to be 12 ft above the contemporary ground-level. Between this and the subsequent sub-period were encountered a pottery and ash-dump on the outside and seemingly occupational debris with three terracotta soakage ring-wells on the inside, suggesting that for some time this part of the rampart had fallen into disuse. In the second sub-period was built a brick-structure serving possibly as a parapet over the rampart. In the next sub-period the height of the rampart was raised by mud-filling, while in the last sub-period was built a brick-structure above that filling (IAR 1958–59: 50; also Sinha 1967).

On the basis of numismatic and other evidence, Period II has been dated to the late centuries BC.

Evidence regarding the habitational remains inside the rampart is very limited. What has been called 'Kachchi Kuti' in the eastern sector near the rampart may generally be a temple site while 'Pakki Kuti' may be a stupa. There was a stupa, called Stupa A, on the eastern edge of the rampart.

Saheth, the site of ancient Jetavana, is a monastery site, comprising shrines, monasteries and stupas, the earliest of which, dated to the Mauryan period, has yielded a stone casket containing bone-relics together with a gold leaf and a silver punch-marked coin (Marshall 1910–11). The recent excavations at the Jetavana site were conducted on the southern and northwestern periphery of the mound. Two periods have been postulated: Period I—first century BC–first century AD and Period II—third–sixth centuries AD. Forty-one structures of burnt brick, mostly remains of walls and cells, divided into six structural phases were found in 1986–87 (IAR 1986–87: 76). In the next season (1987–88: 106–8) a Kushan period tank and a monastic complex were noticed. Rectangular in plan, the tank has an enclosure wall and three terraces.

Ganwaria

Ganwaria and Piphrawa are the city and stupa sites of the ancient city of Kapilavastu in the Basti district of eastern U.P. The long-standing dispute regarding the identification of the capital of the Sakyas, of whom the Buddha's father was the chief, was resolved with the discovery of the monastic sealing of Kapilavastu at Piphrawa in the Archaeological Survey of India excavations at this site and the city site of Ganwaria under K.M. Srivastrava in 1973 (Srivastava 1986). The monastic site of Piphrawa yielded the ruins of three major monasteries, two shrines, a public hall, a votive stupa and the main relic stupa which originally was erected by the Sakyas over the corporeal relics of the Buddha. Measuring 300 m (north–south) and 270 m (east–west), the town site of Ganwaria is now a little more than 8 ha. in extent, but Srivastava (1986: 61) points out that the original extent was much more. The 7 m thick occupational deposit was divided into four periods: Period I—fine grey, black polished and red wares; Period II—NBPW; Period III—Sunga; Period IV—Kushan. It is not that a great deal of evidence regarding town-planning has been obtained. Two monasteries (36 m square and 26 m square) which had monastic cells around a courtyard with a major projected gateway entrance on one side, two shrines, a large structure identified as a 'school' and miscellaneous house-remains constitute the basic structural finds. In the first period of the site the houses were built of mud. The use of burnt bricks became extensive only during the NBPW period and later.

Tilaura Kot

According to Vincent Smith (1924: 167, n.3), Kapilavastu, the Sakya capital in the Nepalese terai was 'certainly represented by Tilaura Kot and neighbouring ruins'. While there is as yet no positive proof, according to P.C. Mukherjee, who dealt extensively with the problem of identification, 'no other ancient site has so much claim on the identification of Kapilavastu as Tilaura, as being situated in the right position and fulfilling all other conditions' (Mukherjee 1901: 50).

The fortified site, as explored by Mukherjee, is roughly rectangular, 'about 1600 feet north to south by 1000 feet east to west' (Mukherjee 1901: 10) with traces of habitation outside the fortification. 'Originally it appears to have been a mud fort, on which subsequently brick walls were raised. The mounds on the ruined walls are easily distinguishable on all the four sides. The brick fort was protected by a deep ditch on all sides, as also by a second mud wall and a second but wider ditch' (Mukherjee 1901: 10).

The 1961–62 excavations (IAR 1961–62: 73–4) have clearly established the stratigraphy of the site. The pre-defence Period I had two phases with the occurrence of NBPW from the beginning. Three terracotta ring-wells were discovered in Phase A. The mud rampart was built in Period II with a moat outside. On the sloping outer face of the rampart there was a fortification wall of bricks and brickbats. 'The contemporaneity or otherwise of the wall with the mud rampart could not definitely be established in view of the absence of a foundation trench for the former and of any occupation on the mud rampart' (IAR 1961–62: 74). No coordinated plan of the habitation inside the rampart has been obtained.

Lauriya-Nandangarh

Lauriya-Nandangarh, which is about 15 miles to the southwest of Bettiah in Champaran in north Bihar, was excavated successively by T. Bloch (1906–7: 118–26, 1904–5: 38–40), N.G. Majumdar (1935–36: 55–66, 1936–37: 47–50) and A. Ghosh (cited in A. Ghosh ed. 1950: 60–1). The site lies on an important route to the Nepalese terai. That the route to the Nepalese terai from the middle Gangetic valley was important in early times is amply clear from the distribution of the Asokan pillars at Basarh, Lauriya-Araraj, Lauriya-Nandangarh, Rampurwa and finally, Lumbini.

The site itself has two components: Lauriya which possesses the Asokan pillar and a number of burial mounds, all indisputably of pre-Mauryan antiquity, and Nandangarh, about 400 m to the southwest, forming an irregular quadrangle to house a huge terraced stupa dated roughly between the first century BC and the second century AD. The Asokan pillar, the burial mounds and the terraced stupa do not in themselves make Lauriya-Nandangarh a city-site but it appears that a considerable area in the vicinity of the terraced stupa was once fortified and Majumdar himself refers to mounds possibly with dwelling remains.

Balirajgarh

So far as archaeological evidence goes, Balirajgarh in Darbhanga, north Bihar, was an extensive fortified habitational centre but it has not yet been identified with any settlement mentioned in early literature. Excavated in 1962–63, the defence wall is found to have

consisted of a mudbrick core with brick encasement, the outer one being four times the width of the inner. The wall was battered and measured 5.18 m at the base and 3.65 m at the top. Three phases of construction including repairs were recognized. The earliest phase consisted of a mudbrick core with battered brick revetments, of which the outer had approximately three times the width of the inner. In the second phase, a brick-concrete ramp was built against the inner face. The third phase witnessed further reinforcement of the ramp in the shape of a 3 m high platform of earth mixed with potsherds, built against the inner face of the fortifications (IAR 1962–63: 5).

The fortification seems to have been built in the second century BC. The remains of a temple (of uncertain date) have been recovered inside the habitation area.

Katragarh

This site in the Muzaffarpur district of Bihar is noted for its Sunga period fortification with three phases of construction. In the first and third phases it was built of burnt bricks whereas in the second phase it is represented by a massive mud core and moat. In the third phase the burnt brick defence wall with sloping sides was 2.60 m at the base. Two watch towers have also been exposed. This site has also not been correlated with any settlement mentioned in literary sources.

Basarh

The identification of ancient Vaisali with the ruins in and around the modern village of Basarh (Muzaffarpur district, Bihar) was first proposed by Cunningham (1963 rep.: 373–6) in 1861–62, and after initial controversy (see Patil 1963: 21–2) the point was finally settled by T. Bloch's excavations in 1903–4 which yielded, among other things, a few inscribed terracotta sealings with the name 'Vaisali'.

The history of Vaisali as a city has been adequately surveyed by Y. Misra (1962). Geographically it was not merely in the heart of a fertile agricultural district but also it lay on the route from Magadha or south Bihar to the Nepalese terai. As the capital of the oligarchical tribe of the Lichchhavis during the time of the Buddha and also as the place where the Second Buddhist Council was held after his death, Vaisali repeatedly figures in Buddhist literature. It is also important in Jaina sources as the birthplace of the first Jaina preceptor, Mahavira. The Puranic tradition is less equivocal and associates it with the legendary king, Visala. Among the later references, Hiuen-Tsang's account is the most extensive.

In 1903–4 Bloch published a map showing the remains of ancient sites in the area, which seem to fall into two main clusters. First, there is an extensive mound, about 6 to 10 ft (1.82–3.04 m) high, locally known as 'Raja Visal ka garh' (fort of King Visal) whose circuit is about 5000 ft (1524 m), closely approximating Hiuen-Tsang's estimate of the periphery of the royal precinct of the city (Patil 1963: 23). Traces of round towers may be observed at the corners and a surrounding ditch, presumably 150–200 ft (45.72–60.96 m) wide, is now filled up and under cultivation. Traces of an embankment across the ditch suggest that the main entrance to this enclosure was in the centre of its southern side. In the vicinity of this major mound there are a few smaller ones, generally identified with some of the Buddhist ruins mentioned by Hiuen-Tsang. In addition, there is a big tank locally known as Khorana Pokhar and generally supposed to be the coronation tank of the ancient Lichchhavis. The second group of ruins lay about two miles to the northwest and comprised primarily an Asokan pillar, an ancient brick-lined tank associated with a Buddhist legend and the remains of a brick stupa.

The city itself was in the area of the first group of ruins though its precise boundaries are now not easy to demarcate. Bloch writes:

According to modern tradition, the four corners of the ancient city of Vaisali are marked by four lingas or Mahadevas, of which the two northern ones are visible and the two southern ones hidden. Hence their name 'Gupta' Mahadeva. The ancient city would thus have formed an irregular quadrangle, the eastern measuring about two-thirds of the western. . . . There are traces of an old earthen rampart between the two 'Gupta' Mahadevas (Bloch 1903–4: 87).

Raja Visal ka garh or the main mound has been subjected to repeated excavations but not with very comprehensive results. The earlier excavations of Cunningham, Bloch and Spooner revealed primarily a wealth of antiquities, a few terracotta ring-wells and an assortment of structures, the earlier group of which was dated by Bloch to not later than the fourth–fifth centuries AD. Spooner's (1913–14) attempt to trace the fortification wall was not successful and he suggested that the mound possessed only an earthen embankment. The fortification wall with its three main periods was, however, traced in 1958–59 (IAR 1958–59: 12). In Period I there was a burnt brick defence wall, about 20 ft wide (*c.* 6 m) and roughly ascribed to the Sunga period, i.e. to the second century BC. In Period II, which was not much later, there was a massive earthen rampart, which was 68 ft (*c.* 21 m) wide at the base and 21 ft (*c.* 6 m) wide at the extant top, with an extant height of 13 ft (*c.* 4 m). The moat was dug during this period. In Period III, dated 'late Kushan-early Gupta' (third–fourth centuries AD) the wall was brick-built again and was 9 ft (less than 3 m) wide, with 'military barracks' attached. Inside the fortified enclosure a network of structures has been revealed and their periodization conforms to that of the defence wall. Building activities seem to have been the most in Period II.

In 1957–58 a tank, generally supposed to be the Lichchhavi coronation tank, came to be excavated. A wall was traced for a considerable stretch at the slope of the tank embankment, and at one place, 2 ft (*c.* 0.61 m) below the foundation level of this wall, a 'concrete platform' was discovered.

The antiquities in the intervening deposit and in the layers underlying the spoil-earth of the tank deposited on its embankment included cast coins and terracotta figurines stylistically assignable to the Sunga age, which were indicative of the date of the wall. The original tank of the Lichchhavis might have been a small one, which was subsequently enlarged and surrounded by a wall, represented by its present remains in about the second century BC when the Lichchhavis might have once more become powerful after the downfall of the Maurya empire (IAR 1957–58: 10).

A small mound to the northwest of the tank, when excavated in 1957–58, revealed a stupa which was originally built of mud but was subsequently encased in burnt bricks. Chronologically this could have been built 'any time' between 600 and 200 BC (IAR 1957–58: 11). The excavators prefer to identify it with the stupa reputedly built by the Lichchhavis over the remains of the Buddha. Limited excavations in other areas (Sinha and Roy 1969) have unearthed primarily the general occupational sequence of the site which begins with the black-and-red ware succeeded by the NBPW.

Maner and Manjhi

Maner is a high mound or a set of mounds overlooking an old bed of the Son, about 32 km to the west of Patna. The site, although subjected to excavations for several years (IAR 1984–85: 11–12, 1985–86: 11–12, 1986–87: 25–6, 1987–88: 11–12) has yielded little, except for showing a sequence beginning with the chalcolithic stage and continuing upto the Pala period from which a large structure has been reported.

Manjhi (IAR 1983–84: 15–16, 1984–85: 12–13) on the left bank of the Ghaghra in the Saran district is a high mound too and shows a similar sequence where a defence wall was apparently constructed in the last phase of the NBPW.

Patna

The Magadhan capital was shifted from Rajagriha to Pataliputra under Udayin, the grandson and successor of Ajatasatru. With the increasing power of the kingdom of Magadha and the development of trade and commerce along the Ganges the site of Pataliputra or modern Patna at the confluence of the Son (which has now shifted about 20 miles to the west but once flowed close by) and the Ganges was obviously considered more suitable as the capital than the older one of Rajgir or Rajagriha which was away from any river traffic. Earlier, Ajatasatru built a fort at the site, perhaps to cope with the Lichchhavis whose territory lay across the river (for a comprehensive discussion, Patil 1963: 373–8).

Pataliputra came to be the meeting point of some of the most important trade routes of ancient India. 'From Pataliputra three great routes radiated to the frontiers of the (Mauryan) empire—the southwestern to Barygaza by Kausambi and Ujjain, the northern to Nepal by Vaisali and Sravasti and the northwestern, the longest, to Bactriana by Mathura and upper valley of the Indus' (H. Chakraborti 1966: 182). Downstream, Pataliputra was connected with Tamralipta in the Ganges delta and thus perhaps with southeast Asia. If the idea of a route to China from the Gangetic valley through Assam and Burma is correct, it was also probably connected with China.

Of the copious literary records of this site the most significant is that of Megasthenes (Majumdar 1960) who refers to the general size and administrative arrangement of the city, the timbered palisade with towers and loopholes for shooting arrows around the periphery, the encircling moat which also served as the sewer, and the Mauryan palace with its pillared hall and gardens. Partly because of this elaborate classical reference and partly because of its great significance in the history of India as the centre of the Mauryan empire, the site of Pataliputra has had scholarly attention since the late eighteenth century (Patil 1963: 378–80). Since the late nineteenth century the site has been subjected to sporadic excavations but modern construction over most of the ancient site and the presence of subsoil water have never allowed the excavations to be extensive.

According to Megasthenes the city was 80 stadia (little more than 9 miles) long and 15 stadia (about 1–1/3 miles) wide, roughly the same size as modern Patna. It is unlikely that the actual demarcation of the boundaries of the ancient and modern cities correspond, though there are 'traces of extensive ruins spread and interspersed over almost the entire length of the modern habitation' (Patil 1963: 380). Of the seventeen-odd discovered ruins of ancient Pataliputra, two—Kumrahar and Bulandibagh—happen to be very significant. At both these places the excavated remains largely substantiate Megasthenes' observations.

The remains at Kumrahar comprise primarily traces of a pillared hall and a series of wooden platforms nearby, both discovered by Spooner in 1913–15 but reinvestigated by Altekar and Misra in 1951–55 (Altekar and Misra 1959). In the pillared hall there are traces of ten rows of pillars with eight pillars in each row. Seventy two of them, in the form of cylindrical shafts of ash with pillar fragments in them, were found by Spooner while eight more were added by Altekar and Misra, with evidence of four additional ones which formed part of a porch. Spooner could not find the bases or pedestals of the pillars but Altekar and Misra found that they were fixed on wooden basements, each 4 ft 6 ins (1.37 m) square, which were laid on a compact layer of blue clay, 6 ins (0.15 m) in thickness. The height of the pillars was about 32$^{1}/_{2}$ ft (9.90 m) with 9 ft (2.74 m) buried inside the plinth. The enormous quantity of ash in the excavated area with burnt-out pieces of wood suggests that both the floor and the roof were made of wood. The shape of the roof has, however, not been determined. The wooden ceiling might have been covered by a brick work and lime-plaster, as both bricks and fragments of lime-plaster have been found in the ruins. No side-wall has been discovered and it is likely that the hall was open on all sides. It was burnt down in the early Sunga period (second century BC). Till now there is no positive proof that there were subsidiary buildings near the pillared hall or that it was surrounded by a boundary wall.

To the southeast of the pillared hall, only about 15 ft (4.57 m) away,

Spooner excavated seven wooden platforms, each 30 ft (*c.* 9 m) long, 5 ft 4 ins (1.62 m) broad and 4 ft 6 ins (1.37 m) high. They lay parallel to each other and extended from north to south. Five platforms were found in line with the rows of pillars of the hall. They were made of logs of 'sal' wood: the horizontal logs were carefully placed and joined together and supported by deeply set vertical pieces both at the edges and the centre. Altekar and Misra found no new platform but suggested on the basis of a study of the stratification that there was once a canal at the spot leading to the Son. 'It is possible to make a new conjecture about the purpose of wooden platforms. They probably supported a broad wooden staircase of about 30 steps, each step being 24 ft in length and 6 inches in height. This staircase was used by distinguished visitors, coming to the Hall by boat' (Altekar and Misra 1959: 25).

At some distance from the complex of the pillared hall Altekar and Misra also found the remains of a Buddhist monastery, called the Arogya-vihara monastery, according to an inscribed terracotta seal and dated on the same basis to the Gupta period. The remains of an apsidal brick chaitya, dated between AD 100 and AD 300, have also been discovered.

In the Bulandibagh area, northwest of Kumrahar, the primary ruins comprise vestiges of a wooden palisade, excavated haphazardly over a number of years but principally by Spooner in 1915–17. There were two parallel walls of wooden uprights (each with a section of 1 ft 3 ins (0.38 m) by 1 ft 10 ins (0.55 m) separated by a width of about 12 ft 4 ins (3.75 m). The space between the two walls was covered, at 22 ft (6.70 m) below the surface, by a floor of squared timbers fitted into the slots of the vertical uprights. The uprights went 5 ft (*c.* 1.55 m) deeper than this floor-level and rested on a bed of gravel foundation. They were found to be about 24 ft (7.31 m) high. Intermittent excavation pits traced this complex for about 350 ft (106.68 m). Initially the alignment was found to be from east to west, but at one point in the east, the lines of upright timbers were north-south, indicating that the wall somewhere here took a bend to the north or south. In later years (1922–23 to 1928–29) M. Ghosh (cited in Patil 1963: 394–5) found a long octagonal post, nearly 16 ins (0.40 m) in diameter, along this wall and he suggested that this might be the post of a gateway in the line of the palisade. He also discovered a wooden drain (6 ft 3 ins and 3 ft 6 ins high/1.90 m and 1.06 m high) running mostly along this wall.

The alignment and the extent of the palisade have never been made clear. The stratigraphy and consequently the precise date also remain uncertain. But on circumstantial evidence this may logically be explained, as has been done by Spooner and others, as the wooden palisade encircling the city in a description given by Megasthenes. Haphazard excavations and accidental discoveries have been made in various parts of the city but these are too disjointed to suggest any coordinated pattern.

Rajgir

When the kingdom of Magadha in its early stage was in feud with its neighbours, Rajagriha, ensconced in a hill-valley about forty miles southeast of Patna, was the capital; it was in a strongly defensible position offering security. Besides, it lay close to the rich mineral and other raw material deposits of modern Bihar, control of which, according to one opinion, could have given Magadha an edge over the other contemporary aspirants to political power. In this connection I emphasize that it is the proximity of Magadha to the entire resource-rich Chhotanagpur plateau which has to be considered here. There is, in fact, no point in drawing attention to the iron ore deposits alone because the major iron ore deposits which lie at the southern edge of this plateau were not used until recently. As the literary sources (Law 1938) suggest, Rajagriha had many historical and mythical associations. On the one hand, it was closely associated with the life of the Buddha, the early Magadhan court and other religious groups like the Jainas and the Ajivikas. On the other, it was supposed to have been established by the legendary king, Jarasandha. The Jarasandha legend referred to in the Mahabharata persists in modern local tradition and it is possible that it evokes a dim prehistoric tribal memory, losing its intelligibility afterwards. On the economic level Rajagriha was a terminal point of the early trade-route linking the middle Gangetic valley with Paithan on the Godavari. I have argued elsewhere (Chakrabarti 1993) that Rajagriha as a trade centre could mediate the raw materials available in the Chotanagpur plateau lying immediately to the south of this first Magadhan capital.

The archaeological investigations at Rajgir began in the middle of the nineteenth century and continued sporadically upto the present, with the result that the basic lay-out of the site is now amply clear and most of the ruins intelligently studied. On the negative side, the explorers have been preoccupied mostly with the problem of the identification of the ruins with the monuments described either by Hiuen-Tsang or in early Buddhist literature, a natural enough trend considering the close association of the site with the Buddhists and their elaborate records. Though a beginning was made in 1950 (A. Ghosh 1950, 1951), very little attention has been paid to the task of tracing the cultural growth of ancient Rajagriha (for details of the argument, see Chakrabarti 1976).

There are actually two cities at the site—Old and New Rajagrihas. Old Rajagriha lay entirely within a valley surrounded by five hills on all sides, each given a name in the Mahabharata and the Jaina tradition. The valley possesses two rivulets, the Sarasvati and the Banganga. New Rajagriha lay in the level plain to the north of the hill-girt valley. D.R. Patil (1963: 436) argues that there is no chronological basis to warrant a division between the Old and New Rajagrihas. In 1961–62 the inner rampart around New Rajagriha was partly excavated and it was found to rest on a basal deposit towards the end of which the NBPW and punch-marked coins appear. Period II has two sub-phases, A and B. The rampart was built to suggest a somewhat late date for the citadel wall of New Raja-griha, and it is possible that the naming of the settlement in two parts, Old and New, reflects a reality.

Along the crest of the hills encircling Old Rajagriha there is a stone fortification wall called the outer fortification. Its plan published by A. Ghosh (1950) differs somewhat from that published by Marshall (1905–6). In Ghosh's plan the fortification extends without any break on all the hill-tops while, according to Marshall, 'the break in the line of fortifications to the east of Chhata giri is a considerable one, and it is pos-sible that the fortifications were never completed at this point . . .' (Marshall 1905–6: 88). Moreover, Ghosh shows a wall extending south-eastwards from the main alignment of the fortification on the Sona hill, which does not appear in Marshall. The total length of the outer forti-fication as it exists in traces may come to about 12–13 miles according to Marshall, while Ghosh speaks of its extension 'over a length of about 25 to 30 miles along the crest of the hills' (Kuraishi 1958: 33).

The faces of the walls are built of massive undressed stones between three and five feet in length, carefully fitted and bonded together, while the core between them is composed of smaller blocks less carefully cut and laid with chips or fragments of stone, packing the interstices between them. No mortar or cement is visible anywhere in the stone work (Marshall 1905–6: 88).

The greatest extant height of this wall, 11–12 ft (3.35–3.65 m), may be observed at the southern extremity of the valley where the rivulet Banganga moves into the plains. Marshall points out that at this level 'the walls are invariably finished off with a course of small stones' (Marshall 1905–6: 88) and as there is no scatter of fallen stones nearby, he assumes this (i.e. 11–12 ft) to be the original height of the wall. Marshall also suggests the existence of some kind of superstructure on top of this but there is no suggestive evidence on this point. Its usual thickness is 17 ft 6 ins (5.33 m). There are a number of bastions of which about sixteen have been observed and of which seven are on either side of the Banganga defile. They also occur on either side of the northern opening of the valley. They are each broadly 47 to 60 ft (14.32 to 18.28 m) long and 34 to 40 ft (10.36 to 12.19 m) broad. 'The defences . . . were further supplemented, possibly at a later date, by separate watch towers erected at various prominent places on the hills. Two conspicuous examples of these exist on the Vaibhara hill. . . . Of the main gates in the outer walls traces of only one on the north are visible' (Marshall 1905–6: 89). Access to the top of the wall was obtained through 'stairs or rather ramps built in the thickness of the wall along its inner face' (Marshall 1905–6: 84).

In the valley itself, below the level of the hills, a ridge of earth and stone, about 4 1/2 miles long, encloses the valley on all sides, and is roughly pentagonal in plan. This is known as the inner fortification of Old Rajagriha. This still remains unexcavated and Patil (1963: 439) points out that this might well have been a mere embankment to protect the settlement from rain water coming down from the hills. No systematic excavation directed towards reconstructing its different cultural phases has yet taken place inside the proper settlement of Old Rajagriha.

Individual ruins like the Maniyar math, 'Bimbisara's jail', etc. have been excavated but these monuments are mostly religious in character and do not add up to any pattern of systematic town-planning. Religious monuments of different periods also abound in the slopes and the periphery of the neighbouring Vaibhara and Gridhrakuta hills. The secular aspect of the city core of Old Rajagriha, however, still remains elusive.

Outside the hill-girt valley, in the level plain to the north, New Rajagriha also has two sets of fortifications. The outer fortification is an irregular pentagon in shape with a periphery of about three miles. It is a massive wall of earth and according to the evidence of Francis Buchanan is 'strengthened by a ditch . . . which seems to have been about 100 feet wide' (cited in Patil 1963: 466). This wall is now fast disappearing. In a fairly well-preserved condition is the inner fortification, enclosing the citadel, a roughly rectangular area of about 70–80 acres (28.32–32.37 ha.). The wall is 15.18 ft (4.57–5.48 m) thick, and is preserved up to a height of 11 ft (3.35 m). It is faced with unhewn blocks of stone set without any mortar, the filling inside being stone rubble and earth. The lime mortar used in the pointing of the joints seems to be from a later period.

There were semi-circular bastions set at regular intervals. There are gaps in the wall in the north, east and west but except in the south, there is no positive proof of a gateway, indicated by an 11 ft (3.35 m) wide passage approached by earthen ramps both on the inside and outside, and flanked by a semi-circular bastion on either side.

The proper stratigraphic sequence of the citadel wall was established in 1961–62. The mud rampart wall was built in Period IIA which was a little later than the initial appearance of NBPW at the site. It was 7.31 m high and was retained on the southern side by a brick wall with a height of 2.15 m. The base of the mud rampart was 40.53 m wide but it was somewhat narrower on its northern side. There was also a moat, the width and depth of which remain undetermined. In Period IIB a brick fortification wall was added to the top (IAR 1961–62: 7–8). In the following year it was established that there was an earthwork in the first phase of the NBPW itself. Period II shows a mud rampart whereas a massive stone fortification appears in Period III. Outside the inner wall but within the outer one in this area one notes quite a few religious structures like the 'Venuvana', 'Ajatasatru stupa', etc. but the secular aspects of the town-planning are not understood. In 1974–75 (IAR 1974–75) nothing much was found except a broad stratigraphy beginning with the NBPW. There is no doubt that Rajagriha, one of the earliest and most important centres of Indian history, deserves far more systematic modern archaeological attention than it has hitherto received.

Champa

One of the six principal cities of India during the time of the Buddha and a place visited both by him and Mahavira, ancient 'Champa' was identified by Cunningham (1963 rep.: 402–3) with Champanagar and Champapur, two modern villages near Bhagalpur (Law 1954: 214–15; H. Chakraborti 1966: 186–7) in south Bihar. It was connected with Pataliputra, Rajagriha, and the early historic settlements of north Bihar on the one hand, and the comparable settlements in the lower Gangetic valley like Pundranagara and Tamralipta on the other. It is also supposed to be a centre of maritime trade to southeast Asia. A comprehensive description of the archaeological aspects of ancient Champa, 5 km west of Bhagalpur, has been given by B.P. Sinha (in A. Ghosh 1989, II: 90). There is a defensive fortification surrounded by a deep moat and the bed of the Ganges. The rampart came up in the first phase of the NBPW which was preceded by a black-and-red ware occupation of the site. The first phase of the rampart wall was built of blackish soil with a gentle slope on the outside. In the second phase it was built by the dumping over of yellow and red soil to form a thick wall. This wall was raised against a 3.80 m wide embankment of burnt brick debris which was possibly meant to prevent erosion by water. The maximum height traced is 5.80 m. Further, a high brick wall was raised right over the rampart to strengthen the overall fortification system. This phase has been placed in the Sunga period. Associated with it is a rammed brick floor with six postholes, which may represent the position of a watchman's room on the rampart. B.P. Sinha states that numerous well-built brick houses of the Sunga-Gupta period have been found at the site, along with an 'exceedingly well-built' plastered drain (25 cm wide, 52 cm deep) in the village outside the fortified area.

There is no dearth of early historical sites in the Bhagalpur area: Oriup (IAR 1966–67: 6–7), Jhimjhimia-Kalisthan near Rajmahal (1987–88: 12–13), etc. The mound of Jhimjhimia-Kalisthan is said to include five villages and this must be a very large site.

LOWER GANGETIC VALLEY
(WEST BENGAL AND BANGLADESH)

In the lower Gangetic valley the distribution of early historical sites falls into a number of geographical areas: the old alluvium of the districts of Dinajpur, Rajsahi, Bagura and Maldaha of pre-1947 Bengal, the confluence of an old course of the Brahmaputra with the Meghna in the upland tract near Dhaka, the deltaic region of the districts of 24 Parganas and Midnapur, and the Rarh tract of the districts of Birbhum, Burdwan and Bankura.

Mahasthangarh

Ancient Pundranagara was identified with modern Mahasthan in the Bagura district of Bangladesh by Cunningham (1963 rep.: 404–5) and this was afterwards corroborated by the local find of an inscription in Mauryan Brahmi which referred to Pundranagara. On the bank of the river Karatoya the ruins at the site comprise a 5000 by 4000 ft (1524 by 1219 m) oblong mound, besides some isolated ones. The area involved is about 185 ha. As Kashinath Dikshit (1929–30: 88) wrote: 'The extent of the ancient city with its suburbs is unequalled by any other ancient site in Bengal . . . and can stand comparison with the ruins of ancient cities in other Gangetic provinces, such as Basarh, Saheth-Maheth and Kosam'.

As far as the specific excavation results are concerned, structural evidence regarding the early historic levels does not exist except for the occurrence of a mud rampart below the burnt brick Gupta fortification at the site (for a detailed discussion on Mahasthangarh and its neighbouring area, see Chakrabarti 1992).

Bangarh

Modern Bangarh (West Dinajpur) has been identified with ancient Kotivarsa, a place mentioned in some literary and epigraphic sources (Law 1954: 230, Goswami 1948), all of which suggest that it was the chief town of an administrative centre of the same name. The site is situated on the bank of the Purnabhava and comprises a number of mounds, the chief of which is a citadel (about 1800 by 1500 ft; about 25 ha.) surrounded by a ditch on three sides, namely, north, east and south and by the river on the west. When excavated, this mound revealed five strata or levels of occupation, the earliest two of which could be assigned to the early historic period. The structural evidence of the fifth stratum comprised only a ring-well while in the succeeding stratum four there were some fragmentary burnt-brick walls, a burnt-brick drain and a cess-pit without any outlet. The finds indicate that this stratum belonged to the second–first centuries BC. The details of excavations of the rampart wall have not been included in the excavation report but according to the excavator the city came to possess by the second–first centuries BC a brick-built rampart wall which was 10 ft 8 ins (3.25 m) wide. A black- and-red ware sherd has been obtained in a recent investigation of the site (Chakrabarti and Chattopadhyay 1992) and it is thus probable that the antiquity of the site goes back to the black-and-red ware level. This is a hypothesis which may be made about Mahasthangarh as well.

Wari-Bateshwar

This site does not show any visible mound but has yielded thousands of silver punch-marked coins and semi-precious stone beads. The total area covers a number of modern villages on an old course of the Brahmaputra near its confluence with the Meghna near Narsingdi in modern Bangladesh. There is no doubt that the site represents a major early historic settlement going back to the third century BC. It has been inferred (Chakrabarti 1992) that this represents a trade centre through which the produce of Assam and the eastern Bengal delta used to meet the commercial traffic with southeast Asia and Rome.

Tamluk

Though the ancient port of Tamralipta or modern Tamluk on the bank of
the Rupnarayan river in the Bengal delta figures in many early literary
sources (H. Chakraborti 1966: 146–50) including Ptolemy (where it is
called Tamalites), archaeologically the site has not been given as much
attention as it deserves. A limited excavation in 1954–56 showed that
over an assemblage of neolithic celts and ill-fired pottery (Period I) there
was an early historic Period II dated to the third–second centuries BC.
Period III was placed in the first two centuries AD. The only structural
evidence of these two periods was a brick-built tank and some terracotta
ring-wells. The succeeding occupation levels continued with interrup-
tions up to the modern period. Though the evidence from excavations is
thus limited and was not in any sense implied by a later work at the site,
the abundant wealth of antiquities collected from the surface at Tamluk
is amply suggestive of the early historic importance of the site.

Chandraketugarh

Chandraketugarh (IAR 1956–57: 29–30, 1957–58: 51–2, 1958–59: 55–
6, 1959–60: 39–40, 1960–61: 50–2, 1961–62: 62–3, 1962–63: 46–7,
1963–64: 63–5, 1964–65: 52–3, 1965–66: 59–60, 1966–67: 48) is an
extensive site on the bank of a dried-up course of the Vidyadhari (24 Parganas district). A rampart wall is clearly visible and the total fortified area
should be more than one square mile. The site has yielded an occupational
sequence beginning with a pre-NBPW level. This distinctive pottery
begins only in Period II. The succeeding two periods are also early
historical while Periods V and VI belong to the Gupta and Pala periods,
respectively. The structural evidence of the first four periods is very
limited but there is ample indication of the use of mud, bamboo and timber
for houses. There are also some terracotta ring-wells and drain-pipes. The
mud-built rampart wall has not as yet been satisfactorily excavated but
a limited cutting traces its beginning to about the second century BC. As
at Tamluk, there is an extensive collection of early historic antiquities
from Chandraketugarh, suggestive of its early importance. The city still
remains to be positively identified with any ancient city mentioned in
Indian literature, but it may be identified with Gange, a place mentioned
both by Periplus and Ptolemy.

Mangalkot, Dihar and Pokharna

The ruins of Mangalkot are spread on the bank of the Kunur river near its
confluence with the Ajay in Burdwan district over an area of roughly

35–40 ha. There is still no positive evidence that the site was enclosed by a rampart although it is possible that segments of an earthen rampart survive in one or two places. The most prominent mound of the site is known locally as 'Vikramadityer Dhibi' which, when excavated, yielded a sequence beginning with black-and-red ware. Extensive burnt-brick structures have been reported from the Gupta period and earlier. The site is noted for its rich early historic antiquities (for a discussion, see Chakrabarti et al, 1993). Dihar lies on the bank of the Dwarakeshwar river near modern Bishnupur. The present mound which has shown black-and-red ware in its earliest phase and an abundance of early historical antiquities including cast copper coins later should not measure more than 15-20 acres (*c.* 8 ha.) but it has been said that the mound was originally much more extensive. This may also be said about the extent of Pokharna which lies on the bank of the Damodar in Bankura. The sequence beginning with black-and-red ware is evident and in the early historic period the place was possibly a major administrative centre of the region. It could have originally comprised an area of 1 km sq.

BRAHMAPUTRA VALLEY (ASSAM)

Literary sources such as the Mahabharata and the Arthasastra unequivocally suggest the significance of the Brahmaputra valley in early historic India. These and other relevant sources have been discussed, among others, by P.C. Choudhury (1966), R.D. Choudhury (1985), N.D. Choudhury (1985), N. Lahiri (1991) and M. Momin (1991). In his illustration of pottery types in a surface collection from Dah Parvatiya, N.D. Choudhury (1985) shows, without underlining its special significance, a 'Sunga bowl'. It seems that careful work in this region should produce archaeological evidence going back to *c.* 200 BC, if not earlier. There is in fact no reason why the Brahmaputra valley should not have major settlements dating from this period, especially in view of the fact that there are early sites both in the Karatoya valley (Mahasthangarh) and in the area of confluence between the Meghna and an old course of the Brahmaputra (Wari Bateshwar).

RAJASTHAN

The primary concentration of early historical sites in Rajasthan is in its comparatively fertile part to the east of the Aravallis. In west Rajasthan this evidence is limited: the sites are spread only along the course of the dried-up Ghaggar. Explorations in this area have yielded positive evidence of the occupation of the valley in the early centuries AD when it seems to have provided a direct passage of communication between Sind and the area around Delhi. The early historical settlements discovered in the valley may be explained in the light of the importance of this passage. One of these settlements, Rangmahal, was excavated by Hanna Rydh (1959) with little specific results except for the identification of a black-painted red ceramic belonging to this period. However, Rangmahal sites have been reported as far east as parts of east Rajasthan and Haryana, and it has been reported (A. Ghosh 1989, II: 369) that some Rangmahal sites are quite extensive and a few have mud fortifications. In east Rajasthan where the evidence of early historic occupation is fairly widespread, systematic excavations of this level have been generally inadequate. The sites that deserve attention are Bairat, Rairh, Sambhar and Nagari.

Bairat

The total area of the ruins at Bairat or ancient Viratanagara, the capital of the Matsyas (Law 1954: 333–4) is supposed to be more than 2½ miles in circuit (Archaeological Survey of India Report, Cunningham Series, vol. II: 245). D.R. Sahni's excavations (Sahni, undated) were confined to an area 'not more than 400 feet by 190 feet' and yielded 'an unexpectedly rich harvest of archaeological remains of the Maurya period and those immediately succeeding it'. Among the finds may be listed an interesting type of temple, a monastery, fragments of Mauryan pillars and miscella-neous antiquities. The point is that Sahni's work was conducted at a Buddhist establishment outside the fortified city of Viratanagara and modern excavations here (IAR 1962–63: 31) were content with establish-ing its mere sequence which began with the PGW.

Rairh

The mound at Rairh (1300 ft by 2500 ft/*c.* 400 by 775 m/*c.* 35 ha.) was excavated by K.N. Puri (undated) and yielded occupational remains ranging from the third–second centuries BC to the second century AD and beyond. A number of soak-wells with terracotta rings and a series of parallel walls with narrow intervals between them seem to have been the only structural evidence discovered during excavations. According to Sahni (undated:3), 'this small town must have been an important centre of Mauryan art and culture'.

Sambhar

The antiquity of Sambhar or ancient Sakambhari (N.L. Dey 1971 rep.: 174), the capital of the Chahamana princes, was pushed back to the early historical period by Sahni's excavations in 1936–38 (Sahni undated). The unearthed structures range in date from the third–second centuries BC to about the tenth century AD, but there is nothing structurally significant about the early remains in the excavation report.

Nagari

Nagari or ancient Madhyamika (Smith 1924: 227–8), the capital of the Sibis, a place important enough to be invaded by the Indo-Greek king, Menander, and mentioned by the grammarian, Patanjali, has been only briefly excavated (Bhandarkar 1929, IAR 1962–63: 19–20). The site possesses a defence wall built in the early centuries AD (probably in the Gupta period). The beginning of occupation at the site goes back to *c.* 400 BC.

MADHYA PRADESH

The geographical nucleus of early urban growth in central India is the Malwa plateau, a rich agricultural territory in itself, with the added advantage of lying on the main communication line between north India on the one hand and the Deccan and west India on the other. The combined evidence of literature and archaeology singles out the following settlements among the rest.

Besnagar

Modern Besnagar or ancient Vidisa (Dey 1971: 35, Law 1954: 336–40, for data on economic life, H. Chakraborti 1966: 192–5) was an important place for a number of reasons. First, it figures as a capital city in three contexts. It was the western capital of the Sunga dynasty under King Pusyamitra and King Agnimitra. Moreover, it has been suggested that it was the capital of east Malwa. It has also been mentioned as the capital of Dasarna country, the Dasarnas being a tribe in the Mahabharata. Its political importance has been further emphasized by a stone pillar at the site set up by a certain Heliodorus who was the envoy of the Indo-Greek king, Antialkidas of Taxila, to the court of King Kasiputra Bhagabhadra of Vidisa. Secondly, it was an important break-point on the north India–Deccan–west India route. Its economic prosperity may be generally deduced from references to its labourers, bankers and artisan-guilds in some dedicatory inscriptions in the stupas of Bharhut and Sanchi. It may also be emphasized that Vidisa seems to have been an important craft centre, particularly noted for ivory, weaving and sharp swords. Finally, on the religious level, Vidisa was, as the Heliodorus pillar testifies, an important early centre of the Bhagavata cult.

The ruins of the site lie primarily in the fork between the converging rivers, Betwa and Bes, but they also extend 'for at least two-thirds of a mile north of the river Bes' (Bhandarkar 1913–14: 186). After a preliminary investigation by Lake in 1910 (cited in ibid.) when nothing earlier than the Gupta period was found, the site was excavated by D.R. Bhandarkar. His attempts were primarily confined to the area around the Heliodorus inscription which, he himself admits, 'is, strictly speaking, outside the confines of the old town of Besnagar which . . . are defined by two rivers the Betwa and the Bes'. At this place he discovered some ruins which belonged to a probable Vasudeva temple while his excavations 'in the heart of the ruins' yielded nothing significant except 'the foundations and walls of old brick dwelling houses with brick pavements in front' probably belonging to the early centuries AD.

M.D. Khare has supplied further details regarding the site (IAR 1963–64: 16–17, 1964–65: 19–20, 1965–66: 23–4, 1975–76: 30–1, 1976–77: 33–4). In the main six habitational periods have been identified, ranging in chronology from the chalcolithic to the post-Gupta period. The early historical period begins in Period II with the NBPW. The most significant structural find in the city area was a massive wall

exposed towards the north and south to a length of 53 m and to an averaging width of 3.75 m. Originally built of dry rubble masonry, it was provided with passages and drains and was twice rebuilt in brick with supporting buttresses. More than half a dozen large-sized stone balls, recovered from either side of the wall and used perhaps as sling stones may perhaps indicate its function also as some sort of a defence wall, besides an enclosure wall of a palace complex (IAR 1964–65).

The stratigraphical details of this wall are not published but it is said to belong to the NBPW phase. Terracotta ring-wells have also been reported from this phase. At the site of the Heliodorus pillar a temple with two phases (the first phase is said to have come to an end in the third century BC), perhaps the probable Vasudeva temple, was discovered.

Pawaya

Ancient Padmavati has been identified with the modern village of Pawaya in the former state of Gwalior (Smith 1924: 300). The site lies in the fork formed by two converging rivers, the Sindh and the Parvati, and thus resembles the site of Vidisa. The total extent of the site has been estimated to be about 4 km. The site has not been excavated but 'the brick remains and fragments of sculptures scattered among them attest to the existence here of an ancient city from at least the first or second century AD down to the late Gupta period' (Garde 1915–16). M.B. Garde also traced the remains of a large and terraced Gupta period temple at the site.

Ujjain

Ancient Ujjayini ranks in importance with Rajagriha, Kausambi, Taksasila and such other cities of ancient India. During the time of the Buddha it was the capital of Avanti, one of the sixteen mahajanapadas whose contemporary reigning king, Pradyota, has been mentioned in early Buddhist sources. The most important point of reference was his relationship with the Gangetic valley princes like Udayana of Kausambi and Bimbisara of Rajagriha. According to one evidence he even waged an unsuccessful war against King Pukkusati of Taxila in the northwest. Subsequently, under the Mauryas, Ujjayini became a viceregal centre. Before his accession to the throne, Asoka, one of whose Minor Rock Edicts refers to Ujjayini, served as a viceroy here. After the Mauryas its important political masters were the Satavahanas of the Deccan and the Saka Kshatrapas of western India, and finally, under Chandragupta II in the fourth century AD it came to acquire a fame for culture and beauty, which is reflected in ancient Indian literature (Law 1944).

The economic and commercial significance of Ujjayini must have to a great extent been responsible for its political and cultural pre-eminence. The route from the Gangetic valley bifurcated here for the Deccan and west India: 'Ujjain gathered up and forwarded the trade between the N.W. India, the Ganges valley, the southern and western India' (H. Chakraborti 1966: 195).

Modern Ujjain or the site of ancient Ujjayini stands on the bank of the Sipra, a tributary of the Chambal. The site came to be briefly excavated in 1938–39 when the remains of a wooden structure, terracotta ring-wells and miscellaneous early historic antiquities were discovered (cited in

Ancient India 9: 160). In 1955–58 (IAR 1955–56: 19, 1956–57: 20–8, 1957–58: 33–6, also Banerjee 1965: 14–15) it was more fully excavated and revealed something of a coherent town-plan and a dependable archaeological sequence.

There are four main cultural periods. Period I yields a black-and-red ware and has been dated 700–500 BC. It antedates the NBPW at the site. This appears in Period II while Period III falls between the Sungas in the second century BC to the Paramaras in the ninth-tenth centuries AD. Period IV is medieval.

The plan of the site shows an irregular oblong measuring 1 by 3/4 mile, and surrounded by a rampart which shows eight openings, presumably all gateways. The river flanks the site almost immediately on the west and distantly on the northern side. On two of the other sides—east and south— there was a moat. The rampart which was made of heaped up clay and battered both inside and outside was built in Period I and lasted up to the end of Period III. In Period I it was 245 ft broad at the base and 132 ft wide at the top. A couple of bamboo baskets and some iron implements including a spade—suggestive of the tools of construction—have been found in the body of the rampart. The rampart was strengthened on the river side (i.e. on the west side) in Period I itself

by the placement of well-cut wooden sleepers or beams in a connected manner for a stretch of nearly 350 ft . . . alongside the river, corresponding in length to an inward bend in the stream. This feature was observed along the northern half of the western face of the ramparts. The sleepers were placed angularly to the flow of the river so as to serve as a buffer to break the force of striking waters. . . . The sleepers were laid, as seen in the trenches, sunk carefully in several courses to form a series of deep, rectangular chambers, intended apparently to hold the dumped clay in position and prevent it from being scoured away (Banerjee 1965: 16).

The wood used for the sleepers has been identified as teak (*Tectona grandis*) and Safed khair (*Acacia feruginea*). The logs vary in length from 13 to 18 ft (3.96 to 5.48 m) and have a 9 ins (0.22 m) square cross-section. In Period II the outer edge of the rampart was reinforced by a 3 ft 9 ins (1.143 m) wide brick wall. The width of the moat was reduced to 129 ft (39.31 m) in Period III.

Inside the fortified habitation area no structural evidence was obtained for Period I. In Period II the houses were made

variously of mud, mud-bricks, stone rubble or burnt bricks. The mud and burnt brick structures were usually built over a plinth of rubble and clay. The flooring too lay on a bed of rubble and was made either of clay, occasionally mixed with mud bricks or brick-dust. The mortar and plaster, where available, were of a smooth paste of clay. The floors were renewed or raised periodically with clay. The houses appeared to have been roofed generally with oblong tiles with double perforations for being fixed in position (IAR 1956–57: 24).

A burnt brick oblong enclosure (34 by 26 ft or 10.36 by 7.92 m) with a low parapet wall, which has been excavated might have served as a re-servoir. A large number of finished and unfinished products inside a mud house suggest that this was a 'workshop for the manufacture of beads of agate and arrowheads and knitting needles of bone' (IAR 1956–57: 28). The building tradition of Period II continued in Period III while terracotta ringed soak-pits, ring-wells, bottomless soakage jars and terracotta drain pipes have been found in both periods.

Malhar

This site in Bilaspur district is supposed to have been a 'flourishing township on the ancient route from Kausambi to the southeastern coast' (IAR 1974–75: 21). Excavations here (IAR 1974–75: 21–2, 1975–76: 23, 1977–78: 30–1) have revealed a sequence beginning with a level bearing punch-marked coins. In the first phase of Period I locally available stone blocks were used as housing material whereas in its second phase burnt bricks were used. An enclosing mud wall has been reported in this period. Excavations in one trench showed three structural phases belonging to the Gupta and later times.

The first structure consisted of small rooms with plinths of slate stones. The second structure with fairly large rooms and a courtyard on the eastern side, running north-south, has the plinth of dressed massive limestone blocks, over which the superstructure of baked bricks was standing. Below these structures was encountered three successive floor levels, made of rammed earth and potsherds, the earliest one resting over the burnt layer. A thick wall of massive round boulders was found in the lowest level of the trench (IAR 1977–78: 31).

Another trench revealed structural activities of the Satavahana and earlier periods. Among the finds are a stone wall enclosing the plinths of a house complex, an earlier house made of slate stone, etc.

Other Sites

There are also a few other excavated city sites in Madhya Pradesh, not-ably Nandur (IAR 1980–81: 37–8, 1981–82: 36–7, 1982–83: 40), Tumain (ancient Tumbavana, IAR 1971–72: 27–8, 1972–73: 15–16), Tripuri

(IAR 1965–66: 21–2, 1966–67: 17–19, 1967–68: 23–4, 1968–69: 11–12) and Maheshwar which lies on the northern bank of the Narmada opposite Navdatoli. Maheshwar has been identified with ancient Mahismati. Regrettably, the details of urban planning from these excavated sites have not been reported, although there are early historic levels at all these sites which are given urban status in literary sources.

GUJARAT

The archaeological horizon marking the beginning of the early historic period in Gujarat seems to be characterized by a black-and-red ware which co-occurs with the late phase of the NBPW. At Broach, for instance, the NBPW occurs in the upper levels of the black-and-red-ware-bearing horizon (IAR 1956–57: 24), an evidence which is more or less repeated at some other sites like Nagal (IAR 1959–60: 19), Prabhas Patan (IAR 1961–62: 11–12), Amreli, etc. One may reasonably presume that the NBPW was introduced in Gujarat when it came within the Mauryan empire either under Chandragupta or Bindusara. In any case the date should be around the very beginning of the third century BC or earlier. With its inclusion in the Mauryan empire, however, Gujarat finds a place in Indian history and from then, particularly with the development of India's Mediterranean trade, the Gujarat coast-line attained a new level of economic prosperity which must have been the most important single factor in the growth of its early historic urbanism.

Considered in detail, however, the archaeological evidence of early historic urban development in Gujarat is still very scanty. Almost all the excavations at this level have been exclusively vertical in nature, revealing hardly anything beyond the archaeological sequence.

Broach

The most important early historic city in Gujarat was ancient Bharukachchha or Bhrigukachchhá of the Indian and Barygaza of the classical sources. Identified with modern Broach on the Narmada estuary this was a port town par excellence. Not only was its immediate hinterland fertile, yielding wheat, rice and cotton, but its connection stretched to Ujjayini in Malwa and Pratisthana in the Deccan, thus touching the arterial routes of traffic in inner India. Evidence contained in Periplus is most explicit, one of its sections being devoted to an elaborate list of the imports and exports of this port (Majumdar 1960:304). It did not, however, cater only to the Mediterranean trade; in some Jatakas it is said to have had connections also with Ceylon and southeast Asia (H. Chakraborti 1966:92), a likely enough phenomenon considering the importance of the Gujarat coast in India's southeast Asian trade over a long period of time.

The excavations at Broach in 1959–60 have yielded extremely limited data. As the excavator puts it:

This high mound on the bank of the Narmada, though extensive and compact, is almost completely sealed for examination by the busy town thriving on it, leaving only the eroded peripheral fringes on the riverside at the eastern and southeastern limits available for excavation (IAR 1959–60: 19).

Of the 25 ft thick cultural deposit, Period I was marked by a black-and-red ware bearing the NBPW in its upper levels. An important feature of this period was a mud rampart with a deep moat on the outer side. No structural evidence was found but there was a cluster of five terracotta ring-wells on the inner fringe of the rampart. Another important aspect was the presence of a large number of finished and unfinished beads of semi-precious stones, suggesting a bead industry. The beginning of this period has been tentatively dated by the excavator to the third century BC. Considering the introduction of the NBPW at the site presumably at the very beginning of the third century BC or earlier, the initial date of the period is likely to be earlier.

Period II continued till the early centuries AD, as evident from the presence of red polished ware. During this period the mud rampart was provided with heavy brick revetments which subsequently collapsed. Period III was medieval.

Other Sites

The archaeological data from the other relevant sites in Gujarat are extremely scanty; even at Dwaraka, an important place in the Krishna tradition, what has been obtained is a mere vertical sequence (Ansari and Mate 1966). Only at Shamlaji (IAR 1961–62: 13–14, R.N. Mehta and A.G. Patel 1967) in the Sabarkantha area of northeastern Gujarat has some semblance of early historic town-planning been found. The site possesses an oblong brick-built fortification measuring 670.50 by 304.80 m. The bastions are visible and in places intact upto a height of 7.62 m from the present ground level. B. Subbarao's limited excavation in 1961–62 showed the site to have possessed four main periods. Period I was pre-defence and dated to the beginning of the Christian era. Period II with two phases in the construction of the defence fortifications was dated AD 100–500, the first phase being in AD 100–300. Periods III and IV ranged from the post-Gupta to the medieval period. The picture is not much clearer at such sites as Panduwala (Kushan period settlement, IAR 1982–83: 99), Timbarva (R.N. Mehta 1955), Vadodara (ancient Vadapadraka, cf. A. Ghosh 1989, II: 457—a large burnt brick structure, Roman bronzes, early Kshatrapa coins) and Karvan (IAR 1974–75: 15–16, 1975–76: 15, 1976–77: 18, 1977–78: 22–3), etc.

MAHARASHTRA

The beginning of the early historic period at Nasik (Period IIA) has been dated around 400 BC (Sankalia and Deo 1955: 20) and this may well be the date of the beginning of the early historic period in the upper Godavari region and Vidarbha. On the basis of evidence contained in the *Suttanipata*, one of the oldest surviving works of the Pali Buddhist canon, the twilight phase may certainly be pushed back to an earlier date. This text refers to the southern trade route linking the Gangetic valley with the Deccan and also to a sage called Bavari who sent his pupils from the Deccan to the Buddha to ask him questions and who became a Buddhist convert in the end (Malalasekera 1960, II: 279–80). On this basis, the Deccan found a place in history in the second half of the sixth century BC. Moreover, the discovery and excavation of a Bharhut-type stupa at Pauni in the Wainganga valley in Vidarbha, which is said to possess a pre-Mauryan core, amply suggests that historical centres in Maharashtra were being developed in the fourth century BC, particularly along the route which connected it with the Gangetic valley. The region gained historic importance in the orbit of history in the second century BC. Not merely did it witness the growth of a political power under the Satavahanas but there were also in about this period Buddhist rock-cut caves like Karle, Bhaja, Kanheri, Pitalkhora, etc., which stood along the Deccanese trade routes and which indicate through their inscriptional details the existence of a well-organized economic structure. This economic base was further strengthened in the early centuries AD by the demands of Indo-Roman trade. Ports like Surparaka and Kalyana came to flourish along the coast while in the interior there were distributing centres like Pratisthana and Tagara, all mentioned in Periplus and Ptolemy (for a comprehensive discussion, see H. Chakraborti 1966: 101–9, 192–203).

The archaeological data regarding these settlements are hopelessly inadequate. Excavations of the early historic levels of sites like Nasik,

Brahmapuri, Ter, Nevasa, Kaundanpur, etc. have merely bracketed the stratigraphic position of these levels.

A place mentioned by Patanjali and called 'nagara' or city in an early local inscription (Sankalia and Deo 1955: 1), Nasik Period II, which ushers in early history, possesses two sub-periods: A, dated *c.* 400–200 BC, and B, dated *c.* 200 BC–AD 50. The few houses which were excavated were mud-walled and there were soakage pits lined with bricks or terracotta rings. Period III is dated *c.* AD 50–200 and possessed burnt brick houses.

The beginning of Brahmapuri (Sankalia and Diksit 1952) on the Panchaganga river may go back to *c.* 200 BC but the settlement seemed to have been prosperous only in the early centuries AD. Four burnt brick houses of this period have been excavated. They were built on a foundation of large pebbles embedded in layers of clay, roofed with tiles and had at least three rooms each, some of them big in size. A room measures 32 ft by 6 ft in House IV. The passages between these houses were irregularly aligned and were narrow, about 2 ft wide.

The inland market town of Tagara (H.Chakraborti 1966: 202–3, for different theories of identification) is generally identified with modern Ter on the river Terna. Although excavated over a number of seasons earlier (IAR 1957-58: 23–4, 1966–67: 25–6, 1967–8: 35, 1968–69: 17–18), the site was re-excavated by S.B. Deo in 1974–75 (IAR 1974–75: 32) and showed three cultural phases. Phase I is marked by the NBPW. Phase II shows 'some sort of wooden barricade with teak plants fixed in position with wooden pins'. The structures of Phase III (Satavahana coins) 'were constructed of baked bricks with floors of hydraulic lime-mortar, tiled roofs and attached soakage wells of terracotta rings'. The habitation at this mound came to an end around the third century AD. An extensive mound (3.24 ha.) which has been reported as 'probably the most intact and most extensive one with Satavahana habitational deposit' was found at Irle, 16 km southeast of Ter in Osmanabad district. In 1987–88 the excavations at Ter revealed some religious structures including a tank of the first century AD (IAR 1987–88: 87–8).

Kaundanpur (Diksit 1968) on the bank of the Wardha or ancient 'Kaundinyapura' was the traditional capital of Vidarbha (Dey 1971: 108). The excavations yielded only a sequence from the megalithic to the Muslim periods including the following levels: Period II (pre-Mauryan), Period III (*c.* 300–100 BC), Period IV (*c.* 150 BC–AD 200) and Period V (*c.* AD 200–250). Brick-built soak-wells were found in Period IV. Structural evidence is equally inadequate in Periods IV and V of Nevasa on the

Pravara; these periods dated *c.* 150 BC–50 BC and *c.* 50 BC–AD 200, respectively. There has been no excavation at Sopara and Kalyan, both sea-ports of undoubted significance near Bombay. Pratisthana on the Godavari, perhaps the most important early historical inland settlement in the Deccan with a very wide trade network extending into the Gangetic valley, has neither been properly surveyed nor excavated (IAR 1965–66: 28–9). The sequence is said to begin with the NBPW mixed with Satavahana coins. The site is said to measure 4 sq. km in extent (A. Ghosh 1989, II: 325). Excavations at Bhokardan (Deo and Gupta 1974) or ancient Bhogavardhana in the Amaravati district did not yield much data of structural significance. Another site, Bhatkuli, which has been mentioned in the Bharhut inscriptions as Bhojakakata, is reported in the same district. Another major site is Adam (IAR 1987–88: 85, also, A. Nath 1991) in Nagpur district which has shown the remains of an earthen rampart with gateways on the eastern flank. The site is said to measure 10 ha. The rampart and the moat came up in Period III, dated between *c.* 1000 and 500 BC and was later reinforced by a stone battlement. Arni in Yeotmal district (IAR 1984–85) shows a mud rampart wall with a stone foundation of the Satavahana period. Arni is unexcavated but Nadner, a fortified settlement in Sehore district, was excavated for two seasons (IAR 1986–87: 58, 1987–88: 80–1), although nothing can be gathered about the nature of the rampart and the moat from the published material. This site has been described as a 'flourishing trade centre of the Avanti kingdom'.

KARNATAKA

Evidence of early history has been obtained from a few places in Karnataka or Mysore. The Mauryan presence is an indisputable historical thread. The township of Isila mentioned in an Asokan minor rock edict at Brahmagiri is supposed to have been a provincial administrative centre of the Mauryas. There is no reason why the location of such a centre should be on the border of the empire; I suspect that Mauryan control extended much further south. There is no special reason to believe, as has been the case so far, that the 'bordering' states of the Cholas, Keralaputras and Satiyaputras, were outside the Mauryan border and not inside. These groups of people may, with perhaps more justification, be interpreted as people constituting the inhabitants of the southern outlying ('bordering', if one prefers) section of the Mauryan empire. There is really no reason why Isila should be placed on the border itself. Whatever it is, we do not know anything about Isila of the third century BC. In the Andhra level, however, there is evidence of a 'road of stone rubble, 17–18 feet wide'. Chandravalli, some miles southwest of Brahmagiri, was another township of the early centuries AD. The details are not known but the ground survey indicates that it was some 800 yards long with about the same width. The finds of Roman coins indicate that Mysore had its share of Indo-Roman trade. There is reference to a port called Byzantium both in Periplus and Ptolemy, identified with modern Vizadrog or Vaijayanti contained in a Karle inscription which refers to a banker of the place (H. Chakraborti 1966: 109–11). The place has revealed occupation going back to the third century BC and at a site called Udayvara near modern Udipi there is evidence of an early historic fortification (IAR 1968-69). At Banavasi (North Kanara district) the mound (over 1 sq. km in extent) is enclosed by a fortification which is made of bricks set on a rubble foundation. This is surrounded by a deep moat (except on the river side) and underwent repairs at least twice with brickbats and large lateritic blocks. This rampart dates from the first century AD. Religious structures have also been reported from the place. Vadgaon-Madhavpur (A. Ghosh 1989, II: 456) in Belgaum district is a very large early historic site (40 ha.) which was excavated in 1972–77. This has yielded a sequence beginning with the third century BC. Brick structures have been reported from Period III, dated from the middle of the first to the second centtury AD. On the left bank of the Bhima and on one of its inward bends, Sannati (Sundara 1988) is a single culture site of the early historical period and is roughly more than 200 ha. in extent. There is a brick fortification wall, 4 m wide and 2–3 m high. The site has been reported to possess two parts, one on the river bank (80 ha.) and the other on a lower level. About 3 km away there are two stupa sites dating from the second century BC to the second century AD. According to A. Sundara no other site is so rich in Buddhist relics in Karnataka.

KERALA

The coastal strip of Kerala, a focal point of India's sea-borne trade through the centuries, has not yet reported a single authenticated early historical site. Considering that the Asokan rock edicts II and XIII refer to 'Keralaputras' and that the region was of historic importance in the classical sources of the early centuries AD, this lack of early historic sites is surprising. It may be explained by the lack of adequate exploration, the shifting mouth of the rivers on which the coastal stations were presumably

situated and the yearly two seasons of monsoon acting against the formation of a suitable habitational deposit.

Armed with an effective knowledge of the monsoons Roman traffic
from the Red Sea area converged directly on the Kerala coast, before
proceeding further to the east. In Periplus, Ptolemy and Pliny a number
of trading stations have been mentioned, the most important of which
seems to be Musiris, generally identified with modern Cranganore.

The Peutinger Tablet, a cartographic representation of the ancient
world dating from the third century AD shows an Augustan temple on the
map beside Musiris. Thus, a careful archaeological search for early historic sites is of importance in Kerala.

TAMILNADU

It is difficult to pinpoint the precise beginning of history in the former
province of Madras or modern Tamilnadu. The earliest fixed point is the
Asokan rock edicts II and XIII which refer to the kingdom or the people
of the Cholas and Pandyas, the former extending along the eastern coast
from Nellore to Pudukottai and the latter centred around Madras and
stretching to the southern tip of the peninsula. Besides, the earliest known
Tamil literature refers explicitly to these two kingdoms. There is a reference to the Pandyas in the works of the Sanskrit grammarian, Katyayana,
who is likely to belong to the fourth century BC, and at about the same time
Megasthenes speaks of Pandaia, the daughter of Heracles ruling that
portion of India which lies to the south and extends to the sea. In Strabo,
King Pandion is said to have sent a mission to Augustus Caesar in 20 BC
(for a discussion, see Smith 1924: 470–1, K.A.N. Sastri 1958, chapters IV
and V). There is little doubt that there were two well-organized kingdoms
in the Coromandel coast dating at least from the post-Mauryan period, if
not earlier. Their twilight period, however, lasts up to the beginning of the
Christian era when both Tamil literature and the classical sources speak
of a concentration of sea-borne trade in the region. It is also from this
period that archaeological evidence becomes historically revealing.

Compared to the archaeological potentiality of the region, however,
the excavated sites are still limited in number: Urayur, Arikamedu,
Kanchipuram and Kaveripattinam, all in the Chola country. The Pandyan
centres like Madura and Korkai remain largely unexcavated. Madura, the
Pandyan capital in the early centuries AD, possesses graphic Tamil literary
descriptions and some classical references (H. Chakraborti 1966: 209–
11). Korkai, identified with a village on the bank of the Tamraparni river
was the earlier capital.

Briefly excavated, Korkai has yielded in its early historic level a brick platform and a terracotta soakage jar. The discovery of innumerable pearl oysters in different levels indicates that the site was an important centre of pearl-fishery (IAR 1968–69). Three periods of the ancient Chola capital have been identified (IAR 1964–65), now within the city limits of modern Tiruchirapalli or Trichinopally. Period I, dated between the third century BC and the first–second centuries AD, is marked by the primary use of megalithic black-and-red, russet-coated, rouletted and Arretine wares, the last two being of Roman affiliation. A few potsherds bear Tamil inscriptions in the Brahmi script of the first–second centuries AD. Period II, dated between the second and fifth–sixth centuries AD, witnessed a decline in the use of the megalithic black-and-red ware. A small burnt brick structure with two adjoining cisterns, which belong to this period, might have had some industrial use, perhaps as dyeing vats. Period III began in about the sixth century AD (for almost similar evidence from Tirukkampuliyar and Alagarai, see Mahalingam 1970).

Excavations in 1945 at Arikamedu (Wheeler 1946), a small fishermen's village on the bank of a lagoon about two miles south of the centre of modern Pondicherry, produced the first securely dated stratigraphic evidence of the presence of Romans in the south and gave in the process south Indian archaeology its first secure chronological datum-line. However, from the point of view of urban planning the results have been inadequate. Even the 1947–48 excavations by Casal did not enlarge the picture to a great extent.

The chronology of early Arikamedu broadly spans the first two centuries AD, although recent opinions favour a beginning about one or two centuries earlier. In the northern sector of the excavated area, 'on the foreshore of the estuary', there was a large brick-structure, more than 150 ft long, which is supposed to have been a warehouse. This building has been dated approximately to the middle and second half of the first century AD. In the southern sector two complexes of pavements called Tanks A and B lay at the edge of two large and apparently unroofed courtyards and were associated with extensive drains or conduits. The general impression is that 'the site was used for industrial purposes involving a constant inflow and outflow of water. It is likely enough, though not proved, that the tanks were used as cisterns or vats for dyeing the muslin which formed one of the most important exports of this part of India in ancient times. The yards may have been used for drying this cloth' (Wheeler 1946). In 1947–48 a sloped brick revetment with a surviving height of 6 ft was traced for about 80 yards in the southern sector. It has been imagined to be the side of a reservoir, but might well be a defensive revetment. The presence of Arretine ware, Roman gems, a lamp, amphorae fragments and glass bowls amply indicates that it was one of the Roman emporia, perhaps the Pouduke emporium mentioned by Ptolemy.

The excavated data at Kaveripattinam are also meagre (A. Ghosh 1989, II: 216); there excavations revealed a massive brick platform (18.28 by 7.62 m) built on natural sand and perhaps a wharf where boats could be tied. There is a radiocarbon date of the third century BC for this structure. Another major structure, although in a different excavated locality, is a water reservoir made of an earthen bund with a brick facade. It is designed with curves to receive the water and let it into a pond. Probably a small channel from the river Kaveri at whose mouth the site is located or one of its offshoots served as the feeding channel of this reservoir. The third major excavated structural complex here represents an entire wing of seven rooms (each 2.4 m sq.) of a Buddhist monastery which had an ornamental structure (a *mandapa*?) nearby. The walls of this structure were found decorated with stucco figures and paintings, one of the former being found in the excavations.

At Kanchipuram (IAR 1962–63, 1969–70, 1970–71, 1971–72, 1972–73, 1973–74, 1974–75, 1975–76) the sequence began with the megalithic black-and-red ware but witnessed the introduction of Roman amphorae and rouletted ware at a later level.

Karaikadu (IAR 1966–67: 21) in South Arcot district is reported to have been a trading station.

ANDHRA

In the Krishna-Godavari delta and its adjacent uplands the twilight period of history decidedly begins in the third–second centuries BC. There are in this region not merely a number of Asokan inscriptions but also the pre-Christian sculptural reliefs at Amaravati, Goli and Jaggayyapeta conforming to the contemporary art-idiom of the Gangetic valley and central India. In the early centuries AD this region came into sharp focus in history. In about this period it witnessed a political consolidation successively under the Satavahanas and Ikshakus, and acquired a significant share in India's contemporary Roman and South-east Asian trade.

One of the results of this political consolidation and the prosperity resulting from trade was the growth of a large number of religious complexes which were mostly Buddhist in character. The discovered sites in the Krishna-Godavari delta stretch between Ganjam and Nellore while in the adjacent uplands they reach as far as Srisailam and Warangal. It is likely that there were five main routes leading to and from the Andhra region: the routes to Kalinga, the South, Karnataka, Maharashtra and Kosala. The fact that the religious settlements were closely linked with the development of trade is suggested by their distribution mainly along these trade-routes.

Nagarjunakonda

Of all these sites the one most extensively excavated is Nagarjunakonda. The capital of the Ikshakus, modern Nagarjunakonda or ancient Vijayapuri was excavated in 1926–31, 1938 and 1954–60. The historical sections of the 1954–60 excavations have only been briefly published while the results of the two earlier excavations have been embodied in two Archaeological Survey of India Memoirs (Longhurst 1938, Ramachandran 1953).

The site lies in a valley which is about 3 miles wide and almost completely enclosed by some off-shoots of the Nallamalai range on all sides except the west where the Krishna serves both as a barrier and a river-passage. Two hill knots are centred in the valley itself: Nagarjuna and Peddakundelagutta hills. A rubble fortification has been explored at the eastern entrance to the valley while another fortification of the same kind has been noticed along the summit of the Siddhaldari hills.

What is known as the Ikshaku citadel lay close to the river-bank and overlay the summit of the Peddakundelagutta hill. It enclosed a roughly trapezoidal area, about 3000 by 2000 ft (914.4 by 609.6 m) and was surrounded by a fortification wall which revealed two building phases. In Phase I it was mud-built, was about 80 ft (24.38 m) wide at the base and rested on the natural soil except for the river-side where it overlay an earlier occupational deposit. In Phase II there was a 9–14 ft (2.74–4.26 m) wide burnt-brick wall built over at places over the remains of the earlier wall. Except the portion overlying the Peddakundelagutta hill this fortified citadel was surrounded by a ditch, 12 ft (3.65 m) deep and 74–132 ft (22.55–40.23 m) wide. There were two main gateways, one each in the east and the west, while a narrow postern gate has been traced on the northern side. Outside the western gate which had a minimum width of 17 ft (5.18 m) there was a brick-wall, 6–7 ft (1.82–2.13 m) high and 3–4 ft (0.91–1.21 m) wide, suggesting an outwork or barbican. The ceramic evidence from the pre-to-post-rampart layers was uniform and conformed to the Ikshaku period.

Close to the eastern gateway have been discovered some barracks and stables and a well-plastered masonry cistern. Near the western gateway a compound wall enclosed some ritualistic structures. The central feature was a four-tiered tank, 27 ft (8.22 m) square at the top and 6–4 ft (1.93 m) square at the bottom. At each level it had short steps on its sides. The total depth of the tank was about 6–8 ft (2.59 m). At a height of about 7 ft (2.13 m) there was a drain connected successively with a closed passage and a narrow slab-covered drain. Bones, possibly of a horse and a goat have been found outside the tank but within the outer enclosure. The tank has been supposed to represent an 'Asvamedha' tank. Another two-tierd small tank, built of carved bricks and roughly tortoise in shape lay to the south of the Asvamedha tank and is also supposed to represent a water-reservoir of ritualistic significance. East of this complex a number of residential structures lying within an enclosure wall may represent the palace area.

Sites have been excavated almost all over the valley outside the Ikshaku citadel. But as the detailed plan of the site remains unpublished it is still not possible to evaluate their significance in terms of the total layout of the city. Certain sectors, however, seem to stand out from the rest.

The ordinary residential area was concentrated to the east of the citadel. The respective width of the streets, lanes and alleys was 25 ft (7.62 m), 15 ft (4.57 m) and 8 ft (2.43 m). A main street divided the area into two parts. The largest of the houses measured 250 by 200 ft (77 by 60.06 m). Large storage jars arranged in rows seem to have been a characteristic feature of the houses. One particular house has been identified as a goldsmith's shop because of its 'terracotta crucibles, a touch-stone, an iron-pestle, terracotta and stone weights, terracotta bangles, ear-rings and oblong moulds with designs for ornaments'.

An important structural complex in this context is what has been called a stadium. It consisted of a central arena, 309 ft (94.18 m) long, 259 ft (78.95 m) wide and 15 ft (4.57 m) deep. It was enclosed on all sides by a flight of steps 2 ft wide and had a pavilion to the west. 'In continuation of the topmost steps, there was a platform all around, the width of which, as noted on the southern side, was 11 feet. On this side six staircases, placed at regular intervals, each measuring 6 feet (1.82 m) in width connected the arena with the platform'. The pavilion had three phases of varying width and in the last phase had an enclosure wall with an entrance on the western side. Rainwater was drained out of the arena by a 2 ft wide drain passing through the northern wall of the stadium.

The structural complexes on the river-side included a cremation ground, a stepped and balustrated ghat on the river and some temples, the most important of which was a Kartikeya temple. Another temple, the

Kuvera temple, lay to the southeast of the citadel. Mention should also be made of 'a canal, 30 ft (9.14 m) wide and 6 ft (1.82 m) deep, running east-west, belonging to the Ikshaku period. With ramps on both sides the canal-bed was traced to a length of 1000 ft (304.8 m). On the southern side of the canal were two mandapas, one a chatuhsala and the other a sixteen-pillared hall'.

The bulk of the excavated structural data, is, however, confined to the Buddhist monastic complexes with their stupas, Chaityas and Viharas. When these data are fully published they are likely to shed light on the condition of Buddhism in the early centuries AD in this part of India.

A fuller appreciation of Nagarjunakonda must await the detailed publication of the historical section of the 1954–60 excavation reports but whatever little has been published amply suggests that here was a settlement, the magnificance of which is all too rare in Indian archaeology.

H. Sarkar (in A. Ghosh 1989, II: 299–303) adds the following details: Structures inside the royal citadel included residential buildings, barracks, stables, cisterns, baths, square wells or soak-pits. The palace has not been identified except for a bathing establishment attached to it. Two ornamental tanks connected with underground drains, wells and paved cisterns formed the core of this establishment. Outside the citadel the rooms arranged in one alignment with a commmon verandah in front were generally built of rubble set in mud. Some of these houses were shops (cf. a goldsmith's shop). Brick-built houses followed the same pattern but in the more spacious, richer houses, rooms were arranged around a central pillared hall.

There is no doubt that the settlements followed a linear pattern and that they came up along broad roads intercepted by cross-roads and bylanes. Some of the wealthy houses came up along the bank of a canal with rubble-built ramps on either side. . . . A novel feature of the Ikshvaku townplanning was the provision of about a dozen wayside resthouses, in the form of pillared halls and public baths. . . . There were about 18 Brahmanical temples . . . situated mostly along the north-flowing Krishna and around the citadel. . . . The Bathing Ghat, fully encased in stone, . . . was a wonder of Ikshvaku architecture. . . . More than 30 Buddhist establishments . . . were exposed. . . . These monasteries were spread throughout the valley except the river-bank.

Satanikota

The main occupational period of the site of Satanikota (Kurnool district, located on the right bank of the Tungabhadra) spanned the mid-first century BC to the mid-third century AD. A rampart, a moat and a gate were found in the first structural phase of the period. The fort followed the natural contour lines of the area and was thus irregular in shape. The main wall was built of stone slabs of irregular sizes (mud mortar) and was 3.2 m wide with 10–13 courses extant. It had a 1.45 m wide facing of burnt brick. On the inner side along the main wall there was a 3 m wide pavement of burnt brickbats. A moat was cut into the natural bedrock as indicated by extensive chisel marks on the sides. The average depth and width of the moat were 3.20 m and 4.25 m, respectively with embankments of boulders and Cuddapah slabs on the outer edge of the moat. The gateway complex facing the south showed a flight of five steps of 3 m width and was flanked by 45 cm wide parapet walls. There are indications of a drawbridge over the moat. Structural complexes with rectangular rooms have been found well inside the fort (N.C. Ghosh 1986).

Vengi

Ancient Vengi, called Peddavegi (West Godavary district), was the capital of the Salankayanas who have been mentioned by Panini. The excavated areas showed three phases: c. fourth–fifth century AD, mid-fifth–end sixth century AD and end sixth–early seventh century AD. Religious structures have been excavated (I.K. Sarma 1988) but there are extensive ruins including a fortified township covering about 6 sq. km. The gravel fortifications called Kotadibbalu (with a moat) encircle an area of one sq. km.

There are a few other interesting early historic sites: Chinnabankur (5 ha. in Karimnagar district); Dhulikatta (18 ha., mud fortification, Karimnagar), Karnamandi (20 ha.) and Peddabankur (Karimnagar). At Dhulikatta there are two huge brick-built gateways and a deep moat. Kotalinga on the Godavary is surrounded by small early historic sites, one of them being Vemnuru, a site of 3/4 ha. It may be noted that except for Karnamandi which is in Adilabad district, most of the sites are in Karimnagar (for details, see V.V. Krishnasastry 1983, Parasher 1992).

Other Andhra Sites

A.H. Longhurst (1983) reports a town-site near the Buddhist stupa of Amaravati and it has been generally accepted as the site of ancient Dhanyakakata, an important trade-mart with references in Amaravati and Karle inscriptions (Kosambi 1955).

It is surrounded on all four sides by a massive embankment of earth and broken brick and stones, about 650 yards on each side, the west side only being a little shorter and irregular owing to a curve in the river-bank. This embankment marks the site of the ancient walls of what must have been the citadel of a city and a place of very considerable strength in early times. A large town no doubt surrounded it (Longhurst 1983: 13). Recent excavations (IAR 1962–63, 63–4, 64–5) have identified six occupational periods at the site, the earliest one going back to the second century BC. On numismatic and palaeographical grounds Period VI has been dated to the second–third centuries AD. Structurally nothing significant has been found except the traces of an Amaravati-type stupa in Period VI but the rouletted and Arretine wares occurred in Period III. There were also soak-pits and drains in this period. Period II revealed 'a gold-smiths's mould, glass-bangles and ear-rings of bewildering variety and shape, undoubtedly imported through oceanic and riverine trade' (IAR 1964–65).

A cutting laid across the western side of the fortified township revealed seven structural phases, of which the earlier six related to the embankment-*cum*-wharf abutting a navigation-channel, and the latest one to the defence-system. The structural details of each phase were as follows: Phase I, navigational-channel, cut into the natural lateritic ridge which also showed occupational deposits in the shape of a series of hearths with ash, etc. . . .; Phase II, a huge wharf raised upon wooden posts as indicated by rows of post-holes; Phase III, brick wharf built along the inner side of the channel with further heightening of the embankment by a mud ramp; Phase IV, brick revetment on both sides of the channel with lateritic gravel as the packing-material; Phase V, reinforcement of the inner side of the channel with further raising of the embankment by the use of sand and sandstone chips and the provision of retaining walls of laterite blocks; Phase VI, repairs to the brick-revetments and sand-fillings of the earlier phases resulting from heavy erosions; and Phase VII, following a period of abandonment, filling up of the channel, and conversion of the embankment into a defence-wall (IAR 1962–63: 1–2).

Excavations at Yeleswaram (A.W. Khan 1962) have also revealed an extensive habitational deposit. The remains are mostly of Buddhist complexes.

At Kondapur (Yazdani 1941) the excavated assemblage belongs primarily to the early centuries AD. The rooms were either 10–12 ft square or rectangular, measuring 10 by 8 ft The floors were occasionally brick-laid but in some cases they were made of well-paved brick-dust or rubble. Perhaps tile was used as roofing material. The site was, in fact, briefly excavated and though a number of interesting antiquities were found, including a gold coin of Augustus, no precise plan of the settlement could be made.

ORISSA

Regarding the early settlements in Orissa where the Asokan inscriptions at Dhauli and Jaugada provide a firm datum-line for the beginning of history, not much is known from the literary and epigraphic sources. The Asokan edicts refer to two Mauryan administrative centres, Tosali and Samapa, none of them identified beyond doubt, except possibly modern Sisupalgarh and Jaugada. Ptolemy refers to a place called 'Paloura or Pakoura, a town' (Majumdar 1960: 367), generally taken to be the Dravidian form of Dantapura, supposedly an ancient capital of Orissa or Kalinga (H. Chakraborti 1966: 143–5). Its identification also remains uncertain.

Archaeologically, only two early historic town-sites have been excavated in Orissa: Sisupalgarh and Jaugada.

Jaugada

Jaugada (ancient Samapa?) on the bank of the Rishikulya river is a fortified, roughly square-shaped area. Each side of the fortification is about half a mile long and possesses two gateways.

Apart from an earlier neolithic celt 'seemingly associated with a black-and-red ware' just above the natural soil, Period I at the site revealed evidence of extensive bead-making and post-holes and patches of floor of rammed gravel or burnt earth. Brick and stone structures were encountered in Period II but in the limited area of digging no detailed plan could be drawn up. The earthen rampart was first built over a 'flimsy occupational debris, consisting of sherds of fine black-and-red ware' on the natural soil. Its extant maximum height is 14 ft 6 ins and the basal width is 70 ft. There was a ditch beyond the rampart but its width and depth could not be ascertained. After this phase the top of the rampart was covered by a thick deposit of earth and soon after there was the construction of a 2 ft high wall of rubble and stone chips with a layer of large boulders—all laid in thick lateritic gravel and clay—against the inner side. The chronology is still tentative but it should go back at least to the third century BC and it continued up to the middle of the fourth century AD or thereabouts (IAR 1956–57).

Sisupalgarh

Sisupalgarh (ancient Tosali?) near modern Bhuvaneswar is also fortified and roughly square-shaped, each arm of the square measuring about three-fourth of a mile. The contours suggest corner-towers and eight gateways, two on each side. Traces of early occupation may be noticed for a considerable area outside the fortification and the general inference is that 'the fort, while being too large for a mere citadel . . . did not accommodate the entire population, a considerable section of which dwelt outside its confines' (B.B. Lal 1949: 64).

The sequence in the habitational area spans the period between 300 BC and AD 350 and is subdivisible into a number of occupational periods. In Period IIA (*c.* 200 BC–AD 100) there was a terracotta ring-well with a stone-paving at the mouth. In Period III (*c.* AD 200–350) the plans of two adjoining houses built of lateritic blocks could be drawn up. These two houses did not have a common partition wall but were separated by a gap of about 2 ft (0.61 m). The northern house had two rooms, 10 by 8 ft and 10 by 9 ft (3.04 by 2.43 m and 3.04 by 2.74 m) with a verandah, 19 by 8 ft (5.79 by 2.43 m) in front.

The defences were first built in Period IIA, supposedly in about the first quarter of the second century BC. In its Phase I it was a massive clay rampart, about 25 ft (7.62 m) high at the excavated point and 110 ft (33.52 m) wide at the base. There was a series of roughly circular holes about 1 ft (0.30 m) deep and 10 ft (30.4 m) wide arranged at a regular interval of 1 ft 10 ins (0.55 m) and covered with a thin layer of clay, on the top of the rampart. Their purpose remains uncertain. In Phase II, a 4 ft 6 ins (1.37 m) thick layer of lateritic gravel was laid on top of the rampart. In Phase III, two brick walls, 26 ft (7.92 m) apart, were built on top of the lateritic gravel and the portion between these walls was filled up by earth. In Phase IV, which does not immediately follow Phase III, a revetment with a stepped exterior was added.

Among the eight gateways only the western gateway was excavated. This gateway complex basically consists of two L-shaped flanks with a 25 ft (7.62 m) wide intervening passage in the form of a ramp. There were two gates, inner and outer, set at a distance of about 100 ft (30.48 m); the door sockets of these gates have been found. A 5 ft 3 ins (1.60 m) wide ancillary passage, connected with the main passage by three steps, flanked the inner gate. There was a guard-room attached to the outer gate. 'The entire system of the gateway may be imagined to have functioned as follows. At a certain fixed hour in the night, the inner gate was closed, stopping all vehicular traffic beyond this point. Pedestrians could, however, get in or out through the ancillary passage. A little later, the outer or main gate was also closed, while the guards at its back probably still remained on duty' (B.B. Lal 1949: 77). The gateway was repaired several times. A remarkably interesting discovery is that of 'early historical habitation extended in a radius of 1 km' from the Dhauli rock-edict spot. Earthen fortifications were also noticed in the neighbourhood.

No other fortified early historic habitational settlement has yet been reported from this region, although there is a possibility of further discoveries.

ASPECTS OF EARLY HISTORIC URBAN PATTERN

Pattern of Growth

In the Northwest the theoretical starting point should be the Achaemenid annexation of the region under Cyrus, perhaps 'a little before 530 BC'. By turning it into a satrapy of their empire the Achaemenids politically consolidated their empire in the Northwest which had been placed as part of the Achaemenid empire within the economic orbit of contemporary West Asia. There was a secure village base in the Northwest long before the coming of the Achaemenids but I believe that the political and economic influence of the Achaemenidian empire served as a major stimulus to the early historic urban growth of this area. No direct evidence, however, is forthcoming: both at Charsada and Taxila the contemporary excavated remains are scanty. But in the case of the Bhir mound, Taxila, Marshall notes that the 22 ft wide First Street dates from the earliest occupation of the site, dated fifth–sixth centuries BC.

The evidence becomes clearer in the succeeding periods. By the time of Alexander's invasion, Charsada came to possess a rampart and a ditch while at the Bhir mound, Taxila, which attracted the curiosity of Alexander's historians and was a Mauryan administrative centre not long after, the settlement reveals a coherent plan.

The succeeding Indo-Greeks and Saka-Parthians gave this urban core a more elaborate and new pattern. Both at Shaikhan, Charsada, and at Sirkap, Taxila, the new Indo-Greek and Saka-Parthian settlements chose in their urban quest new sites where the principles of chess-board planning drawn from the contemporary Hellenistic world could be given clear and logical shape. The Northwest's early historic urban prosperity is likely to have reached its zenith in the Kushan period when India came to acquire close trade-links with the west Asiatic and Roman world on the one hand and with central Asia and China on the other. The Kushan emperors themselves had their northern capital in India at Purusapura or Peshawar. Not much is known about the urban planning of this period. There is almost no evidence from Purusapura, the Kushan capital. The plan of the earlier Indo-Greek and Scytho-Parthian periods continues in the Kushan levels of Shaikhan at Charsada. The Kushan site of Sirsukh at Taxila suggests a fortified urban complex which was distinctly parallelogrammatic in shape. It is also probable—though there is very little direct evidence — that during this period there was, to some extent, a proliferation of small urban settlements in the Northwest, particularly along the trade-routes. There must have been major habitational remains associated with the innumerable stupa sites of the region, although it is the stupa which would have come in for archaeological study.

In adjacent Kashmir, no early historic urban site except Semthan has yet been identified or excavated, but I suggest that a secure urban core could be established in Kashmir only in the Mauryan period, i.e. in the late centuries BC. Subsequently Kashmir was a major focus of India's central Asian trade and it is probable that this trade was one of the basic causative factors of the large scale growth of urban settlements in the valley.

There is no properly excavated early historic urban settlement in the Punjab plains (west of the Sutlej) either. The Milindapanha indicates that there was a city laid out in a chess-board pattern at Sakala or modern Sialkot which was the capital of the Indo-Greek king, Menander (*c.* 155–130 BC). This may be considered a fixed point. But the problem is, how far back can one push the regional urban line beyond this point? Alexander's historians refer to a number of fortified places, each the stronghold of a tribe. One of these, Tulamba in the valley of the Ravi, has been excavated but has yielded very little definitive evidence regarding the settlement. One may, however, suggest that with the beginning of an effective centralized political control under the Mauryas and the consequent increase in contact between the Gangetic valley and the Northwest, the Punjab plains, from the third century BC onwards, came to occupy a place in the early historic urban map of India.

The situation is equally unclear in Sind. The literary data amply indicate the commercial importance of this province in the second century BC. Except at Banbhore where there is a reference to a Scytho-Parthian level of the first century BC, and Bahmanabad-Mansurah which may be equally early, no comparable early horizon has yet been excavated in Sind. The data seem to be clearer in the early centuries AD when Sind was part of the Kushan empire. The still traceable Buddhist religious ruins suggest corresponding secular settlements, though it must be admitted that no such settlement has yet been suitably identified and excavated.

The sequence at Rupar may represent the early historic cultural picture in the Indo-Gangetic divide. Period III at the site is early historic, dated 600–200 BC. There is no evidence of systematic planning in the brief reports but the existence of structural miscellanea like the 3.65 m wide and more than 75 m long burnt-brick retaining wall of an oval shaped reservoir, etc. may suggest a settlement with more than a village status. At Sugh there are traces of fortification but as the site has only been briefly investigated and scantily reported, its date remains uncertain. The Indo-Gangetic divide in the sixth century BC belonged to the economic and cultural orbit of the Gangetic valley and the beginning of the urban growth here is likely to be the result of the factors which were operative in the Gangetic valley. But from the second century BC onwards the political powers with bases in the Northwest like the Indo-Greeks extended their influence over this area which also witnessed, sometime after, the growth of the tribal republics like the Yaudheyas whose coins have been well attested to in different local archaeological sites. Though there is no direct evidence it may be reasonable to infer that during this period urban growth in the Indo-Gangetic divide received a fresh impetus. Along the dried-up Sarasvati valley on the southern fringe of the divide extensive early historic settlements are attested to only in the early centuries AD.

The earliest evidence of a fortification in the upper Gangetic valley comes from Kausambi. According to Sharma, the Kausambi defences came to be built around 1025 BC. But as K.K. Sinha (1973) has argued and as has been discussed earlier, there is not much reasonable basis to push it back so early. In fact, a date around 600 BC should fit in with the present evidence. At Hastinapur no fortification has been reported. The city-walls of Mathura which are as yet unexcavated have been attributed by Piggott to the Kushan period. M.C. Joshi's work has shown that this dates from Period I at the site which has been dated by him between the closing decades of the fourth century to *c.* 200 BC, i.e. the Mauryan period. Similar walls at Sankisa and Chakranagar also remain unexcavated. The beginning of the Ahichchhatra fortification has been dated to the early centuries AD. The defences at Bhita are said to belong to the early Mauryan or pre-Mauryan period.

In the middle Gangetic valley the fortification at Rajghat belongs to 'the middle, if not the earliest phase', of Period I which has been dated 800–200 BC. The earliest phase antedates the NBPW which appears in the middle phase only. So the Rajghat fortification may safely be related to the appearance of the NBPW at the site. At Sravasti the defences were built in Period II, the beginning of which has been dated around 250 BC. At Tilaura-Kot, once identified with Kapilavastu, the beginning of the mud-rampart has been placed in the second century BC. The fortifications at Balirajgarh and Katragarh also seem to be of this date. The fortification wall around the mound of Raja Visal ka garh at Vaishali dates from this period. The stratification of the wooden palisade at Pataliputra is not clear but on the basis of Megasthenes' work, it may be safely assigned to the fourth century BC. The encircling cyclopaean wall of Rajagriha has not been archaeologically dated. The literary sources indicate that it is likely to date at least from the sixth century BC when Bimbisara (*c.* 543–491 BC) was the reigning king. As Bimbisara is not credited with the building of this fortification in the literary accounts one may suppose that it could have been built sometime before his reign. No firm dating evidence is available for the rampart wall of New Rajagriha either. But it is supposed to have been built by Ajatasatru (*c.* 491–451 BC) and thus belongs to the fifth century BC. The radiocarbon dates are too erratic to permit a precise dating. The fortification is clearly associated with the appearance of the NBPW at the site.

In the lower Gangetic valley, the antiquity of Mahasthangarh or Pundranagara may be reasonably pushed back to the third century BC because of the find of an inscription in Mauryan Brahmi. A mud fortification wall is clearly visible below the Gupta brick fortification wall, and although this mud wall remains undated there is no doubt about its being early. At Bangarh or ancient Kotivarsa there was a brick-built rampart wall in its fourth stratum dated to the Sunga period or roughly to the second century BC. The mud rampart wall at Chandraketugarh has been inadequately explored but a limited cutting traces it to the second century BC. Period II of Tamluk or Tamralipta, the first early historic period at the site, has been found to belong to the third-second centuries BC. There is no reason why the first urban centres in the Brahmaputra valley should be dated later.

Archaeological data of the early historic period are meagre in east Rajasthan. At none of the excavated sites—Bairat, Rairh, Sambhar, Nagari—has the early historic material been dated earlier than the third–second centuries BC. D.R. Sahni calls Bairat an important Mauryan township. Nagari or ancient Madhyamika possesses a defence wall built in the early centuries AD.

At Vidisa in central India the early historic level begins with the

NBPW. The precise date is uncertain but considering that the first phase of the temple excavated near the Heliodorus pillar comes to an end in the third century BC the beginning may be pushed back earlier. At Ujjayini the rampart came to be built in Period I, the beginning of which has been dated by the excavator around 700–500 BC. The main basis of this dating seems to be the occurrence of a sherd of the Painted Grey Ware in the core of the Ujjayini rampart. This is not much of an evidence to go by and to put the Ujjayini rampart on par with the Kausambi defences, I prefer to date its beginning around 600 BC or possibly a little earlier.

In Gujarat the early historic data seem to be available from the third–fourth centuries BC onwards. Excavated material is most inadequate but the settlements seem to indicate a period of prosperity only in the early centuries AD when the Gujarat coast was open to the Indo-Roman trade. At Shamlaji in north-eastern Gujarat, the only early historic site in the region to reveal some semblance of planning, the first phase of the rampart has been dated AD 100–300.

At Nasik in Maharashtra the early historic occupation is supposed to go back to 400 BC. The epigraphic sources, however, reveal Nasik as an important settlement as early as in the second century BC. At the other excavated sites also (cf. Brahmapuri, Kaundanpur, etc.) the early historic level dates from the pre-Christian era but the settlements seem to have prospered only in the early centuries AD.

In Mysore also the situation seems to be similar. Isila or Brahmagiri was a Mauryan administrative centre but almost nothing is archaeologically known about the Mauryan level. No specific data are available even from the succeeding Andhra period except the remains of a 17–18 ft wide road of stone rubble.

Kerala is entirely devoid of the relevant archaeological data but the literary evidence is secure enough to suggest urban settlements in the Kerala coast in the early centuries AD.

In Madras the early historic level may go back to the third century BC as it does at Urayur, an early Chola capital, but it is only in the early years of the Christian era that the data become clear and suggest the existence of urban settlements such as Arikamedu and Kaveripattinam.

The early historic settlements in Andhra decidedly begin in the third–second centuries BC but as excavations at Nagarjunakonda indicate, prosperity came only in the early centuries AD.

In Orissa the fortified settlements of Jaugada and Sisupalgarh both go back to the third–second centuries BC.

The foregoing resume of evidence should reveal that the archaeological data on the early historic urban growth in India are strictly limited. There is not a single properly excavated urban site in many regions of India where the excavations conducted on the early historic levels have been almost exclusively vertical in nature. Kashmir, the Punjab plains, Sind, the Indo-Gangetic divide, the Brahmaputra valley, Rajasthan, Gujarat, Mysore, Kerala and Madras should come under this category. To piece together the evidence of urban growth in these regions one has to depend exclusively on the nature of the archaeological sequence and a few other types of archaeological and literary data—epigraphs, well-dated specific literary references, etc. Even in the areas which possess some horizontally excavated urban settlements the data are not free from limitations. In some cases the publication of excavated findings has been brief. The excavations at Ahichchhatra, Sravasti, Ujjayini, Nagarjunakonda and a few other places are cases in point. And, even where the publication is fuller, certain significant problems remain to be solved. For instance, despite a large number of publications on Rajagriha no attempt has yet been made to date its cyclopaean wall archaeologically. Or, as one notes in the case of the Bhir mound, Taxila, there has been no specific effort to find out if the settlement was fortified or not.

These limitations notwithstanding, the data seem to suggest the following broad pattern.

The earlier evidence of fortified urban settlements seems to be from Ujjayini, Kausambi, Varanasi (Rajghat), Rajagriha and Champa. The beginning of none of these fortifications is very precisely dated but all of them decidedly go back to about 600 BC. And, in each case, there is a possibility of their being somewhat earlier. The chronological line adopted here is 700–600 BC. The early historic urban growth in India, thus, began along a belt that stretched from Rajagriha to Ujjayini through Kausambi.

If the evidence from Hastinapur and Rupar is any indication, an urban core came to be established in the upper Gangetic valley and the Indo-Gangetic divide soon after or at about the same time. This was also the period when the Achaemenid annexation of the Northwest may have given rise to an urban nucleus there.

The third–second centuries BC seem to mark the next phase of growth. This period witnessed the further growth of settlements in the areas which had already come within the urban fold in the preceding phase. One may note, for instance, excavated settlements showing a coherent plan in the Northwest, the beginning of defence fortifications at Bhita in the upper Gangetic valley, Tilaura-Kot in the Nepalese terai, Balirajgarh and

Vaisali in the middle Gangetic valley, etc. The basic importance of this stage, however, seems to be the fact that during this period many new regions, where the precise beginning of the early historic period is still uncertain, came to develop or were about to develop a clear and unmistakable urban base. The regions which should fall in this category are the Punjab plains, Sind, Brahmaputra valley, lower Gangetic valley, Rajasthan, Gujarat, Maharashtra and Orissa. This was also the twilight period of early history in Mysore, Kerala, Madras and Andhra.

The third and final phase of urban growth in our chosen period seems to have developed in the early centuries AD, characterized by a general urban prosperity throughout the subcontinent. One also detects now indisputable evidence of urban settlements in areas like Mysore, Kerala, Madras and Andhra where previous evidence seems to be vague and doubtful.

At this point a pertinent problem is: can we correlate this early historic urban growth-process, primarily postulated on the basis of archaeological data, to what we know of the political and economic development of India of the corresponding periods? Considering the evidence, the answer should be in the affirmative.

Places like Rajagriha, Rajghat, Kausambi and Ujjayini, which represent the first phase of early historic urban growth, were the capitals of the kingdoms of Magadha, Kasi, Vatsa and Avanti (Raychaudhuri 1953: 197–215). These kingdoms were among the first centralized political structures of which we possess some cognizable and unambiguous literary evidence. In the literary sources all of them came to be in sharp focus by the sixth century BC. Moreover, these places were also linked by one of the earliest well-defined trade-routes of India. Thirdly, though archaeological evidence of early historic writing on non-perishable materials like stone does not occur before the third century BC, its beginning on perishable materials like palm-leaves may logically be placed a few centuries earlier. The point is that my postulated date of 700–600 BC as the first chronological line of early historic urban growth does not at all seem to be out of context. There is no doubt about the NBPW being as early as 700 BC at Sringavarapura. This incidentally bears out Marshall's dating of this ware to the eighth century BC on the basis of stratification at Bhita.

It may, however, be pointed out that the literary data refer to some other contemporary political entities besides the kingdoms of Magadha, Kasi, Vatsa and Avanti and mention in those contexts some important settlements as well. All that can be said is that the archaeological data do not seem to suggest anything specific regarding their importance during that period. Two major instances in this context may be those of Sravasti and Vaisali. Sravasti was the capital of the kingdom of Kosala, quite a powerful kingdom of the sixth century BC. Vaisali was no less important as the capital of the Lichchhavis during the time of Buddha. None of them reveals any archaeological evidence of urban planning from the level of this period. The fortification at both these sites belongs only to the third–second centuries BC. There is, of course, no reason to assume that all early historic urban centres had to be fortified. There are many sites which are not fortified.

The postulated next phase in the third–second centuries BC also was a period of considerable political and economic significance. The Mauryan hegemony which lasted from the closing years of the fourth century BC to the beginning of the second, was instrumental in bringing most of India within the well-knit political and economic entity of an empire. Moreover, this was also the period when India came to forge close links with the West, and perhaps Southeast Asia. The second century BC witnessed the Mauryan disintegration but was marked by the growth of effective regional powers and the penetration of alien rulers like the Indo-Greeks. It was only reasonable that the economic and political dynamism of this entire period found expression in an extension of the urban base.

In the early centuries AD, the postulated third and final phase of early historic urban growth, the most important single factor of stimulus was possibly trade which was both land-based and maritime, supplemented by close trade contacts with Central Asia, China and Southeast Asia.

One may, in fact, safely assert that the archaeological pattern of the early historic urban growth in India is in no phase divorced from the corresponding political and economic realities of the country.

Elements of Size and Planning

A clear estimate of size is available only for a few of the sites. The relevant data, adduced earlier, may now be represented in the following form:

Charsada   : The mounds spread over an area of four miles (6.436 km) but they represent the remains of two, probably three, different cities of different periods.

Pataliputra   : Old ruins are spread almost all over the modern built-in area which is roughly of the same size as that mentioned by Megasthenes; 80 stadia (little more than 9 miles or 14.48 km) long and 15 stadia (about 1½ miles or 2.4135 km) wide.

Rajagriha : The inner fortification of Old Rajagriha has a periphery of about 4½miles or 7.23 km. New Rajagriha possesses a periphery of about 3 miles or 4.827 km.

Mahasthangarh : The mound measures about 5000 × 4000 ft. The periphery is, thus, roughly about 3^1/2 miles or 5.635 km.

Bangarh : The fortified 'citadel' is about 1800 × 1500 ft, the periphery being more than a mile.

Chandraketugarh : It has a periphery of about 4 miles or 6.436 km.

Bairat : It is about 2^1/2 miles (4.01 km) in circuit.

Pawaya : The total area covers some 2 square miles (3.20 km).

Ujjayini : The fortified enclosure measures 1 by 3/4 mile; the perimeter is about 3^1/2 miles (5.635 km).

Shamlaji : The fortified enclosure measures 670.50 × 304.80 m; the perimeter is little more than a mile (20.42 ha.).

Chandravalli : It is about 800 yards (731.52 m) square; a little less than 2 miles in perimeter (53.47 ha.).

Nagarjunakonda : The fortified enclosure measures 3000 by 2000 ft (914.4 × 609.6 m). The valley is about 3 miles (4.82 km) wide (55.69 ha.).

Taxila : A more or less connected plan has been obtained for about 3 acres of the Bhir mound. The periphery of the Saka-Parthian Sirkap is more than 3 miles (4.827 km). The Kushan Sirsukh measures 1500 × 1100 yards (1371.6 by 1005.84 m/ 137.85 ha.); the periphery is, thus, about 3 miles.

Sugh : The fortification possesses a periphery of about 4 miles (6.636 km).

Hastinapur : The mounds extend half a mile north-south and hardly quarter of a mile east-west. The periphery, thus, is about 1^1/2 miles (2.4135 km).

Sankisa	:	It is about 3½ miles (5.6315 km) in periphery.
Chakranagar	:	About 3 miles (4.827 km) in circuit.
Ahichchhatra	:	It has a perimeter of about 3¹/₂ miles (5.6315 km).
Kausambi	:	The fortification possesses a periphery of about 4 miles (6.436 km). The mounds both inside and outside the fortification spread over an area of about eight square miles (more than 20 sq. km).
Sravasti	:	The city site of Maheth possesses a periphery of more than 3 miles (4.827 km).
Tilaura-Kot	:	The fortified site measures 1600 by 1000 ft (487.68 by 304.8 m). The periphery, thus, is about a mile.
Vaisali	:	The circuit of the fortified mound, Raja Visal ka garh, is about a mile (1.609 km).
Dhanyakakata	:	The fortification encloses an area of 650 yards square (35.29 ha.). The perimeter is little more than a mile.
Jaugada	:	It is about two miles (3.21 km) in periphery.
Sisupalgarh	:	It is about three miles (4.82 km) in periphery.

The foregoing data are admittedly inadequate. One may, however, note that a total periphery of 3–4 miles seems to be rather common among the major settlements. Occasionally, habitations spread outside the enclosed area (cf. Kausambi, Sravasti). The total built-in areas of Kausambi and Pataliputra, if the estimates are correct, seem to be outstanding in that context.

The usual physical shape of the city seems to be square or oblong; the latter seems to be more common while an instance of a square shape may be observed in Sisupalgarh. In some cases the alignment of the enclosing fortification has followed the lie of the land and has resulted in a shape which does not wholly conform to the usual pattern. The walls around Sirkap where the hill-features have been taken advantage of and Sravasti where the city-site resembles a semi-circular crescent along the Rapti are cases in point. Where the city-sites are spread all over a narrow hill-girt valley as they are in Rajgir and Nagarjunakonda, the shape of the valley has determined the general lay-out. The walled enclosure in the shape of a rough isosceles triangle seems to be a lone feature, applicable only to Ahichchhatra. The elliptical outer ring of wall at Mathura also seems to be a peculiarity of that site alone.

The city lay within one, or in some cases, two rings of fortification. The fortification is not evident at some sites like the Bhir mound and Hastinapur. One, however, feels that in these cases it has not been properly looked for. There are quite a few instances of two rings of enclosing walls. In Sirkap a spur of the Hathial within the city-site was specifically ringed off and perhaps served as an acropolis. There is also a feeling that the excavated rampart, enclosing about 15 acres in Charsada, belonged to an inner citadel complex and did not represent the entire city. The explored quadrangular-shaped rampart around the Katra area in Mathura may represent a citadel. There is a reference to an inner citadel in Chakranagar. It is also probable that the fortification around the Raja Visal ka garh mound suggests a citadel area and that the city of Vaisali as a whole had an outer ring of wall. In New Rajagriha the presently observable fortification encloses 70–80 acres and belongs to the inner ring of defence. But there is also an outer ring of wall which is fast disappearing. In Old Rajagriha the fortification along the hill-top is prominent enough but in the valley itself there is an enclosing ridge of earth and stone which may be part of an inner fortification. The Ikshaku citadel in the Nagarjunakonda valley forms only a part of the total built-in area but in this case there is no enclosing outer fortification. The hills and the river Krishna serve this purpose. Only the vulnerable points have been walled off. In Kausambi there is an outer ring of defence about a mile away from the main excavated complex. In the rest of the excavated sites there seems to be only one ring of wall.

Every excavated fortification is found to possess a number of constructional phases. In most cases the core was of mud dug out of the surrounding land, with burnt-brick revetments added later on. When the date is comparatively late, the exclusive use of burnt-bricks may be noted right from the beginning (cf. Vaisali, Bangarh, Shamlaji, etc.). Where stone was easily available stone blocks or rubble were used instead of burnt-bricks (cf. Sirkap, Sirsukh, the outer fortification of Old Rajagriha, lateritic slabs used over the earthen rampart in Sisupalgarh, etc.). The width and height of the fortification varied from place to place. The width of the earthen rampart had, of course, to be wider than the burnt-brick ones. A basal width of about 245 ft (74,676 m) can be noticed in the earthen rampart of Ujjayini while the burnt-brick wall in Bangarh is only 8–10 ins wide. The use of wooden sleepers set in the body of the rampart to preserve it from the scouring action of the river has been noted in Ujjayini and Rajghat. The protective bastions arranged at regular intervals along the wall may be considered an invariable feature of the fortification. A moat, occasionally of considerable width, usually encircles a settlement except on the river-side, where the settlement is on the bank of a river. It may be noted that the moats were not an invariable feature. For instance, there is no moat around Sirkap and Old Rajagriha where the features of the land make any specially excavated moat redundant. Separate watch-towers seem to be rare except in Kausambi and Old Rajagriha. The evidence suggests that there was always more than one gateway on each side of the rampart. The gateways were as a rule (as is evident from the excavated specimens) carefully laid out and possessed guard-rooms as a feature. In all excavated cases they were wide enough to permit vehicular traffic.

The data regarding the internal arrangement of streets are very scanty. A more or less intelligible idea has been obtained from Shaikhan, Bhir mound, Sirkap, Bhita and Nagarjunakonda. Isolated streets have been briefly excavated in some other sites as well but they hardly add up to a coherent pattern.

It may be emphasized at the outset that the sites of Shaikhan and Sirkap are a class apart. A glance at the available plans of these two settlements suggests that almost the entire urban area in these cases has been subdivided into a number of blocks by a series of parallel streets. This chess-board pattern is not known to occur in any other excavated site in India and it may be considered solely as an extension of the contemporary concept of classical planning in this country.

The plan of the exposed portion of the Bhir mound may be representative of the more usual mode of arrangement of the internal streets in an Indian city. Four streets and five lanes have been excavated in this place. Even the main street which is 22 ft wide has a distinct northwest-southeast slant. The width of the other streets varies from between 8 ft (2.43 m) and 17 ft (5.18 m). They are more winding and possess open square areas in places. The lanes are considerably narrower, occasionally not wider than narrow alleys. The two streets excavated in Bhita are roughly straight and mutually parallel but it may be added that they have been excavated for a very limited portion. One of them was about 30 ft wide while the other was somewhat narrower. In Nagarjunakonda a main street divides the ordinary residential area to the east of the Ikshaku citadel into two parts. The respective width of the streets, lanes and alleys (the detailed plan of which is unpublished) is 2 ft (7.62 m), 15 ft (4.572 m) and 8 ft (2.4384 m). In Brahmapuri the passage between the houses has been noted to be 2 ft (0.6096 m), though one cannot be sure if this served as an alley. The same feature has been observed in Sisupalgarh also.

There has been no evidence yet to suggest that the streets were systematically paved for any significant length. Occasionally, however, local patches of hard material have been observed during excavations. In Brahmagiri a rubble-paved street which is 17–18 ft wide is found to belong to the Andhra level.

Evidence of a systematic street drainage system is not very extensive. In the Fourth Street and Lane I of the Bhir mound there are traces of covered surface drains, made of limestone and *kanjur* and at times lined with slabs of slate,but they do not seem to be connected with any large drain in the main street. The obvious inference is that the streets had to serve as water-courses during the rains, a feature not entirely unknown in India today. This also applies to the Indo-Greek and Saka-Parthian Sirkap. In Hastinapur III there is some evidence of civic drains. One of the excavated burnt-brick drains was 3 ft (0.9144 m) deep, possessed a brick-lined floor and was traced for a length of 24 ft (7.3152 m). No drain has been reported along the two excavated streets in Bhita. Drains have been reported from Nagarjunakonda but the published evidence does not make clear whether they were civic drains or normal household drains.

Some other civic traits of a general nature have been observed in the Bhir mound. Round refuge-bins were set in the squares and streets. It is likely that they were regularly cleared. In the Bhir mound there were rough stone-pillars, about 3 ft high above the ground, preventing the corners of the houses from being damaged by passing carts or chariots.

As the data are not representative from all over India it is not possible to make a systematic study of the house-patterns. A house in a well-to-do area of the Bhir mound occupied about 3600 sq. ft (334.45 sq. m) of which about 700 sq. ft (65.032 sq. m) were taken up by an open courtyard. On the ground floor there were 15–20 rooms, most of which were small with windows perhaps high up in the walls. There is no positive evidence regarding the type of roofs but they were probably flat. In areas with a greater amount of rainfall, the roofs of mud houses were likely to be sloping but the general plan of the houses conformed to the usual plan of arranging rooms around one or more than one courtyard. Some houses in Kausambi and Bhita are observed to have had two sections: the sections adjoining the road may have been meant for business purposes while the inner section may have been reserved for domestic functions. There is evidence of road-side shops in some sites like the Bhir mound, Kausambi, Bhita, Nagarjunakonda, etc. Evidence of a different type of house-planning has been obtained from Brahmagiri where one of the fully cleared houses had three small rooms bounded by a long corridor-like room. The use of grooved terracotta tiles which were fixed on to the rafters with iron-nails has been noted here. In Sisupalgarh also a house had two rooms with a verandah in front. The data on the foundation of houses have been surveyed by Sankalia. He concludes that they were conditioned primarily by two factors: 'The availability of the raw material, and secondly, the adaptability to the environmental conditions—climatic, geographical, etc. in each case'. The flooring material varied but a spread of brickbats covered by mud and lime-plasters seems to be common. It is probable that the house-patterns possessed regional variations as they do now.

Individual households had an adequate arrangement for drainage. A key item in this regard was the soak-well of different forms, commonly made of terracotta rings. These occur in almost all the early historic sites of India and according to Sankalia (1966: 157) 'may well become a top-object of Indian culture between 5th century BC and 1st century AD'. The entire evidence has been comprehensively discussed by Pande (1966). The most extensive data from one place are from the Bhir mound where Marshall has observed five of these types of wells. 'Sewage . . . was thrown down the private soak-wells which were maintained in every house. As a rule there was one such soak-well in each courtyard and one for the privy, bathroom, wash-house or kitchen' (Marshall 1951, I: 94). Surface drains built of brick or stone have also been observed in some individual houses in different sites. Pottery drain-pipes with spigot-and-faucet joints seem to have been widely distributed.

Literary Data on Town-planning

There are ample literary data on town-planning for this period. These have been dealt with in various places but a comprehensive summary has been made by Amita Ray (1964). In this section I propose to analyse the salient points of these literary data and try to find out how far they correspond to the picture obtained through archaeology.

The texts primarily utilized by Ray in her summary are the early Buddhist texts, particularly the Jatakas, the Milindapanha, the Jaina sutras, Panini's *Astadhyayi*, Kautilya's *Arthasastra*, the Puranas, particularly the *Agnipurana*, the *Manasara* and the epics. It may be mentioned that the evidence contained in the Jaina sutras, the Puranas and the Manasara referred to a period later than our chosen time-span upto AD 300 but they may partly reflect the earlier tradition. It is also difficult to assign specific dates to the Jatakas, the Milindapanha, the Arthasastra and the epics but there is little doubt that they were collated before AD 300. In addition, in the present context, evidence contained in the early Tamil literature will be taken into account.

There is no dearth of reference to contemporary cities in the Jatakas but except in broad outline the evidence does not contain details of town-planning. All that one is able to gather is that any city of importance lay within an enclosing wall, itself within a moat. There were gateways on each side, superimposed by a tower. The city of Vaisali is said to have possessed three rings of walls. The internal arrangement of the roads has not been especially alluded to but there are references to both civic and household drains.

As far as the elements of basic planning are concerned, evidence in the Milindapanha is much more specific, and this evidence is worth quoting in detail:

> . . . the architect of a city, when he wants to build one, would first search out a pleasant spot of ground . . . and would proceed to build there a city fine and regular, measured out into suitable quarters, with trenches and ramparts thrown up around it, with strong gateways, watch-towers and battlements, with wide squares and open places and junctions (where two roads meet) and cross-ways (where four roads meet) . . . with regular lines of open shops, well provided with parks and gardens, and lakes, and lotus ponds, and walls, adorned with many kinds of temples to the gods, free from every fault. And then when the city stood there in all its glory, he would go away to some other land (Sacred Books of the East 36, Pt. II).

The itinerant architect here has perhaps been endowed with more responsibility than he actually possessed but the entire passage reminds one of a chess-board type of city, the type which could be planned on a drawing-board. Archaeologically this type does not seem to extend in India beyond the Punjab plains and it may be suggested that the town-plan mentioned in the Milindapanha possesses only a regional validity.

What is significant in the Jaina sutras is a careful, almost loving, description of the city-moats, ramparts, shops, markets, cross-roads, etc. The moats were broad at the top and cut deep down. The ramparts were solidly built and spread in bow-like curves. They possessed buttresses, bastions, paths, doors with strong door-leaves and bolts, gates, towers and high roads. Internally there were pleasure parks, gardens, pools and tanks. There were different kinds of shops, and craftsmen thronged the market lanes. The roads were lined with houses on either side.

In Panini's Astadhyayi the moat, the gate and the rampart constituted the important parts of a city. The city-gates were named after the names of the cities towards which they opened, a practice which is still noticed in the names of the gates of some medieval Indian cities. A regular planning is suggested by some references to the residential buildings and business premises, intersection of streets, storehouses, royal council-halls and places for dramatic performances.

After going through two of Kautilya's chapters on the laying-out of forts and cities (Shamasastri 1960: 50–5) one is left with a feeling that Kautilya was dwelling more on an ideal fort or city than referring to any specific reality. Kautilya's ideal city was by every standard a strictly regimented one, a place where everything was determined by caste and social hierarchy. There should be little doubt that Kautilya's ideal city conformed to his notion of statecraft where everything had its well-appointed place in the autocratic running of the state-machinery.

Kautilya's abstract design of an ideal city continues also in such texts as the *Agnipurana, Manasara, Sukranitisara*, etc. The Agnipurana arranges different occupational and caste-groups, shops, temples and such other features in different areas of the city. There are, of course, references to the square or rectangular shape of a city with gates, main streets, drains, rampart, moat, etc. but the over-all descriptive pattern remains idealistic. In the Manasara one is impressed by its theoretical concern for classification (cf. cities of eight different classes, the prescribed measurements of the smallest and largest cities, etc.) but the basic idea of a socially well-regulated place does not seem to have changed. The theme persists also in the Sukranitisara though Ray says that it differs somewhat from the other texts in its placing of the council-house at the centre of the city instead of the palace.

There are many literary allusions to the cities, including those in the epics. The magnificence apart, the basic concepts of early historic town-planning—moat, rampart, a coherent lay-out of streets—remain the same.

The point which should be clear even from the foregoing cursory survey of the literary data is that in its basic details the literary image corresponds to the archaeological reality. The basic shape and lay-out of the early historic Indian cities, as contained in the literary sources, is clearly observable in the archaeological records. Regarding the internal social arrangement and such other details the archaeological data have *ipso facto* to remain silent.

There has as yet emerged no clear archaeological picture of planning from South India. The evidence contained in early Tamil literature, however, is so extensive that one feels that it is authentic (Ayyar 1915, Pillai 1967). Cities like Puhar, Kanchi, Madura and some others have been described in loving detail. The basic shape of the city which emerges is that of a well-fortified, moat-encircled place with well-defined roads, palaces, shops and temples, in fact an image which accords well with what we know from archaeology in the rest of India. But the essential charm of the description of a city in early Tamil literature lies in its ability to convey a vivid urban image, an image built on small, yet realistic, well-knit details. Such an image will, of course, elude archaeological records but from this point of view, early Tamil literature occupies an almost unique place in the annals of Indian literature.

Urban Character

Archaeological data regarding early historic Indian cities, an analysis of their pattern of growth and elements of their planning are futile if a basic problem is not considered at this stage. Were the settlements, which have in the present context been listed as urban, really urban centres or mere over-sized villages? This problem has never been tackled in detail but has occasionally been raised.

In one sense the problem does not seem to lead us anywhere. From the third century BC we get indisputable archaeological evidence of writing in early historic India and the general assumption is that the antiquity of writing on perishable materials should be pushed back a few centuries earlier. It has been noted in the present work that Phase I of the early historic Indian urban growth corresponds to the seventh–sixth centuries BC and that it ties up with an important political-cultural phase of the country, covering at least south Bihar, central India, upper Gangetic valley, Indo-Gangetic divide and Northwest India. Theoretically at least there should be no hesitation in describing the India of this phase and these geographical zones as urban. The political, economic and cultural vicissitudes of the country from the third century BC are largely clear on the basis of textual data alone. To deny an urban status to the primary settlements of early historic India would, in fact, mean that the early historic civilization of India was one which possessed no cities. A close analysis of the archaeological data alone would, however, warrant a complete negation of such an idea.

A number of points may be suggested at the archaeological level. First, one may emphasize the physical magnitude of the settlements. As has been noted, a periphery of 3–4 miles, applicable to the walled enclosure only, seems to be common, in the case of the major settlements at least. As the corresponding data on the village-sites are almost non-existent it is difficult to discern how this peripheral extent stands in contrast to that of the village-sites. But to anyone familiar with both these types of settlements in the field there should be no doubt that the city-sites represented a new scale of physical magnitude beyond the scope of any contemporary village settlement.

This physical magnitude is reflected not merely in the areal spread but also in a cardinal feature of city-planning, the rampart and its associated details. It is not that a village may not have a defensive palisade but the city-ramparts which have been excavated suggest by their massiveness, constructional care and elaborately laid out gateways, bastions, moats and other defensive measures, that they were meant to defend and mark out a type of settlement whose significance in the social, political and economic landscape was far greater than that of a village.

Archaeological evidence of the internal lay-out of cities is admittedly inadequate but where available, it is suggestive. Even if one sets aside the data from Sirkap and Shaikhan where the streets are laid out according to a grid pattern, one should not ignore the evidence from the Bhir mound which is likely to reflect more truly the planning of a typically Indian city. The streets and lanes at that site may not conform to any neatly aligned pattern but its 22 ft wide main street does not by any stretch of imagination fall in the category of a village street. This is also true of the excavated streets at Bhita which measure about 30 ft in width or the 25 ft wide main streets east of the Ikshaku citadel at Nagarjunakonda. In this connection it may also be pointed out that a systematic civic drainage system may not have been wide-spread but it doubtlessly existed, as is evident at sites like the Bhir mound, Hastinapur and Nagarjunakonda.

Another feature which needs emphasis here is that within the city a distinct area was marked out as the palace complex, quite often with its own defence system. The evidence is limited but where it is clear this seems to be the general picture. The point is that one does not expect this type of planning in a village.

So far as the excavated houses are concerned, one notes that there is nothing particularly distinctive constructionally or materially to separate them from a village-house except perhaps their general commodiousness (cf. the houses at the Bhir mound, Bhita, Nagarjunakonda, etc.) and a seemingly more frequent use of burnt-bricks or stones as constructional material. At the same time it may be emphasized that no early historic city anywhere was exactly a 'city of palaces'; even in the Greek cities of the fifth century BC and later, 'the houses were lightly built of wood and sun-dried clay: so flimsy were the walls that the quickest way for a burglar to enter a house was by digging through the wall. Residentially speaking, the biggest cities were little better at first than overgrown villages . . .' (Mumford 1961: 129–30).

The excavated evidence is not extensive enough to permit any elaborate inference regarding the different occupational groups and other aspects of the social situation in an early historic Indian city. To dwell on only a few pieces of evidence, a shell-worker's shop has been excavated in the Bhir mound. The evidence of a bead-industry is explicit in Ujjayini. There is a goldsmith's shop in Nagarjunakonda. Arikamedu yields some evidence of dyeing. A house in Bhita has been called a 'house of the guild' on the basis of a locally found inscribed terracotta seal. Quite a number of antiquities from different settlements (cf. Taxila, Arikamedu, Nagarjunakonda, etc.) suggest foreign trade. The discovery of a large number of coins in the city-sites may also be indicative of their general economic prosperity. What is highly suggestive is that some of the early coin-types of India, have, in fact, been grouped after the names of different cities whose economic organizations were responsible for their circulation (for some examples, Allan 1936).

It is precisely in this context that epigraphical data, also a kind of archaeological record, are most helpful. To take only a few instances, the early inscriptions from Mathura refer to occupational groups such as bankers, iron-mongers, dyers, perfumers, workers in metal, goldsmiths, actors, dancers and courtesans. The Sanchi inscriptions refer to bankers, clerks, merchants, royal scribes, musicians, weavers, ivory-workers, foremen of artisans, surveyors, carpenters, and horsekeepers. The Bharhut records refer to arrow-makers, troopers, gardeners and sculptors. The Jogimara cave inscription refers to a copyist from Varanasi besides mentioning a *devadasi* or temple courtesan. The Sohgaura copper-plate inscription refers to the 'great officials' of Sravasti. The early inscriptions from west India also possess a number of such references. The Kanheri inscriptions refer to merchants, jewellers, goldsmiths, etc. from the two west coast port-cities of Kalyan and Sopara. There are similar references in the donative records of Bhaja, Karle, Amaravati and Pauni—in fact, of many other places of this period. Considered as a whole, the archaeological data are suggestive enough of the economic organization and diversity centred in the cities of early historic India (these data are listed by Luders, 1912).

Two other aspects of contemporary urban centres need attention. First, most of these excavated sites have yielded art-objects in varying quantities. Besides, as the donative records indicate, the city-dwellers contributed to the making of the contemporary Buddhist stupas which in their engraved scenes reflect adequately the art-tradition of the period. What is relevant here is that the art-tradition of early historic India is an urban art-tradition. Pieces of Mauryan art have been thought to be the products of the urban, centralized court-ideology of the Mauryas but even when a noticeable popular participation in the making of art objects is discerned in the succeeding periods, the urban element remains a constant, distinct factor. This urbanism is manifest not merely in the wide variety of non-village themes which cover almost all aspects, both playful and serious, of human life but also in the inherent plastic treatment of these themes which display a sensuous and sophisticated awareness of the human body itself. What Coomaraswamy wrote about western Indian art from *c.* 200 BC to AD 20 is true of the early historic Indian art in general.

The whole approach, like that of early Indian art generally, is realistic, i.e. without *arriere pensee* or idealization. The main interest is neither spiritual nor ethical, but altogether directed to human life; luxury and pleasure are represented, interrupted only by death, and these are nothing but practical facts, endorsed by the inherently sensual quality of the plastic language (Coomaraswamy 1965).

Secondly, it may also be noted that most of the early historic urban centres were religious centres in some form. There have been very few places where religious complexes like stupas, monasteries and temples have not been excavated either inside or in the vicinity of the city. Of the contemporary religions, Buddhism and Jainism in particular seem to be closely linked with the urban centres and urban occupational groups like merchants, etc. The location of important Buddhist complexes within easy reach of the cities or along the trade-routes frequented by city-merchants amply corroborate this. In fact, Max Weber's assertion, 'like Jainism,but even more clearly, Buddhism presents itself as a product of the time of urban development, of urban kingship and the city nobles' (Weber 1958: 204) is clearly borne out by the archaeological data.

None of the foregoing facts should come as a surprise to any student of early Indian history but taken collectively, they do suggest that the urban centres of the period represented a new complexity and scale of human settlement and were also the focal points of the contemporary politico-military, economic, cultural and religious life. So far as the physical and social structures and the functions of these settlements are concerned they were decidedly urban and not merely oversized villages. In this context one notes that this structural-functional approach has been adopted by Sjoberg in his analysis of the pre-industrial cities (Sjoberg 1960: 12).

An extensive summary of the relevant literary data is beyond the scope of the present work which is only concerned with putting forward an archaeological perspective. A brief but good summary of these is available in Bose's *Social and Rural Economy of Northern India, c. 600* BC– AD *200*. His discovery is that the contemporary cities were the media of politico-economic, religious and spiritual expression, and were an educative force as well (Bose 1961, I: 193–224). The literary data, thus, broadly substantiate the picture formed through an archaeological analysis.

The literary data also indicate that there was a definite urban consciousness in early historic India. 'Nagaraka' or 'city-dweller' seems to be a familiar term. Vatsyayana's ornate erotica seems to have been written primarily with this class in mind. There is at least one Jataka story (*Nakkhatta-Jataka*) (Cowell 1957, I: 124–6) which is a significant pointer in this direction. There one finds some villagers saying that the city-dwellers lacked common decency.

The rural–urban dichotomy was a sociological fact and existed in the people's consciousness just as it does today. This, of course, is not deducible from the archaeological data (for a discussion on the rural–urban dichotomy in the early historic Indian context, see Bose 1961, I: 225–6).

Chapter Six

Problems and Perspectives

In the preceding chapters we have systematically reviewed the basic
archaeological data related to the development and features of urban
centres in different parts of the Indian subcontinent both in the protohistoric
and early historic periods. I do not claim to have been able to isolate all
or perhaps even most of the urban sites but the current situation in
different geographical areas has certainly been assessed. Since, at the
time of writing, *Indian Archaeology—A Review* was available only up to
1987–88, we cannot claim that even our 'current situation' is quite current. However a large mass of data covering a wide chronological and
geographical range has been analysed in the preceding chapters, and
some thought may be given here to the elucidation of these data as the
archaeological source of the history of urban centres in ancient India.

We have to be aware of the following issues. First, in a large number
of cases the settlement perspective is not clear. Though detailed explorations have been undertaken in many areas, especially in the context of
the Indus civilization and the neolithic-chalcolithic and Iron Age cultures
of inner India, there are still some major uncertainties. We have been
concerned primarily with the sequence of horizontal site spreads or distribution in a given area: a specific number of sites of a particular period or
cultural level to be followed by a specific number of sites which belong
to the succeeding cultural phase, and so on. It is, of course, possible to
make on this basis some salient observations on the location and distribution of sites of various phases in a particular area. On the basis of the
study of surface scatters scholars have also tried to make a distinction
between 'industrial' and 'non-industrial' sites. These are no doubt useful
exercises but they still do not free us from some major working problems.
For instance, the picture of a steady growth in the number and size of these
settlements in the surveyed areas may be more deceptive than we are
willing to admit. Most of these sites are multi-cultural sites; how do we
estimate the sizes of these settlements in different periods? In the Indian
context where most of the ancient village and urban settlements incorpo-

rate directly, or in their vicinity, modern habitations, it needs a very brave person to be even vaguely confident of the areas of successive occupations at a site on the basis of surface scatters. Secondly, surface scatters of slag, pottery kilns and debris of various manufacturing activities do not necessarily indicate in the Indian context that the site did not have agriculture as its major function. Most of the modern Indian villages have different occupational groups living within their boundaries but this does not take away the significance of agriculture in their economy. Some villages, of course, are more famous because of the larger number of potters, metalsmiths and other craftsmen in them but it may be stated that such villages form only a small percentage of the total number of villages in an area and perhaps it is unwise to jump to conclusions about the function of a particular settlement mainly on the basis of surface scatters. To come back to the main point, we can assess the contrasts or variations between sites of different periods in a given area only in terms of time-blocks. For instance, we can say that the general size of settlements in the black-and-red ware phase of West Bengal went upto 8–10 acres whereas in the succeeding early historic stage a limited number of settlements measured appreciably more in extent, going up to 250 acres in one or more cases. However, we should note that the black-and-red ware phase, as we understand it today, covers a history of about a thousand years (approximately from the middle of the second millennium to the middle of the first millennium BC) in itself, and more if we consider the point that most of these black-and-red ware settlements contain early historic material too in their surface scatters. So, it is only a handful of settlements which show a great increase in their size. The point is that unless one is dealing with a situation where one set of single culture occupational sites is followed by a different set of such sites, it is difficult to arrange them in a linear progression towards urban formations. This is also true of the 'urban history' of a particular urban settlement. Many of our early historic urban settlements contain remains right from the protohistoric period to the Gupta, post-Gupta and later periods. We know the sequence but do we know anything of the horizontal succession of settlements of different periods within the overall framework of a particular city-site? The answer has to be in the negative, because, for one thing, most of the urban sites we have dealt with are known through their cultural sequences, and for another, even where excavations have been fairly detailed, as in the Mauryan Bhir mound, the exposures have been concentrated only on one or two periods and not on the different phases of the city.

The settlement perspective is not clear for a host of other reasons too.

For instance, whereas the estimates of the sizes of individual settlements offer a good indication of the settlement hierarchy of a given period, sometimes the evidence furnished by settlement-sizes can be quite ambiguous. The case of a number of Harappan and related settlements with apparently very large occupational areas in the Mansa taluk of the Bhatinda district comes to mind. In any case, because the settlement perspective is not clear in its detailed nuances, the picture we have of ancient urban development in India is essentially a static one.

Considering the limitations of the usual ground survey of sites and the inferences made therefrom, is there any way of getting round them and trying to impart a fuller understanding of the ancient landscape? As far as I have been able to understand in the light of my experience, a detailed study of the agricultural geography of a given area with reference to the location of its ancient settlements may provide some insight into the basic character and functioning of these settlements. As most of our ancient sites are overwhelmingly rural, this approach is likely to prove useful. In the same way, the study of the sources of different raw materials that one encounters in surface scatters of different sites in a given area may give an indication of their intra- and inter-regional contacts. On the basis of excavated materials such a study has been undertaken by N. Lahiri in the protohistoric and early historic (up to *c*. 200 BC) contexts of the subcontinent as a whole, but there is great scope for undertaking studies of this type on the basis of carefully assessed surface finds in different areas. The issue and the approaches I have outlined here do not call for large excavations, but they need small-scale investigations on the ground, sorting out one local issue after another.

A considerable amount of basic ground data is now available in Indian archaeology; settlement distribution maps of various areas are quite impressive, but the trouble is that the associated field-data are not published in many cases. For instance, the Harappan and related sites which one now finds plotted between the Hakra course and the Yamuna must be considered one of the achievements of post-1947 archaeology in the subcontinent, but the fact remains that we know very little about them because nobody has bothered to publish the detailed field notes on these sites or tried to work out the basic agricultural geography of the entire region in relation to these sites. Apart from working out the landscape of ancient rural settlements in relation to their agricultural character and intra- and inter-regional contacts for raw materials, we should perhaps try to weave the few urban settlements of such areas into these landscapes as administrative centres, redistributive centres of the local agricultural pro-

duce and some raw materials, craft-activity centres and finally as religious and trade centres. In each case, close contact with the ground is
essential. As a preliminary, we must know about the local routes in detail
and also about the inter-regional lines of movement passing through the
area. It is unlikely that all this will be achieved in a short time-span but
nonetheless our efforts should be directed towards achieving these goals.
There have been limited excavations of city-sites but merely large-scale
exposures of big sites are not necessary in this context. A proper settlement perspective is essential and the present, increasingly popular
settlement studies can be expanded by considering a few ground realities.
While studying such ground realities, historians can take advantage of the
data furnished in various inscriptions of the period, but both the archaeological and more orthodox historical aims are more or less the same in this
context, i.e. the context of the general rural landscape of ancient India
without which its urban landscape cannot be meaningfully understood in
any way. I endorse what B.D. Chattopadhyay (1990: 125–6) has argued
in the context of his early medieval village settlements:

Viewing rural settlements and, by implication, village communities as isolates
does not, for one thing, take cognizance of settlement hierarchies, and such
hierarchies, it needs to be stressed, do not necessarily imply distinction between
urban and rural settlements alone. Hierarchies could exist in rural space, and
since settlement size is not always a satisfactory determinant of hierarchy, the
concept of hierarchy can be considered in terms of both how rural residents were
socially organized and how differentially individual villages existed in rural
landscape. Rural space did not consist of single units in a vacuum; nor did it
extend to horizontal infinity. There may have been different levels at which
individual units, with variations within them, could intersect. Viewing rural
settlements not simply as undifferentiated land mass would lead to acknowledg-
ing the possibility of the existence of nodes even in rural space and of change.
Change, of course, would relate to historical processes which could originate at
the rural level or elsewhere.

The second major issue of importance is the general limitation of the
work done on the urban settlements themselves. In this regard the Harappan cities have been treated better than the early historic ones. The excavations on most of the Harappan cities have been detailed, bringing out
the basic data on planning. In the case of the Harappan cities the basic
problem seems to be that of publication. The result of years of competent
work at Kalibangan, Banawali and other lesser places remains unpublished, and whereas there should be detailed annual bulletins on the
ongoing work at such an important—and in many ways unique—site as

Dholavira, we are getting information only in driblets. However, it is in the context of early historic cities that the level of investigation has been abysmally low for many years; barring Taxila, Bhita and perhaps Nagarjunakonda, there is not a single early historic site in the subcontinent which has been subjected to detailed, horizontal, phase by phase exposures. Although we now know more of the archaeological sequences and distribution of various types of sites in the subcontinent, our knowledge of its early historic cities has not significantly increased since the time of Marshall. No modern nation state of the subcontinent has yet bothered, through prolonged, detailed and systematically published excavations to bring to life the image of an ancient city in the post-1947 era. There are no doubt valid historical reasons for this state of affairs. In modern India, for instance, much of the time and money available has gone into making our protohistoric past alive, and this is more or less true of Pakistan. In Bangladesh and Nepal the structural sites representing stupas and temples have remained centres of attraction. but no early historic settlement, except perhaps Nagarjunakonda and Kausambi has drawn the attention of archaeologists, and as things stand at present, data on the early historic part of the Nagarjunakonda excavations are still awaiting publication, and the results of many years of work at Kausambi have been bogged down in unsavoury controversies. It is difficult to imagine an early historic settlement grander in scale or richer in historical association than Kausambi, and this site ought to have been taken up for detailed year-by-year excavations by a nationally organized team in post-Independence India. Mahasthangarh in modern Bangladesh is another rare, large and undisturbed early historical site, the normal occupational levels of which have still not been excavated. However, it is not merely the lack of detailed horizontal exposures of early historic sites which is worrying. The level on which the investigations have been conducted at many of these sites is worrying too. In the case of fortified settlements the work has generally been limited to cutting across the defences and the attempt to relate this cutting to the stratigraphy of the occupational remains in the habitation area. The emphasis has exclusively been on dating, especially the dating of the defences and in no case has there been a conscious effort to understand the basic details of the settlement as a whole. Even when prolonged excavations have taken place, as in the case of Chandraketugarh, the results have not been edifying from the point of view of urban planning, because in this particular case, excavations were concentrated on a temple area in a locality known as Khana Mihirer Dhibi. I must hasten to add that there are many reasons for the apathetic situation, some of them being the lack of money, time and (in many cases) suitable infrastructure. As a result even the basic task of exploration has not yet been attempted in some cases; for instance, Pawaya or ancient Padmavati in central India (Gwalior) which is said to measure 4 sq. km in extent has not been investigated since 1936–37. There are many examples like this (cf. a site near Rajmahal which is supposed to cover a few villages of the area: Jhimjhimaiya-Kalisthan).

In this work I have been concerned with only the excavated archaeological data from various sites in various areas. I would like to emphasize that this is only one of the possible dimensions of the investigation of early historic city sites. In a series of publications which I have cited at appropriate places, B.C. Law has examined the literary references to some of the major sites like Rajagriha, Ahichchhatra, etc. The early history of an individual city (Kausambi) was dealt with by N.N. Ghosh. More recently, the contributors to the volume on Mathura, entitled *Mathura, the Cultural Heritage* (D. Srinivasan 1989) have explored in some detail the historical background, society and economy, religious sects, numismatics, archaeology, language and literature, epigraphy, art and iconography, although one would have liked a detailed section on the settlement perspective of the Mathura region as a whole. Detailed, multi-dimensional exercises to explore the cultural history of an ancient Indian city are laudable academic endeavours and one hopes that exercises such as the one at Mathura will be attempted both at the individual and collective level in the context of other major early historic urban settlements.

There is still a major problem in the domain of literary references to ancient Indian settlements, especially cities. In a previous chapter I have pointed out that the literary evidence on ancient Indian town-planning corresponds, on a general level, to the basic image which emerges from the archaeological data. In his book entitled *Urban Centres and Urbanisation as Reflected in the Pali Vinaya and Sutta Pitakas* K.T.S. Sarao (1990) has highlighted this particular dimension in great detail on the basis of the early Buddhist literary sources selected by him. He begins by establishing the main functions of various types of settlements mentioned in this literature:

Settlement	Type	Main Function
Kuti/Nivesa	rural	shelter
Gama	rural	multiple, but limited
Nigama	urban	commercial
Nagara	urban	multiple

Pura	urban	defence-cum-administration
Pattana	urban	commercial
Puta-bhedanam	urban	commercial
Rajadhani	urban	political
Mahanagara	urban	multiple

Sarao (1990) then proceeds to describe some settlements on the basis of textual references. He believes that the following settlements have been identified on the ground:

Aggalapura (Taria Sujan in U.P.?), Alavi (Newal near Kanauj?), Allakappa (Nandangarh near Betiah?), Amaravati (the stupa site), Andhapura (Bezwada in Andhra?), Anoma (?), Arittha (Shorkot in Panjab?), Atthakanagara (Hathagaon on the Baghmati river near Pataliputra), Varanasi, Bhaddiya (Bhadariya near Bhagalpur?), Dantapura (Orissa-Andhra border?), Devadaha (near Piphrawa?), Dhannavati (Dhannagaon in Gaya), Dvaraka (modern Dwaraka), Erakachchha (Eran), Gaya, Hamsavati (Hanswa in U.P.), Hatthipura (Hastinapur), Indapatta (Indra-prastha), Jetuttara (Nagari near Chitorgarh), Kajangala (Kankjole near Rajmahal), Kampilla (Kampil), Kannakujja (Kanauj), Kapilavatthu (Ganwaria), Kavirapattana (Kaveripattanam), Kekaya (Girjak in Panjab), Kesaputta (Kesariya near Basarh), Khemaka (Khemrajpur in Basti), Koliyanagara (Koraon Dih near Basti), Kosambi (Kausambi), Kukkuta (Peshawar), Kumbhavati (Nasik?), Kusinara (Kusinagara in U.P.), Machchikasanda (Masaon Dih near Benares), Madhura (Mathura), Mahissati (Mahismati on the Narmada), Mithila (Janakapura in Nepal terai), Nagara (Nagar on the Beas, Himachal Pradesh), Nalanda, Nagaraka (Nagara in the Rapti valley, U.P.), Pannakata (Palghat in Kerala?), Pataliputta, Rajagaha, Ramagama (Deokali east of the Ganges), Roruka (Alor in Sindh), Sadhuka (Nawabganj in Barabanki, U.P.), Sakala (Sialkot), Sahajati (Bhita), Saketa (Ayodhya), Samkassa (Sankisa), Sarana (Saran Khas in north Bihar), Savatthi (Sravasti), Sena_Nigama (Bakraur), Setavya (Satiaba and Basedita near Sravasti), Sihapura (Sihor in Gujarat), Sobhavati (Khopoa Dih in Basti), Soreyya (Soron near Atranjikhera), Sotthivati (near Banda?), Sumsumaragiri (Chunar), Supparaka (Sopara), Takkara (Ter?), Takkasila, Thuna (Thaneswar), Udumbara (Pathankot?), Ujjeni (Ujjayini), Ukkavela (Sonpur in Bihar?), Vamsa/Vanasa (Tumain near Gwalior), Varana (Bulandshahr), Vedisa (Vidisha), Veranja (Atranjikhera?), Vesali (Basarh) and Vethadipa (Betiah?).

In addition to these 'identified' settlements, Sarao mentions fifty-two unidentified ones. These were all mostly urban settlements of different types. They are spread over a very wide area, from Taxila in Panjab to

Kaveripattinam in the south and from Gujarat to Bihar. However, except in the cases where the problem of identification has been solved by the discovery of a suitable inscribed material, no suggested identification is beyond pure speculation. The problem of the identification of ancient Indian cities is far from being over; the names of different settlements given in the literary and epigraphic sources of a given area should be carefully studied in the light of the available archaeological data of that area. This calls for many years of patient work. Sarao (1990) further gives a list of the frequency of urban settlements in the Pali Vinaya and Sutta Pitakas, and in this list he mentions 173 urban settlements. He builds up a neat order of inter-related settlements:

The overwhelming dominance of capital settlements, the clear hierarchical ordering of settlements and the concentration of urban settlements is worthy of notice. Differentiation based on size was accompanied by a clear delineation of functions, and the smaller ones by their unique roles; villages served as primary agricultural producers, *nigamas* participated in trade and redistribution. The capitals not only performed all these functions but also supported elite residence, large religious establishments, civic and ceremonial structures (Sarao 1990).

Another major problem is to determine if there was an 'urban decay' in the Gupta and post-Gupta periods, as propounded by R.S. Sharma (1987). One of the major points to be appreciated about the preindustrial cities is that they served some distinct politico-administrative, religious, cultural and economic functions in relation to the villages in their hinterlands. This is what Nissen implies by his idea of 'centre' and 'surrounding' (chapter 1). To argue that such functions ceased to be relevant in the context of Gupta and post-Gupta India is not logical and based on facts. As far as the literary evidence is concerned, one has only to remember the description of Ujjayini in the *Meghadutam* of Kalidasa who has been generally placed in the Gupta period. To say that urban centres ceased to exist in the Gupta period or that they became subject to a process of decay specifically from that period onwards flies straight in the face of the contemporary literary image of the cities. Secondly, Sharma, while trying to underline the factor of decay, argues that the material remains in the form of structures, etc. in the excavated levels of the period are not at all impressive and that this suggests 'decay'. The main argument is that the excavated structures of the period are not made of good quality bricks. Also, such burnt brick structures are generally limited in number. As this is an archaeological argument, I may point out the following facts. First, it is not at all true that the excavated Gupta period remains from our major sites are by and large devoid of good quality brick constructions. At Mahasthangarh, for instance, there is a burnt-brick fortification wall of the Gupta period, and miscellaneous structural remains of the period have been excavated at many sites in north India. However, the point is—and one supposes that this is Sharma's main argument—that the excavated structural remains of the period at most of our sites do not impress one with quantity, or in some cases, even with quality. As far as quality is concerned, the use of bricks dug up from the earlier levels has been pointed out. The occurrence of 're-used bricks' in the structures of the period may suggest that the hey-day of urban prosperity was over. Answers to such problems are fairly straightforward. Has there been any excavation which aimed at the horizontal exposure of the Gupta period level at the site? In any case, horizontal exposures of our historic sites have been singularly rare in recent years, and what we know of the Gupta period in terms of its excavated remains must be considered negligible in the long run. Moreover, how do we date the Gupta period in the archaeological sequence of the Gangetic valley and elsewhere? I raise this question because it is my belief that the divisions between the different dynastic groups (i.e. the Maurya, Sunga, Kushan and Gupta dynasties) in our north Indian archaeological columns are not always very clear, a good part of the exercise being subjective. The distinction between the Kushan and the Gupta periods is not at all sharp in the archaeological sequence, and what we get in most cases is a routine labelling exercise based on 'field intuition', and rarely on the basis of well-dated and stratified antiquities. One should be wary of jumping to conclusions about the cultural prosperity or the lack of it during the Gupta period on the basis of the excavated data. It is not also generally appreciated that by the time the Gupta and post-Gupta levels are reached in our early historic sequence, the mound becomes fairly high, depending on the local situation, and it is probable that the main settlement of the period is no longer on top of the mound but has shifted to a more level ground elsewhere. While assessing the location of major occupational remains of this period, this feature needs careful consideration. So, it is not really a question of looking for whatever Gupta and post-Gupta structures exist on top of the excavated mound and jumping to conclusions on that basis but taking a whole lot of settlement issues into consideration before passing judgement on the settlement features of that age.

The more orthodox historical data against Sharma's hypothesis have been carefully summarized by Sheena Punja (1990) on the basis of B.D. Chattopadhyay's researches.

From epigraphic evidence it is clear that sites existed which show certain 'urban' traits and that there were distinct differences between these and 'rural' settlements. Sites like Tattanandapura (identified with Ahar in Bulandshahar),

Siyadoni (near Lalitpur in Jhansi district), and Gopagiri (Gwalior), among others, testified through epigraphic evidence, seem to exhibit evidence for the existence of guilds, merchants, traders involved in overland and inland trade, large settlements, well-planned roads and houses, and dense population. Apart from the new sites, certain earlier sites like Varanasi and Ahichchhatra survived right up to medieval times. Epigraphic evidence further shows that terms for different settlements, i.e. *grama, pura, nagara* (or distinction between rural and urban settlements) that existed in early historical times continued during this period. There is evidence of foreign trade in inscriptions and literary texts, so the complete cessation of trade cannot be adhered to totally.

There is no doubt that certain sites declined or were deserted after the early historical period, but there were others which emerged. The nature of early medieval settlements was different from their predecessors, being more rooted in their regional contexts; they acted as nodal points in local exchange networks, corresponding to different ties of regional power—unlike the early historical towns, which were directly linked up with centres of authority with supra-regional loci. Hence, rather than talking of an urban decay, it would be more fruitful to try and understand the change in the nature and location of settlements in the Gupta and post-Gupta periods.

In the present volume I have offered a coherent account of the early urban history of India with reference to a host of related issues—distribution, context, sequence, chronology, physical features, historical character, and so on. But I have also tried to offer in this volume a wholly archaeological and indigenous framework of early cultural development in the subcontinent, beginning with the Indus civilization. In the context of this civilization I have made the following hypothesis:

With the growth of villages in the Indus and related alluvium, Baluchistan, Kirthar piedmont and Sind Kohistan became separated as an orbit from the cultural development in the valley, which got more or less nucleated in the Cholistan area of the Sarasvati-Hakra drainage. Much regarding its beginning is uncertain but there is perhaps no point in denying that the sites of the Hakra ware complex in Cholistan date from the fifth millennium BC. In my discussion I have accepted Louis Flam's reconstruction of the palaeogeography of Sind: the Indus and the Hakra channels joining lower down in Sind and flowing jointly into the present Rann of Kutch which must then have made the modern Kutch peninsula an island. There is no guarantee, of course, that the palaeochannels which Flam observes in aerial photographs and satellite imageries are dated—or even can be precisely dated—but the fact remains that this reconstruction is as good as another, and in fact makes sense in the light of the historical testimony that the present flow of the Indus via Sukkur and Rorhi is a much later development. Flam's distribution maps may also underline the fact that the distribution of the Hakra complex and the early Harappan Kot Diji level was in no way oriented towards the Kirthar piedmont and beyond, which became the focus of the Amri culture. The arrowline of succession from the Hakra complex to the early Harappan and thence to the mature Harappan is crystal clear from the simple distributional point of view in Cholistan, and it is there that the origin of the Indus civilization must be considered to have taken place. I suggest two lines of dispersal after its origin: one towards the Indus, and the other along the course of the combined Hakra-Indus flow towards Kutch. Apart from being a major craft centre in the heart of the most prosperous agricultural area of Sind, Mohenjodaro could also serve a purpose similar to that of Shikarpur in the nineteenth century and earlier when the entire Bolan trade used to come through the Kachchi plain to this area of Sind. This must also have attracted the trade coming overland from Iran through the western section of Baluchistan. Cotton, grazing land and semi-precious stones of Kutch must also have attracted the Indus civilization people at this stage. The sites in Indian Rajasthan, Haryana and Panjab were parts of a secondary expansion towards the Siwalik piedmont along the drainage lines of the Sarasvati-Drishadvati. Another line of secondary expansion was towards the peninsula of Saurashtra and mainland Gujarat. The expansion towards Harappa could be a part of the possible movement upstream from the Multan area in the central Indus valley. I suggest that there was not a homogeneous Harappan empire; on the contrary, if we look at the later political history of the entire region, we are likely to argue in favour of the idea of a number of separate kingdoms throughout the Harappan distribution zone. I have further argued that we need not expect the existence of an Egyptian or Mesopotamian-type of kingship in the Harappan context. The Harappan kings were more likely to preempt the later day historical pattern of kingship circumscribed within the social and religious ideals of duty towards subjects. Quite naturally they do not loom large in the archaeological record. Those who doubt this assumption may recollect the fact that had it not been for Asoka's inscriptions, there would have been no archaeological evidence of the great Indian monarch.

I have suggested two factors which played a catalytic role in the development of the Indus civilization: the ability to harness the power of the rivers before they could settle in the floodplains by devising a system of overflow irrigation, and the intensification of craft activity as evidenced by the stupendous metallurgical activity in northeast Rajasthan dating from even before the early Harappan stage. The evidence of an irrigation system in Sind was, in fact, argued by Marcia Fentress in her article in Misra and Bellwood 1986, although she did not try to establish any link between the origin of this irrigation method which continued upto the early years of the twentieth century and the origin of the Indus civilization. The situation, as I have shown citing the relevant gazetteers, is clear as regards the Indus, whereas there is no specific evidence from the Hakra stretch in Cholistan. However, in the light of the French postulate of irrigation canals upstream in Haryana, the development of an irrigation network is a logical postulate in the context of the Hakra too. The later excavations at Ganeshwar have demonstrated the entire sequence of metallurgical development in the copper-rich northeast region of Rajasthan, beginning with a mesolithic stage, and the fact that about 2000 copper artifacts have been documented in the not-so-extensive excavations of a single site and that more than 80 such sites have been recorded in this region is good enough proof of this metallurgical activity which led to the general intensification of all craft activities in the early Harappan stage.

Regarding the decline of the Harappan civilization I have pointed out that in the areas of its secondary expansion, i.e. in the large tracts of the Indo-Gangetic divide, the upper Doab, the Saurashtra peninsula and mainland Gujarat, the early Harappans and the mature Harappans were essentially imposed on hunter-gatherers, and this fact in itself must be considered an impediment in the process of striking deep urban roots in these areas. Once the civilization in its heartland weakened due to the slow but inexorable process of the drying up of the Sarasvati-Hakra channel and had to transform itself into a number of densely distributed but much smaller agricultural communities, the process could not but affect the entire Harappan distribution area, and Harappan urbanism, as we know it in its mature form, was easily lost.

From this 'late' phase onwards the Harappans moved in two directions: one towards the Doab and the other towards Maharashtra and Malwa. I have argued that they interacted with the regional hunter-gatherers, and the neolithic-chalcolithic communities of the second millennium BC in inner India were primarily the result of this interaction. The Harappans introduced a higher productive system to the hunter-gatherers of inner India, and incorporated them within it. In view of the fact that the process of incorporating the hunter-gatherers within the fold of the caste structure or the Hindu productive system has continued to this day, the hypothesis I have offered perhaps makes more sense than is generally admitted.

To come to a more specific and tangible issue, some transitional levels between the early Harappan and the mature Harappan have now emerged at such sites as Banawali, Harappa and Dholavira. Once the details are published, we shall be better able to examine the process which led to the emergence of the Indus civilization. Meanwhile, on the basis of personal information which has been very kindly supplied by R.S. Bisht I reproduce below the basic stratigraphic sequence of Dholavira, beginning with its lowest level.

Period I — terracotta cakes, perforated ware and other varieties of pottery, blades of chert and chalcedony, evidence of copper-working, 11 m wide fortification wall, 65 cm thick occupational deposit.

Period II — the earlier pottery types continue but with more shapes, profusion of beads, further 2.30 m added to the width of the fortification wall, 90 cm thick occupational deposit.

Period III — typical Harappan pottery shapes appear but are not dominant, evidence of more industrial activities, drill-bits for bead-making, 3 seals without inscriptions but with motifs (in one case pipal leaf motif), peripheral wall added, the construction of a 'middle town' and 'citadel' with 'ceremonial' ground between the two, a series of water-reservoirs built towards the later phase, the width of fortification further increased by 4.50 m, 3.30–3.60 m thick occupational deposit.

Period IV — many seals, lower town added, peripheral wall extended, special clay material with stone chips added for fortification, a radiocarbon date of 2323 BC uncalibrated from the lower part of the deposit, natural disturbance (earthquake?) at the end of the phase, 4.50 m thick occupational deposit.

Period V — phase of decline, the settlement not properly maintained, 0.80–1.00 m thick occupational deposit.

Period VI — rickety houses, seals without figures but with inscriptions, Rojdi pottery, 0.70 m thick occupational deposit.

Period of desertion—0.35 m thick deposit.

The location of the radiocarbon date giving a calibrated version around 2800 BC is interesting and seems to agree with my premise that Kutch was within the earliest phase of the distribution of the Indus civilization. Also, the scheme I have offered explains why the Indus civilization must have had a long chronology instead of a short one.

In the field of early history I propose to take up only two issues. One is the problem of 'state formation' in early historic India and the other is the issue of early historic urban growth in the context of the Deccan. These issues have long been discussed by Indian scholars, and I propose to put down my own observations on them.

As far as the process of state formation in early historic India is concerned, the concentration of archaeological sites in different parts of the Doab and Gangetic valley suggests that some kind of state structure must have existed from the late Harappan period onwards. The sheer density of sites in the Gangetic valley seems to suggest this. What is remarkable in this context is that not merely the Gangetic valley but the entire area of distribution of the traditional 'sixteen mahajanapadas' from Gandhara to the Deccan was well-covered by sites of different magnitude by the second half of the second millennium BC. The base of the regional political units must have been laid down by then, although it is a different matter whether these units represented 'chiefdoms' or states ruled by kings. Those who are familiar with India's political history must remember how H.C. Raychaudhuri (1953) cogently showed the correlation between later Vedic literature and early Buddhist literature as far as the growth of political units in the Indo-Gangetic divide and the Gangetic valley is concerned. I dare not offer any chronological sequence of this development, as Romila Thapar has done in *From Lineage to State*. Although her discussion is excellent within the parameters accepted by her, I cannot accept these literary parameters because we do not think that the literary traditions which have survived in the context of early India represent homogeneous or unitary texts of different clear-cut periods. However much the serialization of these texts and the picture of a chronological evolution of Indian society and economy may appeal to our love of harmony and neatly ordered succession of events, the postulated chronologies for these texts do not make sense in the light of the archaeological data. The picture of the growth of Harappan civilization in the Sarasvati valley in Cholistan, and its gradual absorption in, and positive effect on, the main flow of Indian cultural development, which I have presented in the present volume, does make some sense of the Indian literary tradition. I admit that this tradition is only composed of disparate strands of different periods, with which the generally accepted chronological frameworks of these texts do not bear any relationship.

The point I propose to outline in the context of the Deccan has been emphasized by Aloka Parasher (1992). This is a hypothesis which makes one rethink about the oft-quoted premise regarding the influence of trade on the growth of urban centres in the Deccan. Parasher writes:

That a surplus had been generated by the well-settled communities of the central Deccan during the early centuries AD is evident enough from the structures they built to store it, as also the other manifestations of urban life. However, as delineated above, the early history of habitation and cultural evolution in this region had helped in gradually transforming pockets of the food-gathering economy particularly from the Megalithic phases of habitation. These have been generally found in close proximity of the early historical sites. The expansion of the agrarian base was therefore linked with the proliferation of early historical sites in the region. It is in this phase that it can be postulated that there was an increase in population. In the sites under discussion the maximum number of iron implements have been recovered from Peddabankur and Kondapur. The impact and the use of the iron technology must, nevertheless, be understood in the context of a limited ecological base, where because of the non-availability of fertile tracts, other than along the river, large scale agricultural operations were not possible. Village settlements thus continued to be dependent on other modes of production such as pastoralism, gathering and fishing. But what is particularly striking is that even small settlements in the mid-Godavari valley give evidence of the production of iron objects. In this way it would be possible to suggest that the existence of social groups, organized most possibly on kinship lines were involved in the craft production of smelting and forging of iron. Thus we submit that trade in these parts was stimulated not so much by the export of an agricultural surplus, but rather by the supply of iron objects and other related commodities, a process which began in protohistoric times (Parasher 1992: 475–6).

The emphasis is on craft-activity and agricultural expansion in the background of the early historic urban phenomenon in the Deccan. Trade was no doubt a sustaining factor but was perhaps not a catalytic one.

That there cannot be any mechanical one-to-one explanation of a phenomenon as complex as the growth of cities was directly driven home to us in the context of West Bengal. That the black-and-red ware settlement phase of the region merged into the phase of early historic cities is not in doubt, but the point is that the black-and-red ware settlement phase itself comprises a history of about a thousand years. How much do we know of its developmental sequence except for some obvious inferences made on the basis of archaeological stratigraphy? The maximum size during this phase was 8–10 acres, but the early historic settlements of the region go up to 250 acres in extent and even this spread must have had a history of a few hundred years. Again, do we know much of this history? The point is that we have no answer to the question as to how such a drastic change in the settlement size was possible from the black-and-red ware to the early historic periods in the context of West Bengal. Moreover, detailed ground surveys can always throw up surprises regarding the density and distribution of urban sites in a given area. For instance, we have only recently realized that there were at least ten early historic urban centres in the estuarine and coastal area of West Bengal.

It is imponderables such as these which make all hypotheses regarding early urban growth very tentative. The present volume has explained how tentative our range of data and explanation is in the context of ancient India.

References

Adams, R.M. 1960a, The Origin of the Cities, *Scientific American*, 203, pp. 153–68.

—— 1960b, Factors Influencing the Rise of Civilization in the Alluvium: Illustrated by Mesopotamia, *City Invincible* (eds C.H. Kraeling and R.M. Adams), Chicago, pp. 24–34.

—— 1965, *The Evolution of Urban Society*, Rochester.

—— 1981, *Heartland of Cities*, Chicago.

Agrawal, D.P. 1982, *The Archaeology of India*, London.

—— 1992, *Man and Environment in India Through the Ages*, Delhi.

Agrawal, R.C. and V. Kumar, 1982, Ganeshwar-Jodhpura Culture: New Traits in Indian Archaeology, *Harappan Civilization* (hereafter *HC*) (ed. G.L. Possehl), Delhi, pp.125–34.

Ali, A.M. 1941, The Problem of Desiccation of the Ghaggar Plain, *Indian Geographical Review*, pp.166–77.

—— 1966, *The Geography of the Puranas*, Delhi.

Allchin, F.R. 1960, *Piklihal Excavations*, Hyderabad.

—— 1961, *Utnur Excavations*, Hyderabad.

—— 1963, *Neolithic Cattlekeepers of South India*, Cambridge.

—— 1989, City and State Formation in South Asia, *South Asian Studies* (hereafter *SAS*), 5, pp. 1–16.

—— 1990, Patterns of City Formation in Early Historic India, *SAS*, 6, pp. 163–73.

Allchin, B. and F.R. Allchin 1968, *The Birth of Indian Civilization*, Harmondsworth.

—— 1982, *The Rise of Civilization in India and Pakistan*, Cambridge.

Allchin, F.R. and Dilip K. Chakrabarti (eds) 1979, *A Sourcebook of Indian Archaeology*, I, Delhi.

Allchin, F.R. and J.R. Knox 1981, Preliminary Report on the Excavations at Tarakai Qila, *South Asian Archaeology 1979* (ed. H. Hartel), Berlin, pp. 245–50.

Allchin, F.R. *et al.* 1986, *Lewan and the Bannu Basin*, Oxford.

Altekar, A.S. and V.K. Misra 1959, *Report on the Kumrahar Excavations 1951–55*, 1959.

Ansari, Z.D. and M.S. Mate 1966, *Excavations at Dwarka*, Pune.

Ansari, Z.D. and M.K. Dhavalikar 1975, *Excavations at Kayatha*, Pune.

Ayyar, C.P.V. 1915, *Town-planning in Ancient Dekkan*, Madras.

Bala, M. 1992, *Archaeology of Panjab*, Delhi.

Ball, Warwick 1989, *South Asian Studies*, p. 5.

Banerjee, N.R. 1986, *Naqda Excavations*, Delhi.

Bhan, K.K. 1992, Late Harappan Gujarat, *Eastern Anthropologist* (hereafter *EA*), 45, pp. 173–93.

Bhan, S. 1972, *Prehistoric Archaeology of the Sarasvati and Drishadvati Valleys* (Haryana), M.S. University of Baroda, Ph.D. thesis.

——— 1973, The Sequence and Spread of Prehistoric Cultures in the Upper Saraswati Basin, *Radiocarbon and Indian Archaeology* (eds D.P. Agrawal and A. Ghosh), Bombay, pp. 252–63.

——— and J.G. Shaffer 1978, New Discoveries in Northern Haryana, *Man and Environment* (*ME*), 2, pp. 59–68.

Bhandarkar, D.R. 1917, Excavations at Besnagar, *AR ASI 1913–14*, Calcutta, pp. 186–226.

——— 1929, *The Archaeological Remains and Excavations at Nagari*, Calcutta.

Bhattacharya, T. 1963, *The Canons of Indian Art*, Calcutta.

Biagi, Paolo and M. Cremaschi 1990, Geoarchaeological Investigations on the Rorhi Hills, *South Asian Archaeology 1987*, vol. I, pp. 31–42.

Bisht, R.S. 1982, Excavations at Banawali: 1974–77, *HC*, pp. 113–24.

——— 1984, Structural Remains and Town-planning of Banawali, *FIC*, pp. 89–98.

——— 1987, Further Excavation at Banawali: 1983–84, *Archaeology and History*, vol. I (eds B.D. Chattopadhyay and B.M. Pande), Delhi, pp. 135–56.

——— 1989, The Harappan Colonization of the Kutch: An Ergonomic Study with Reference to Dholavira and Surkotada, *History and Art* (eds K. Deva and L. Gopal), Delhi, pp. 267–72.

——— 1991, Dholavira: New Horizons of the Indus Civilization, *Puratattva*, 20, pp. 71–82.

Bose, A.N. 1961, *Social and Economic History of Northern India*, I, Calcutta.

Braidwood, R. 1950, *The Near East and the Foundations for Civilization*, Oregon.

——— 1957, Jericho and its Setting in Near Eastern History. *Antiquity*, 31, pp. 73–81.

Casal, J.-M. 1964a, Fresh Digging at Amri, *Pakistan Archaeology* (hereafter *PA*), I, pp. 57–65.

——— 1964b, *Fouilles d' Amri*, 2 vols, Paris.

——— 1966, Nindowari, A Chalcolithic Site in South Baluchistan. *PA*, 3, pp. 10–21.

Chakrabarti, Dilip K. 1976, Rajagriha, *World Archaeology*, 7, pp. 261–8.

——— Origin of the Indus Civilization: Theories and Problem, *Frontiers of the Indus Civilization* (hereafter *FIC*) (eds B.B. Lal and S.P.Gupta), Delhi, pp. 43–50.

——— 1984, The Archaeology of the Iron Age and the Early Historical Period of Kashmir, *ME*, 8, pp. 109–16.

————— 1988a, *Theoretical Issues in Indian Archaeology*, Delhi.

————— 1988b, The Problems of Urbanization and Rural-Urban Differentiation, *Rural Life and Folk Culture in Ancient India* (ed. U.N. Roy), Allahabad, pp. 1–11.

————— 1988c, *A History of Indian Archaeology from the Beginning to 1947*, Delhi.

————— 1990, *The External Trade of the Indus Civilization*, Delhi.

————— 1992, *Ancient Bangladesh*, Delhi.

————— 1992, *The Early Use of Iron in India*, Delhi.

————— 1993, *Archaeology of Eastern India: Chhota-Nagpur Plateau and West Bengal*, Delhi.

Chakrabarti, Dilip K. and R.K. Chattopadhyay 1992, Notes on the Archaeology of Maldaha and Dinajpur Districts, *SAS*, 8.

Chakrabarti, Dilip K., G. Sengupta, R.K. Chattopadhyay and Nayanjot Lahiri 1993, Black-and-Red Ware Settlements of West Bengal, *SAS*, 9.

Chakraborti, H.P. 1966, *Trade and Commerce of Ancient India*, Calcutta.

Chattopadhyay, B.D. 1990, *Aspects of Rural Settlements and Rural Society in Early Medieval India*, Calcutta.

Chaturvedi, S.N. 1985, Advance of Vindhyan Neolithic, *ME*, 9, pp. 101–8.

Childe, V.G. 1941, *Man Makes Himself*, London.

————— 1950, The Urban Revolution, *Town Planning Review*, 21, pp. 3–17.

————— 1952, *New Light on the Most Ancient East*, London.

————— 1952, *What Happened in History*, Harmondsworth.

————— 1957, Civilization, Cities and Towns, *Antiquity*, 31, pp. 36–7.

————— 1958, *The Prehistory of European Society*, Harmondsworth.

Chitalwala, Y.M. 1989, Minor Antiquities, *Harappan Civilization and Rojdi* (G.L. Possehl and M.H. Raval), Delhi.

Choudhury, N.D. 1985, *Historical Archaeology of Central Assam*, Delhi.

Choudhury, P.C. 1966, *The History and Civilization of the People of Assam to the Twelfth Century A.D.*, Gauhati.

Choudhury, R.D. 1985, *Archaeology of the Brahmaputra Valley*, Delhi.

Coomaraswamy, A.K. 1930, Early Indian Architecture, *Eastern Art*, 2, pp. 209–35.

————— 1931, Early Indian Architecture, *Eastern Art*, 3, pp. 181–217.

————— 1965 (rep.).*History of Indian and Indonesian Art*, New York.

Courbin, P. 1988, *What is Archaeology. An Essay on the Nature of Archaeological Research*, London.

Couseus, H. 1929, *The Antiquities of Sind*, Calcutta.

Cowell, E.B. (ed.) 1957, *The Jataka Stories*, vol. I, London.

Crawford, H. 1991, *The Sumerians*, Cambridge.

Cunningham, A. 1963 (rep.), *The Ancient Geography of India*, Varanasi.

————— 1966 (rep.), *ASI Report for the Year 1871–72*, Varanasi.

Dales, G.F. 1962, Harappan Outposts on the Makran Coast, *Antiquity*, 6, pp. 86–92.

——— 1964, The Mythical Massacre at Mohenjodaro, *Expedition*, 6, pp. 36–43.

——— 1965, New Investigations at Mohenjodaro, *Archaeology*, 18, pp. 145–50.

——— 1965, A Suggested Chronology for Afghanistan, Baluchistan and the Indus Valley, *Chronologies in Old World Archaeology* (ed. R.W. Ehrich), Chicago, pp. 257–84.

——— 1966, The Decline of the Harappans, *Scientific American*, 214, pp. 92–100.

——— 1979, The Balakot Project: Summary of Four Years of Excavation in Pakistan, *ME*, 3, pp. 45–53.

——— 1992, Recent Excavations at Harappa, *EA*, 45, pp. 21–37.

——— and J.M. Kenoyer 1989, Excavation at Harappa—1988, *PA*, 24, pp. 68–176.

Dales, G.F. and R.L. Raikes 1968, The Mohenjodaro Floods: A Rejoinder, *American Anthropologist*, 70, pp. 957–61.

Dani, A.H. 1960, *Prehistory and Protohistory of Eastern India*, Calcutta.

——— 1964–65, Shaikhan Dheri Excavation, *Ancient Pakistan*, 2, pp. 17–214.

——— 1970–71, Excavation in the Gomal Valley, *Ancient Pakistan*, 5, pp. 1–77.

Daniel, Glyn 1968, *The First Civilizations, the Archaeology of Their Origins*, London.

Dasgupta, P.C. 1965, *Excavations at Pandu Rajar Dhibi*, Calcutta.

Davies, K. 1966, Urban Research and its Significance, *Urban Research Methods* (ed. J. Gibbs), Delhi, pp. xi–xxii.

Dey, N.L. 1971 (rep.), *A Geographical Dictionary of Ancient India*, Delhi.

Dhavalikar, M.K. 1982, Daimabad Bronzes, *HC*, pp.421–6.

——— 1984, Sub-Indus Cultures of Central and Western India, *FIC*, pp. 243–51.

——— 1988, *The First Farmers of the Deccan*, Pune.

Dhavalikar, M.K., V. Sinde and S. Atre 1988, *Excavations at Kaothe*, Pune.

Dhavalikar, M.K., H.D. Sankalia and Z.D. Ansari 1988, *Excavations at Inamgaon*, Pune.

Dhavalikar, M.K. and G.L. Possehl 1992, The Pre-Harappan Period at Prabhas Patan and the Pre-Harappan Phase in Gujarat, *ME*, 17, pp. 71–8.

Dikshit, Kailash Nath 1979, The Ochre Coloured Ware Settlements in Ganga-Yamuna Doab, *EIP*, Delhi, pp. 285–99.

——— 1984, The Sothi Complex: Old Records and Fresh Observations, *FIC*, pp. 531–7.

Diksit, Kasi Nath 1935, Excavations in Bengal, Mahasthan, *AR ASI 1929–30*, Delhi, pp. 88–97.

Diksit, M.G. 1955, *Tripuri—1952*, Nagpur.

——— 1968, *Excavations at Kaundinyapura*, Bombay.

During-Caspers, E.C.L. 1991, The Indus Script in the Light of the Cultural

Interaction with the Near East and the Recent Reappraisal of the Dating of the Harappan Culture, *Aksayanivi: Essays Presented to Dr. Debala Mitra* (ed. G. Bhattacharya), Delhi, pp. 1–14.

———— 1992, Some Thoughts on the Indus Script, *Indian Art and Archaeology* (eds E.M. Raven and K.R. Van Kooij), Leiden, pp. 54–67.

Durkheim, E. 1964, Sociology and its Scientific Field, *Essays on Sociology and Philosophy* (ed. K.H. Wolff), New York, pp. 354–75.

Durrani, F.A. 1988, Excavations in the Gomal Valley, Rehman Dheri Excavations, Report No. 1, *Ancient Pakistan*, vol. 6.

Dutt, B.B. 1925, *Town-Planning in Ancient India*, Calcutta.

Erdosy, G. 1988, *Urbanisation in Early Historic India*, Oxford.

Fagan, P. 1900, *Gazetteer of the Montgomery District*, Lahore.

Fairservis, W.W.A. 1956, *Excavations in the Quetta Valley, West Pakistan*, New York.

———— 1967, The Origin, Character and Decline of an Early Civilization, *American Museum Novitates*, no. 2302, New York.

———— 1971, *The Roots of Ancient India*, London.

———— 1982, Ahladino, An Excavation of a Small Harappan Site, *HC*, pp. 107–12.

Fentress, M. 1982, From Jhelum to Yamuna: City and Settlement in the Second and Third Millennium BC, *HC*, pp. 245–60.

———— 1984, The Indus 'Granaries': Illusion, Imagination and Archaeological Reconstruction, *Studies in the Archaeology and Palaeoanthroplogy of South Asia* (eds K.A.R. Kennedy and G.L. Possehl), Delhi, pp. 89–97.

Flam, L. 1981, Towards An Ecological Analysis of Prehistoric Settlement Pattern in Sind, Pakistan, *ME*, 5, pp. 52–8.

———— 1984, The Palaeogeography and Prehistoric Settlement Patterns of the Lower Indus Valley, *Studies in the Archaeology and Palaeoanthropology of South Asia* (eds K.A.R. Kennedy and G.L. Possehl), Delhi, pp. 77–82.

———— 1986, Recent Explorations in Sind, *Studies in the Archaeology of India and Pakistan*, Delhi, pp. 65–89.

Foote, R.B. 1914, *The Foote Catalogue of Prehistoric and Protohistoric Antiquities*, Madras.

Francfort, H-P. 1984, The Harappan Settlement of Shortughai, *FIC*, pp. 301–10.

———— 1989, *Fouilles de Shortughai*, 2 vols, Paris.

———— 1992, Evidence for Harappan Irrigation System in Haryana and Rajasthan, *EA*, 45, pp. 87–103.

Frankfort, H. 1951, *The Birth of Civilization in the Near East*, London.

Garde, M.B. 1918, The Site of Padmavati, *AR ASI 1915–16*, pp. 100–8.

Gaur, R.C. 1973, Lal Qila Excavations and the O.C.P. Problem, *Radiocarbon and Indian Archaeology* (eds D.P. Agrawal and A. Ghosh), Bombay, pp.154–62.

———— 1983, *Atranjikhera Excavations*, Delhi.

Ghosh, A. 1948, Taxila (Sirkap), 1944–45, *Ancient India*, 4, pp. 41–84.

———— 1951, Rajgir 1950, *Ancient India*, 7, pp. 66–78.

———— 1962, The Archaeological Background, *Memoir of the Anthropological Survey of India*, 9, pp. 1–5.

———— 1965, The Indus Civilization—its Origins, Authors, Extent and Chronology, *Indian Archaeology: 1964* (eds V.N. Misra and M.S. Mate), Pune, pp. 113–56.

———— 1973, *The City in Early Historical India*, Simla.

———— (ed.) 1989, *Encyclopaedia of Indian Archaeology*, II, Delhi.

Ghosh, A. and K.C. Panigrahi 1946, Pottery of Ahichchhatra (U.P.), *Ancient India*, I, pp. 37–59.

Ghosh, A. and Dilip K. Chakrabarti 1968, Prehistoric Metal Stage in West Bengal, *Bulletin of the Cultural Research Institute*, 7, pp. 11–23.

Ghosh, N.N. 1935, *Early History of Kausambi*, Allahabad.

Gordon, D.H. 1958, *Prehistoric Background of Indian Culture*, Bombay.

Goswami, K.G., 1948, *Excavations at Bangarh*, Calcutta.

Hassan, F. 1981, *Demographic Archaeology*, New York.

Heine-Geldern, R. 1956, The Origin of Ancient Civilizations and Toynbee's Theories, *Diogenes*, 13, pp. 81–99.

Hooja, Rima 1988, *The Ahar Culture*, Oxford.

Jacobsen, T. 1960, Comments, *City Invincible* (eds C.H. Kraeling and R.M. Adams), Chicago, p. 243.

Jacobson, J. 1986, The Harappan Civilization: An Early State, *Studies in the Archaeology of India and Pakistan* (ed. J. Jacobson), Delhi, pp.137–74.

Jansen, M. 1979, Architectural Problems of the Harappa Culture, *South Asian Archaeology 1977*, pp. 405–32.

———— 1984, Architectural Remains in Mohenjodaro, *FIC*, pp. 75–88.

———— 1987, Preliminary Results of 'Forma Urbis' Research at Mohenjodaro, *Interim Reports*, vol. 2 (eds M. Hansen and G. Urban), Aachen, pp. 9–22.

———— 1989, Water Supply and Sewage Disposal at Mohenjodaro, *World Archaeology*, 21, pp. 177–92.

———— 1991, The Concept of Space in Harappan City Planning—Mohenjodaro, *Concepts of Space, Ancient and Modern* (ed. K. Vatsyayan), Delhi, pp. 75–81.

Jarrige, J-F. 1989, Excavations at Nausharo 1987–88, *PA*, 24, pp. 21–67.

———— and R. Meadow 1980, The Antecedents of Civilization in the Indus Valley, *Scientific American*, 243, pp. 122–33.

Jettmar, K. 1967, An Iron Cheek Piece of a Shaffle Found at Timargarha, *Ancient Pakistan*, 3, pp. 203–9.

Joshi, J.P. 1991, Settlement Patterns in the Third, Second and First Millennia in India, with Special Reference to Recent Discoveries in Punjab, *The Cultural Heritage of an Indian Village*, London, pp. 11–18.

Joshi, J.P., M. Bala and J. Ram 1984, The Indus Civilization: A Reconsideration on the Basis of Distribution Maps, *FIC*, pp. 511–30.

Joshi, M.C. 1989, Mathura, *Mathura the Cultural Heritage* (ed. D.M. Srinivasan), Delhi.

Kaw, R.N. 1974, The Neolithic Culture in Kashmir, *Essays in Indian Protohistory* (eds D.P. Agrawal and Dilip K. Chakrabarti), Delhi, pp. 219–28.

Kenoyer, J.M. 1991, The Indus Valley Tradition of Pakistan and Western India, *Journal of World Prehistory*, 5, pp. 331–85.

———— 1992, Harappan Craft, Specialization and the Question of Urban Segregation and Stratification, *EA*, 45, pp. 39–53.

Kesarwani, A. 1984, Harappan Gateways: A Functional Reassessment, *FIC*, pp. 63–74.

Khan, A.W. 1960, *Yeleswaram Excavations*, Hyderabad.

Khan, F.A. 1964, Excavations at Kot Diji, *PA*, 1, pp. 39–43.

———— 1965, Excavations at Kot Diji, *PA*, 2, pp. 11–85.

Khan, F., J.R. Knox and K.D. Thomas 1991, *Explorations and Excavations in Bannu District, Northwest Frontier Province, Pakistan 198–88*, London.

Khare, M.D. 1982, Chalcolithic Besnagar, *IANP*, pp.220–3.

Kosambi, D.D. 1955, Dhenukakata, *Journal of the Asiatic Society of Bombay*, 30, pp. 50–71.

———— 1962, *Myth and Reality*, Bombay.

Krishnasastry, V.V., *The Proto- and Early Historic Cultures of Andhra Pradesh*.

Kroeber, A. 1940, Stimulus Diffusion, *American Anthropologist*, 42, pp. 1–20.

Kumar, Giriraj 1982, Houseplanning in the Chalcolithic Malwa, *IANP*, pp. 238–44.

Lahiri, Nayanjot 1990, Harappa as a Centre of Trade and Traderoutes, *Indian Economic and Social History Review*, 27, pp. 40–4.

———— 1991, *Pre-Ahom Assam*, Delhi.

———— 1992, *The Archaeology of Indian Traderoutes*, Delhi.

Lal, B.B. 1949, Sisupalgarh 1948, *Ancient India*, 5, pp. 62–105.

———— 1951, Further copper hoards . . ., *Ancient India*, 7, pp. 20–39.

———— 1953, Protohistoric Investigations, *Ancient India*, 9, pp. 80–102.

———— 1955, Excavation at Hastinapur . . ., *Ancient India*, 10–11, pp. 6–151.

———— 1979, Kalibangan and the Indus Civilization, *Essays in Indian Protohistory* (eds D.P. Agrawal and Dilip K. Chakrabarti), Delhi, pp. 65–97.

———— 1985a, Paper on Syena-chiti, Kausambi, *Puratattva*.

———— 1985b, Paper on the Udayana Palace, Kausambi, *Puratattva*.

———— 1993, *Sringavarapura Excavations*, Delhi.

Lal, B.B. and B.K. Thapar 1967, Excavation at Kalibangan, *Cultural Forum*, 9, pp. 78–88.

Lal, M. 1984a, Summary of Four Seasons of Exploration in Kanpur District, *ME*, 7, pp. 61–80.

———— 1984b, *Settlement History and Rise of Civilization in the Ganga-Yamuna Doab*, Delhi.

———— 1986, Iron Tools, Forest Clearance and Urbanization in the Gangetic Plains, *ME*, 10, pp. 83–90.

Lamberg-Karlovsky, C.C. 1972, Trade Mechanisms in Indus-Mesopotamian Interrelations, *JAOS*, 92, pp. 222–9.

———— and Tosi, M. 1973, Tracks on the Earliest History of the Iranian Plateau: Shahr-i-Sokhta and Tepe Yahya, *East and West*, 23, pp. 21–53.

Lambrick, H.T. 1967a, The Mohenjodaro Floods, *Antiquity*, 41, p. 228.

———— 1967b, The Indus Floodplain and the Indus Civilization, 133, pp. 484–95.

———— 1971, Stratigraphy at Mohenjodaro, *Journal of the Oriental Institute*, 20, pp. 363–9.

Law, B.C. 1922, *Historical Gleanings*, Calcutta.

———— 1935, *Sravasti in Ancient Literature*, Delhi.

———— 1938, *Rajagriha in Ancient Literature*, Delhi.

———— 1939, *Kausambi in Ancient Literature*, Delhi.

———— 1942, *Panchalas and their Capital Ahichchhatra*, Delhi.

———— 1944, *Ujjayini in Ancient India*, Gwalior.

———— 1950, *Indological Studies*, Calcutta.

———— 1954, *Historical Geography of Ancient India*, Paris.

———— 1969, Sakala: An Ancient Indian City, *East and West*, 19, pp. 401–9.

Leshnik, L.S. (n.d.) (1966?), Early Settled Farmers of Central India, *Year Book of the South Asia Institute*, Heidelberg, pp. 43–55.

Luders, H. 1912, A List of Brahmi Inscriptions, *Epigraphia Indica*, 10, Appendix.

Mackay, E. 1938, *Further Excavations at Mohenjodaro*, 2 vols, Delhi.

———— 1943, *Chanhudaro Excavations*, New Haven.

———— 1948, *Early Indus Civilizations*, London.

Mahalingam, T.V. 1970, *Report on the Excavations in the Lower Kaveri Valley*, Madras.

Majumdar, G.G. and S.N. Rajguru 1963, Early Mining and Metallurgy in Rajasthan (part 1), Copper Around Udaipur, *Bulletin of the Deccan College Research Institute*, 23, pp. 31–3.

———— 1966, *Ashmound Excavations at Kupgal*, Pune.

Majumdar, N.G. 1934, *Explorations in Sind*, Delhi.

Majumdar, R.C. 1960, *The Classical Accounts of India*, Calcutta.

Majumdar-Sastri, S.N. 1927, *McCrindle's Ancient India as Described by Ptolemy*, Calcutta.

Malalasekera, Y.P. 1960, *Dictionary of Pali Proper Names*, 2 vols, London.

Marshall, J. 1902–3, Excavations at Charsada, *AR ASI*, pp. 141–84.

———— 1909, Rajagriha and its Remains, *AR ASI, 1905–6*, pp. 86–106.

———— 1915, Excavations at Bhita, *AR ASI 1911–12*, pp. 29–94.

———— (ed.) 1931, *Mohenjodaro and the Indus Civilization*, 3 vols, London.

———— *Taxila*, 3 vols, Cambridge.

Masson, V.M. 1968, The Urban Revolution in Southern Turkmenia, *Antiquity*, 42, pp. 178–87.

Mehta, R.N. 1955, *Excavations at Timbarva*, Baroda.

———— 1968, *Excavation at Nagara*, Baroda.

———— 1982, Some Rural Harappan Settlements in Gujarat, *HC*, pp. 167–74.

———— 1984, Valabhi—A Station of Harappan Cattle-breeders, *FIC*, pp. 227–30.

Mellaart, J. 1965, Catal-Huyuk, a Neolithic City in Anatolia, *Proc. Brit. Acad.*, 51, pp. 201–13.

———— 1966, Catal-Huyuk—the World's Oldest City, *Illustrated London News*, 248, pp. 26–7.

Misra, V.N. 1967, *Pre- and Protohistory of the Berach Basin*, Pune.

Mockler, E. 1877, On Ruins in Makran, *JRAS*, 9, pp. 121–34.

Momin, K. 1984, Village Harappans in Kheda District of Gujarat, *FIC*, pp. 231–4.

Momin, M. 1991, Paper in *Archaeology of Northeastern India* (eds J.P. Singh and G. Sengupta), Delhi.

Moorti, U.S. 1991, Evidence of Social Differentiation and Sociopolitical Organization during the Megalithic Period in South India, *Puratattva*, 20, pp. 1–64.

Mughal, R. 1967, Excavations at Tulamba, *PA*, 4, pp. 11–152.

———— 1971, *The Early Harappan Period in the Great Indus Valley and Northern Baluchistan*, Ann Arbor.

———— 1973, *Present State of Research on the Indus Valley Civilization*, Karachi.

———— 1974, New Evidence of the Early Harappan Culture from Jalilpur, Pakistan, *Archaeology*, 27, pp. 106–13.

———— 1990a, Further Evidence of the Early Harappan Culture in the Greater Indus Valley: 1971–90, *SAS*, 5, pp. 174–99.

———— 1990b, The Decline of the Indus Civilization and the Late Harappan Period in the Indus Valley, *Lahore Museum Bulletin*, pp. 1–17.

———— 1992, The Consequences of River Changes for the Harappan Settlements in Cholistan, *EA*, 45, pp. 105–15.

Mumford, L. 1960, Concluding Address, *City Invincible*, pp. 224–6.

———— 1961, *The City in History*, London.

Nagar, M. 1985, The Use of Wild Plant Foods by Aboriginal Communities in Central India, *Rec. Adv. in Indo-Pacific Prehistory* (eds V.N. Misra and P. Bellwood), Delhi, pp. 337–42.

Narain, A.K. and T.N. Roy 1976, *Excavations at Rajghat*, part I, Varanasi.

———— 1977, *Excavations at Rajghat*, part II, Varanasi.

Narain, A.K. and P. Singh 1977, *Excavations at Rajghat*, part III, Varanasi.

Narain, L.A. 1970–71, The Neolithic Settlement at Chirand, *Journal of the Bihar Research Society*, 56, pp. 1–35.

———— 1979, Paper in *Essays in Indian Protohistory* (eds D.P. Agrawal and D.K. Chakrabarti), Delhi.

Narasimhaiah, B. 1980, *Neolithic and Megalithic Cultures in Tamil Nadu*, Delhi.

Nautiyal, K.M. and B.M. Khanduri 1990, *Puratattva*, Delhi.

Nissen, H.J. 1988, *The Early History of the Ancient Near East 9000–2000 B.C.*, Chicago.

Paddayya, K. 1973, *Investigations into the Neolithic Culture of the Shorapur Doab, South India*, Leiden.

Pande, B.M. 1966, Ring-Wells in Ancient India, *Bulletin of Deccan College Research Institute*, Pune, pp. 207–19.

———— 1970, The Neolithic in Kashmir: New Discoveries, *The Anthropologist*, 17, pp. 25–41.

———— 1990, Archaeology of Thanesar, *Puratattva*, 19, pp. 1–5.

Pandey, S.K. 1982, Chalcolithic Eran and its Chronology, *IANP*, pp. 249–56.

Parasher, A. 1992, Nature of Society and Civilization in Early Deccan, *Indian Economic and Social History Review*, 29, pp. 437–78.

Patil, D.R. 1963, *The Antiquarian Remains in Bihar*, Patna.

Pearson, H.W. 1957, The Economy has no Surplus: A Critique of the Theory of Surplus, *Trade and Market in the Early Empires* (eds K.Polanyi *et al.*), Glencoe, pp. 320–41.

Piggott, S. 1945, *Some Ancient Cities of India*, Bombay.

———— 1950, *Prehistoric India*, Harmondsworth.

Pillai, J.M.S. 1967, *A History of Tamil Literature with Texts and Translations*, Annamalainagar.

Pithawala, M.B. 1936, *A Geographical Analysis of the Lower Indus Plain (Sind)*, part I, Karachi.

———— 1959, *A Physical and Economic Geography of Sind*, Karachi.

Plenderleith, H.J. 1965, Mohenjodaro—A 5000 Year Old Heritage Menaced by Destruction, *UNESCO Courier*, pp. 22–6.

Possehl, G.L. 1988, Radiocarbon Dates from South Asia, *ME*, 12, pp. 169–96.

———— and M.H. Raval 1989, *Harappan Civilization and Rojdi*, Delhi.

———— 1991, *A Report on the Excavations at Babarkot 1990–91*, Delhi, mimeographed.

———— 1990, Revolution in the Urban Revolution: The Emergence of Indus Urbanism, *Annual Review of Anthropology*, 19, pp. 261–82.

———— 1991, Paper in Berlin Conference of South Asian Archaeologists in Europe.

———— and P. Rissman, 1992, The Chronology of Pre-Historic India, *Chronologies in Old World Archaeology* (ed. R.W. Ehrich), vol. I, Chicago, pp. 465–90; vol. II, pp. 447–74.

Prasad, K. 1984, *Cities, Crafts and Commerce Under the Kushans*, Delhi.

Puri, B.N. 1966, *Cities of Ancient India*, Meerat.

Puri, K.N. (n.d.), *Excavations at Rairh*, Jaipur.

Raikes, R.L. 1963, The End of the Ancient Cities of the Indus Civilization in Sind and Baluchistan, *American Anthropologist*, 65, pp. 655–9.

———— 1964, The End of the Ancient Cities of the Indus, *American Anthropologist*, 66, pp. 284–99.

———— 1965, The Mohenjodaro Floods, *Antiquity*, 39, pp. 196–203.

—— 1967a, The Mohenjodaro Floods: Reposte, *Antiquity*, 41, pp. 309–10.

—— 1967b, *Water, Weather and Prehistory*, London.

—— 1968, Kalibangan: Death from Natural Causes, *Antiquity*, 42, pp. 286–91.

—— and R.H. Dyson 1961, The Prehistoric Climate of Baluchistan and the Indus Valley, *American Anthropologist*, 63, pp. 265–81.

Ramachandran, T.N. 1953, *Nagarjunakonda*, Delhi.

Rami Reddy, V. 1978, *A Study of the Neolithic Culture of Southwestern Andhra Pradesh*, Hyderabad.

Rao, M.S.N. 1965, Survival of Certain Neolithic Elements Among the Boyas of Tekkalakota, *Anthropos*, 60, pp. 480–1.

—— 1971, *Protohistoric Tungabhadra Valley*, Dharwar.

—— and K.C. Malhotra 1965, *The Stone Age Hill-Dwellers of Tekkalakota*, Pune.

Rao, M.S.N. and S. Nagaraju 1974, *Excavations at Hemmige*, Mysore.

Rao, S.R. 1963, Excavation at Rangpur and Other Explorations in Gujarat, *Ancient India*, 18–19, pp. 5–207.

—— 1979, *Lothal, a Harappan Port Town*, Delhi.

—— 1991, *Dawn and Devolution of Indus Civilization*, Delhi.

Rapson, E.J. (ed.) 1962, *The Cambridge History of India*, I, Delhi.

Ratnagar, S. 1981, *Encounters, the Westerly Trade of the Harappa Civilization*, Delhi.

—— 1991, *Enquiries into the Political Organization of Harappan Society*, Pune.

Ray, A. 1964, *Villages, Towns and Secular Buildings in Ancient India*, Calcutta.

Raychaudhuri, H.C. 1953, *Political History of Ancient India*, Calcutta.

Roy, U.N. 1965, *Pracin Bharat Mein Nagara Tatha Nagara Jivana* (in Hindi), Allahabad.

Redfield, R. 1962, The Cultural Role of Cities, *Human Nature and the Study of Society, the Papers of Robert Redfield* (ed. M. Redfield), Chicago, pp. 326–50.

—— 1963, *Peasant Society and Culture*, Chicago.

—— 1965, *The Primitive World and its Transformations*, Ithaca.

Redman, C.L. 1978, Mesopotamian Urban Ecology: The Systematic Context of the Emergence of Urbanism, *Social Archaeology, Beyond Subsistence and Dating* (ed. C.L. Redman *et al.*), New York, pp. 329–47.

Renfrew, C. 1984, *Approaches to Social Archaeology*, Edinburgh.

—— and P. Bahn 1991, *Archaeology*, London.

Rissman, P. and G.M. Chitalwala 1991, *Oriyo Timbo*, Delhi.

Rydh, H. 1959, *Rangmahal*, London.

Sahni, D.R. (n.d.), *Archaeological Remains and Excavations at Bairat*, Jaipur.

Sahni, M.R. 1956, Biological Evidence Bearing on the Decline of the Indus Valley Civilization, *Journal of the Palaeontological Society of India*, 1, pp. 101–7.

Sahu, B.P. 1988, *From Hunters to Breeders: Faunal Background of Ancient India*, Delhi.

Sali, S.A. 1986, *Daimabad*, Delhi.

Sankalia, H.D. 1969, *Mesolithic and Pre-Mesolithic Industries from the Excavations at Sanganakallu, Bellary*, Pune.

———— 1974, *Prehistory and Protohistory of India and Pakistan*, Pune.

———— and M.G. Diksit 1952, *Excavations at Brahmapuri (Kolhapur)*, Pune.

Sankalia, H.D. and S.B. Deo, 1955, *Report on the Excavation at Nasik and Jorwe*, Pune.

Sankalia, H.D., B. Subbarao and S.B. Deo 1958, *The Excavations at Maheshwar and Navdatoli 1952–53*, Baroda.

Sankalia, H.D., S.B. Deo and Z.D. Ansari 1960, *From History to Prehistory at Nevasa (1954–56)*, Pune.

———— 1969, *Excavations at Ahar*, Pune.

———— 1971, *Chalcolithic Navdatoli*, Pune.

Sarao, K.T.S. 1989, *The Origin and Nature of Ancient Indian Buddhism*, Delhi.

———— 1990, *Urban Centres and Urbanisation as Reflected in the Pali Vinaya and Sutta Pitakas*, Delhi.

Sarcina, A. 1979, Paper in *South Asian Archaeology*, 1977.

Sastri, T.V.G., K. Bai and J.V.P. Rao 1984, *Veerapuram*, Hyderabad.

Schmandt-Besserat, D. 1992, *Before Writing*, 2 vols, Austin.

Shaffer, J.G. 1978, *Prehistoric Baluchistan*, Delhi.

———— 1986, Cultural Development in the Eastern Punjab, *Studies in the Archaeology of India and Pakistan* (ed. J. Jacobson), Delhi, pp. 195–235.

———— 1992, The Indus Valley, Baluchistan and Helmand Traditions, Neolithic Through Bronze Age, *Chronologies in World Archaeology* (ed. R.W. Ehrich), 2 vols, Chicago.

Shah, U.P. 1960, Lothal—A Port?, *Journ. of the Orient Inst*, Baroda, 9, pp. 310–20.

Sharif, M. 1969, Excavation at Bhir Mound, Taxila, *PA*, 6, pp. 7–99.

Sharma, A.K. 1991, Antiquity of Iron from Gufkral, *Recent Advances in Marine Archaeology* (hereafter *RAMA*), pp. 181–2.

Sharma. G.R. 1958, Excavations at Kausambi, 1949–55, *Annual Bibliography of Indian Archaeology*, 16, pp. xxxvi–xlv.

———— 1960, *The Excavations at Kausambi (1957–59)*, Allahabad.

Sharma, R.S. 1987, *Urban Decay in India*, Delhi.

Sharma. T.C. 1967, A note on the Neolithic Pottery of Assam, *Man*, 2, pp. 126–8.

Sharma, Y.D. 1964, Protohistoric Remains, *Archaeological Remains, Monuments and Museums*, part I, Delhi.

Sheshadri, R. 1992, Paper on Copper Metallurgy, *ME*, vol. 16.

Singh, B.P. 1990, Early Farming Communities of Kaimur Foot-hills, *Puratattva*, 19, pp. 6–18.

Singh. O.K. and R.K. Ranjit Singh 1990, A Preliminary Report on an Archaeological Exploration at Singtom, Chandel District, Manipur, *ME*, 15, pp. 103–6

Singh, P. 1992–93, Excavations at Imlidih—1992, *Bharati*, 19, pp. 1–10.

Singhvi, A.K., D.P. Agrawal and K.S.V. Nambi 1991, Thermo-luminescence Dating: An Update or Application to Indian Archaeology (ed. S.R. Rao), *RAMA*, Dona Paula.

Sinha, B.K. 1991, Excavations at Golabai Sasan, District Puri, Orissa, *Puratattva*, 21, pp. 74–6.

Sinha, K.K. 1967, *Excavations at Sravasti 1959*, Varanasi.

——— 1973, Stratigraphy and Chronology of Early Kausambi, *Radiocarbon and Indian Archaeology* (eds D.P. Agrawal and A. Ghosh), Bombay.

Sjoberg, G. 1960, *The Preindustrial City: Past and Present*, Illinois.

Smith, V. 1924, *The Early History of India*, Oxford.

Snead, R.E. 1967, Recent Morphological Changes Along the Coast of West Pakistan, *Annals of the Association of American Geographers*, 57, pp. 550–65.

Spengler, O. 1954, *The Decline of the West*, vol. II, London.

Spooner, D.B. 1917, Excavations at Basarh, *AR ASI 1913–14*, Delhi, pp. 99–185.

Srinivasan, D. (ed.) 1989, *Mathura—The Cultural Heritage*, Delhi.

Srivastava, B. 1968, *Trade and Commerce in Ancient India*, Varanasi.

Srivastava, K.M. 1986, *Discovery of Kapilavastu*, Delhi.

Stein, A. 1929, *An Archaeological Tour in Waziristan and Northern Baluchistan*, Calcutta.

——— 1931, *An Archaeological Tour in Gedrosia*, Calcutta.

——— 1942, A Survey of Ancient Sites Along the 'Lost' Sarasvati River, *Geographical Journal*, 99, pp. 173–82.

Subbarao, B. 1948, *Stone Age Cultures of Bellary*, Puna.

Subrahmanyam, R. 1975, *Nagarjunakonda (1954–60)*, vol. I, Delhi.

Sukthankar, S. 1920, Selection of Literary References to Taxila Gleaned from Indian Sources, *AR ASI 1914–15*, pp. 36–41.

Sundara, A. 1968, Protohistoric Sites in Bijapur District, *Journal of Karnataka University (Social Sciences)*, 4, pp. 1–23.

——— 1971, Chalcolithic Phase of the Upper Krishna Valley, *Studies in Indian History and Culture* (eds S.H. Ritti and B.R. Gopal), Dharwar, pp. 13–36.

Tessitori, L.P. 1919, Progress Report . . ., *Journal of Proceedings of the Asiatic Society of Bengal*, 15, pp. 5–79.

Thakur, V. 1981, *Urbanisation in Ancient India*, Delhi.

Thapar, B.K. 1957, Maski 1954, *Ancient India*, 13, pp. 4–142.

——— 1964–65, Prakash 1955, *Ancient India*, 20-1, pp. 5–167.

Trivedi, H.K. 1982, Study of Awra Pottery, *IANP*, pp. 245–8.

Ucko, P., R. Tringham and G. Dimbleby 1972, *Man, Settlement and Urbanism*, London.

Vats, M.S. 1940, *Excavations at Harappa*, Delhi.

Venkatachar, C.S. 1933, *Census of India 1931*, vol. 20, *Central Indian Agency*, part I, Calcutta.

Verardi, G. 1987, Preliminary Report on the Stupa and the Monastery of Mohenjodaro, *IR*, vol. 2, pp. 45–58.

Verma, B.S. 1971, Excavations at Chirand: New Light on the Indian Neolithic Culture-complex, *Puratattva*, 4, pp. 18–22.

Weber, M. 1958, *The Religion of India*, Glencoe.

Weber, S. 1991, *Plants and Harappan Subsistence*, Delhi.

Wheeler, R.E.M. 1947, Harappa 1946: The Defences and Cemetery R 37, *Ancient India*, 3, pp. 58–130.

—— 1947–48, Brahmagiri and Chandravalli, *Ancient India*, 4, pp. 180–310.

—— 1950, What Matters in Archaeology? *Antiquity*, 24, pp. 122–30.

—— 1956, The First Towns, *Antiquity*, 30, pp. 132–6.

—— 1962, *Charsada*, London.

Wilson, J.A. 1963, *The Culture of Ancient Egypt*, Chicago.

—— 1968, *The Indus Civilization* (3rd edn), Cambridge.

Wirth, L. 1938, Urbanism as a Way of Life, *American Journal of Sociology*, 44, pp. 1–24.

Worman, E.C. 1949, The 'Neolithic' Problem in the Prehistory of India, *Journal of the Washington Academy of Sciences*, 39, pp. 181–201.

Wright, R. 1989, Paper in *South Asian Archaeology 1985*.

Index

Adams, R.M. 5–8
Agrawal, D.P. 27–8, 79–80, 113
Agrawala, R.C. 144–5
Ahar 145–8
Aims of this work 9
Ali, S.M. 79
Allchin, B. and F.R. 21, 27, 126
Allchin, F.R. 2, 155
Altekar, V.S. and Misra, V.K. 210–11
Ambkheri 133
Amreli 226
Amri 33
Ancient Indian cities, academics on 1–2
Ansari, Z.A. 150
Arikamedu 232
Atranjikhera 160–2
Avra 148
Ayyar, C.P.V. 1

Babarkot 135
Bahn, P. 7
Bala, Madhu 52, 87, 143
Balakot 56–7
Balu 40
Baluchistan as a geographical area 53, 55
Banavasi 231
Banerjee, R.D. 61
Bannu basin 35
Bargaon 133
Bet Dwaraka 136–7
Bhagawanpura 133
Bhan, K.K. 95–6, 134, 137
Bhan, S. 87–8
Bhandarkar, D.R. 221
Bhokardan 230
Bisht, R.S. 87–8, 92, 94, 96, 103–4,
    110–11
Bloch, T. 205
Bose, A.N. 193, 262

Brahminabad 183–4
Braidwood, R.J. 4
Brunswig, J.H. 114
Buchanan, F. 214
Burzahom 143, 181

Canal system in Haryana 50–1
Casal, J.M. 16
Chakrabarti, D.K. 2, 11, 24, 27
Chakravarty, P.L. 145
Chattopadhyay, B.D. 266, 271
Childe, V.G. 3–5, 8, 14
Chirand 158
Cholistan as a geographical area 78–9
Choudhury, N.D. 219
Choudhury, R.D. 219
Chronology of the early Harappan 41–3
Concentration of sites in Mansa
    taluk 109–10
Construction process of
    Mohenjodaro 62–4
Coomaraswamy, A.K. 1, 261
Courbin, P. 9
Courty, M.A. 45–6
Cousens, H. 184
Craft-specialization in Indus urbanism
    51–2
Cunningham, A. 182–3, 190, 198, 202,
    206, 208, 216

DK area, Mohanjodaro 72–5
Dabarkot 56
Dadheri 133
Daimabad 151
Dales, G.F. 17, 58, 62, 83, 86, 107, 126
Dangwada 148
Dani, A.H. 142, 157, 173
Daniel, G. 5
Daojali Hading 157

Datta, J.M. 116
Davies, K. 2
Desiccation of the Ghaggar plain 79–80
Dhavalikar, M.K. 136, 150, 152–3, 163–4
Dikshit, Kasinath 216
Dikshit, K.N. 94, 110, 161
Distinctive and unique character of the Indus civilization 10–14
During-Caspers, E.C.L. 26
Durkheim, E. 3
Dutt, B.B. 1
Dyson, R. 55, 119

Early Harappan at Banawali 39–40
Early Harappan at Harappa 36–7
Early Harappan at Kalibangan 38–9
Early Harappan at Kunal, Mahorana 40
Early Harappan in Panjab, Rajasthan, Haryana 35–41
Edith Shahr 57
Eran 148
Erdosy, G. 9
Explanation of the origin of the Indus civilization 46–52

Fairservis, W.A. 19–20, 55, 57
Fentress, Marcia 69, 82, 274
Flam, L. 28–9, 31–3
Flannery, K. 7
Formulation of the problem of origin of the Indus civilization 14–28
Francfort, H. 51, 79, 87–8
Frankfort, H. 5, 52

Gamanwala 31
Ganeshwar 52, 143–5
Gaur, R.C. 160, 169, 188
Ghaligai 142
Ghosh, A. 1, 16, 81, 86, 126, 205, 213
Ghosh, M. 211
Ghosh, N.N. 194
Gilund 145–8
Golbai Sasan 157
Gomal valley 34–5
Gordon, D.H. 15
Gufkral 142–3, 181
Gujarat geographical elements 94–5
Gumla 34

HR area, Mohenjodaro 70–2
Hakra ware sites 29–30
Harappan sites in Baluchistan 56–9
Hassan, Fekri 52
Hathial 36
Heine-Geldern, R. 15
Hooja, Rima 146–7
Hulas 133
Hydrographic setting of the Indus and Ghaggar-Hakra plains 43–6

Immediate antecedence of the Indus civilization 29–43
Inamgaon 152
Irrigation canals in protohistoric Haryana 87–8

Jacobson, T. 6
Jainal-Naula 186
Jaiwali 31
Jalilpur 30
Jansen, M. 62–5, 68, 75–6, 118, 120, 122
Jhang 36
Joshi, J.P. 52, 87–8, 102, 132, 143
Joshi, M.C. 190, 244
Judeirjodaro 56

Kachhi plain 29
Kalibangan 'eastern mound' 91–2
Kalibangan 'western mound' 90–1
Kanchipuram 232
Kanewal 138
Kaothe 150
Karvan 227
Kaspapyros 182
Katpalon 133
Kaundinyapur 230
Kaveripattinam 232
Kayatha 148
Kenoyer, J.M. 83, 86
Kenyon, K. 4
Khadinwala 36
Khan, F.A. 15, 77
Khare, M.D. 222
Kirthar-Kohistan 32–3
Knox, R. 41
Koldihawa 159

Kondapur 239
Korkai 232
Kosambi, D.D. 68, 167
Kot Diji 33–4
Kot Diji horizon in Cholistan and
    Sind 30–4
Kroeber, A.L. 15
Kulli (early Kulli) 31–2
Kumar, Vijay 145
Kuntasi 135
Kupgal 155

Lahiri, Nayanjot 83, 108, 110, 153, 163,
    219
Lal, B.B. 89–90, 126, 160, 187, 193,
    198–200
Lal, M. 2, 162, 169
Lamberg-Karlovsky, C.C. 24
Lambrick, H.T. 117
Law, B.C. 194
Leshnik, L. 101
Lewan 35
Location of Mohenjodaro in relation to
    trade routes 107–8
Long chronology of the Indus civilization
    114–15
Longhurst, A.H. 238

Mackay, E. 61, 65–7, 69–77, 83, 112,
    118–22, 130
Majumdar, N.G. 15, 76–7, 107, 129–30,
    205
Makran coast 106–7
Malhotra, K.C. 154
Mansa taluk sites 40, 109
Marshall, J. 11–14, 60–1, 65–6, 68–70,
    85, 111–12, 122, 124, 172, 175–81,
    198–9, 213, 242
Masson, V.M. 6
Mehrgarh 28–9
Mehta, R.N. 137–8
Meluhha debate 47–8
Misra, Y. 207
Mitathal 38
Mockler, Major 57
Mohrana 133
Momin, K. 137
Moneer, Q.M. 75
Moneer area, Mohenjodaro 75–6

Moorti, U.S. 168
Moradhwaj 186
Mound AB, Harappa 83–4
Mound E, Harappa 86
Mound F, Harappa 84–6
Mughal, R. 22–4, 29–31, 81, 96, 108,
    131–2
Mumford, L. 4, 6

Nagal 226
Nagar 133
Nagda 148
Nagwada 41
Narasimhaiah, B. 154
Nasik 228–9
Nausharo 56
Nautiyal, K.P. 186
Navdatoli 148
Negation of external trade as a causative
    factor of Indus urbanism 47–8
Nesadi 137
Niai Buthi 57
Nindowari 57
Nissen, H.J. 7, 270

Oriyo Timbo 137

Paddayya, K. 155
Padri 135
Pandu Rajar Dhibi 158
Parasher, Aloka 276
Pathani Damb 56
Patil, D.R. 213–14
Pauni 228–9
Pearson, H.W. 6
Piggott, S. 1, 15, 72, 124, 190
Piklihal 155
Possehl, G.L. 47, 95–6, 136
Prabhas Patan 136
Prasad, K. 2
Pre-Harappan in Gujarat 41
Pre-industrial agricultural geography of
    Sind 49–50
Punja, Sheena 271
Puri, B.N. 1
Puri, K.N. 220
Purola 187

Raikes, R.L. 55, 79, 89, 119, 127–9

Ram, Jassu 37, 143
Rami Reddy, V. 155
Rangmahal 186
Rao, M.S.N. 154
Rao, S.R. 97, 99–101, 130, 134, 136
Ratnagar, Shireen 26–7, 82, 139
Raval, M.H. 95
Ray, Amita 1, 255
Raychoudhury, H.C. 276
Redfield, R. 2, 5
Redman, C.L. 52
Rehman Dheri 34–5
Renfrew, C. 7–9
Rohira 133
Rojdi 135–6
Roy, U.N. 1
Rydh, Hanna 220

Sahni, D.R. 192, 220, 245
Sahni, M.R. 127
Sahu, B.P. 163
Sakala 183
Sali, S.A. 150–1
Sanganakallu 155
Sanghol 133, 186
Sankalia, H.D. 149–50, 162–3
Saraikhola 35
Sarao, K.T.S. 2, 268–9
Sarcina, Anna 118
Sarkar, H. 237
Sastri, H. 191
Schmandt-Besserat, D. 10
Semthan 182
Shaffer, J.G. 9, 94
Shamlaji 227
Senuar 138
Sharma, G.R. 194–8, 244
Sharma, R.S. 2, 270
Sharma, T.C. 158
Sharma, Y.D. 94
Sheri Khan Tarakai 35
Shortughai plain 52, 106–7
Sind: physiographic units and prehistoric
    climate 59–60
Singanapalli 150
Singh, B.P. 158
Sinha, B.P. 215–16
Sinha, K.K. 244
Siswal 40

Sjoberg, G. 261
Smith, V. 183, 202, 205
Snead, R.E. 59
Sotka-koh 58–9
Soundara Rajan, K.V. 102
Spate, O.H.K. 184, 187
Spengler, O. 2
Spooner, D.P. 208, 210–11
Srivastava, B. 191
Srivastava, K.M. 204
Stein, A. 55, 57, 80, 89
Summary of the hypothesis regarding the
    place of the Indus civilization in Indian
    history 272–5
Sutkagendor 57–8

Tagara 228–9
Taradih 158
Tarakai Qila 35
Tekkalakota 155
Tessitori, L.P. 80
Thakur, V. 1
Thaneshwar 186
Thapar, B.K. 89
Thapar, Romila 276
Thapli 186
Timbarva 227
Tosi, M. 25

Urayur 232
Urban, Th. 75
Urbanism in archaeological literature 2–9

Vadodara 227
Vats, M.S. 84–6, 122
Vigel, J.Ph. 203
Virabhadra 186
VS area, Mohenjodaro 72

Wakankar, V.S. 148–9
Weber, S. 96
Weiner, Sheela 26
Western Panjab geography 82
Wheeler, R.E.M. 60–1, 68, 83–4, 112–
    13, 122, 124, 126–8, 173
Wilson, J.A. 5
Worman, E.C. 151
Wright, Rita 26

Yeleswaram 239